THE
FAST TRACK

—————— ~ ——————

The Insider's Guide
to Winning Jobs in
Management Consulting,
Investment Banking,
and Securities Trading

—————— ~ ——————

MARIAM NAFICY

BROADWAY BOOKS
NEW YORK

BROADWAY

Broadway Books titles may be purchased for business or promotional use or for special sales. For information, please write to: Special Markets Department, Bantam Doubleday Dell Publishing Group, Inc., 1540 Broadway, New York, NY 10036.

BROADWAY BOOKS and its logo, a letter B bisected on the diagonal, are trademarks of Broadway Books, a division of Bantam Doubleday Dell Publishing Group, Inc.

Library of Congress Cataloging-in-Publication Data

Naficy, Mariam, 1970–
      The fast track : the insider's guide to winning jobs in
  management consulting, investment banking, and securities trading /
  Mariam Naficy. — 1st ed.
          p.   cm.
      Includes index.
      ISBN 0-7679-0040-5 (pbk.)
      1. Business consultants —Vocational guidance.   2. Investment
  bankers —Vocational guidance.   3. Brokers —Vocational guidance.
  I. Title.
  HD69.C6N33   1997
  650.14— dc21   97-20959
                                                                       CIP

Designed by Stanley S. Drate/Folio Graphics Co., Inc.
Back cover photo: John Perino

98   99   00   01   10   9   8   7   6   5   4   3   2

for Mary and Hossein Naficy,
and
for Michael Mader

CONTENTS

*pseudonym

*pseudonym

THE RECRUITER'S PERSPECTIVE:
Andrea Terzi Baum
Vice President, Goldman, Sachs & Co.

THE RECRUITER'S PERSPECTIVE:
Kate Byrne
Head of Global Recruiting, Monitor Company

6

WHO THE FIRMS ARE
LOOKING FOR

Critical skills • Specific skills sought for consulting, investment banking, and
sales and trading

INSIDER INTERVIEW: SPOTLIGHT ON DAILY WORK IN INVESTMENT BANKING:
Beth Bradley*
Former Analyst, major-bracket investment bank
based in New York

7

RÉSUMÉ AND COVER LETTER:
THE PACKAGING

How the recruiter evaluates your résumé • General strategies • Writing a
winning cover letter • Sample cover letter: before and after • Writing a
winning résumé • Sample resume: before and after

8

BEFORE THE INTERVIEW

Logistics • Headlining • Preparation worksheet • Your wardrobe • Sample
evaluation form • Methods of communication

*pseudonym

9

THE INTERVIEW:
ANSWERING THE QUESTIONS   185

The introduction • Personality questions • 10 common interview gaffes •
Résumé questions • Communications questions • Business questions • Your
questions • The final-round interview • Appendix A: comprehensive lists of
interview questions

AFTER THE INTERVIEW IS OVER:
WHAT HAPPENS BEHIND CLOSED DOORS

A composite of actual sessions in which consultants
evaluate candidates.

10

THE MANAGEMENT
CONSULTING CASE QUESTION   206

Standard case questions • Number questions • Brain teasers • Frameworks •
Practice case 1 • Practice case 2 • More practice questions

INSIDER INTERVIEW:
Bob Simonelli*
Former Consultant, Bain & Company, Inc.

11

CHOOSING THE RIGHT JOB   223

The nuts and bolts of the offer • Companies' sales techniques • What to watch
for • Ten tall tales • What's negotiable • How to evaluate the money • Culture
and people • Appendix A: Questions to ask during sell day

INSIDER INTERVIEW:
Rajesh Gupta*
Former Analyst, strategy consulting firm

*pseudonym

INSIDER INTERVIEW:
Gillian Chen*
Former Analyst, bulge-bracket investment bank

PROFILES OF THE LEADING CONSULTING FIRMS   243

OTHER WORTHY MENTIONS   285

PROFILES OF THE LEADING INVESTMENT BANKS   289

OTHER WORTHY MENTIONS   332

*pseudonym

ACKNOWLEDGMENTS

The Fast Track is in many ways the product of a collaborative effort, and there are several people who should be recognized for their part in it. My friends in the Class of 1998 at Stanford Business School provided critical information and helped me survive school and write a book at the same time. Professors George Parker and Joel Podolny of Stanford reviewed and commented on selected chapters. Former colleagues at Goldman Sachs and Gemini Consulting went out of their way to assist me.

Anjali Crawford, Hilary Johnson, Doug Koo, Kathy Koo, Kellyann MacLean, Davin McAndrews, Todd Owens, and Varsha Rao spent hours reading the manuscript and contributed important suggestions. Dom DeMarco, Dwight Eyrick, and traders at Merrill, J.P. Morgan, and Goldman fine-tuned my thinking on sales and trading. Maurice Werdegar, a great mentor and businessperson, provided critical encouragement from the beginning.

Daniel Greenberg and Jim Levine, my agents, saw value in the book when it was still a concept and found a home for it with the right editor—Lauren Marino, who guided me through the publication process with understanding and expertise.

I am very grateful to Andrea Terzi Baum, Kate Byrne, Kenichi Ohmae, and Addison Piper, who granted interviews for the book.

I owe a great debt to many others who have reviewed this book and granted interviews but whom, to preserve anonymity, I cannot thank by name. To all the "Insiders"—you know who you are—thank you for generously sharing your experiences with others who come after you.

As always, I was inspired by Hossein and Mary Naficy, Yassy Naficy, Sophie Sun, and Horst and Eva Mader.

Finally, I am grateful to Michael Mader for stepping down this path with me. *The Fast Track* is as much his as it is mine; it would not exist at all had it not been for his unending support and steadfast belief in me and in this book.

THE FAST TRACK

~ 1 ~

THE GOLD RUSH

In the winter of 1990, I, like other seniors, was facing the question of what to do after college. Progression through school had been a lock-step process: You left each spring knowing you'd return in the fall. Now, looking out at the "real" world, there seemed to be relatively little structure and many choices. Only a few careers had an obvious starting point, and these I gravitated toward. I dutifully filled out law school applications, thinking that perhaps I would make a good lawyer. But a nagging voice was telling me not to commit to any lifelong career that I didn't understand.

Older college friends had disappeared into the worlds of "investment banking" and "management consulting" and had occasionally resurfaced on campus with stories of diverse work, foreign travel, and big salaries. My friends were *analysts,* positions they had won through campus recruiting. Analyst programs were structured yet seemed to offer a good deal of variety in assignments. My interest was piqued. I could *postpone* the Big Career Decision until I learned more. I turned down law school and instead joined the annual campus mating dance of students and recruiters.

I battled through a grueling recruiting season, totaling about seventy-five interviews with various banks and consulting firms. After the seventieth or so, I didn't care any more what job I got. I just wanted the interviews to end. After comparing job offers in banking and consulting, I accepted a position at a New York investment bank.

I made the transition from rural campus town to Wall Street in August 1991. A liberal arts major, I didn't understand the meaning of "stock" or "bond" or what investment bankers really did every day. I was too young

1

to drink legally. But I soon found myself in meetings with chief officers of corporations and selling bonds in $10 million chunks over the telephone. I wasn't climbing a learning curve; I was hauling myself up a learning pole. Over the next two years, I would help raise hundreds of millions of dollars for clients, travel on business to Spain, Sweden, and England, develop a good understanding of finance and accounting, and get paid about $100,000 in total for the experience.

But my original interest in consulting still called to me—I wanted the exposure to strategic decision-making that this field would provide. After two years in investment banking, I joined a management consulting firm. I advised Fortune 500 companies on important strategies, including planning joint ventures and figuring out markets for new products. I traveled extensively, became familiar with the day-to-day workings of corporations, and was paid even more than in banking.

Now, looking back at these "fast-track" jobs, their intangible value has far transcended any money I earned. I developed a knowledge of accounting and finance and how to analyze a company's competitive position and industry structure. But most importantly, I rotated through projects in different industries and concerning different issues. I became aware of the business world and what exists within it.

Why is breadth of experience important? In making decisions, we draw data from what we have already experienced. This data, of course, is a biased sample; no person has done everything. The fewer issues we have been exposed to, the smaller our sphere of awareness is likely to be—and the more biased our sample.

This has serious implications for career planning. In our first jobs, we're pruning branches off our career decision tree—we're eliminating certain options, perhaps never to revisit them again. To do so without as broad a base of experience as possible means that we may reject certain paths or lock ourselves into others simply out of ignorance: ignorance about careers that exist, ignorance about the pros and cons of those careers, and ignorance about what types of work suit us as individuals. Save the specialization and deep knowledge for later; get the breadth of exposure now.

A RECRUITER'S PERSPECTIVE

At both the bank and the consulting firm I worked for, I was assigned recruiting duties in addition to client work. (In this book I use the terms "banking" and "bankers" for "investment banking" and "investment bankers." However, this shortened form does not include commercial banking, a distinction explained in Chapter 3.) Every winter my colleagues and I thumbed through thick piles of résumés from people around the country. Now, on the other side of the interview table, I realized how lucky I had been to land a job in the first place. Most leading firms screen thousands of applicants each year. Goldman Sachs, for example, receives over 6,000 résumés annually for its approximately 130 undergraduate investment banking positions. Forty to 50 percent of graduating MBAs rush into investment banking or consulting, and an even larger number apply.

From my new vantage point, I could see that many job applicants had good qualifications but ruled themselves out through simple mistakes, while successful applicants had made a special effort to get an "inside scoop" on the industries and the recruiting process. Clearly, the perspective that we recruiters took for granted—our knowledge of what the jobs entailed and what constituted appropriate behavior and useful skills—was not getting across to the majority of job applicants.

The purpose of this book is to provide my viewpoint and others' viewpoints on investment banking, securities sales and trading, and management consulting—and to share more detailed and candid information than is typically available through official channels.

This book answers several questions that I heard repeatedly as a recruiter in both investment banking and management consulting:

- Can you explain in plain English what management consulting, investment banking, and securities sales and trading mean?
- What are the benefits of working in these fields?
- What do bankers and consultants do every day?
- How would you describe the culture and working environment?
- What are recruiters looking for?
- What types of questions are asked during interviews?
- How can I improve my chances of getting a job?
- What are the differences among firms?
- What does it take to succeed in banking and consulting?
- What options would I have after working in these industries?

WHAT ARE INVESTMENT BANKING AND MANAGEMENT CONSULTING?

Management consulting and investment banking may seem like an odd pairing, but they have one important thing in common: Both involve providing advice to the top management of major corporations.

Both consulting and banking are *service industries:* They provide business services, not tangible products, to other companies. Investment bankers help companies raise or invest capital; they work with financial managers such as the chief financial officer (CFO), treasurer, or investment manager of a company. Management consultants help companies make strategic or operating decisions; they work with managers of strategy or operations—anyone from the chief executive officer (CEO) to the head of a division or product line.

In a business that primarily sells knowledge, a firm's competitive asset is its people. Firms' reputations are established based on how good its people are: The better a firm's people, the more valuable its advice will seem and the more business it will win away from competitors. Banks and consulting firms are alike in that they seek the highest-quality businesspeople they can find: people who are personable, intelligent, and hard-working. The firms select the best candidates through a rigorous process and pay them extremely well in order to retain them. What most people notice about banking and consulting—a difficult selection process and enormous salaries—are outgrowths of their need to find and retain the best businesspeople.

What sets banking and consulting apart is that they have developed the most uniform, consistent recruiting of any profession at top college and business school campuses. Banks and consulting firms offer a steady number of job openings and conduct a standard interview process each year. They have created a recruiting tradition: Read Michael Lewis's description of the 1981 recruiting season at Princeton in his book *Liar's Poker,* and you'll find that recruiting sounds very much like it is today.

This is not to say that banking, trading, and consulting are all the same: Investment banking could be described as buttoned-down and patrician, sales and trading as street-smart and fast-paced, consulting as highly intellectual and less transaction oriented. Of all the three fields, sales and trading least resembles the other two. Although sales and trading has slightly different human resource needs, it is included anyway in this book because it is highly lucrative and hires a large number of young professionals. Sales and trading is technically a separate service from investment banking but is performed by the institutions known as investment banks. For brevity's sake, this book includes sales and trading under the umbrella term "investment banking" unless otherwise mentioned. The qualities unique to sales and trading are covered in Chapter 3 and should be carefully reviewed by job-hunters.

THE JOBS AVAILABLE

Banking and consulting have practically identical structures for bringing in fresh blood. Every major American bank or consulting firm offers entry-level positions to recent college and business school graduates. Although titles vary from firm to firm, here's a summary of typical entry-level positions, which are covered in Chapters 2 and 3 in more depth:

- *College graduates are hired as "analysts."* Analyst positions are finite job offers that last two to three years; most analysts then leave for business school or other careers. Very few are promoted to a post-MBA position. Analysts support senior employees by performing business research and analysis, writing, building computer spreadsheets, interacting with clients, and doing logistical and presentation work. Many companies offer summer analyst positions to sophomores or juniors, which can lead to offers of full-time employment upon graduation.

- *MBAs or law students are hired as "associates."* Associate positions are long-term. Associates manage teams of junior employees and perform analysis to advise corporations on financial or other business issues. They participate heavily in client meetings, have a high level of contact with senior clients, and eventually develop expertise in a particular service or industry. Some firms only hire MBAs from the top fifteen business schools as associates; those holding MBAs from other business schools may be hired as analysts or into intermediate positions between analyst and associate.

- *Those holding master's degrees in other subjects or who have had minimal experience in business are usually hired as analysts, but each firm's policy differs.* Some firms have intermediate levels between the analyst and associate positions that are designed for people with more experience or education than an undergraduate.

What They're Paid

In 1997, entry-level compensation at the most prestigious firms looked approximately like this:

	Investment Banking		Management Consulting	
	Base Salary	Signing Bonus*	Base Salary	Signing Bonus
Undergraduate Student ("Analyst")	38,000	2,000	40,000	2,000
MBA Student ("Associate")	77,000	20,000	87,000	21,000

To calculate these numbers, salaries of five top firms in each industry were averaged. The salaries are closely clustered together; for example, the consulting firm MBA salaries are within a $5,000 range. These numbers *do not* include annual bonus, which is extra. Most investment banks, for example, guarantee MBA students an additional $20,000 annual bonus in their first December at the firm.

*Signing bonus is a one-time bonus received when joining the company.

Sources: Interviews with students and career counselors.

WHY PEOPLE DO IT

So what do investment banking and management consulting hold for you? Why do so many MBAs and college students rush into these fields? In return for analytically challenging work and long hours, banks and consulting firms offer young employees training with high-quality managers and an enhanced professional reputation.

Bankers and consultants receive the choicest of introductions to the business world. New recruits participate in formal training programs, in which accounting, finance, and the use of computer software applications are taught. Learning also takes place on the job. Through a broad range of projects, high levels of responsibility, and exposure to managers with experience, bankers and consultants become well versed in business concepts, vocabulary, and etiquette—training that amounts to a kind of finishing school. Most have an opportunity to travel on business, sometimes overseas. Analysts and associates are able to interact with extremely bright and sociable peers. Recent college graduates benefit from a rare early exposure to current high-level business thinking and ambitious career paths.

Consulting and investment banking alumni occupy the best business schools, the senior ranks of Corporate America, and the hottest entrepreneurial ventures. The simple act of taking a job in consulting or investment banking, therefore, confers two additional assets: a bond with a group of outstanding businesspeople and a seal of recognition of having passed a difficult screening process. How can these assets help you in your career? Eventually, most analysts and associates move on to other jobs and companies, forming a network of connections in varied fields. Their shared experience in banking or consulting serves as a reference point around which they maintain relationships with each other.

Whether they deserve it or not, bankers and consultants enjoy a measure of instant status: Future employers, business schools, and others automatically assume that these professionals are top performers and have had excellent business training. An analyst position, for example, typically represents a "ticket" to a top business school because of the universally acknowledged training the position provides. Like alumni of a prestigious school, bankers and consultants who graduate from their firms continue to enjoy enhanced reputations and a network of contacts.

HOW DO BANKING AND CONSULTING COMPARE TO OTHER JOBS?

In making a career decision, it's a good idea to evaluate investment banking and management consulting relative to other career options. Here's a comparison based on several factors that are important to job-seekers.

People and Culture: Since the recruiting process in banking and consulting is more selective than in most businesses, you'll find people with outstanding academic records, people whose interpersonal skills and extracurricular accomplishments dazzle. The bottom line: a consistently high quality of people. Although culture varies among companies, most firms share competitiveness and standards of excellence that come from putting a bunch of overachievers in the same room.

Work: The work tends to be intense, highly analytical, and intellectually challenging. Performance standards and attention to detail are extremely high. One typo in a ten-page document is considered a grave error in investment banking.

Responsibility: Both consultants and investment bankers fulfill responsibilities that are unusually high powered for their age; stories of twenty-three-year-olds interacting with the treasurers of Fortune 500 companies or leading meetings on projects with million-dollar consequences are common. Working teams are lean, which means that you'll find yourself substituting for your supervisor in complex and critical situations.

Quality of Life: Hours are much longer, especially in investment banking, than in most business jobs. Investment bankers tend to work eighty to one hundred hours per week, and consultants typically work fifty to eighty hours per week. Weekend work is considered normal. Travel is very frequent. A strong work ethic and sacrifices of "outside life" are expected in banking and consulting.

Opportunity for Promotion: For undergraduates, opportunities for promotion are limited because they are expected to return to graduate school for an advanced degree. The exception is securities sales and trading, which typically promotes undergraduates without an MBA. Business school graduates face intense competition in moving up the ladder, because their peer group is of such a high quality. If you're hoping to be a big fish in a small pond, you should consider another career. In addition, many firms employ an "up-or-out" policy, which means you can't stay at one level forever.

Geographic Location: Like other business services industries such as advertising or accounting, banking and consulting tend to be clustered in major urban centers. Investment banks are located in major financial centers, overwhelmingly in New York City and to a lesser degree in Chicago, San Francisco, Los Angeles, Atlanta, and Minneapolis. Consultants are more evenly spread out but are still clustered in urban centers such as Boston, New York, Washington, D.C., San Francisco, Chicago, Los Angeles, and Atlanta. West Coast slots in both industries are limited and highly coveted.

Opportunities for Career Change: Future employers see investment banking experience as valuable for finance-related jobs, from working in the finance department of a corporation such as Pepsi or Disney to evaluating investment opportunities at an LBO or private equity firm. Consulting experience is seen as valuable background for strategic planning or general management, and consultants sometimes find these positions through the contacts they have made with clients. Consultants often join fast-growing start-up companies because they are constantly scanning for and evaluating new business ideas. Both consultants and bankers find it difficult to transfer to a function such as line management or marketing of a corporation if they have had no prior experience in these areas. The majority of undergraduate-level bankers and consultants return to business or law school.

WHO FITS THE BILL?

Aware of the huge rewards of investment banking, securities sales and trading, and management consulting, thousands of people apply for jobs in these fields each year. Job offer rates at major firms are well below 10 percent.

This figure may seem daunting, but let's deflate a couple of myths regarding who can be hired by an investment bank or a consulting firm. *Contrary to popular belief, banks and consulting firms frequently hire candidates who have no business or economics background.*

You also may have heard that firms "target" their recruiting at a handful of schools. This varies among companies. Some companies select students from a narrow range of schools; others purposely avoid taking students just from name-brand schools. In addition, although firms organize recruiting visits to only selected campuses, they will review résumés from students at any school. Outstanding students at reputable schools that are not targeted by investment banks or consulting firms still have a good shot at getting jobs in banking or consulting if they are persistent and present their credentials well.

Furthermore, there are no hard-and-fast rules about grade point averages required to win a job. There are differences in requirements between securities sales and trading, investment banking, and consulting. The likelihood of being hired into securities sales and trading from a "nontargeted" school or with a lower GPA, for example, is much greater than being hired into investment banking or management consulting. The ranks of securities sales and trading are more diverse, whereas graduates of "good schools" dominate investment banking and certain types of management consulting.

What *is* required by all three industries is a unique combination of academic performance, communications skills, personality, and presence. Because the desired blend of these characteristics is so precise, recruiting processes are more strenuous than those in other industries. Forget everything you've learned about recruiting in other business fields: Consulting and banking have their own unique set of rules and traditions.

NAVIGATING THROUGH THIS BOOK

This book has three main sections: how to understand the industries, how to get a job, and how to choose a job.

If you read anything in this book, it should be Chapters 2 and 3—these are critical to understanding the jobs before you apply for them and before you accept them.

To get a feel for the lifestyle, culture, and daily work in investment banking and management consulting, what could be better than "talking" with insiders? To this end, conversations with industry insiders are interspersed throughout the book. Most of these professionals were interviewed anonymously in order to provide you with the most unbiased information possible, and their names and identities have been disguised.

KEEPING YOUR SANITY

I returned, and saw under the sun, that . . . time and chance happeneth to them all.

—Ecclesiastes

A word of advice as you undertake the strenuous recruiting process: Luck is a factor in landing a banking or consulting job. As in the college or business school admissions process, a candidate can be accepted at one firm and denied a job at another firm of equal stature. Expect many rejections, and don't take them personally. Pick yourself up and try again. When you're dealing with a game of odds, persistence is obviously the key to eventually winning. And persistence *is* under your control.

Finally, although you should put great effort into finding a job, there is a point where the process can be taken too seriously. That's when you'll lose all perspective and start making errors in judgment, perhaps forgetting your overall goals or priorities. Take a break once in a while, take a step back, and view this process from afar. Doing so will keep you from burning out.

Good luck with the job hunt—and with your pursuit of the fast track.

VIEW FROM THE TOP

Addison (Tad) L. Piper
Chairman and CEO, Piper Jaffray Cos., Inc.

Tad Piper's office is a corner office, but not a typical one. It is simple and surprisingly small, decorated with bright Native American art and unobtrusive white furniture. One can look in from the corridor outside through glass walls. Photos of Piper's family in a myriad of frames line the sideboard by his desk.

Piper is the chairman of the board and chief executive officer of Piper Jaffray, the investment bank. In many ways, his office is an appropriate symbol of a firm that prides itself on its close-knit family of bankers, down-to-earth personalities, and accessibility of even the most senior managers. Piper Jaffray provides large and medium-size companies with investment banking, asset management, and retail distribution services.

Tad Piper joined Piper Jaffray in 1969 and eventually served as assistant syndicate manager, director of securities trading, and director of sales and marketing. He was named chairman of the management committee in 1982 and chief executive officer in 1983. He holds a BA in economics from Williams College and an MBA from Stanford University.

When you joined the firm, what was it like?

It was dramatically smaller—that was twenty-five years ago. Piper Jaffray was small, entrepreneurial, and most of our business was centered in the Midwest. But we were already beginning our expansion outside our traditional territory, which was the upper Midwest.

What are some of the major challenges you face in managing this firm?

It sounds trite, but it's true: We don't have any assets at this company other than the people walking in the door everyday. So our challenge continues to be to find and keep challenged the best people. I think that if we do that, even if the investment banking environment continues to change, we will find the right opportunities.

Is your business a relationship business?

It is. We think that in the final analysis, corporations are looking for investment bankers who really understand their industry and what's affecting them on a day-to-day basis. Who know what their competition is doing and can provide an ongoing resource to them well beyond just doing transactions for them, and who will become an important adjunct to their team. It's really important for us to be networked into their industry and know how to use our resources to their advantage.

So you end up taking a very broad perspective on their industry?

You distinguish yourself by becoming an industry expert: knowing your clients' business well, knowing how to use your resources to their advantage. The key is industry expertise, because on the other side of every transaction there's a buyer looking for an interesting investment idea. They too want you to have expertise so that you can put the investment you're recommending to them in the context of an industry—how does this particular company stack up against its competition? What is the future of this particular industry?

Do you think that clients' demand for industry experts will change the types of people investment banks need?

Well, yes and no. Because of the need for industry expertise, there is a trend toward hiring people who have come out of relevant industries—either right out of that industry or after graduate school. We'll look for somebody who is very knowledgeable in a technology area or a medical area, because they've had a head start on understanding the industry or networking in the industry.

However, it's not an insurmountable disadvantage for someone who didn't start in a relevant industry. It's just that it is a very competitive business, so to get that head start is really helpful for the client and therefore for the person's career.

If someone were to walk into this room for an interview with you, what qualities would you be looking for?

Typically the kind of person who ends up being successful is someone who has distinguished themselves in some way. We ask ourselves, what is this person's record? What is motivating him? They have to be a good student because the intellectual challenges in this business are pretty high. And our clients are knowledgeable and intelligent, so our bankers need to match up well with them. But they also distinguish themselves in other ways in addition to carrying a rigorous academic load—they've worked their way through college. They've done something in their lives to show that they're achievers. People who are successful here are aggressive—in the good sense of the word. I say aggressive as opposed to passive. Because there's aggressive that isn't particularly attractive. They're high-energy, high-activity-level people. They have shown an ability to juggle a fair number of things at once.

What distinguishes good investment bankers from great ones?

The great ones do two things. They become an invaluable part of the client's management resources, both in financing the growth of their business and in

helping them strategically. When the client thinks of someone who is important to helping them in running their business, their investment banker at
Piper Jaffray should be someone who is on that list.

But also the great bankers really know how to use our resources to the
client's best advantage. They know how to use our research analysts, our trading people, our sales people, our senior management, so that they don't always
have to be the focus. So that they don't only become invaluable to the client
but *Piper Jaffray* becomes invaluable to the client.

What advice would you give to someone just starting in the business?

There's an old bromide that holds true: There's no substitute for hard work.
There are no shortcuts, no easy way. We're in an industry where some people
seem to become successful fairly quickly. The reality is that they got there in
part because they were lucky. They also worked hard, they worked smart.
Someone just starting should learn about the resources available to them.

They should find a mentor—quickly. And if you've got the wrong mentor,
change. Often the obvious mentor, the one that's willing to spend time with
you, isn't the right mentor. The best mentors are often the busiest people who
are juggling lots of balls, and what you want to do is be one of the balls they're
juggling. The ones who have time to spend with you may not be very successful, and that's the reason they have time to spend with you. Look for people
that you admire and think are successful, and absorb what they're doing like
a sponge.

*Do you think there's a difference in the qualities needed to be successful in,
say, corporate finance versus the trading floor?*

I think the essential skills are the same, but what you do every day is quite
different. The immediacy of the moment on the trading floor is essential. The
dynamism of what's happening every day, every moment, and the need to "get
it done now" is certainly different than some of the long-term relationship
building you do on the investment banking side. Often in investment banking
the development of a relationship that results in a revenue transaction can be
over a fairly lengthy period of time. But the skills necessary to do the jobs are
similar. A good trader also has wonderful relationships with his or her clients.
The ability to build trust and credibility in a relationship is the same on the
trading floor as it is in investment banking.

*Are results less attributable to the individual in investment banking than in
trading?*

At Piper Jaffray, the days of the "star" investment banker are over. It's so
competitive out there right now that you really have to have a whole team in

place to impress the client that you're the one they want to do business with. Does that mean one-on-one relationships aren't important? No. What you want to have is several combinations of one-on-one banker-client relationships. The investment banker has got to have the right support to help him or her make that relationship work. The days of reading about the star person who's doing the huge M&A [merger and acquisition] transactions aren't completely over, because there are some incredibly talented individuals out there who have that kind of lure, but to build a business with that approach is difficult.

What advice would you give someone who's trying to break into investment banking, especially outside of the on-campus recruiting process?

We have a lot of people who come through nontraditional sources. Typically they come through someone who works here already. They establish a friendship with somebody outside the work environment either through a social, athletic, or volunteer activity. They begin networking that way, they learn more about our industry and find out it's something that intrigues them.

Or, we meet somebody during our industry networking—not the investment banking industry but the industries we're covering. And we suggest to them that it would be appropriate for them to think about switching over to investment banking. We're looking for great people, and those people don't always walk in the door. Part of our job here is to find great people, not wait for them to find us. It works both ways.

What advice would you give to someone trying to sort out which offer to take?

It's such a personal decision. I'm a firm believer in finding an environment in which you think you'll thrive. That doesn't mean the best-name firm or even apparently the best financial offer to start with. The best decisions are made based on asking yourself: What's going to fit for me best, do I like the people, do I respect the people, am I going to be challenged and given opportunities as soon as I'm able to demonstrate capability, will they let me assume more responsibility as soon as I'm able to handle it, are they going to treat me with respect, is my work going to be valued?

How would you describe Piper Jaffray's culture?

The feedback I get is that culture is important here. A lot of people are here because they feel the environment has a lot of the qualities I just described. They feel respected and valued, and they're given lots of opportunities. We have a very nonhierarchical structure here, we believe in partnership, team effort, and ready access. People here are nice people. And they're not stamped out of a mold.

They're not all from name-brand schools?

Not necessarily. Although we have a lot of the name-brand product here, not all the people who have the right characteristics went to name-brand schools. I think our culture is quite different from New York investment banking. I think people here work just as hard or harder, so it's not like "Come to the Midwest, so that you don't have to work quite as hard." But I think the environment in which we work is more supportive, both to their career and to their outside activities. It's less dog-eat-dog and more conducive to feeling good about the environment in which you're working so you're not competing against the people you're sitting next to.

I think we're more understanding here, frankly, of family and personal issues. These are part of people's lives. Raising families and doing volunteer work, we think, are also important to a person's career and longevity here. I think we're pretty understanding about things that are not strictly work-related. We understand that the whole person is important. It seems to me if people are evaluating where they want to work, if they make the assumption that they will be successful and therefore financially rewarded no matter where they go, they should seek then other things that round out their career experience and that are nonfinancial.

It seems that nonfinancial rewards are becoming more and more important to job-seekers.

I hear that from my own kids. It's not just the financial rewards, it's feeling good about myself and my company, that my company values me as a whole person and not just what I produce. Having said that, you still need to work hard. Investment banking is competitive. Our good people are spending a lot of time on airplanes and in the office. You need to be excited and stimulated by that. If somebody came to me and said, "I want to be an investment banker but I don't want to travel," I'd say, "Thank you very much for coming in." I spend half my time on airplanes, out trying to win clients all day, every day. There's no substitute for face-to-face. So you spend a fair amount of time away from home. You have to be excited and stimulated by that. That's a lifestyle issue. I don't begrudge people who don't want to do it, it's just that investment banking isn't what they should do.

Anything else that you'd like to tell the readers of this book?

Well, I've been asked many times, if I weren't doing what I'm doing, what would I do? And I can't even think of anything else. This is a wonderful business. It is very challenging, very intellectually stimulating, and there are opportunities to meet all kinds of creative, interesting people. It's fascinating, fun, and rewarding in the broadest sense of the word. So I'm obviously sold on this business, and I would encourage people who have the characteristics we've been talking about to actively pursue investment banking.

General advice? If I were starting again in business I would look for a career that's fun. We spend too much time working to not enjoy it. Look for something that's really going to excite you, so that you feel energized every day and you'll get up saying, "Okay, what am I going to do today?" There are too many people I know who are my age who have spent a career not being very happy, wishing that they were doing something else but feeling trapped. So, seek a career that you think you'll really enjoy. I've been in banking for about twenty-seven years, and I'm as excited about it today as I was when I started.

Be your own person. Be less concerned about monetary compensation. I mean, it is important—we're all here to make a living—but if you find something you're successful at and enjoying, the financial rewards are going to be adequate. Everybody has a different measure of the money they think is adequate, but the other part of the equation is more important. If you're enjoying your work, you're going to be good at it and will be compensated. In the final analysis, the financial reward is only a piece of the reward. My observation is that people who enjoy their lives the most are those who enjoy what they do.

VIEW FROM THE TOP

Kenichi Ohmae

Former Director and Chairman of Asia Pacific Council, McKinsey & Co.

Kenichi Ohmae defies expectations. Often credited with inventing the profession of management consulting in Japan, Ohmae spent twenty-three years at McKinsey & Co., the world's most prestigious consulting firm. There, he didn't advise just anybody: Clients included the prime minister of Malaysia, the CEOs of Asia's most important companies, and other heads of state. He is regarded as one of the world's foremost thinkers on global strategy.

Ohmae is a modern "Renaissance man": While working full-time as a consultant, he wrote more than sixty books (an average of about three books per year), many of which became international bestsellers. His books include *The End of the Nation State* (1995), *The Evolving Global Economy* (1995), and *The Mind of the Strategist* (1982).

Ohmae holds a Ph.D in nuclear engineering from M.I.T. In his spare time, he plays the clarinet, records CDs with professional musicians, rides his motorcycle, and somehow manages to spend time on interests such as reforming Japan's socio-political system.

There's one thing he's *not*—shy with his opinions.

What were some early career decisions you made, and how did you make them?

I had a degree in nuclear engineering, and in those days I didn't have much of a choice. I became an engineer, working for Hitachi in Japan. Then I made the decision to leave the field of nuclear engineering—this was probably the most important choice I made. Very accidentally my résumé came to the attention of a headhunter. The headhunter called me and said that there was this management consulting firm that had opened an office in Tokyo but didn't have any people, and they wanted to interview me. I didn't know what management consulting was and had never heard of McKinsey, but I decided to talk with them. McKinsey didn't know what to make of me either—I didn't have any business education, I didn't even know what "price" and "cost" were.

I later found out that only one in eight McKinsey people who interviewed me actually voted strongly in favor of giving me a job. But they didn't have much of a choice, because they needed people.

When I arrived at McKinsey, I began teaching myself the profession of consulting. I compiled all of what I had learned into an internal memorandum so that I could pass this on to other consultants. By chance, *President* magazine in Japan wanted to interview a senior director at McKinsey, and I supplied the memorandum to the magazine to give them some background on consulting. I was then asked if I was willing to publish it. This internal memo eventually became the bestseller *The Mind of the Strategist*. At the age of thirty-one I found myself touring around, giving lectures, and trying to explain to Japan the field of management consulting. In my early years, I was sleeping about four hours each night. In Japan at the time, if you were a young man in business you weren't treated very well, you weren't even invited into the executive suites. But this book, and the others I wrote after it, gave me an advantage in dealing with much older Japanese executives.

What advice would you give to college students who are trying to sort out their career options?

I have always chosen the more difficult path, and this is what I would advise young people to do as well. When you know the answer to all the questions, then you know that this path is more certain and that you would learn and grow more by taking another path with greater unknowns.

What benefits or drawbacks does management consulting present to the recent graduate who's interested in a business career?

I would advise recent graduates to go ahead and join a consulting firm. At McKinsey, we have distilled decades of research into training materials for new consultants. I sort of envy this new generation of consultants, because we didn't have any books, or internal guides, when I started. But now a young person can be exposed to hundreds of management issues and top-level strategic thinking. These are very powerful tools. I would recommend consulting over taking a job in one company in industry, where a recent graduate may work on just one or two management issues.

But I think there is a disadvantage to joining consulting now, which is that you don't have a chance to think through these frameworks or solutions as if you were inventing them yourself. If you treat this as a cookie-cutter process, then your brain won't be as well trained. Always develop an inquisitive mind. At the root of consulting or any other profession is the ability to ask questions and figure out an approach to coming up with solutions. That is at the root of problem-solving.

If you can solve problems that no one else can, there is an opportunity to make money. The value of some outside advisor being able to come up with an approach to finding solutions for institutions is so high that there is always room for such a person.

Any specific advice about a career in consulting?

Join smaller offices, because smaller offices are much better in giving you the opportunities to work on larger problems. The smaller offices have the advantage of letting you see the forest instead of just the trees. I had the advantage of having no office at all.

What do you think makes a great consultant?

Interpersonal relationships are a very important aspect of consulting. Consulting is a very human, interface-intensive profession. If you don't like people, or people don't like you, then you can't do consulting. At the end of the day, consulting means sharing your vision with the chief executive. A lot of times a chief executive can agree that what you're saying makes sense. But unless he or she has ultimate confidence in you as a person, they will not follow your advice. So interpersonal skills are really the key. I have seen *so* many smart people at McKinsey: Many of them can solve problems, many of them can come up with beautiful analyses. For them the solutions are so obvious that they talk as if the solutions are obvious. And CEOs get offended. Because it's less obvious to the CEOs. You can turn off chief executives or managers so easily by the attitude that solutions are obvious. Therefore, you have to develop a sensitivity, develop sympathy with the person in question. Think on her behalf: If you were in her shoes, what would you do? You have to think like her and live like her and see what you come up with.

One reason I think I've been able to relate well to CEOs is that I was very close to my grandparents. And I also was a tourist guide for six years, and my typical clients were older American retirees. So I was not only close to my own grandparents, but I was very familiar with these other old folks. I had a clear advantage in that I was very comfortable with older people. At McKinsey, my colleagues were surprised that I could convert older executives to my camp within a very short period of time. They thought I could get into bed with them if I wanted to!

I respect older people, I respect where they've come from and how far they've come. And that's helped me relate to them. If you have an appreciation for what they've done, and in addition you can give some fresh perspective and come up with nonthreatening possibilities that they can take ownership of, then that's better than just giving them the solution and telling them that they have to accept it. So as a young man or woman, you have to develop the skill of knowing how to deal with decision makers. That people skill is something that I cannot find in many young, intelligent people.

Another element in consulting is that you have to feel comfortable building yourself as a result of building small blocks. It's not your company, it's somebody else's company. It's not your problem, it's somebody else's problem. The engagement is finite, maybe six months or three months. If you feel that you need to be building a company or department over twenty years, and that's your joy, then consulting isn't right for you. Consulting means short-term projects, and that's it. So each experience has to become the nutrition for developing yourself as a person. To become a better problem-solver, and a better manager.

I have seen a lot of consultants in their forties who are not very well established in society, not very accepted in chief executives' ranks. They make good money if they've stayed in the consulting industry for ten or fifteen years. But their social status or prestige, as opposed to their status within the firm, is at odds. They don't have impact on society, they don't have impact on a group of CEOs. They have stopped growing at thirty-five or maybe forty. They are the most uninteresting people at fifty. Only a few consultants grow to have impact commensurate with their income and the internal positions they hold. We at McKinsey have only seen a half-dozen such guys, you know, high-impact guys, around the world. Very few people grow beyond the minimum necessary survival skills to be a consultant. Very few grow to become socially very influential, and more should—they can contribute to society in very important areas. They can develop strategies for governments, they can develop economic recommendations, they can recommend health reforms or political reforms—any of these. But you have to really keep pushing new frontiers to become someone like that. Otherwise, you end up dull and old.

Do you think you can develop charisma, or do you think you need to be born with it?

I would advise young people to have the assumption from day one that charisma can be developed. Otherwise, you give up too early in the game. And that's not good. It's hard to explain how charisma comes about. I myself was a totally secluded, almost reclusive, engineer before I joined consulting, and my associates tell me now that I have charisma. Before, I wasn't even associating with others, not even watching TV, not reading the papers. I was able to explain the relationship between a neutron and a proton but not the relationship between John and Mary. Now I can tell you what's happening in the world, I can tell you what's happening in human society. This is the result of doing the right things, so the best advice I can give is to believe that charisma can be developed. I think every year is fresh, and you should keep trying something new and make new efforts every year. By year thirty you'll be a good man, and by year forty you'll be a terrific man.

You have a very broad set of interests, everything from politics to education. Where do these interests come from?

I have this strange obsession with death. I've always thought about how I would die. Early on in high school, I guess I wanted to die. But when I died, I wanted to have no regrets. The day I die could be today or tomorrow. So every year, every day, I ask myself if I would have regrets for not having done this or that, and I always do things that I feel that I will retrospectively not regret. That's why I have tried my best each year, in January, to come up with a new issue that I will devote myself to in the next one year. It's usually completely unrelated to consulting. Some years ago, my goal was to understand China better. At other times, it was corporate marriages or the reform of Japan. One year I asked myself, what if the chairman of Japan were to come to me and ask me to fix Japan Inc.? Then I came up with a book called *The Reform of Heisei;* and other related books to transform Japan into a modern society. I ended up retiring from McKinsey to pursue this course of action on a full-time basis. It was originally one of my self-imposed projects. One theme a year. You learn a great deal. Education and educational reform is my more recent theme. If I come up with themes, they usually result in something like writing a book. But the objective is not to produce something, but to give me an opportunity to think about issues that I'm not familiar with. Basically, it's evidence that I'm still alive and kicking. That's how I live.

Young men and women have every privilege to fail, and I advise them to fail many times. Because when they become important, failure becomes expensive. When they're young, failure is cheap.

How has consulting affected your lifestyle?

Over the past twenty-five years I have been on the road most of the time. I take about twenty to twenty-five overseas trips a year. Over 500 or 600 trips in sum. Very rarely do I spend two days in one place. It's a very heavy toll on family life and friends. I developed early on a method for dividing my time into four: one is professional time, one is family time, one is society time, and the last is my personal time. I play the clarinet, I ride motorcycles, I play active sports in my personal time. I have my family time, I always make a point of going out to dinner with my wife at least once a week. With my two sons, I normally communicate on the Internet, but make a point of spending my vacation time with them, either skiing in Whistler, where we have a house, or playing water sports at our house on Australia's Gold Coast. Lifestyle-wise, my wife also plays music, so we give concerts a couple times a year. My wife, Jeannette, and I have always kept up with music. We have published a couple of CDs, and we give concerts with accomplished musicians, which forces me to continue to do this.

In my society time, I devote myself to thinking about reforming society, my country, and the world. Because I am a citizen. And as a citizen of Tokyo, Japan, and the world, I want to use the expertise that I have developed over time to help societies. That's my pro-bono contribution to society.

What does all this do to me? It cuts into my sleeping time. I sleep a little bit more than I used to, but I have developed an inability to sleep long hours.

Any thoughts for what you'll be devoting yourself to over the next few years?

As I said, I don't want to have any regrets when I die. The only thing that I think at this time that I'd regret is the society component, because I have already had a pretty good life. But, my home country, Japan, is going down the tubes, and there are so many things one can do to reform the country. It could be so much better of a country and member of the world community, and yet they seem to be going in the wrong direction. For this reason, in the future, I will probably spend more time trying to fix Japanese society. I ran for the Governorship of Tokyo in 1995 as my means of devoting more time for the reform of Japan. But I did not make it. Japan is not yet ready for a broad scope of reforms. That is understandable. Frankly, I don't want to be a politician myself and do the things that as a politician you have to do. If you go motorbiking in the mountains or jet-skiing as a government official, it's not received very well here! I'm not going to give up those lifestyle things. I've decided to find someone who can be the "skipper" of Japan and work for him. After all, that is the role of a top management consultant. That's what I'll spend more time on during the next decade.

2

MANAGEMENT CONSULTING:
AN OVERVIEW

DEFINING CONSULTING

Ask consultants what they do for a living and you'll get a vague answer: *We provide guidance on critical management issues to corporations.* Which might leave you wondering "What types of management issues? What types of guidance?"

Consultants basically serve as doctors to large, Fortune 500 corporations. Consultants examine a company's situation, diagnose the source of a problem, prescribe solutions, and help the company implement changes. To do this, consultants use a combination of analytical tools and quantitative and qualitative information.

The looseness of a consultant's job description reflects the unclear boundaries of the industry. To some, management consulting refers only to providing companies with advice on strategy and internal operations. To others, guidance on *any* business area—finance, human resources, and so on—qualifies as consulting. The consultant's job description becomes vague when all these types of advice are included.

In this book, I will set parameters on a definition of management consulting in order to explain the industry clearly. I will focus on those firms that most typically hire graduates fresh out of college or graduate school and that have developed the most systematic recruiting procedures. I therefore refer to management consultants as those consultants who help companies make decisions in the following areas:

- *strategy:* a company's external focus. Determining how a company should behave in its business environment and which broad goals it should set, given internal capabilities and external influences such as customers, competitors, and suppliers.
- *operations:* a company's internal focus. Determining how a company can operate optimally—its organization, processes, and policies—given its resources and strategy.
- *information technology:* developing technology strategy and systems that support, inform, and enable a company to achieve its overall strategic goals.

Management consulting employs approximately 225,000 people worldwide. The industry generated over $45 billion in worldwide sales in 1996[1] and is projected to grow at a compound annual rate of 13 percent through 1999.[2] The long arm of consulting shows: Practically every firm in the Fortune and Global Fortune 500 has hired a consulting firm.

A BRIEF HISTORY

Consulting has its roots both in older professions such as law and accounting and in the work of turn-of-the-century engineers and economists such as Frederick Taylor and Josef Schumpeter.[3] An early pioneer, Edwin Booz founded Booz•Allen & Hamilton in 1914 to provide economic and business analysis to corporations. His early clients included Goodyear Tire & Rubber and the Canadian Pacific Railroad. McKinsey & Co., also a pioneer, was started by an accountant in 1926 to provide professional help with management problems.[4] Marvin Bower, McKinsey's patriarch, joined the firm in 1933 and guided it with a clear mission: "to provide advice on managing to top executives, and to do it with the professional standards of a leading law firm."[5] Management consulting still enjoys a prestigious reputation and high standards of professionalism.

Despite its influence in the business community today, management consulting is a relatively young industry. The oldest consulting firm was founded in the late 1800s and faced no competition for decades. During the 1940s consultants advised companies on how to increase production, as U.S. industrial capacity was critical to war efforts. In the mid-1960s new consulting firms began to enter the market, offering advice on corporate strategy in an attempt to meet emerging competition from European businesses. In the early 1970s strategy "boutiques" pioneered the development of consulting products—specific tools such as the "experience curve" and the "portfolio matrix"—to help managers solve problems. This innovation raised the stakes for other firms that had until then sold themselves on the basis of their superior intelli-

Selected Management Consulting Firms*

Firm	Estimated 1996 Management Consulting Revenues ($ millions)
Andersen Consulting	5,300
McKinsey & Co.	2,100
Ernst & Young	2,100
Coopers & Lybrand	1,918
Deloitte & Touche	1,550
KPMG Peat Marwick	1,380
Arthur Andersen	1,380
Mercer Consulting Group	1,159
Towers Perrin	903
A.T. Kearney	870
Price Waterhouse	840
IBM Consulting Group	730
Booz·Allen & Hamilton	720
Watson Wyatt Worldwide	656
The Boston Consulting Group	600
Gemini Consulting	600
Arthur D. Little, Inc.	574
Bain & Company	450
CSC Index	200
Monitor Company	181

Industry Facts:
1996 Total Worldwide Revenues: $45 billion (including $21 billion in U.S.)
People Employed: 225,000 worldwide
Projected Compound Annual Growth Rate: 13% through 1999

*Revenues for fiscal year 1996. Mercer Consulting Group figure includes both William M. Mercer and Mercer Management Consulting.

Source: *Consultants News*, author's analysis, company interviews.

gence. Further changes occurred in the late 1980s and early 1990s when consulting firms built generalist capabilities through mergers and acquisitions. Restructurings and leveraged buyouts placed heavy debt burdens on American corporations, which had to increase cash flow by decreasing costs. To cut costs, consultants were called in to help downsize and "reengineer" corporations. In the mid-1990s consultants came full circle and again focused on generating growth.

Every year consultants invent new management tools that become popular fads, only to watch them replaced by new tools within a year or two. Scan the list of books at the end of this chapter and you will find many written by consulting firms to promote their own business commandments.

Throughout these changes consulting firms have consistently and selectively recruited on undergraduate and business school campuses, fueling the hype surrounding consulting. Top graduates compete for consulting jobs, which earn them prestige and the highest starting salaries of any industry.

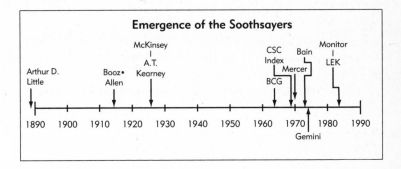

Riding the Gravy Train: Typical Consultants' Salaries

Level	Avg. Starting Salary	+	Annual Bonus	+	Signing Bonus	+	Profit Sharing
Manager	$100,000		0–40% of base		N/A		5–10% of salary
Associate	$ 87,000		0–30% of base		$21,000		5–10% of salary
Analyst	$ 40,000		0–10% of base		$2,000		5–10% of salary

Sources: Interviews with students and career counselors, author's analysis.

Emergence of the Soothsayers

McKinsey · A.T. Kearney · Arthur D. Little · Booz•Allen · CSC Index · Bain · Monitor · LEK · Mercer · BCG · Gemini

1890 1900 1910 1920 1930 1940 1950 1960 1970 1980 1990

THE CLIENTS

Consulting firms can afford to pay sky-high salaries because they charge clients as much as $200,000 a month. Since their costs tick upward regularly as salary checks go out the door, consulting firms strive to keep over 60 percent of their employees "utilized," in other words billable to clients at any given time.[6] Each client is served by a team of consultants composed of several senior and junior members. As in the legal profession, different members of the team bill at different rates. For example, clients might be billed at a rate of $100 per hour, or $4,000 per week, for a twenty-two-year-old analyst right out of college, while the rate for a senior manager might be $500 per hour, or $20,000 per week. What clients buy this expensive advice? Typically, they are large corporations with names you would recognize, such as:

- AT&T
- Avon Products
- Bell Atlantic
- British Telecom

- Burger King
- CIGNA
- Coca-Cola
- DuPont
- Fresh Choice Restaurants
- Rolls-Royce
- Sony
- Whirlpool
- Wisconsin Power & Light

More rarely, clients are governments, small businesses, or nonprofit entities. Who hires consultants? Executives ranging from chief executive officers (CEOs) to department heads hire consultants. As a consultant, you'll work with a team of colleagues and client employees to address a problem that the executive is wrestling with.

Why does the executive hire a consulting firm? Consultants perform work that the company is too busy to do or finds economical to outsource; many companies find it cheaper to hire consultants occasionally for special projects than to keep an entire strategic planning staff on payroll. Consultants also are hired for their:

- *Fresh perspective:* New ideas often spring from a consultant's outside perspective.

- *Knowledge, data, or expertise:* Clients won't otherwise have access to the expertise and data that consultants have gathered in helping other businesses.

- *Ability to make difficult decisions* (i.e., do the dirty work): Clients can use consultants as a front for cost-cutting or layoffs, and ask them to make these changes.

- *Ability to change an organization:* Consultants have processes and human resource tools that enable them to implement change smoothly.

- *Objectivity and immunity from politics:* Consultants can recommend the right changes rather than being influenced by preconceived notions or internal politics. (However, they do need to be aware of the politics within the client company.)

It is not unusual for a large corporation to hire several consultants at once, assigning each a different business issue. Consultants sometimes find themselves working jointly on a project with competing firms.

You might think that Corporate America eventually would tire of paying for advice, especially in economically difficult times. But the strength of the

The Consulting Process

SELLING A PROJECT
The consulting process begins when a corporate executive calls a consultant for advice or when a consultant calls on a client. In many cases, the corporate executive already has a long-standing relationship with the consultant. The consultant (usually a high-ranking partner) meets with the client to discuss the problem, and sometimes brings along a colleague who specializes in a relevant area.

STAFFING A PROJECT
Once the executive agrees to hire the consultant, the consulting firm mobilizes a project team. The team includes a project manager with previous experience in the industry, several associates and analysts with diverse backgrounds, and client employees with relevant knowledge.

ANALYZING THE CLIENT'S PROBLEM
After moving into offices on the client's premises, the team launches into an analysis, interviewing client employees, generating hypotheses that will guide their research, and diagnosing the heart of the client's problem. The team formulates a solution to the problem.

ACHIEVING BUY-IN
In order to gather support in the client's firm, the team must present its findings to client employees along the way. By the time the team formally presents its recommendations for change, most key clients already have given the team constructive input and agreed to support them. If the client doesn't agree with the recommendations, the consultants must go back and fine-tune their analysis.

IMPLEMENTING A SOLUTION
Once the consultant's team has come up with a solution the client supports, the client extends the consultants' contract to implement their recommendations. (This occurs about 30 to 50 percent of the time.) The consulting firm then takes a fresh look at staffing needs for the implementation phase, perhaps bringing on additional consultants who have particular operations or process experience.

How Many Consultants Does It Take to Fix a Corporation?

AT&T spent over $290 million on consultants from 1990 to 1993, including advice from these firms:

Firm	Fees from AT&T ($M)	Firm	Fees from AT&T ($M)
McKinsey	79.1	Geopartners	10.1
Monitor	76.5	CSC Index	7.0
Andersen	56.7	A.T. Kearney	5.0
Mercer	24.8	Booz•Allen	4.3
BCG	22.9	Deloitte & Touche	4.0

Source: *Business Week*

---

consulting industry continues nevertheless. Companies depend on consultants in sickness and in health, for richer or poorer. In bad times, consultants are hired to cut costs, and in good times, they are hired to spur growth. The consulting field is extraordinarily creative in its ability to generate new products to keep the industry "fresh" and client demand piqued. In this way, consultants are somewhat isolated from business cyclicality. Currently, growth in the consulting industry is being driven by client demand for large technology projects and by increased demand overseas.

WHAT PROBLEMS DO CONSULTANTS SOLVE?

Let's get into types of issues consultants work on, since this will drive your experience. Project length, amount of client interaction, and daily duties are all affected by the issues your team is analyzing. Management consultants are hired to work on three major categories of issues: *strategy, operations,* and *information technology.*

STRATEGY CONSULTING

When you think of strategy, think of a company's *external* focus. Strategy determines a company's relation to its outside environment. Consultants help shape a company's destination based on the company's internal capabilities and external influences such as competitors, customers, allies, and suppliers. As can be expected, strategy consultants work with very high-level corporate executives who are in charge of setting the direction of their company.

As a strategy consultant, you could help clients explore possibilities of growth, research and respond to competitors or unfavorable market trends, segment the markets for a company's products, assess the structural attractiveness of an industry, consider potential alliances with other companies, and come up with a strategy for mergers and acquisitions and financing.

Examples of strategic problems that consultants could be asked to solve are:

- Our chemicals division sales decreased suddenly last year. What is the source of the problem and what can we do to reverse it?
- Our company is wondering whether we should buy or continue to make printed circuit boards for use in the PCs we manufacture. Which strategic factors should we consider before outsourcing? How should we restructure our organization if we outsource?
- We want to expand our Java coffeehouses into new markets. How should we go about choosing and entering these markets?
- Our satellite technology could be used to provide telephone service in Bali. What other markets in Asia would be attractive? Would this market be profitable in the long term? How can we leverage our basic technology to provide other telecommunications services?
- We run a large salmon estuary. We are considering shifting our focus to value-added products, such as smoked salmon. How would our competitors respond?

Of course, often there is a fine line between analyzing strategy and operations because a strategic decision often requires changes in the way a company operates. In particular, organizational issues such as major restructuring or downsizing could be categorized as either strategic or operational in nature.

OPERATIONS/PROCESS CONSULTING

When you think of operations, think of a company's *internal* focus—its optimal procedures, analytical tools, processes, organization, productivity, and costs. The daily operations of a company are what accomplishes overall goals: If strategy determines the destination, effective operations enable a company to reach that destination.

As an operations consultant, you could help clients restructure their organization, optimize their logistics, improve the performance of their service or manufacturing process, improve the quality of their output, or reduce operating or inventory holding costs.

Operations consulting has a strong implementation bent. When people speak of operations or "process" consulting, often what is implied is that in addition to making recommendations to a client, consultants make change happen within the client's organization. For this reason, operations projects often last longer than pure strategy projects. Operations consultants become very familiar with how companies operate on a daily basis, how managers make decisions, and how operating decisions impact profitability.

"Reengineering" (also known as BPR, or business process reengineering), a hot consulting trend of the early 1990s, was a classic example of operations consulting. CSC Index reportedly described reengineering to recruits this way: "Reengineering involves looking at inputs and desired outputs, and finding the best process for the middle."[7]

Many business functions act together to enable a company to operate. As an operations consultant, you could tackle issues within marketing, sales, supply, logistics, or distribution functions, for example. Two areas often are broken out into separate consulting industry categories: information technology and human resources (i.e., compensation and benefits). These are considered large consulting market segments of their own.

Examples of operational issues that consultants advise clients on are:

- How can we achieve and sustain world-class manufacturing productivity and performance?
- Inventory levels at our distribution center are always inadequate, causing major delays in replenishment at our retail stores. What is causing this problem, and what type of solution should we implement?
- Are we efficiently allocating our supply of metal to our nationwide automobile factories so that we minimize costs and downtime? If not, how can we optimize our allocation?
- Our semiconductor sales force is receiving poor ratings from customers. Which key service criteria are we missing? How can we improve our service?
- How can we restructure and reduce the size of our credit card organization yet minimize negative effects on our culture and morale?

INFORMATION TECHNOLOGY/SYSTEMS CONSULTING

Information technology (IT) consultants find ways to apply technology to achieve a client's business goals. To do this, they either work with a company's information systems department or its senior financial or operating officers. Information technology could reasonably be categorized as an operations issue—computer systems are one tool a manager uses to operate a company. However, we break out IT consulting because it is an enormous segment of the consulting industry. Systems consulting revenues account for a much bigger part of the market than strategy consulting, for example, and are growing at a faster rate. What's driving this growth? With the shift in corporate systems from mainframes to PCs, corporations are facing an increasingly complex task in integrating disparate systems and managing large-scale technology projects. Facing uncertainty, they're bringing in the consultants.

Systems consulting involves several steps:

1. Strategy: creating technology strategy that links to a firm's overall strategy and operations
2. Development: designing custom software

Consultant-Speak

Here's a translation of a few well-known approaches consultants use:

Activity-Based Costing (ABC): Assigns overhead costs to customers and products based on the amount of activity and resources spent on these customers and products. Leads to enhanced understanding of customer and product profitability. (See "On the Job: A Case Example.")

Balanced Scorecard: Enhances performance measurement by creating a scorecard based on a balance of four perspectives—customer, internal, financial, and future. Allows companies to measure both daily performance and long-term strategy.

Economic Value Added (EVA) analysis: Measures the return on total capital invested in a company. To improve accountability for delivering value to shareholders, operating income is compared to the cost of the capital invested.

Reengineering: The radical redesign of a company's processes, organization, and culture. Traditional vertical divisions such as sales, marketing, and production are reorganized around processes such as taking an order, delivering products, and collecting payments.

Supply Chain Management: Manages supplier relationships in order to gain competitive advantage in cost, service, and quality. Streamlines logistics and procurement; integrates business functions with suppliers.

Total Quality Management: Teaches that quality, like everything else, has an intrinsic value and is extremely important to customers; spreads customer orientation throughout company; empowers employees to fix problems in order to sustain world-class quality of products, services, and processes; sets goal of meeting rigorous quality standards; emphasizes continuous improvement.

3. Integration: creating interfaces to make disparate systems compatible
4. Management: assuming all or part of a client's IT operations

As they progress toward later steps, consultants need less general business knowledge and more industry and technical knowledge.

Examples of information technology issues that face clients are:

- How can we use technology to improve our competitive position?
- We will be shifting our customer focus from individuals to businesses. What are the IT implications of this change, and how can we manage them?
- Our Grub pet food brand managers do not have access to daily regional sales information and customer profitability data. How can we help them?
- The local government wants to improve its tax accounting and billing process. How can they use systems to do this?

- How can we design a software package to reduce labor costs in the customer service area?
- We need to improve the speed of our billing process. Can you build us a system that integrates our accounting database and customer database?

Consulting projects can fall purely into the strategy, operations, or IT categories or be sweeping enough to fall into several categories. For example, a CEO might hire a consultant to increase company-wide profitability by 5 percent. To accomplish this goal, consultants might perform both strategic work (decide that the company needs to produce a new product), operations work (adapt the manufacturing process to best make this new product), and information technology work (build an information system that allows the company to provide better customer service to those buying the new product).

What Skills and Knowledge Will I Develop in Consulting?

Knowledge of:
- how a business operates
- different industries and the relevant business models within them
- how to break down and analyze complex business problems
- how to articulate ideas clearly and compellingly
- how to prioritize and complete work under time constraints
- how to make decisions under informational constraints
- how to develop credibility with people more senior than you
- how to work effectively as part of a business team

COMPANY ORGANIZATION

Unless a firm is small or specialized, it organizes consultants into divisions. These divisions typically serve as a consultant's "home base"—divisions oversee recruiting, staffing, evaluation, and training. Consulting firms are organized into divisions in order to build specialized expertise, operate more efficiently, and give the consultant a sense of belonging to a smaller business unit.

Consulting firms organize their people around one or more of the following affiliations:

- *Geography/Office.* Divisions can be continental (North America vs. Europe), regional (Asia/Pacific vs. Latin America), or city-based (San Francisco vs. New York)

- *Industry.* Sectors can include financial services, consumer products, energy and chemicals, multimedia/communications, and "diversified industries"

- *Functional Expertise.* Strategy, operations, information technology, organizational development, and financial advisory services (such as mergers and acquisitions) are among the most common functional distinctions

Each firm is structured differently. (See company profiles at the end of the book.) Booz•Allen & Hamilton is organized around industry groups. Consultants at Bain & Company, on the other hand, are more strongly affiliated with geographic groups. The level of decentralization—the autonomy given to divisions—also differs from one firm to another. Bain, for example, is known for its collection of fairly independent, "entrepreneurial" offices.[8]

THE PROJECT AND THE TEAM

Although your division serves as your home base, as a consultant you will find that your professional life revolves around your client project (also known as your "engagement" or "case").

Consultants are assigned to work on one or two projects at a time. Increasingly asked by clients to implement change, consultants typically spend two to four days per week on-site at a client's offices. This means that, as a consultant, your perspective on your job is heavily influenced by your current project: The client's office becomes your office and your project teammates become your closest colleagues for the duration of the case.

Projects last anywhere from a few weeks to over a year, with the average falling in the three- to seven-month range. Projects involving analysis and recommendation typically are shorter than projects involving implementation of recommendations, because making change happen within an organization depends on the cooperation of client employees and can be time-consuming.

In addition, the more an engagement focuses on a company's operations rather than its strategy, the more time consultants will spend working on-site: Consultants can perform strategic analysis at their own offices because it entails independent research, but they examine operations most efficiently on the client's premises.

One unusual aspect of the consultant's job is the high level of change that occurs in daily tasks and environment. A reward of project-based work is the constant learning that occurs as consultants move from one project to the next, with an entirely different set of clients, colleagues, and business issues. Unlike other business professions, a consultant's job changes greatly every few months.

How does working in project teams affect the consultant? Your team becomes your professional life for the duration of the project, especially if you are working on client premises. If you are happy with the team, you are likely to have high job satisfaction. Good teamwork is critical to each project's success; this is why teamwork is emphasized again and again as an important factor in the consulting culture. Be prepared to demonstrate a team player attitude in your interviews.

Project teams are typically staffed with three to fifteen consultants from different hierarchical levels. As an undergraduate or graduate student with no business experience, you can expect to be hired as an *analyst*. As a graduate school student with an advanced degree in business, law, or engineering, you can expect to be hired as an *associate*. Typically, a *vice-president* or *partner* is responsible for the overall client relationship but does not spend time on-site with the project team. The project is managed on a daily basis by a *manager* and is staffed with several associates and analysts. The next chart, based on discussions with insiders, summarizes the typical pecking order within a consulting firm.

Firms try hard to keep a project's staff turnover to a minimum, because clients are concerned about the efficiency of a changing team. However, on extremely long projects (a year or more), consultants are sometimes "rolled off" to another project if they have spent what is considered too much time on one project to be objective.

Level (Typical Titles)	Initial Role
Senior Vice President, Partner	Helps determine direction of firm, leads business development in entire sectors, contributes significantly to firm's thought leadership
Vice President, Officer	Builds client relationships, develops analytical tools, oversees overall quality of services, determines internal administrative policies, provides thought leadership
Manager, Principal	Manages day-to-day project activities, provides project-specific thought leadership, responsible for project results and productivity, acts as leading on-site contact with clients
Associate, Consultant, Senior Consultant	Manages portions of a project, generates hypotheses, writes documents, develops recommendations, conducts some research, presents results to clients
Analyst, Business Analyst, Junior Consultant	Gathers and interprets data to support hypotheses, develops computerized analytical models, works with junior clients, supports associates at client presentations

ON THE JOB: A CASE EXAMPLE

You've heard about the types of problems that consultants solve, but exactly what do they do to solve them? In management consulting, you could divide up daily work into several major categories: planning and logistics, research, analysis, communication, and implementation. Here's a simplified example of these categories on a consulting project.

> *Prometheus Shoes makes high-performance athletic shoes and supplies them to three department stores. Prometheus is wondering how much business sense it makes to serve all three, and hires McCambridge consultants to help them decide which of their customers is most attractive. McCambridge will revamp the company's current accounting system by building an activity-based costing computer model. McCambridge's computer model will assign costs to each customer based on the amount of company resources the company truly spends serving the customer, and then it will calculate how much profit is made on each customer. Some customers, for example, may require a great deal more marketing support. Others may order frequent, smaller shipments, which would cause the company to spend more on order processing. Prometheus's current cost system does not measure these expenses on a customer basis.*

PLANNING

Planning and coordinating are an important part of a consultant's job, particularly at the beginning of a project. Associates are involved in the staffing of a project, the building of a workplan and timetable for an entire team, and the coordination of client documents. Analysts plan their research around the availability of data, organizing their time to meet their responsibilities, and work with administrative staff to produce client documents in a timely manner. This could include everything from drawing graphs and charts and editing text to helping photocopy, bind, and mail presentations.

> *An associate and an analyst from McCambridge have been assigned to the Prometheus team. The client has also assigned key employees to the project team. During the first week on the project, everyone gets to know each other, through a dinner at a local restaurant. With the clients and the project manager, the associate plans the overall scope of the project around the clients' goals. She decides which products will be analyzed, which steps need to be taken, and how long the project will take. The analyst is assigned a discrete piece of work and lays out his own workplan.*

RESEARCH

Consultants perform research on a client's products, industry, and operations. Typically, consultants begin by extensively interviewing clients to gain their perspective on the company, the industry, and the issue of concern. Interviews can take place with clients at many levels—everyone from a top executive to a line manager. Consultants make use of reports already generated by clients or by consulting colleagues. Analysts and associates also spend time talking to industry experts, research firms, and government agencies or reading reports written by independent organizations. Primary research involves interviews with competitors or customers in one-on-one conversations, focus groups, or surveys. Research is hypothesis-driven: Approaching a problem with a hypothesis helps consultants focus their analysis and ask the right questions from the very beginning of a project.

> *The McCambridge consultants spend their next two weeks interviewing executives throughout the company to understand the client's current cost allocation methods and its views on which costs might be misallocated. After sales employees recount stories of small last-minute orders from Foster's Department Stores, the McCambridge team forms a hypothesis: Foster's is costing the company a great deal of money in terms of customer service and order processing. However, the current cost accounting system is not reflecting this. Based on this hypothesis, the team designs the rest of the project to ensure that order processing, delivery, and customer service costs will be examined very closely.*
>
> *The McCambridge analyst designs and writes interview forms to gather data on how much time the sales, purchase order, and delivery departments are spending on each customer and how much time they work in total. By finding out what percentage of their time they spend on Foster's, the analyst figures, he will be able to allocate a certain portion of their salaries and department costs to the Foster's account.*

ANALYSIS

Consultants analyze their research to come up with recommendations for the client. Analysis involves dissecting seemingly unrelated data in order to discover patterns and meanings behind it. Afterward, consultants synthesize these findings into major points upon which the client can act and that relate to the client's high-level concerns. Consultants perform many types of analysis, from building spreadsheets to predict the growth of a new market, to developing a framework with which a client can segment its customer base.

> *The McCambridge associate helps the analyst design the overall framework of the computer model that the analyst will build in Microsoft Excel. A data dump from Prometheus's internal cost system is fed into the model, with total costs of the sales, order processing, delivery, and other "overhead" departments.*
>
> *The analyst calculates the cost of an hour of a Prometheus employee's time by dividing total expenses by total employee hours in each department. Then the model assigns costs to each of the three department stores based on the survey responses of how much time each employee spends on orders re-*

lated to each store. Just as the McCambridge consultants suspected, Foster's is consuming a lot of company resources: Even though it accounts for only 15 percent of total units shipped, the store actually consumes 25 percent of overhead costs. This is because the store makes small, last-minute orders very frequently, and Prometheus's cost of processing each order and delivering each shipment is the same no matter what its size. Allocating overhead costs just based on total units shipped underestimated the cost of serving Foster's. Furthermore, the Foster's account is not profitable.

COMMUNICATION

Consultants must articulate their ideas clearly and compellingly and present them to clients in several ways. In most cases, consultants have reviewed their progress informally with clients along the way through memos, conversations, and meetings. End-of-project presentations combine both written and verbal presentations. Consultants make "panel sets" or "presentations" (typically, a set of overhead slides) that summarize their findings clearly and use graphics to communicate; they then distribute these books and refer to them while making a formal presentation of the work to a group of clients.

The McCambridge consultants are now in crunch mode: All week they work at a furious pace on a presentation to be made to their most senior client at Prometheus.

The McCambridge consultants will recommend in their presentation that:

- *Prometheus either cut the costs of serving Foster's or discontinue serving the store.*
- *Prometheus must consider how the marketplace will perceive dropping a customer, since it wants to be perceived as building long-term relationships with customers.*
- *If Prometheus chooses to retain Foster's, it can cut the cost of serving Foster's as well as the other department stores.*

At 10 P.M. the night before the presentation, the analysis and writing of the report has finally been completed. The analyst and associate stay up late to make sure that twenty error-free copies of the report are put together. The next morning the associate presents the document to the client and fields questions about the recommendations. That same week the analyst holds a training session to teach clients how to use the profitability model, so that they can continue to use it without their assistance. The analyst crafts a clear explanation of the model, uses overhead slides and a computer to demonstrate it, and answers each client's questions.

IMPLEMENTATION

Increasingly, consultants do not leave the client with a book of recommendations; they stick around to help the client make changes. For many consultants, this is the most satisfying step in the business.

The McCambridge team now faces the next step: Prometheus liked their cost-cutting ideas and wants them to implement these changes. The associate and analyst are asked to stay on the team for another three months to work on this phase of the project. Again they come up with a workplan and schedule. They interview employees in the order processing, delivery, and sales departments in more depth to come up with ideas of how to reduce time spent on Foster's as well as how to reduce overall total costs. After research and analysis, McCambridge suggests that the sales force shows the profitability results to Foster's in an effort to encourage that store to make bigger but fewer purchases. This will be positioned as a strategic "partnership" with the Foster's account. McCambridge also suggests methods of lowering order processing time and costs. The McCambridge team writes the document that Prometheus salespeople use in their meetings with Foster's, implements cost reductions in order processing, and demonstrates to the client the reduction in cost (and increase in profitability) achieved.

THE ROLE OF AN ANALYST

So where do analysts fit in? Analysts typically have undergraduate degrees with strong academic records. Their majors are in a variety of areas, from business and finance to art history and English.

Most firms hire analysts with the expectation that they will spend two or three years in consulting and then leave for graduate school. Be aware that differing career paths and beginning salaries can exist within the same firm: Andersen Consulting, for example, offers different career paths depending on whether an undergraduate is hired into the technology or strategy practices. Analysts typically are paid a base salary, a small signing bonus, and relocation costs if necessary. They also earn an annual bonus based on performance.

During their short tenure in consulting, analysts are treated as generalists, meaning that they could be assigned to any industry: Though they can express preferences and be assigned to their preferred industry if convenient, they are available for any project that needs them. A few firms veer from this model and assign all consultants to specific industry groups. An analyst's beginning responsibilities include:

- Gathering data through primary and secondary research to support hypotheses

- Interpreting data

- Building analytical computer models

- Supporting associates and answering questions at presentations

- Gaining general understanding of different industries and consulting methodologies

Assignments might include researching competitors, forecasting industry growth, analyzing industry structure, and performing profitability analysis. An analyst's level of client interaction depends on the specific firm. Analysts working on operational issues rather than strategy issues have more contact with clients, since the entire team works at the client's offices and interactions are likely to be with clients lower down in the corporate hierarchy.

After six to eight months, an analyst begins to take on a more senior role. This is ensured by the fact that a whole "class" of analysts departs for business school, leaving the younger class to take their place as experienced analysts. An experienced analyst's responsibilities can include:

- At some firms, managing small teams of clients

- Continuing to gather and analyze data, but with less guidance; developing frameworks for analyzing data

- Writing reports and presentations

- Developing specialized knowledge of certain industries and consulting methodologies

- Presenting results to clients

- Managing minor workstreams of projects

- Leading undergraduate recruiting efforts

Many firms promote outstanding analysts to a "senior analyst" or "experienced analyst" position for their third year at the firm. Exceptional analysts can be promoted to the associate (post-MBA) position without having to obtain a graduate degree. However, this practice varies widely according to the firm; analyst promotion is much more common at Monitor Company than at other consulting firms, for example.

Analysts from leading firms usually can obtain acceptances from at least one of the top brand-name business schools in the United States (e.g., Harvard, Kellogg, Stanford, or Wharton), because schools value analysts' training and experience with high-level business issues. Most firms will extend *associate* job offers to outstanding departing analysts, offering to reimburse business school tuition if they return after completing their MBA.

Not all analysts move on to business school: Many choose to take jobs in client corporations, attend graduate school in a nonbusiness field such as law or international relations, or join entrepreneurial companies.

Very few consulting firms offer *summer analyst* positions to college juniors.

(Check the company profiles at the end of the book). Summer analysts are usually paid a full-time analyst's salary, prorated for the period worked.

THE ROLE OF AN ASSOCIATE

Associates, also called *senior consultants,* typically possess graduate degrees with strong academic records. Firms regularly hire associates from the top business and law schools in the United States and from INSEAD in Europe. Candidates from second-tier business schools or from nonbusiness graduate schools are not always hired as associates; sometimes they are hired as analysts or into intermediate positions between analysts and associates. Just as at the analyst level, there can be differing career paths and beginning salaries within the same firm: Andersen Consulting, for example, offers different titles depending on whether you are hired into their technology or strategy practice.

Associates typically are paid a base salary, a large signing bonus (about equal to 25 percent of their base salary), and relocation costs if necessary. They also earn an annual bonus based on performance. As an associate, you may indicate an area of interest or future specialization. At most firms, though, you begin as a generalist and can expect to be assigned to projects in a wide range of industries according to the firm's needs.

An associate's early responsibilities include:

- Leading client working sessions

- Designing and conducting primary research to support hypotheses

- Presenting tightly defined portions of formal presentations

- Managing minor workstreams of projects

- Informally coaching junior consultants

- Gaining broad understanding of consulting methodologies

Depending on how structured their firm is, experienced associates begin to take on more sales and project management responsibilities. Usually they are considered for promotion to manager/principal after three to four years, although they will be expected to be performing at the manager/principal level several months before their promotion.

An associate's later responsibilities might include:

- Managing client relationships

- Managing major portions of projects

- Acting as lead presenter at formal client presentations

- Innovating and adding to the firm's toolkit of methodologies

- Formally acting as mentor to junior consultants

- Developing hypotheses that direct projects

- Leading business school recruiting efforts

Many associates enter consulting with the goal of staying until they are promoted to manager and then leaving for a plum job in the business world, perhaps obtained through a client contact. Others leave for entrepreneurial ventures because their knowledge of strategy helps them identify market opportunities.

Headhunters frequently call on associates to offer them opportunities in industry or at other consulting firms. Insiders report that associates shopping for another job have the most negotiating power if they wait until they have been promoted to manager before leaving.

Most consulting firms offer *summer associate* positions to first-year MBA students and some law students. Summer associates usually are paid a full-time associate's salary, prorated for the period worked.

LIFE AS A CONSULTANT

Several factors influence a consultant's lifestyle and job satisfaction.

TRAVEL

Most consultants spend an average of three to four days on their client's premises. If the client is located out of town, consultants fly to the client's location and spend two to three nights in a hotel every week for months. One consultant reported that he spent so little time in his hometown that he literally didn't need an apartment; instead he stayed in hotels or with friends and left his possessions with his parents. Consultants can end up seeing more of their clients than of anyone back at the home office. On the positive side, travel allows all levels of consultants to develop professional relationships with clients (and boost their frequent flyer accounts to obscene levels). On the negative side, travel keeps consultants away from friends and family for several days a week.

The travel model differs among firms; pure strategy firms or those that assign consultants to more than one project at a time tend to require consultants to travel less. This is because strategy work involves external research and can be performed best in the consulting office. In addition, if you have two clients, you can't spend most of your week at one client's offices.

STAFFING PROCESS

Most firms tell applicants that staffing is a decision made with both the firm's and the consultant's input. The reality, however, is that staffing is constrained by timing and project availability. A consultant who wants to be staffed on a consumer products project, for example, cannot necessarily be held idle until such a project is sold, especially if the consultant is junior and has no particular industry expertise. As a consultant gains in seniority, he or she has more control over staffing assignments.

Insiders report that many staffing decisions are made politically: The more higher-ups you know who can specifically request you for a project or protect you until your favored project is sold, the better you will do in the staffing game. Hoping to work overseas? Your chances are improved if your firm has a strong presence in the region in which you are interested, if you speak a foreign language fluently, and if you possess expertise relevant to a specific international assignment. Then you still must present an argument for why you are a better match for an overseas project than a consultant based in the project's region.

COMPANY SPIRIT

Consultants keep in touch with their colleagues through administrative projects, firm-wide or division events, training sessions, and social gatherings. Consultants whose firms require four days of travel a week, however, complain that they do not have the opportunity to develop the same level of company spirit and camaraderie as consultants at firms that require less travel.

WORKING HOURS

How hard do consultants work? In an average week they work fifty to seventy hours, fewer hours than an investment banker but still more than in most other businesses. Consultants' hours do not follow any rigid framework; instead, they vary according to project cycles. Just before client deadlines, consultants can work up to eighty to ninety hours per week.

COMPENSATION AND EVALUATION

A major upside of consulting is that your supervisors change with each project, making your overall performance appraisal less dependent on one person and therefore more objective.

Performance criteria usually include the following: client satisfaction with work, interpersonal skills/teamwork, work ethic, mastery of consulting "tools," expertise developed in one or more industries, communications skills (verbal and written), leadership and development of others, and contribution to company well-being (e.g., recruiting). Most consulting firms employ an "up-or-out" policy—if you're not good enough to be promoted, you're eventually counseled out. Analysts (the pre-MBA position) are an exception, as they are expected to return to business school anyway after a few years.

Consultants typically are evaluated after each project and on an annual or semiannual summary basis. Associates and managers receive annual raises based on this evaluation, while analysts receive raises more frequently. At some firms, analysts receive raises of 5 to 15 percent every six months[9] because they are at the firm only for a short time. An undergraduate who joins the firm with an annual starting salary of $40,000, for example, may see her salary ratcheted up in $2,000 to $6,000 increments every six months, depending on performance. Bonuses are determined by both the company's overall performance and by individual performance.

A major perk that consultants receive is the reimbursement of all travel expenses. This means that basic expenses such as meals, dry-cleaning, and even phone bills incurred while working at client locations are paid for by the client. Reimbursed expenses can add up to a lot of extra money for consultants, on top of their already high salaries.

TRAINING

Most consultancies do not expect their analysts and associates to arrive expert in consulting or in other industries. People are the important differentiating and competitive asset to a consulting firm; firms that recognize this invest substantially in their consultants. Firms typically provide several weeks of initial training to incoming "classes" of analysts and associates. Then, periodic ongoing training for consultants is organized around hierarchy levels, home offices, and industry affiliations. For example, a firm might fly all consultants currently working on oil and gas industry projects to Florida for a three-day industry training session. Or the New York office of a firm might organize a two-day retreat in which broad issues are discussed and training is given. Many firms assign a mentor or "big buddy" to new consultants to provide informal coaching.

TIME OFF

What maintains consultants' sanity? The downtime they have between projects, caused by the imperfect timing of the staffing process. Being "on the beach" is a major perk of the consulting industry. You're still getting paid a large salary and if you're senior enough, you can stay at home and wait for a staffing phone call. In addition, firms usually grant two weeks of vacation to junior consultants. Most firms encourage staff members' taking time off to rejuvenate. A few firms, notably Monitor, McKinsey, and Gemini, allow senior consultants to take sabbaticals similar to those in academia. Consultants often devote their leaves of absence to writing books, spending time with their children, or even starting businesses.

CULTURE

Although consulting firms can differ dramatically, they share certain cultural elements:

Top Ten Things a Consultant Shouldn't Tell a Client
by Michael Rosenstein

10. That was my first guess as well, but then I really thought about it.
9. You should see the hotel I'm staying at.
8. Hey, I just realized that I was in junior high when you started working here.
7. I like this office space. I'll have them put me in here when you're gone.
6. My rental car looks nicer than that junker you're driving.
5. Sure it'll work; I learned it in business school.
4. So what do you need me to tell you?
3. Of course it's right; the spreadsheet says so.
2. I could just tell you the answer, but we're committed to a three-month project.
1. What are you, stupid?

- Teamwork is critical to the success of projects; consultants need to be willing to put their personal interests aside for the good of the team's results and to volunteer to help a colleague when needed, even if it means going home at midnight instead of 10 P.M. The consulting culture places heavy emphasis on being supportive of colleagues.

- Performance and quality standards are set much higher than those in many business environments, which makes sense given that consultants theoretically are being paid to do work that companies cannot do themselves. Consultants are expected to become facile with extremely complex concepts, work long hours with a smile on their face, possess exceptional interpersonal and team-building skills, and perform work with exacting rigor and attention to detail. The "up-or-out" promotion policy encourages consultants to keep their eyes on the ball. You're only as good as your last project.

- Because performance standards are high, recruiting standards are high as well. No one hears consultants complaining about the quality of their colleagues—most consultants are smart, well-rounded achievers.

- Change is a constant. Rote processes don't exist, since there is no such thing as an identical client problem or project. As a new consultant, you can expect to work on projects in a broad range of industries and with a broad range of people in your first year. Even project assignments can change several times in the course of a few hours.

- Working teams are lean, which translates into early responsibility for consultants. The learn-as-you-go mentality is prevalent.

- *Fortune* magazine describes McKinsey as "mostly male, and mostly white."[10] This is true of all consulting firms, where female and minority representation at top levels is sparse. However, the consensus of those who have worked both inside and outside consulting is that the working environment at most consultancies is generally female- and minority-friendly relative to other business fields. Consulting firms promote each "class" that enters the firm together on a lockstep basis, and this process helps ensure fair evaluation for women and minorities.

- As the adage goes, if you don't like the colors gray or navy blue, don't join consulting. Although more progressive than Corporate America, the consulting industry still serves Corporate America. If you're a consultant working on client premises, the client's (sometimes very traditional) culture becomes yours for the duration of the project.

- Top-level consultants have strong ties to academia, which trickles down into the rest of the firm; you will find a great respect for problem-solving, intellectuals, and academic theories in consulting. Many business school professors either provide advice to or act as adjunct staff to consulting firms.

HOW TO TELL FIRMS APART WHEN THEY SOUND THE SAME

So maybe now you're interested in a consulting career. How do you choose which firm to work for? Many consulting firms would have you and their clients believe that they excel at providing "one-stop shopping"—advice on all types of business issues. However, there is a difference between what firms say they can do and what they actually are good at doing (and have been hired to do). Consultancies traditionally have been segmented according to areas of core strength and focus. Very few firms are truly strong in several categories.

The next chart sorts out firms based on what types of work each is traditionally known for—strategy, operations, information technology, and/or specialty consulting niches.[11]

Strategy-Based Generalist Firms provide advice to companies on a range of issues, including strategy, operations, and sometimes information technology (IT). The firms in this category are multinational and renowned. Many firms in this category began as strategy boutiques and added on other services during the 1980s. Because of their roots in strategy, the culture within generalist firms most closely resembles that of strategy firms.

If you're considering this group, pay close attention to whether a firm

Types of Consulting Firms

Category	Examples	Focus	Typical Hires
Strategy-Based Generalists	The Boston Consulting Group, Booz•Allen, McKinsey	Roots in strategy but strong in both operations and strategy	All firms have structured analyst and associate positions; hire undergraduates, MBAs, and other students with high grades from leading schools, good work ethic, leadership and interpersonal skills.
Operations-Based Generalists	A.T. Kearney, Andersen Consulting, CSC Index, Deloitte & Touche, Gemini, KPMG, Price Waterhouse	Large, roots are in operations and IT work but starting to beef up strategy sales	All firms have structured associate (post-MBA) positions, some have analyst (undergrad) positions. May hire fewer traditional MBAs and more industry veterans than Strategy firms. Interpersonal skills and work ethic important.
Strategy Boutiques	Bain & Company, BCG, Mercer, Monitor	Mid-sized or small, tend to do more strategy than operations; no IT work	All firms have structured associate and analyst positions; hire undergraduates and MBAs with high grades, good work ethic. School reputation is very important.
Specialists	ICF, Kurt Salmon Associates, Oracle, Pitaglio Rabin Todd McGrath, Regis McKenna	Specialize in an industry or a functional area	Regular hires include both MBAs and corporate veterans with industry or functional experience. Some undergrads are hired, but analyst positions are less formalized and vary greatly according to firm.

hires consultants into specific divisions or not. This will decide whether you gain a well-rounded experience or specialized knowledge in one industry.

People: Strategy-Based Generalists hire mostly on campus. Grades and the quality of educational institution attended are very important in getting an interview. Generalist firms have begun to institute formal programs to hire graduate students from engineering, law, and other nonbusiness fields. McKinsey, for example, actively recruits Ph.D.'s and post-docs.

Operations-Based Generalists are sometimes called the *Big Eight firms* because many of them are the consulting arms of audit-tax companies: Andersen Consulting, Deloitte & Touche, Ernst & Young, KPMG Peat Marwick, Coopers & Lybrand, Price Waterhouse, and Grant Thornton fall into this category. The firms in this group are extremely large and have an expansive network of international offices. Many win business either directly because of client relationships formed by the audit-tax sister divisions or because of the name recognition that the audit-tax divisions have already built.

Typically, the Operations-Based Generalists have made a living providing advice on operational and information technology issues. IT consulting represents 30 to 50 percent of this group's sales, and KPMG Peat Marwick and CSC Index have particularly strong IT practices.[12] At Andersen Consulting, strategy work accounts for 19 percent of the firm's revenues; information technology, for 70 percent; and operations, 10 percent.[13] However, the Operations-Based Generalists are competing to differentiate themselves and break away from each other. Many of these firms are aggressively trying to develop strategy consulting businesses that have been the domain of such firms as McKinsey and the Boston Consulting Group in the past.

Because of their enormous experience in operations and information technology consulting, the Operation-Based Generalists are skilled in managing behavioral and other aspects of corporate change. They are considered the masters of implementation—in other words, rolling up their sleeves and getting into the gritty business of turning consulting recommendations into reality. Operations-Based Generalists spend a great deal of time at client locations. The ability to implement change and to be price competitive against the more name-brand firms likely will give the Operations-Based Generalists an advantage over the next few years.

People: Operations-Based Generalists hire people for both their operations and IT consulting businesses. For IT work, they recruit heavily at a wide range of undergraduate schools to fulfill their need for armies of programmers. For operations work, they hire on campus and also recruit "gray-hairs" with significant industry experience. According to insiders, these veterans bring with them cultural traits that make operations firms more like traditional Corporate America. Operations-Based Generalists hire from a wider range of schools than strategy boutiques or generalist firms. Interpersonal skills are particularly important to these firms, which pride themselves on their ability to motivate change. To make change happen, consultants must spend a great deal of time working alongside client employees and must be able to get along with different people.

Strategy Boutiques' core strength is providing advice on strategy to companies in a range of industries. Strategy firms are known for taking a bird's-eye view, advising CEOs and other senior managers on high-level issues. Boutiques don't try to do everything; they stick closely to strategy work and do not perform "reengineering" or other sweeping operational change projects unless it is a natural outgrowth of a suggested strategy. This group is blue-chip and exclusive, partly a reflection of the high-level clients that typically buy strategy work.

Strategy groups make use of problem-solving toolkits that can be reapplied in many different industries. These firms maintain relationships with business school professors to gain a steady supply of fresh management theories.

People: Strategy boutiques hire mainly from the campuses of top undergraduate and MBA institutions. In new hires, strategy groups traditionally have favored analytical skills and the ability to learn quickly over specific knowledge or experience. To buy the brightest minds possible, strategy firms offer highly competitive salaries.

Industry and Functional Specialist firms are relatively small, founded as spinoffs of larger firms or springing up around one or two individuals with a particular expertise. Specialist firms aren't trying to sell everything. Instead, they serve clients in a particular *industry,* such as consumer products (Kurt Salmon Associates), electronics (Pittaglio Rabin Todd McGrath), or financial institutions (First Manhattan Group); or advise them on a particular *functional area,* such as marketing (Yankelovich Partners), human resources (Towers Perrin), or litigation (Cornerstone Research). Public policy and economics consulting firms in this category include Putnam, Hayes & Bartlett, and ICF International. The small specialist firms are less international in their clientele base than the big strategy and generalist firms.

People: Specialist firms hire people with skills relevant to their specialty—economists, engineers, attorneys, and people who have spent entire careers in specific industries. Because of their small size, specialist firms are less likely to launch formal recruiting efforts on campuses. However, they continually hire graduate students and some undergraduates. Consulting applicants interested in working in specific industries or functional areas would do best to research proactively and approach relevant specialist firms.

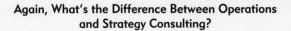

Again, What's the Difference Between Operations and Strategy Consulting?

Michael Porter, the business school professor who authored the consultant's bible *Competitive Strategy*, describes the essence of strategy as planning a company's relation to its environment.

Strategic planning, in Porter's view, includes "developing a broad formula for how a business is going to compete, what its goals should be, and what policies will be needed to carry out those goals." Those policies ensure that corporate departments are working toward a common set of goals.

Consultants themselves have a hard time agreeing on the difference between operations and strategy consulting. Here's one attempt at distinguishing the two:

Source: Porter, *Competitive Strategy*; author's analysis.

Strategic Work:
- Occupies a CEO or unit president
- Shapes the overall mission of a company
- Sets goals that will accomplish a company's mission
- Determines company's external position

Operations Work:
- Occupies a business line manager or the head of a functional area, such as logistics or sales
- Focuses on the processes that accomplish high-level goals
- Is internally focused
- Often involves implementing change within a company

CONSULTING TRENDS

Understanding the direction in which the consulting industry is moving will help you sound knowledgeable in your interviews. Here's what industry observers are saying about current trends.

GLOBALIZATION

Overseas demand for American consulting services is booming because American consultants "control the deepest reserve of knowledge on how to manage globally and build worldwide networks of information technology," and the top multinationals of Europe, Asia, and Latin America "hunger for that know-how."[14] Growth in consulting revenues is now higher overseas than in the United States. In particular, demand for consulting services is booming in Europe and South America.

In response, American consulting firms are spawning offices overseas, often by acquiring local firms with established connections and name recognition.

Most large American firms now earn over half their revenues outside the United States. In order to leverage their global expertise, consultancies are drawing from offices worldwide to staff projects. This situation may mean more opportunities for international work for you, the consultant.

CORPORATE FOCUS ON GROWTH

Reengineering is finished as the consulting industry's hot product; in the mid-1990s, American corporations turned toward growth as their new focus. Human enablers of growth, especially organizational learning, will take their place in the consulting spotlight. Consulting firms have increasingly developed tools to help companies expand their businesses.

PACKAGED SOLUTIONS

McKinsey's Pentagon™ product and Gemini's Transformation™ product are examples of a trend toward offering "end-to-end" consulting solutions that integrate everything from strategic advice to systems implementation.

Diversification is taking place in all consulting categories. IT firms such as EDS and IBM have recognized the potential to consolidate client relationships by selling "upstream" services on top of their traditional computer work, although they face some client skepticism. Strategy firms are seizing the opportunity to sell large projects that focus on operations issues. For the consultant, this trend may spell the opportunity to work on a greater variety of issues.

INDUSTRY CONSOLIDATION

A by-product of the trend toward offering packaged solutions is the rush to merge or acquire. In order to offer integrated solutions, firms are acquiring capabilities that they don't already have. Among the 1995 merger and acquisition activities: Cambridge Technology Partners acquired Systems Consulting Group, EDS acquired strategy firm A.T. Kearney, and Gemini Consulting formed a joint venture organization with Regis McKenna, a specialist in the high-technology arena (although this has since disbanded).

PRICE COMPETITION

Clients are becoming more savvy and more value-conscious; they are less likely to remain loyal to one consulting firm and more likely to shop around. Consulting firms, perhaps with the exception of McKinsey, have had to compete for business on price.

◇   **INDUSTRY LINGO**   ◇

Activity-Based Costing (ABC): assigns overhead costs to customers and products based on the amount of activity and resources spent on these customers and products. Leads to enhanced understanding of customer and product profitability.

Back-of-the-Envelope Calculation: A rough, on-the-spot estimate

Balanced Scorecard: Enhances performance measurement by creating a scorecard based on a balance of four perspectives—customer, internal, financial, and future. Allows companies to measure both daily performance and long-term strategy.

Big Picture: The larger, or overall, perspective

Big Six: The top six audit-tax companies (Ernst & Young, KPMG Peat Marwick, Coopers & Lybrand, Deloitte & Touche, Price Waterhouse, and Grant Thornton), all of which have consulting practices

Buy-in: Agreement from others

Case: A consulting project (also known as an "engagement")

Case Team: Project team, usually composed of three to fifteen consultants

Cycle Time Reduction: Decreasing the time it takes to complete a business process

Deliverables: Tangible outputs or results promised to clients

Economic Value Added (EVA): Measures the return on total capital invested in a company. Operating income is compared to the cost of capital invested.

Engagement: Consulting project

Functional Area: One of the major functions performed in operating a business (for example, marketing, finance, or sales)

Industry or "Corporate America": Consultants' term for the companies that they serve (everyone besides a consultant)

IT and IS: Abbreviations for "information technology" and "information systems"

Methodology: An analytical tool or approach used to solve a client's problem (e.g., activity-based costing)

On the beach: Not currently staffed on a client project

On-site: Working at the client's offices

Porter's Five Forces: Harvard Business School Professor Michael Porter's famous explanation of the five forces that drive industry competition: potential entrants, suppliers, substitutes, buyers, and competitors

Reengineering/Business Process Reengineering: A concept pioneered by Michael Hammer and James Champy, consultants at CSC Index, which advocates the redesign of a company's organization around processes instead of in traditional vertical units

Report-out: An update to the client on project status

Review: Your periodic job performance review

Slides (aka Acetates, Transparencies, Panel Sets, Presentations): Overhead projection slides, the consultant's method of choice to document and present findings

Supply Chain Management: Manages supplier relationships in order to gain competitive advantage in cost, service, and quality. Streamlines logistics and procurement; integrates business functions with suppliers.

Toolkit: A collection of methodologies or tools that consultants can use to help solve a problem

Total Quality Management (TQM): Sustaining world-class quality of products, service, processes, people, and objectives

Workstream: One section of an overall client project

Consult the Web site for this book, www.thefasttrack.com, for an updated list of information on the industry.

∼   RECOMMENDED READING   ∼

"Booz•Allen & Hamilton: Vision 2000." Harvard Business School case, March 25, 1996. This is a great inside look at how consulting firms operate. Order through Harvard's Web site at www.hbsp.harvard.edu.

Byrne, John A. "The Craze for Consultants." *Business Week,* July 25, 1994.

Huey, John. "How McKinsey Does It." *Fortune,* November 1, 1993.

"Inside Andersen's Army of Advice." *Fortune,* October 4, 1993.

Lewis, Michael. "Consultacrats." *The New York Times Magazine,* December 24, 1995.

"The McKinsey Mystique." *Business Week,* September 20, 1993.

Porter, Michael E. *Competitive Strategy.* New York: Free Press, 1980. The classic; look up Porter's "five forces" in the first chapter for help with your consulting case interview.

"Strategic Planning: After a Decade of Gritty Downsizing, Big Thinkers Are Back in Corporate Vogue." *Business Week,* August 26, 1996.

"Trimming the Fat: A Survey of Management Consultancy." *The Economist,* March 22, 1997. Essential reading for future consultants.

Turner, Arthur N. "Consulting Is More Than Giving Advice." *Harvard Business Review,* September-October 1982.

White, Joseph B. "Consulting Firms Break Revenue Records." *The Wall Street Journal,* March 3, 1997.

∼   INDUSTRY SOURCES   ∼

Consultants and Consulting Organizations Directory, 1997. New York: GALE Publishing.

Consultants News. Fitzwilliam, NH: Kennedy Publications. (603) 585-3101 or (800) 531-1026. The most reliable source of news on the industry.

The Directory of Management Consultants, 1995–1996. Fitzwilliam, NH: Kennedy Publications. A useful index of consulting firms.

Dun's Consulting Directory, 1997. Bethlehem, PA: Dun & Bradstreet Information Services.

Harvard Business School Management Consulting Club. *Career Guide: Management Consulting 1997.* Boston: Harvard Business School Press, 1997. A useful index of management consulting firms.

Harvard Business School Publishing: www.hbsp.harvard.edu. Search for consulting-related cases under "Cases and Teaching Materials"—they are incredibly informative and well priced.

Management Consulting Online: www.cob.ohio-state.edu/dept/fin/jobs/mco/mco.html. The most comprehensive Internet site on management consulting. A great source of information on international and smaller firms.

The Wall Street Journal and *Business Week* offer the most frequent coverage of the consulting industry among the popular business press.

 FOR THE DIEHARDS

Whether they've actually read them or not, consultants usually have the following books on their office shelves.

Gouillart, Francis J., and James N. Kelly. *Transforming the Organization.* New York: McGraw-Hill, Inc., 1995. Gemini consultants compare a company to an organism and describe a holistic approach to "treat" it.

Hamel, Gary, and C. K. Prahalad. *Competing for the Future.* Cambridge, MA: Harvard Business School Press, 1994. Two business school professors argue that for healthy growth, a company needs to anticipate the future and embrace new ways of thinking in order to meet challenges.

Hammer, Michael, and James Champy. *Reengineering the Corporation.* New York: HarperBusiness, 1993. CSC Index consultants coin the term "reengineering" to describe their radical redesign of a company's processes, organization, and culture.

Micklethwait, John, and Adrian Wooldridge. *The Witch Doctors: Making Sense of the Management Gurus.* New York: Times Books, 1996.

Reichheld, Frederick. *The Loyalty Effect.* Cambridge, MA: Harvard Business School Press, 1996. Bain & Company consultant argues that for companies to retain loyal customers, they need to retain loyal employees.

Senge, Peter. *The Fifth Discipline.* New York: Doubleday, 1994. How to create a "learning" organization.

Treacy, Michael, and Fred Wiersema. *The Discipline of Market Leaders.* New York: Addison-Wesley Publishing Co., 1995. Another duo from CSC Index argues that companies can dominate their markets by narrowing their focus.

Harvard Business Review articles on relevant consulting theories:

"The Core Competence of the Corporation," C. K. Prahalad and Gary Hamel, May-June 1990.

"Strategic Intent," C. K. Prahalad and Gary Hamel, May-June 1989.
"Reengineering Work: Don't Automate, Obliterate," Michael Hammer, July-August 1990.

~   **NOTES**   ~

[1]*Consultants News*, March 1997, July 1996.
[2]*Consultants News*, September 1995.
[3]"About Consulting," McKinsey & Company Web site, 1997.
[4]"How McKinsey Does It," *Fortune*, November 1, 1993.
[5]Ibid.
[6]*Consultants News*, September 1996.
[7]Interview with a Stanford University student recruited by CSC Index, September 1995.
[8]Interview with a Bain & Company consultant, March 1996.
[9]Interviews with consultants.
[10]"How McKinsey Does It."
[11]Compiled through interviews with consultants at firms in each category.
[12]*Consultants News*, September 1995.
[13]Ibid.
[14]"Hired Guns Packing High-Powered Know-How," *Business Week*, November 18, 1994.

INSIDER INTERVIEW

Roger Steinman*
Associate, McKinsey & Company, Inc.

R oger has worked in both investment banking and management consulting.

— ~ —

How did you make the decision to join McKinsey after business school?

The truthful answer, unfortunately, is that when I was looking for a summer job between my two years in business school, I only interviewed with one consulting firm—McKinsey—and only out of respect for a classmate of mine who said that McKinsey was a really good firm and that I should talk to them. So I went to talk to them thinking, God, I don't want to do consulting. They gave me an offer in about two days. After I spent the summer with McKinsey, I got a full-time offer for after business school. I talked to BCG, several LBO

*Name has been changed to protect privacy.

and money management firms, and some software start-ups. Nothing seemed better than the opportunities McKinsey could provide.

Now that you're in it, what surprises you about management consulting?

I didn't realize how emotionally attached you can become to your clients. You really want them to succeed. There's more gratification in consulting than I ever expected.

How would you describe the differences between working in investment banking and consulting?

They're very different, actually. Investment banking involves being given data that you process in a similar way each time. There's a high premium placed on accuracy, and there's not much real problem-solving. In banking, the problem is always defined for you. You don't get a broad business perspective; you learn a lot about finance and accounting. In consulting, there's a lot more broad business thinking and problem-solving. You have to define a problem yourself, which you never see in banking. I've personally found consulting much more challenging. Intellectually, because consultants are constantly thrown into new situations that they know nothing about. And on the people side, because consultants have a lot more client contact at the junior level.

Which do you like better?

Because of the greater intellectual stimulus, I enjoy consulting more. There's also a much healthier environment in consulting, especially regarding lifestyle. McKinsey has been a lot more humane and caring than the investment bank I worked for. Investment in people is much higher in consulting. Very, very heavy emphasis on professional development. Which is refreshing compared to investment banking, where the attitude is "If you're strong, you'll still be swimming at the end of the day."

Do you think McKinsey hired the smartest people from your business school class?

No, not necessarily. McKinsey is selective and hires the smartest people it can, but there are also other institutional reasons for McKinsey's success. A key one is that McKinsey gives people responsibility early on. They take the leashes off. When you let people stretch, you achieve powerful results.

What have you learned from your colleagues?

I actually learn a lot from my teammates every day, on a broad spectrum of issues. From big things like how to take costs out of a business or double a business's revenue, to how to improve my communication skills.

What do you not like about consulting?

Well, there are a couple of big downsides. There's always the possibility that you'll have to travel extensively. Also, because there's a push for high-quality work, there's an internal bias for longer hours relative to other business jobs.

There's something perverse about thinking of oneself as a professional consultant, because over time you wonder what it adds up to. You can never really explain to your grandmother what you do—you have the empty feeling of not having done something real. Which, in the final analysis, probably couldn't be further from the truth. But there's a big difference between telling someone what to do and actually going and doing it.

Finally, staffing is a bit of a black box. As a junior person, it's not clear that you can pick and choose your engagements. And there's a range of quality in engagements.

In your opinion, what are typical associate career paths in consulting?

I'll give you the typical consultant's answer: It depends. Associates *do* leave, and it's my guess that there's a fairly high attrition rate between the second and fourth years. Because after four years, it makes sense to stay on and try to make partner. Once you're a partner here, it's a pretty cushy life.

Many people who leave take staff roles in corporations, either in corporate development or marketing. Another big chunk of people do entrepreneurial things. McKinsey is an interesting place, because although the entrepreneurial dream is temporarily squashed here, entrepreneurial ideas flow through the halls constantly. We're always bouncing ideas off each other and giving each other feedback.

How would you describe the people in consulting?

One thing everyone here shares is intellectual curiosity. If you give them some fun little logic problem, almost everyone here will be willing to take five minutes to sit down and figure it out.

The people here also have a pretty nonhierarchical attitude when it comes to problem-solving: An analyst's idea is as good as an engagement director's. That's unbelievably honored. In investment banking, an analyst was only supposed to speak up if his number was questioned. Junior people are there just to support the senior people. In consulting, if you don't speak up you're underperforming. The *team* drives and presents the answers and makes the decisions, and senior people are just equal members of the team. The hierarchy is much flatter.

How would you rate the managerial skills of your supervisors?

Most people at McKinsey don't really need to be managed. It's a different dynamic—we're coached. I get a lot of feedback daily on how I could do things better. I think this is heavily institutionalized; managers are graded on how well they coach others.

Can you describe one of your typical days on the job?

I meet with my three client team members first thing in the morning to discuss our progress and daily tasks. In the late morning I meet with my engagement manager to understand what's going on with the rest of the team and communicate our progress. After lunch I spend the afternoon calling and meeting with people to get critical information. The early evening is then spent modifying analyses and preparing for the next day.

What are your hours like? Are they better than in investment banking?

My hours now are about 50 percent better than they were in investment banking. I work ten to twelve hours a day, and I have never worked a weekend. I've been strongly discouraged from working weekends.

Where do you see this job leading for you?

Working in consulting gets me closer to my end goal—and plus it's a lot of fun and a lot of money. Ultimately, my goal is to start my own company that creates jobs that have dignity and purpose to them while creating a product that consumers need. The reason that I want to do that entrepreneurially rather than within a large corporation is that I would like to have control over human resources policies. I think I have substantively different views than most major corporations, specifically regarding the distribution of profit between shareholders and employees.

How does McKinsey help you get closer to that end goal?

First, I'm on an accelerated learning curve here in terms of developing poise, communication skills, and big-picture perspective. I am also learning how to strip costs out of a business and grow revenues. These skills will be important to me later on in my own business.

Anything else you want to tell people about your experience?

There are a couple of key skills that consulting does not develop for you. Most important, decision making. We're not as strong as we might be at making decisions. You often find situations in which five McKinsey people can't decide which restaurant to go to. Second, we don't develop skills in hiring and firing people. We never have to make these decisions and be held accountable for them. And third, we don't ever deal with motivational issues, because people here are all highly motivated. All you'd have to say to get someone working harder is "You could be doing a better job." Whereas in Corporate America, success requires an ability to be an inspiring and motivating leader.

One thing consulting *does* do for you is that you get to work on high-level projects at a young age, which you'd never get if you were working in a normal line job. And you get to work on the most pressing issues in a lot of different businesses. Which is all a great experience. People always make jokes about our generation switching jobs a lot; well, consulting is like institutionalized job-switching.

INSIDER INTERVIEW: SPOTLIGHT ON SYSTEMS CONSULTING

Trevor Watkins*
Former Analyst, Andersen Consulting

Trevor worked for two and a half years as an analyst on information technology projects. Andersen has a strategy consulting division but hires most undergraduates into its technology consulting area (which provides advice to corporations on their internal computer systems and other information technology) or in its process or change management areas.

What was your background before consulting and how did you choose this career?

I went to [a Northeastern college] and was an economics major. I held a lot of leadership positions and did extracurriculars: I played baseball and was on the fraternity council. I did a lot of Greek activities. I was accepted into a three-day conference Andersen held for students between their junior and senior years. That opened my eyes to Andersen.

So you didn't have any systems background before Andersen?

No. And that's pretty standard. Andersen prefers a mixture of people. During the training program, people like me were a little more stressed out than those

*Name has been changed to protect privacy.

who had a systems background. It was really a different language for us. But we were all at about the same point when we finished.

In your opinion, what were the typical career paths at Andersen?

You can stay and grow without an MBA. It's been three years since my start date at Andersen, and there are twelve people out of nineteen left from my original start group. I didn't notice people with an MBA moving any faster than people without one. Maybe the advantage for someone with an MBA was that their first promotion would come six months sooner and they would start off with a better pay rate.

How did your responsibilities change over time?

In the systems group, you come in as a programmer. You learn the logic and the tools, and a testing methodology. When I walked into my first project I was just doing coding. You get used to that and you develop a comfort level with the client and the client environment. Then you move into testing and working more one-on-one with the client. Later on, I was moved to a different project where I took on more of a design role. So when new programmers came in and needed some structure, I provided that structure and supervised them.

After a year and a half or so, you can speak intelligently about problems a client is having and how to resolve them. You have to be able to see things from a client's point of view. It's a stretch to expect a client who isn't familiar with your software to understand how to use it. So you have to be able to explain it well. In my last six months at the firm, I would meet with the client daily to deal with issues like defining a plan, coming to an understanding with the client, and then going back to my team to discuss an approach and divvy up tasks. As you go along, more questions develop, and then you bring the client in. Sometimes the client will call a meeting and bring in five people, then they'll turn to you for information. So what's great is you're twenty-four years old, and you're dealing with people that are much older but don't have the expertise, so they're looking to you to make recommendations and lead meetings.

That was a lot of fun. But there were other times when the client isn't around and there's a lot of data that has to be worked with. Especially when their system is live, it's a lot of hard work and investigation just to find out what's going on.

Can you describe in laymen's terms a typical project?

We developed a tax software system. Our system would take the data from tax returns and business tax returns, and sales taxes. It would process data, validate it, and then determine whether there was a refund due. If there was, the system would physically print a check, and then send it. It would also track delinquent taxpayers.

The nature of this project was that we would present it to the client and do the best to accommodate them, but the truth of the matter was that the cost and time of truly customizing this system was too high for them. It was cheaper and faster for them to modify their end, and take on our structure. So in that case, that was a limitation for them. In some private companies with more advanced systems, there's more flexibility.

~ 3 ~

INVESTMENT BANKING, SALES AND TRADING:
AN OVERVIEW

The investment banker was a breed apart, a member of a master race of deal makers. He possessed vast, almost unimaginable talent and ambition. If he had a dog, it snarled. He had two little red sports cars yet wanted four. To get them, he was, for a man in a suit, surprisingly willing to cause trouble.

> —Michael Lewis, *Liar's Poker*

DEFINING INVESTMENT BANKING

A great deal of mythology has been built up around the profession of investment banking. Behind it lies the daily reality—sometimes glamorous, at other times mundane. Investment banks serve two major constituencies: organizations that need capital in order to operate, and institutional investors that have capital to invest. Investment banks act as middlemen; they help companies and governments raise money at reasonable rates and help investors find a good return.

Investment banks perform the following major functions:

- Act as matchmakers between those who have capital and those who need it.
- Lend and invest the bank's own capital
- Provide and execute financial advice for organizations
- Develop research and opinions on securities, markets, economies

Basic Vocabulary

Knowing these terms will help you understand this chapter.

Companies raise capital by selling (issuing) *securities*—stocks, bonds, or others—to investors. Companies raising capital are called *issuers*.

Security: Evidence that you have loaned or invested money (e.g., a stock or bond).

Equity: An ownership interest in a company. Also *stocks,* the physical evidence of ownership. *Equity markets* refers to the stock markets.

Debt: An obligation to pay back money owed. Also *bonds,* the physical evidence of obligation. *Debt markets* refers to the bond markets. *Fixed income securities* is another name for bonds, because of the fixed interest a bondholder receives.

Capital markets: The markets in securities with a maturity of over one year—for example, long-term debt or equity securities.

Derivatives: New, hybrid securities created from underlying, more basic securities. Options, swaps, and futures are examples of derivatives.

High-yield bonds: Otherwise known as junk bonds; pay high interest to bondholders because the credit quality of the issuer is poorer and risk is therefore greater.

Initial Public Offering (IPO): Selling shares of a privately held company to the public for the first time.

Private placement: A stock or bond issue sold directly by a company to an investor, but which is not registered with the Securities and Exchange Commission, underwritten by an investment bank, or offered to the public.

- Buy and sell securities on behalf of investor clients
- Manage investment portfolios
- Trade stocks and bonds on their own behalf in order to make a profit

Investment banks are most famous for providing the service of *underwriting*—they will buy the stocks or bonds that a client is selling and resell these immediately to investors. In doing so, investment banks place themselves at risk, since they may not find buyers. Why do they do this? They provide the assurance of raising the entire amount of money a company needs.

CLIENTS

Who are the clients paying millions of dollars of fees to investment banks? As noted, they can be split into two groups: issuers and investors.

GROUP 1: ISSUERS
ORGANIZATIONS THAT NEED CAPITAL AND ADVICE ON THEIR FINANCING

Just about every government or large corporation in the United States calls on investment banks to raise capital and get advice on managing its finances. *The investment banking department within an investment bank works directly with these clients.*

Corporations and other institutions raise capital by issuing (selling) securities to investors. Depending on the financial performance and needs of the issuer, investment banks can use a variety of instruments to raise money, ranging from basic stocks and bonds to complex derivatives or asset-backed securities.

Looking for examples of the clients investment bankers serve? Large, New York–based investment banks are likely to serve large companies with sophisticated financial knowledge and needs who frequently tap the capital markets. Smaller banks or those with a special focus are more likely to call on a young, fast-growing company that sticks to issuing less complex securities, such as plain-vanilla stock. Clients can be as different as in this comparison of J.P. Morgan, one of the largest investment banks in the country, and Robertson Stephens, which focuses on serving clients in fast-growing industries.

Client Lists

ROBERTSON STEPHENS & COMPANY	J.P. MORGAN & CO.
Ascend Communications	American Brands
Chiron	Clorox
Cirrus Logic	Dow Chemical
E-Trade	Equitable Life Assurance
Horizon Healthcare	Johnson & Johnson
The Men's Wearhouse	McDonald's
Nellcor	MEMC Electonic Materials
Pixar Animation Studios	PepsiCo
United Waste Systems	Republic of France
Whole Foods Market	Telekom Malaysia

Source: Robertson Stephens; "An Introduction to Robertson Stephens," 1996 company brochure; J.P. Morgan Annual Reports, 1991 and 1995

GROUP 2: INVESTORS
ORGANIZATIONS THAT WANT TO INVEST CAPITAL

Investment banks also serve corporations ("institutional investors") and wealthy individuals ("high-net-worth individuals") who want to invest money. Institutional investors include pension funds, insurance companies, and others who, due to the business they are in, have large deposits of cash to manage. The sales and trading department within an investment bank works directly with all these investors. Investments banks do *not* serve everyday individuals ("retail" investors). (Some banks, such as Smith Barney, Merrill Lynch, Morgan Stanley, Dean Witter, have strong retail businesses. Salespeople who cover retail investors are known as stockbrokers. However, this book focuses on career paths within *institutional* sales and trading.)

Examples of institutional investors that salespeople and traders serve are:

- CALPERS (pension fund)
- CIGNA (insurance company)
- Fidelity Investments (mutual fund)

Investors have different investment philosophies, return goals, and risk tolerance. They therefore invest in different securities, from basic stocks and bonds to more complex securities.

What's the Difference Between My Neighborhood Bank and an Investment Bank?

Banks are part of the overall financial services industry and can be divided into two main groups: investment banks and commercial banks. What distinguishes investment banks from commercial banks is the Glass-Steagall Act of 1934. This law prohibits investment banks from taking consumer deposits and commercial banks from underwriting securities. Investment banks primarily serve *institutions*, such as companies or governments, and very wealthy individuals. Commercial banks serve institutions, but also *individuals* like you and me.

THE PAST AND CURRENT LANDSCAPE

For all its current power and glory, the American investment banking industry has its origins along a modest dirt road built in the 1600s. The road, Wall Street, originally ran alongside a wall of brush and mud built by the Dutch to keep Native Americans out of their New York trading post. Wall Street, conveniently located close to ports on both sides of Manhattan, became *the* center for commercial exchange in the United States. Early merchants traded commodities such as furs, currencies, and tobacco on Wall Street. In the late 1700s, as the newly formed U.S. government began to issue bonds and banks and insurance companies issued stock, merchants began to trade securities at 22 Wall Street.

In 1792 a group of brokers formed and agreed to abide by the rules of an organization that evolved to become the New York Stock Exchange. Under a buttonwood tree, in a coffeehouse, on window ledges, or in the middle of the street, enterprising brokers placed their trades before finally moving indoors to more decorous settings in the 1800s. Major brokerage houses sprang up in the mid-1800s to help investors deal in the booming securities markets.

Initially, the U.S. government did not enforce a separation between commercial and investment banking. However, the 1929 stock market crash, failure of banks, and subsequent loss of individuals' savings during the Great Depression prompted Congress to enact the Glass-Steagall Act, which split commercial from investment banking to protect consumers. Banks had to choose between the two functions: Morgan Stanley, for one, was created as an investment banking spin-off from J.P. Morgan. In the early 1930s, the Securities and Exchange Commission (SEC) was created to enforce the new securities laws. The SEC still ensures that investors have access to important information concerning public securities and regulates anyone involved in trading securities or providing investment advice.

Change is a constant in the investment banking industry. Prestigious banks disappear overnight, acquired by competitors, while new banks spring into successful existence. Yet as you look back over the past 200 years, you'll see that successful investment banks have been founded at fairly even intervals. This history sharply contrasts with that of management consulting, which experienced its major growth in the 1960s and 1970s.

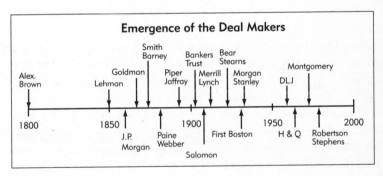

Today the biggest changes affecting the industry are globalization and the gradual collapse of the Glass-Steagall Act. The division between commercial and investment banking is tumbling down, and commercial banks are entering investment banking turf. Several commercial banks have been granted permission to conduct investment banking activities. Foreign giants such as Germany's Deutsche Bank and Switzerland's UBS are spending wads of money to grow their investment banking operations in the United States and woo talent away from U.S.-based investment banks.

Large commercial banks with vast reserves of cash present a competitive challenge to investment banks. For one, they can use their deep capital reserves

The Bank Roll

Bank	1996 Revenues ($ millions)
Merrill Lynch & Co., Inc.	12,961
Smith Barney Inc.	6,295
Goldman, Sachs & Co.	6,129
Morgan Stanley & Co.	5,776
Credit Suisse First Boston, Inc.	5,307
J.P. Morgan & Co., Inc.	5,153
Salomon Brothers Inc.	4,367
Lehman Brothers Inc.	3,444
The Bear Stearns Cos., Inc.	2,982
Montgomery Securities	705
Hambrecht & Quist Group	390
Robertson Stephens & Co.	350

Fiscal year 1996 revenues net of interest expense.

Sources: Annual reports, interviews with firms.

to win underwriting mandates. Well-capitalized firms can afford to make big promises to clients: If they commit to raising money for a client at aggressive terms and under an aggresive time schedule but the market does not comply, the firms have enough capital to follow through on their commitment and sustain a loss.

Industry observers predict the ascendancy of the universal commercial bank and increased competition in the investment banking industry. Existing investment banks are being forced to deepen their reserves of capital, either by going public or by merging with another company. Larger institutions will fare better in this new competitive landscape, while medium-size and small firms that cannot find partners will be at risk of being gobbled up. The industry is already seeing consolidation: Small boutiques such as Wolfensohn and Gleacher have been acquired by larger banks seeking to round out their investment banking skills. Morgan Stanley and Dean Witter announced a merger in 1997 that would create a powerful entity with both investment banking experience and a retail sales network. Bankers Trust also announced its purchase of Alex. Brown, the nation's oldest investment bank, in its quest to become a full-service investment bank. And Bank of America announced its purchase of Robertson Stephens. Increased competition will in particular drive down the price of services that do not require great transaction expertise but can be performed by a newcomer: low-margin debt transactions, for example, rather than high-margin IPOs.

In 1996 the securities industry consisted of over 7,600 firms that generated approximately $90 billion in annual revenues.[1] The industry is highly concentrated, with the top ten firms comprising over 70 percent of total industry revenues.[2]

OVERVIEW OF AN INVESTMENT BANKING TRANSACTION

Let's walk through the steps of a typical stock offering, in which many different areas of an investment bank work together to raise capital for a client (this would be an example of an "issuer," or a "Group 1" client mentioned earlier).

WINNING THE DEAL
The WorldView Company, a giant media conglomerate, plans to raise $150 million in capital by issuing stock. WorldView invites the ABC Bank, along with First Boston, Goldman Sachs, and others, to bid for the business. ABC explains to WorldView's CFO their view on the appropriate price for the stock, and that ABC's experience with similar media stock offerings and their distribution network make them the best choice for the deal. ABC wins the business.

THE INITIAL GAME PLAN
A team of investment bankers is put together from ABC's Corporate Finance group. They hold an "all-hands" organizational meeting with WorldView's CFO and Treasurer to review the client's financing goals and timetable. The team discusses an appropriate price for the shares.

PREPARING TO LAUNCH
After reviewing their alternatives, the team decides to issue common stock and to sell it at $22 per share. The Corporate Finance team prepares a prospectus to market the offering and files registration materials with the SEC.

THE RIGHT PRICE AND STRUCTURE
The Corporate Finance team calls on colleagues in Equity Research and Sales and Trading to predict the market's reaction to the offering and develop a price and marketing plan. Corporate Finance also talks to the syndicate desk, which provides an opinion on pricing and structure. The syndicate desk is responsible for the pricing of all public equity underwritten by ABC.

UNDERWRITING THE DEAL
In the final hours, the price of the shares is finally set. The syndicate desk underwrites (buys) the equity along with a group of other investment banks. The client receives net proceeds from the sale of the equity.

SELLING THE SECURITIES
WorldView shares are released to the sales force, which distributes prospectuses and sells shares to investors.

TRADING THE SECURITIES
The WorldView shares trade on the public market, with ABC's traders making a market (providing liquidity to investors) in the shares.

Now we'll look at an example of how the departments of an investment bank work together to carry out this type of transaction.

ROADMAP OF AN INVESTMENT BANK

Most banks organize themselves on three dimensions: functions, products, and clients.[3] People within the bank specialize along one of these dimensions. The following chart presents some examples.

FUNCTIONS	PRODUCTS	CLIENTS/INDUSTRIES
Investment Banking	Equity	Telecommunications
Mergers and Acquisitions	Fixed Income	Oil and Gas
Sales and Trading	Real Estate	Financial Institutions
Research	Private Placements	Northeastern U.S.

During the recruiting process, you will receive glossy brochures from banks that may overwhelm you with a confusing array of department names. Take out that organizational chart you couldn't understand and follow along. Notice that banks basically use two different approaches in organizing their people. In one approach, people are assigned to a functional area, then to product specialties or client groups:

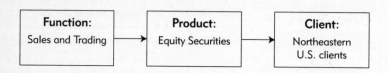

Another approach is to assign people to product areas first, then to functional and client areas:

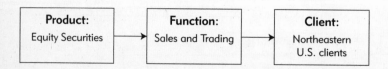

However, the vast majority of banks use a mix of organizational approaches, and this is where confusion arises. A simplified picture of a large investment bank looks like this:

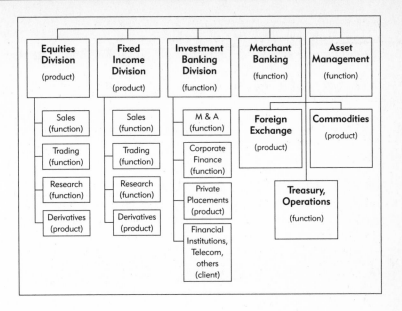

In this book, we focus on two major functional areas: investment banking and securities sales and trading. In *Liar's Poker,* Michael Lewis offers this explanation of the cultural difference between the two areas. (Lewis himself entered Salomon Brothers through sales and trading.) "[T]he trading floor, where stocks and bonds are bought and sold, is the rough-and-tumble center of moneymaking and risk taking. . . . Corporate finance, which services the corporations and governments that borrow money, and that are known as 'clients,' is, by comparison, a refined and unworldly place."

Why are we focusing on these two areas? Investment banking and sales and trading are true "fast tracks" within an investment bank—they are consistently lucrative and present challenging, high-profile work opportunities. But more important, these areas hire the largest number of new graduates. Investment banking departments, in particular, have developed a standard procedure for hiring and training both MBAs and college graduates. (Sales and trading departments tend to have a less structured hiring program but nonetheless hire a large number of recent graduates every year.) Simply put, it is easiest to break into an investment bank through investment banking or securities sales and trading.

Investment banking is a catch-all term for raising capital and providing financial advice to corporations or governments, the "Group 1" clients described earlier. The title "investment banker" refers only to the people who serve this function. Investment banking areas include:

- *Corporate Finance:* helps companies raise capital through debt and equity.

- *Mergers and Acquisitions (M&A):* advises a corporation in the process of merging with, acquiring, or selling a business.
- *Real Estate:* provides advice on real estate transactions and strategies.

Securities sales and trading are the areas that serve the "Group 2" clients described earlier.

- *Sales:* involves acting as a liaison with institutional investors and providing them with a variety of services, including advice on investments and assistance in buying and selling securities. Typically there are many more sales positions available than trading positions.
- *Trading:* buying and selling securities on the secondary markets. There are two main types of trading. In *proprietary trading,* traders take risks with the bank's own capital, placing trades on behalf of the bank to earn profit. This trading is not customer-related. In *client-driven trading,* traders fulfill clients' "buy" and "sell" orders in order to provide them with flexibility.

As a job-seeker, you shouldn't ignore the great job opportunities in research, asset management, or other functions within an investment bank. Much of the recruiting information contained in this book, especially résumé preparation and choosing the right job, applies to other areas within an investment bank. But the areas outside investment banking and sales and trading have less structured recruiting processes; getting a job in those areas will take a more tailored approach, research, and persistence. To be safe, contact firms directly for specific information on off-the-beaten-path jobs.

Next, let's take a closer look at work performed in our areas of focus.

THE INVESTMENT BANKING FUNCTION

At its heart, investment banking is a relationship business. Investment bankers build long-term relationships with large corporations in the hope of acting as their advisor on all financial matters. This is the group of clients mentioned earlier. For their guidance in raising cash or negotiating a merger, investment bankers earn fees based on a percentage of the total sum of money that changes hands.

As a result of the relationship nature of their business, investment bankers often must call on CFOs and other corporate chieftains. Investment bankers are therefore buttoned-down, well educated, and polished enough to fit in at the highest business echelons. The investment banking division is blue-chip, conservative, and populated with graduates of top-tier colleges and MBA programs.

Investment banking includes several major activities: raising capital and providing advice on mergers and acquisitions (M&A) and other financial issues. Structurally, this usually translates into an investment banking division with two main groups: corporate finance and M&A.

CORPORATE FINANCE

Corporate finance is the service of helping an institution manage its finances, and this includes a wide range of services. However, corporate finance groups are best known for raising capital for corporations. In doing so, investment bankers help the corporation determine how much money to raise, which type of security to issue, how and when to enter the market, and how to price the securities. In order to prepare an issue of securities for sale, investment bankers perform an in-depth study of the company, a process called *due diligence*, in order to assure investors and the SEC that they have adequately researched the company. They prepare an *offering memorandum* or *prospectus*, documents that explain the company and the securities offered to investors. Bankers help the corporation tell its "story" to the investor market through *roadshows* and other marketing efforts.

Finally, the bank buys the corporations' securities for immediate resale to investors (the service of *underwriting*). It does this to ensure that the company will receive the money it needs. In doing so, the bank takes on a measure of risk, since the possibility exists that it will not be able to resell the securities. A bank shares this risk by organizing a *syndicate*—a group of investment banks that together underwrite the transaction and then resell securities to investors. However, investment bankers do not actually sell the stocks and bonds themselves. Colleagues in sales and training handle the sales process.

Corporate finance departments help clients solve other financial challenges, including buying back stock that has already been issued, analyzing how their stock is trading in the public market, and completing refinancings.

Wondering if you'll like corporate finance? Corporate financiers get exposed to a great breadth of products since they are serving clients' general finance needs. The downside of working in corporate finance is that you may not come to understand any one type of product very well; in addition, usually you will specialize in serving one industry, such as automotive companies or consumer products manufacturers.

Corporate Finance Case Example: An investment bank is awarded the business of taking public Traditions, a privately held greeting-card company. Traditions wants to raise money by selling shares of its stock to the public for the first time ever. It wants to sell about 2 million shares at roughly $15 per share, for a total offering of $30 million. The investment bankers talk to salespeople and traders to determine current market and trading information, work closely with equity research analysts, and use comparable stock ratios and other financial data to come up with a range of possible prices per share for Traditions. Bankers and Traditions executives then write a prospectus, reviewing it with lawyers. The bankers coordinate with their colleagues in sales to organize a roadshow in which the bankers travel around the country with Traditions executives to explain the company's business to institutional investors. Finally, after the prospectus is filed with the Securities and Exchange Commission, the IPO is launched. Final pricing is determined hours before the stock is for sale.

MERGERS AND ACQUISITIONS (M&A)

M&A is the service of advising a corporation on the process of merging with, acquiring, or divesting (selling) a business or business assets. Again, these corporations are part of Group 1, mentioned earlier—the clients who call on an investment bank for general financial advice. Mergers and acquisitions are undertaken to achieve strategic goals; a company wants to fill a gap in its product line or geographic territory, or wants to dominate a market by buying a competitor, for example. As an M&A investment banker, you would represent the buying company, the selling company, or one of the merging companies. Companies hire investment banks in order to place a value on the business being sold; to find the right partner, seller, or buyer; to make sure they get a fair deal; and to arrange financing to pay for the transaction.

M&A is considered the most glamorous and intellectual area of investment banking because it involves strategic thinking and complex deals—after all, you're marrying or divorcing large, important corporations. Every M&A deal is different, and the M&A investment banker often must manage transactions that involve multiple buyers or sellers.

If investment bankers are representing the buyer, they analyze the company for sale through a due diligence process and come up with an assessment of the company's value and an appropriate premium to be paid for it. They use a variety of information to estimate value: the stock market's valuation of the sale company itself if it is public, market valuation of similar companies, prices that have been paid for similar companies in terms of multiples of their cash flow, and *discounted cash flow* or other analysis of the sale company.

M&A bankers also must negotiate and structure the terms and payment of the transaction. The payment for an acquisition or merger can be made in cash, debt, equity, or a combination of all of these. Investment bankers inform their client of standard practice (if any) in the industry, what is feasible, and what in their opinion would be the best financing structure for the client.

If investment bankers are representing the seller, they prepare a *selling memorandum* that describes the company, including a description of the business and key competitors, projected financials, experience of its management team, and potential risks. They plan a marketing approach for the sale of the company. Representing the selling company is more process-oriented and less modeling intensive than representing the buying company since there is less guesswork involved; investment bankers on the sell-side have access to the company's financial information and in general come up with fewer estimates than on the buy-side. Senior M&A bankers search for potential acquirers by placing phone calls to contacts at appropriate companies and inquiring whether they would be interested in receiving a selling memorandum. Finally, the bankers coordinate the negotiation and due diligence process with final bidders.

Wondering if you'll like mergers and acquisitions? M&A is a good area for those who can't decide between management consulting and investment banking, because it represents a mix between financial and strategic thinking. Because coming up with a valuation involves making financial projections, M&A analysts and associates must build computer models that portray the company being sold under many different future scenarios. M&A bankers therefore build famously good spreadsheet skills and truly become comfortable with accounting and financial statement analysis.

The downside of M&A is its unpredictable and long hours. M&A analysts work an average of 90 hours per week; during crunch times, which can last for several weeks, they work 95 to 110 hours per week. In addition, M&A bankers are more removed from the securities markets than corporate finance or capital markets bankers.

Mergers and Acquisitions Case Example: The Flight Shoe Company bought a cereal subsidiary during the 1980s. The shoe-cereal marriage didn't work, and now Flight wants to sell off its cereal division. Flight calls its bankers, who recommend auctioning the division off rather than negotiating the sale with one buyer because Flight prefers a high sales price over confidentiality. (Opening up the sales process through a broader auction will decrease the confidentiality of the deal.) A team of bankers analyze the cereal industry. They perform a discounted cash flow analysis and other analyses on the cereal division and come up with a range of values that the division is worth. The central part of the transaction is the bankers' marketing efforts: They craft a strong marketing "story," put together a list of interested buyers, make sales calls, send out a selling memorandum, arrange for a competitive bidding, then negotiate over price and terms with the final bidders.

OTHER INVESTMENT BANKING AREAS

As an investment banker, you could also be assigned to a group within investment banking that provides specialized services to clients. These are either product specialty groups or client specialty groups. The most common of these specialty groups include capital markets, real estate, and structured finance.

Capital Markets: This group acts as a liaison between the trading floor and corporate finance. Physically situated on the trading floor, capital markets provides real-time public bond and stock market information to investment bankers and their clients. Capital markets bankers spend dedicated time to develop knowledge of products and the public securities markets and to work with corporate finance and their clients to market and price a deal. The downside of the area is that you may specialize earlier than you want to. In addition, the fast pace and culture of the trading floor are not comfortable for everyone.

Real Estate: The service of planning and executing real estate strategies for large institutions. Real estate bankers help companies manage their real estate assets, whether through sales or purchasing of properties or securitizing mortgages and properties. This area also sometimes makes investments in clients' real estate projects or advises institutions on meeting their real estate needs.

Structured Finance: The investment bankers in this area are called in to raise money for institutions through complex, asset-backed (securitized) instruments. For example, a bank trying to raise capital might take 100 mortgages it has written, pool them, and issue securities guaranteed by that pool. Examples of typical asset-backed securities include those backed by credit card receivables, auto loan receivables, or mortgages.

What's the Difference Between a "Public" and a "Private" Offering?

Most salespeople and traders buy and sell securities that are publicly traded. But companies have the option to issue securities in either *private* or *public* securities markets:

- In a private offering, the investment bank earns an agent fee for selling securities quietly to large, savvy institutional investors who perform their own extensive research on the issuer. The issuer and the investment bank do not need to disclose information about the deal to the SEC or to the public, and individual investors are not able to purchase the securities. This allows the issuer to talk in-depth to a small group of investors who will understand a complex story.
- In a public offering, the bank underwrites the deal, buying securities first and reselling them to investors in the public market. The company must register the deal with the SEC and make information available to the public. Individual investors are able to purchase the securities.

THE SALES AND TRADING FUNCTIONS

All major investment banks have sales and trading departments. These departments serve two clients: their own bank, for whom they trade to make money, and their clients, whose investing and trading needs they serve. Although salespeople and traders buy and sell not only securities but also commodities, currencies, and other products, we will focus here on *securities* sales and trading.

Liar's Poker, Bombardiers by Po Bronson, and other books have all focused on the extremes that make sales and trading so different from any other job and so fascinating to the outsider. What makes sales and trading unusual? The fortunes of salespeople and traders are tied to market fluctuations. Extraordinary sums of money are made and lost very quickly. The high-stakes, market-driven nature of sales and trading has generated a culture that is extreme: Moods display wide fluctuations, people move and speak rapidly, and there is no time for etiquette. Personal charisma is critical in moving up, and those who win the floor's power struggles are those who can produce money and amass allies. Performance measurement is very objective: You'll know immediately if you're performing well, since you'll know how much money you've made for the firm. Therefore, compensation can be tied quickly and accurately to your performance.

What exactly *is* the trading floor? The trading floor of an investment bank is different from the floor of a *listed exchange* such as the New York Stock Exchange, which is an independent organization. The trading floor is a floor of an investment bank with few rooms or dividing walls, just endless rows of desks with computers piled on top of them. The floor is almost completely taken up by salespeople and traders. It is an enormous plain across which news and opinions sweep quickly.

What's the difference between a salesperson and a trader? The trader has the ability to commit his firm's capital and to buy and sell securities, whereas the salesperson doesn't. Securities salespeople and traders typically are divided into those who work with "equity" (stocks) and those who work with "fixed income" (debt, or bonds). Within these divisions, there is further product and client specialization.

Salespeople and traders play distinct but symbiotic roles.

SALES

The salespeople, also called the *institutional sales force,* cover institutional investors. (Most banks have a separate department that caters to wealthy individuals, but otherwise have no retail business.) The salesperson's mandate is very broad: He is to use all the firm's resources to serve an investor's needs.

After developing an idea of a customer's investment preferences, the salesperson will provide the customer with market information and investment advice (gleaned from colleagues in trading or research).

Salespeople recommend both securities that their firm has underwritten as well as securities that it has not. The salesperson will help the customer buy and sell securities by acting as a liaison with traders, who actually *execute* the orders. The salesperson is given some credit for client purchases or sales that he has brought to the firm, even though the salesperson himself does not actually execute the transaction. This is because the firm earns a commission on the transaction. Salespeoples' annual bonuses reflect the "credits" they earn for these client transactions.

To prevent conflict-of-interest situations, such as the salesperson recommending securities the firm has underwritten against the investor's best interests, there is a "wall" between the investment banking side of the investment bank and the sales and trading side.

Salespeople call on ten to twenty institutions each, interacting with a client who has investment responsibility. Beyond the debt-equity distinction, a salesperson is either a generalist covering several types of products (treasury bonds, corporate bonds), or a specialist covering just one product. Generally, investment banks set up specialist groups for more complex products, such as mortgage-backed debt or convertible bonds. Salespeople who serve a small institutional investor will play a generalist role, since small institutions have fewer staff liaisons with the investment bank to cover all products.

Because salespeople from rival banks also call on the client, each salesperson searches for ways to encourage the client to take his calls and value a business relationship with him. Salespeople have different styles of serving clients: Some use a relationship approach, while others like to use an analytical approach and provide clients with data.

At the equity departments of large banks, the salesperson's position is sometimes separated into two roles: the *sales trader* and the *research salesperson,* who work together to cover an account. If the client is a mutual fund, such as Fidelity Investments, for example, the research salesperson will advise the portfolio manager at Fidelity on what stocks to buy, or help him understand how market developments will affect the value of certain stocks. The sales trader will actually carry out the transaction and take a "buy" or "sell" order from Fidelity's trader.

Wondering if you'll like sales? Successful salespeople are able to express themselves well, build rapport with others, display good judgment and tact—and not care if they get a phone slammed down on them thirty to forty times a day. Junior salespeople perform backup work for others for several months, then are assigned small accounts of their own, with the idea of limiting the damage they can do to the firm when untrained.

TRADING

As mentioned earlier, traders differ from salespeople in that they take risks with the firm's capital. In other words, they are able to buy and sell securities. There are two main types of traders: proprietary and client-driven.

Client-driven traders buy and sell securities in response to investor clients' needs. They will sometimes buy securities from a client even if they can't immediately find another investor to take the other side of the transaction. Traders therefore take risk on the client's behalf. This provides the client with liquidity, which is important because it increases the flexibility of their investment strategies and reduces their risk.

Proprietary traders buy and sell securities with the direct purpose of earning profit for the firm based on movements in the securities' prices. They are not involved in client trading flows. Proprietary traders manage risk, liquidity, and interest rate exposure. Most important, they watch for profit-making opportunities as markets move.

Client-driven and proprietary traders never work together or communicate, in order to protect the firms' clients. Otherwise, there could be a problem of "front-running": A proprietary trader knows that a client is about to place a big purchase order of a certain stock, for example, so he buys some for himself first in order to gain when the client's order drives up the price.

Securities traders deal in products ranging from straight equity or debt to derivatives, convertibles, and other complex securities. Typically, traders work with just one product and/or maturity range. On the trading floor, they are grouped according to specialty. Specialty areas are called "desks," as in the Foreign Exchange Desk or the Equity Convertible Desk, so-called because of the physical arrangement of desks by product area.

Wondering if you'll like trading? Over time, traders develop an instinctual feel for trading patterns, market interrelationships, and market dynamics. Successful traders typically are ambitious, entrepreneurial, and good at quantitative exercises or games. They are able to take calculated risks, make quick decisions, and work well under pressure.

The degree to which traders are involved in the structuring of a security (that is, deciding on the form and terms of the security) depends on the complexity of the security. With mortgage-backed securities or other complex securities in which the structure determines whether the security gets sold or not, the trader often is called upon for advice before the securities are even issued. Some trading areas see more active trading than others; in areas with larger deal flow, it is unlikely that the trader will be performing much analysis, because he has little downtime between trades.

Client-driven traders and salespeople have a mutually beneficial relationship. Salespeople provide traders with information on investment opportunities and market demand for securities. Client-driven traders provide salespeople with price quotes on securities and provide liquidity to the latter's customers by buying securities they want to sell. Salespeople earn commissions when a trader makes a trade on information they've provided. Here is an example of how they work together.

Case Example: Say there's a merger announcement. Company A is buying Company B. A pension fund already owns 1 million shares of Company B and doesn't want to be a part of this deal—it wants to sell its shares. This pension fund is covered by a saleswoman at Morgan Stanley. The pension fund calls up the Morgan Stanley saleswoman and tells her to sell the 1 million shares of Company B. The saleswoman at Morgan Stanley knows that Bob Jones is one of the big arbitrage traders on the street. She'll call Bob up and say, "I've got a million shares to go at one-eighth below the market price. Do you want any?" Bob tells her that he'll take 300,000 shares. Bob pays the Morgan Stanley saleswoman a commission on the shares he buys. The saleswoman makes her living by knowing Bob and other traders. If the saleswoman sells the security directly to an investor, she'll only get commission on one side, from the seller. If she sells to Bob or another trader, she'll make more because she gets a commission from both the buyer and the seller.

THE CORPORATE LADDER

So where would you fit in within a bank? In investment banking, people are assigned to teams to carry out client transactions. A *partner* or *senior vice president* is called on to win the business mandate and act as the highest-level contact with the client, but he does not spend much time on the transaction. The team includes a *vice president,* who keeps an eye on the overall quality of a project and makes recommendations to the client.

And this is where you come in. As a recent business or law school graduate, you're hired as an *associate*—you'll help manage the project, perform analysis, and make execution decisions on a day-to-day basis. As a recent college graduate, you're hired as an *analyst*—you'll do most of the number-crunching, analysis, and writing to get the job done.

In sales and trading, roles and titles are much less standardized. There are typically five or six *senior traders* and one or two *junior traders* on each desk. The head of the desk, who supervises all traders, is usually a *managing director.* If you're a graduate student, expect to be hired as an associate or as a trader or salesperson, but you will complete several months of apprenticeship before actually taking on trading or sales responsibility. If you're an undergraduate student, things become even less standardized. This represents opportunity. Some banks actually have investment banking–style "analyst" programs for undergraduates in sales and trading, while others don't. If there is no clear hiring program, college graduates are hired as clerks or assistants and gradually work their way up to full sales and trading positions without an MBA.

On page 80 is a summary of the responsibilities of each hierarchy level.

Working relationships in investment banking differ from those in management consulting: Consultants, even junior ones, work separately on very different issues, which they bring together at the end of the day. Bankers, on the other hand, work together on the same issues.

YOUR ROLE IN INVESTMENT BANKING

ANALYSTS

If you have just graduated from college, you will be applying for an *analyst* position in investment banking. Analysts typically have undergraduate degrees from leading colleges and good academic records and extracurriculars. They have degrees in a surprisingly diverse array of subjects. The firms provide basic training in finance and accounting at the beginning of the analyst program. Many analysts don't fully understand financial theories, but they rely on their HP calculators and Excel spreadsheets to perform calculations for them.

An analyst is typically paid a base salary, a small signing bonus, and relocation costs if necessary. You also earn a large annual bonus based on performance. A bonus can represent as much as 30 to 40 percent of your total compensation. An analyst experience in investment banking is often described as "boot camp," since analysts transition from relatively relaxed college lives to extremely high standards of work ethic, judgment, accuracy, and timeliness. A first-year analyst would be responsible for:

- Working under the close supervision of an associate to execute transactions
- Gathering data to be used in models or other analysis
- Building computer-based analytical models to calculate numbers, such as projected financial results or interest payments
- Coordinating the production and mailing of financial documents
- Participating in the firm's recruiting efforts

As you progress, you will become more efficient at performing basic tasks, which will free up your time to take on more advanced tasks. In addition, you will work with less supervision and will be able to direct yourself because you know what you should be doing.

A second-year or third-year analyst would be responsible for:

- Fielding client telephone calls and participating in client meetings alone, answering their questions about a transaction or a market

INVESTMENT BANKING LEVEL (TYPICAL TITLES)	INITIAL ROLE	SALES AND TRADING LEVEL (TYPICAL TITLES)	INITIAL ROLE
Partner, Managing Director	Helps determine direction of firm, leads business development in entire sectors or product lines, helps build relationships with extremely important clients, serves as liaison with government and other external officials	Partner, Managing Director	Same as at left
Senior Vice President, Principal, Director	Builds key client relationships, heads internal groups or departments, develops products or businesses, determines internal administrative policies	Vice President, Principal, Director	Builds key client relationships, heads sales or trading areas, develops products or businesses, represents group and provides expertise at client and internal meetings
Vice President	Sells deals, manages overall quality of deals, provides product or market expertise, responsible for deal results, acts as contact with highest-level clients	Senior Trader/ Salesperson	Responsible for having a view of product's market and being able to explain it, maintains positions, makes money, oversees junior people, maintains client relationships
Associate	Manages day-to-day execution of a deal, acts as main contact with clients, writes and delivers presentations, provides latest information on markets, develops expertise in products and markets	Junior Trader/ Salesperson	Supervised by a senior trader, watches senior trader's positions when he is away from desk, begins to develop trading techniques and view of market, develops some relationships with clients
Analyst, Business Analyst, Financial Analyst, Junior Analyst	Gathers data, develops computer-based financial models, develops and produces client presentations, works with junior clients, supports associates at client presentations and in executing deals	Intern, Clerk, Assistant	Gathers data, supports traders or salespeople, performs clerical or administrative work, observes markets and asks questions in order to develop familiarity with products

---

Breaking the Bank

INVESTMENT BANKING LEVEL	"ALL-IN" PAY (STARTING SALARY + BONUS)*
CEO	$5,000,000 to $9,000,000
Managing Director	$1,000,000 to $4,000,000
•	
•	
•	
First-Year Vice President	$450,000 to $600,000
Third-Year Associate	$280,000 to $370,000
Second-Year Associate	$175,000 to $240,000
First-Year Associate	$95,000 to $130,000
Third-Year Analyst	$60,000 to $90,000
Second-Year Analyst	$50,000 to $65,000
First-Year Analyst	$48,000 to $55,000

Note: Figures based on investment banking. Sales and trading bonuses show greater fluctuation but reach similar levels. Sales and trading pay is related to bottom-line performance, so levels could be achieved earlier or later than in investment banking.

*Typical pay at major investment banks. In special situations, such as a bank trying to build up a practice by hiring away from competitors, pay can vastly exceed these ranges.

Sources: Interviews with insiders, business school career offices, author's analysis, New York Times.

- Providing guidance to newer analysts
- Presenting material during client meetings
- Substituting for an associate in representing the firm on selected client meetings or conference calls
- Creating documents without supervision
- Traveling alone to visit clients

As an analyst, you're rewarded for skill in execution: accuracy, timeliness, and quick thinking. This is because any mistake in your numbers can have a large, immediate financial impact on a client. Transactions and capital markets are time-sensitive, so delays in completing a transaction also can have a significant impact on a client. Having said this, analysts enjoy the greatest job security at the bank because they represent the least expensive work resources. Analysts are rarely fired.

Most analysts leave after two years, returning to business school or taking finance-related jobs in other industries or companies. Analysts typically are admitted at one of the top brand-name business schools in the United States (Harvard, Kellogg, Stanford, or Wharton). Some analysts join venture capital firms, leveraged buy-out shops, or other financial boutiques. Others gain significant responsibility in other securities fields or within the finance function of a corporation. Since they are younger, analysts find it easier than associates to transition to nonfinancial fields such as marketing, management consulting, or strategic planning, because they are willing to start again at the bottom of the ladder.

Firms invite outstanding analysts to stay for a third year. Compensation rises significantly for that year, to the point that it is close to a new associate's pay. Many third-year analysts are able to choose a different location to work in, even overseas. Chances of getting into a top business school are enhanced because of the additional year of experience and because the third year becomes a type of screening: Business schools are aware that top performers are invited to stay at the firm. (Of course, a third year is neither a prerequisite nor a guarantee of acceptance.) Few banks offer business school tuition reimbursement for returning analysts.

Highly exceptional analysts can be promoted to the associate (post-MBA) position without a graduate degree. However, this is very rare.

ASSOCIATES

If you have just graduated from a leading business school, you will be applying for an *associate* position in investment banking. The vast majority of associates in investment banking have graduate degrees. Those who don't are rare former analysts who have been promoted. Firms have varying policies: some actively recruit associates at only the top ten business schools and from INSEAD in Europe, while others recruit associates from a wider range of business and law programs. Firms typically offer analyst or senior analyst positions to candidates at business schools not in the top tier or candidates with graduate degrees in mathematics, economics, or other nonbusiness fields.

An associate is paid a base salary, a large signing bonus, and relocation costs if necessary. You also will earn a large annual bonus based on performance. As an associate in investment banking, you are assigned to a functional, product, or client specialization. Your early responsibilities will include:

- Executing day-to-day details of a transaction with supervision

- Supervising analyst(s) on transaction team, checking their work

- Acting as daily contact with client

- Developing expertise in your specialization

- Shaping financial documents and presentations

- Participating in firm's associate recruiting efforts

As you progress, you begin to take on more client relationship responsibilities. At many investment banks, your initial assignment will last two or three years, after which you might be put on "mobility": You'll be assigned to another area in order to develop well-rounded knowledge.

Later responsibilities would include:

- Leading client meetings and conference calls

- Managing deals with little supervision

- Calling on clients to pitch business, alone or with senior bankers

- Providing guidance to new associates

- Assisting vice president in management of group: providing advice on staffing, hiring, marketing decisions

On average, associates are promoted to vice president after three to five years. Exceptional performers eventually are promoted to partner or managing director levels, where they earn millions of dollars per year. As a senior investment banker, you're rewarded for salesmanship, client management skills, and expertise in products or markets. The bank is depending on your ability to sell and complete transactions to the client's satisfaction and to add value to the client based on your previous experience. A larger proportion of your compensation is bonus-based, reflecting the higher emphasis placed on sales and bottom-line results. There is less job security for senior bankers, but a lot of company-hopping. Senior bankers frequently move between different investment banks in order to win promotions and higher pay.

Bankers can call on their friends at other firms for information on job opportunities, as banking is a very tightly knit industry. High-level investment bankers are sometimes hired for CFO or treasurer positions at client corporations. However, it is hard for a career investment banker to change paths completely to a function such as marketing or operations.

See page 84 for an example of two typical work days for an investment banking associate and analyst.

YOUR ROLE IN SALES AND TRADING

Hiring and titles are much less structured in sales and trading than in investment banking. Large, well-organized companies such as Goldman Sachs and Morgan Stanley have corporate finance–style positions for MBAs and for undergraduates planning to return to business school when the program is over. But recent college students are not hired as salespeople or traders—they are hired as assistants and then work their way up to full sales and trading positions. Many more positions are available in sales than in trading.

The trading floor is close to being a meritocracy. Unlike in investment banking, there is no absolute need for an MBA in order to be promoted. In fact, many sales and trading divisions are struggling with the issue of what

2 Days in the Career of an Investment Banking Analyst

How good are good days and how bad are bad days? In this example, an investment banking analyst (Ted) works with an associate (Susan) on a private placement of bonds for Pyramid Corp., a long-standing client of the firm's. Susan and Ted are both in the debt private placement group at ABC Bank.

MONDAY—A GOOD DAY

8:00 A.M. Ted arrives at the office and skims *The Wall Street Journal* over gourmet coffee and a bagel.

9:00 A.M. Ted calls a senior VP at Tri-State Insurance, an institutional investor, to discuss the current state of the private placement market. The Tri-State VP tells Ted about a major deal that is being brought to the market by another bank. This is a great scoop: Ted's managers in the private placement group will be interested to hear about it.

10:00 A.M. Susan comes over to tell Ted that they have been assigned to the Pyramid deal.

Noon. Susan and Ted take an investor to lunch at Bouley, one of the best restaurants in New York.

2:00 P.M. The team (Phil, a VP; Susan; and Ted) has a kickoff meeting to review Pyramid's background and what they want out of the deal. Ted is asked his opinion of the current state of the private placement market. The team discusses their outlook on how Pyramid's offering will be received by the market and the interest rates Pyramid will have to pay. They agree on the interest rate range they will recommend in order to get the bonds sold. They also discuss how many investors they will approach and how quickly the bonds can be placed. The team will meet with Pyramid on Wednesday to present their ideas; Ted is asked to put together a presentation for the meeting.

4:00 P.M. Ted works on the Pyramid presentation and puts the marked-up pages into Production, the company's typing center.

5:00 P.M. Ted calls home to catch up with his parents. Sandeep, another VP, walks by and tells Ted that he wants to take him to San Francisco next week for an investor conference.

7:00 P.M. Ted is on his way to meet college friends for dinner at Carmine's. Afterward, they'll hit a few bars.

Midnight. Ted is asleep, dreaming of another day like this one.

TUESDAY—A BAD DAY

7:30 A.M. Ted arrives at his desk to find a pile of articles that Sandeep wants him to read and summarize this morning in preparation for the investor conference. Breakfast will have to wait—Ted substitutes with a Coke from a nearby machine.

9:00 A.M. Ted is asked to sit in on a three-hour conference call to help answer investors' questions about a major client's finances. Ted must answer these questions accurately. He is asked a tough question about the client's inventories that he can't answer and promises to get back to investors this afternoon.

Noon. Ted and Susan order in a sandwich and eat at their desks. ABC bank had arranged Pyramid's previous private placement and has old marketing documents on hand; Susan and Ted locate these documents and read through them to understand the company better.

1:00 P.M. Interest rates rise suddenly; Ted has to recalculate the interest rates ABC Bank is suggesting to Pyramid and change the presentation.

3:00 P.M. Uh-oh. Ted finds major word processing errors in the Pyramid presentation. Ted rushes to Production to submit further edits and plead with them to get the changes turned around in a few hours.

5:00 P.M. A VP walks out of his office and heads straight for Ted's desk— bad news. Geo Oil & Gas has invited ABC Bank to compete for a private placement assignment. The VP asks Ted to put together a pitch book describing ABC's capabilities and have it ready by tomorrow morning.

6:00 P.M. Ted picks up the Pyramid presentation, checks it one last time, and sends it to Phil's home by courier.

7:00 P.M. Ted orders in food, then starts putting together the pitch book for Geo. He submits the book to Production by 11:00 P.M., then waits for the book to be finished. He takes a quick nap at his desk.

1:00 A.M. Ted picks up the finished pitch books from Production, checks each page of each book, then takes a taxi home, where he crawls into bed exhausted. But it's been a productive day.

value to place on an MBA, given that the right to trade traditionally has been earned through experience—observing and learning from senior traders—and the MBA does not replace this experience. Insiders report that MBAs and undergraduates start with very similar responsibilities in sales and trading. Promotion is based purely on accomplishment, and an undergraduate conceivably could rise faster than an MBA who started at the same time.

There is truly a wide variety of backgrounds on the trading floor. Some people have graduate degrees, others don't. Salespeople are more likely than traders to have graduate degrees from top schools, but both pools are more heterogeneous than investment bankers. There is a recent trend toward hiring salespeople and traders from the same MBA programs as investment bankers.

Salespeople and traders have a strong desire to make money and often have shown previous interest in economics, business, mathematics, or other quantitative fields. In sales, it is important to be able to explain complex ideas and persuade someone to take an action. In trading, you need the ability to make quick decisions, to work under pressure, and to be comfortable with quantitative analysis and computers. Past experiences that have prepared people to be successful in sales and trading include bridge, card-counting, prior telemarketing or sales experience, sports, and even Mormon proselytizing.

Beginners in sales and trading go through a formalized, classroomlike training for a few weeks or months. After completing the training program, new hires either become assistants on a trading desk or rotate through various industry coverage and product specialty groups. They might spend a few weeks or months on each desk, seeking a good match for a permanent assignment. Rotation provides you, the beginner, with exposure to many types of products and a sense of which desks you would enjoy working on. Afterward you are permanently assigned to one desk. During your rotation or as an assistant, your activities would include:

- Gathering information and opinions on the market and on securities

- Developing a feel for markets and knowledge of specialty products

- Supporting junior and senior traders in a range of tasks (interns have been known to carry out menial tasks, such as fetching coffee or lunch)

As you progress from an apprentice-type position to a junior trader position, your responsibilities would change to:

- Covering senior traders' positions when they're away from the desk

- Begin developing in-depth knowledge of a product and a trading strategy for that product

- Placing smaller trades under supervision

Junior *salespeople* would:

- Cover smaller sales accounts

- Begin developing an understanding of various securities products

- Try to develop smaller sales accounts into bigger ones

- Build relationships with accounts, get a feel for their investment preferences and strategies

As an intern or junior trader or salesperson, you are rewarded for excellent interpersonal skills, enthusiasm for the job, quickness, and hard work. Since you are not trading fully and are not expected to know your product yet, you add value by supporting the senior traders around you with a positive attitude.

As a senior trader or salesperson, you are rewarded for making money. For traders, this involves developing a point of view on your products and markets and executing a successful trading strategy around this viewpoint. For salespeople, success involves having an excellent breadth of knowledge of products and markets, developing new accounts through strong sales and interpersonal skills, and developing connections and working well with both traders and clients.

Salespeople and traders tend to exit the business at an earlier age than investment bankers, due to the demanding environment of the trading floor. Insiders report that they like to stay in one specialty area during their career in order to advance quickly; if they move to another area, they must build expertise all over again.

Like investment bankers, salespeople and traders experience a great deal of interfirm mobility. Their options outside sales and trading, however, are limited. They can switch over to the buy side of the market, so that they are working for the institutional investors that were once their clients. However, transitioning even to an advisory (non–transaction-oriented) finance position is very difficult—investment banking or finance positions in Corporate America are not options for former traders.

TASKS PERFORMED

Work at an investment bank can be broken down into the following categories:

Research: Collecting data or opinions on companies, industries, or markets through primary or secondary sources. In investment banking, this would entail going to the bank's library and locating a company's annual report or credit ratings, for use in writing an offering memorandum, or talking to the bank's research department to find out what research analysts are predicting for the company and its industry. In sales and trading, research might include going to a daily morning review by a bank economist to find out the latest forecast and indicators or getting an update on bond inventory for use in determining pricing and selling of securities.

Analysis: Once data is collected, it is synthesized and analyzed in quantitative and qualitative ways. In investment banking, analysis might include building a spreadsheet to project future cash flows of a division to be sold, or using current bond prices to calculate the all-in cost to a client of issuing debt. In sales and trading, analysis might include following M&A activity for possible arbitrage opportunities, monitoring the market for broad changes that would signal investment opportunities, or developing an opinion as to a market's direction.

Communication: Bankers communicate with clients in written or verbal form on a daily basis. In investment banking, for example, associates and analysts write offering memoranda and prospectuses used to market securities to investors and meet with clients and lawyers to hammer out the terms of an agreement. In sales and trading, communicating with clients is a constant; this includes salespeople exchanging information with a client on portfolio needs and the bank's securities offerings or traders exchanging views on the market with each other.

Presentation: In investment banking, analysis and conclusions are often presented to clients and others in written form, which entails the production of documents. Analysts and associates prepare "pitch books," for example, which describe their firm's abilities in a product area and that are used in the selling process. For the pitch book, an analyst might produce graphs like the "league table," which shows the firm's ranking against competitors in the area of IPO underwriting. All documents must be photocopied, bound, and sent to appropriate recipients; analysts and associates coordinate these activities with the bank's production department or administrative staff.

Execution: This entails performing the specific steps involved in carrying out a transaction. In investment banking, it would include registering a securities offering with the SEC or distributing prospectuses to potential investors. Execution is central to sales and trading, and includes the syndicate desk pricing a new issue, salespeople calling investors to market a new issue of securities, and traders working with their bank loan department to finance their purchase of a block of securities.

LIFE INSIDE AN INVESTMENT BANK

Several key factors will drive your job satisfaction and lifestyle.

Group Assignment: Nothing drives a banker's or trader's experience more than his group assignment. Once you join an investment bank, you are asked to specialize in a function, product, or group of clients. Investment bankers often remain in a group for two or three years before rotating to another group. Analysts spend their entire tenure at the firm within one group. Salespeople and traders either stay in one area for their entire careers or rotate among product areas every few years.

Your group is your "home base": The group's senior managers make assignments, evaluations, and other key decisions. Groups can range in size from five to seventy-five people. Unlike in management consulting, where colleagues change every few months with a new project, you will spend every day of your experience with the colleagues within your group in an investment bank. Since you'll have fewer colleagues, you'll have more of a chance to build mentoring relationships with supervisors. Your ability to fit in with your group will largely determine your success or failure.

What's more, groups tend to be fairly isolated from one another and develop distinct cultures and traditions. *The culture of the group you're assigned to will have a greater impact on your experience than the culture of the investment bank as a whole;* you can have a vastly different experience at the same bank depending on the group you are assigned to.

Finally, typical team structures differ from group to group. Who's on your team will determine how much responsibility you get. For example, a team that includes several analysts might allow a second-year analyst to take on more responsibility. An associate may get more responsibility in a group in which there are few vice presidents.

Working Hours: The amount you'll work in investment banking cannot be overstated. Most people think they understand the hours before they arrive, but they still are shocked by the reality. One analyst reported that he bought fifty pairs of underwear because he had no time to do laundry: When he needed a fresh pair, he'd break open a new package.

Investment bankers work longer hours than salespeople and traders. Investment banking analysts and associates work eighty hours per week on average and one-hundred hours per week at peak times. Hours depend on what stage of a deal you're in. Weekend work is guaranteed. M&A department hours are known for being the most brutal.

Sales and traders consistently work fifty to seventy hours per week. Their hours are more regular because of their market orientation; every day, you must be in the office by the time the markets open. Traders in equity products tend to have shorter hours than traders in debt products, getting in at 8:00 A.M. and leaving at around 4:30 P.M. Debt traders typically work from 6:00 A.M. to 5:00 or 6:00 P.M.

Deal Assignments: Once in their group, investment bankers experience variety because they are assigned to different deals. You're likely to be working on several deals at once, all in different stages. Each deal lasts only three to four months at most. With each deal comes a different deal team, the group of bankers assigned to execute the deal. The deal team usually is composed of bankers from your specialty group, so that after several deals you probably will have worked with everyone in your group at least once.

Investment banking deals are short and trading transactions can happen instantaneously, so there is a great deal of variety in the projects you work on.

Finding a Mentor: Bankers aren't assigned formal, senior mentors to help coach them through their first months in the industry. But the bankers who are most successful are those who have identified and built a relationship with a mentor who is fairly senior. A mentor can be your advocate to senior management, making sure your accomplishments are recognized, your mistakes are downplayed, and you are receiving the assignments you want. A mentor can provide you with valuable career advice.

Compensation and Evaluation: Compensation and evaluation are fundamentally driven by quantitative, "harder" measures. Senior bankers and traders, especially, are evaluated based on profit or sales they bring in and technical skills they possess.

Performance ratings are relative, and bankers are ranked against their peers at each level. A class of investment banking analysts, for example, might be divided into three groups, with the bulk of analysts falling into the middle category. Bonuses are then distributed depending on rank. Analysts are given overall performance measures, but reviewers' comments often are kept anonymous.

Investment banking analysts are evaluated and granted bonuses twice a year, while associates are reviewed once a year. Annual raises are based on relative performance. An MBA graduate who joins the firm with an annual base salary of $75,000 might see his salary increased to $85,000 for the second year. Bulge-bracket firms such as Morgan Stanley and Goldman Sachs pay less than up-and-coming banks that have to pay high amounts to attract high-quality people.

Regionalism: Conventional wisdom has it that bankers who are vying for fast-track careers and CEO positions must stick closely to a bank's headquarters, where management decisions are made. The bulge-bracket firms are head-

quartered in New York, but several large firms are based in Chicago, Minneapolis, and the San Francisco Bay Area.

Camaraderie: The extent to which bankers feel a bond with their colleagues
depends on the firm and the group they work for. Bankers at smaller boutiques
report a "family feeling" and a high level of unity among peers. Reports from
larger firms are mixed and are dependent on individual departments. The
greatest rapport tends to build in areas in which there are a large pool of
analysts or associates working in a common area and on similar work, such as
M&A.

There are occasional events, such as Christmas parties, during which bankers are able to mix with colleagues from across the firm. More common, however, are department events, such as parties at partners' homes or dinner and
dance events at local nightclubs.

Training: Typically, new associate and analyst "classes" enter the firm in August and are immediately immersed in a group training session with their
peers that lasts several weeks. This training session covers topics such as accounting and finance for analysts or in-depth securities training or bond math
for associates. After this session is over, bankers are grouped in individual
department training sessions, where they receive training in their specialty.
Some banks, instead of assigning bankers immediately to a department, rotate
them through various departments to train them in a variety of fields and
allow a better match between banker and department. Rotation periods are
common practice in sales and trading.

Vacation, What Vacation?: As a starting analyst or associate, you're typically
given two to three weeks of vacation each year. But few actually take their full
vacation; doing so tends to be frowned upon. Since bankers usually are staffed
simultaneously on several deals, all in different stages, it is difficult for them
to break away without it having a noticeable impact. Vacation is most easily
taken around Christmas, when clients are on vacation and the pace of deals
slows down.

CULTURE

- Performance standards are extremely high; you will be surrounded by
  top-notch people who want to put a 100 percent effort into their jobs.
  You will be expected to work very long hours, maintain your calm under
  extreme pressure, perform work with rigor and attention to detail, and
  uphold high ethical standards.

- A work-hard, play-hard mentality is prevalent: Bankers throw themselves into their "play" activities with as much energy as they do their

work. Bankers admire well-rounded people with good intellect rather than super-intellectuals with limited personal interests. You'll find a lot of bankers running the New York Marathon or squeezing in workouts as early as 5:30 A.M. or as late as 9:30 P.M.

- A sink-or-swim mentality also exists. Weakness, excuses, and laziness will stunt your career, while strength, a "can-do" attitude, and hard work are revered. You are expected to make sacrifices and take care of yourself, and there is not much sympathy for personal problems.

- "Softer" interpersonal skills sometimes are neglected because of the great time pressures that bankers and traders face. Tied to the markets or to the timing of transactions, bankers and traders often do not have the time to think about the way they communicate. Especially on the trading floor, thoughts may be communicated more abruptly than in other business settings.

- Be forewarned: This industry can be difficult for women and minorities. There exists a wide range of cultures from politically correct to "locker room" behavior, but expect a more male-dominated culture the closer you get to the trading floor. As a business, the securities industry is notoriously slow to promote women. Minorities and women are scarce at top ranks, particularly in sales and trading areas, although banks are trying hard to change this. Less than 10 percent of the partners and managing directors at Wall Street's leading firms are women.[4] The women who have climbed the highest have gone off the beaten path: They have taken the less-coveted administrative, management, and re-search jobs.

- Those who like structure and stability in their everyday lives will like investment banking. Process and hierarchy are fairly well defined, except perhaps at smaller, leaner banks.

HOW TO TELL THE FIRMS APART

So maybe now you're interested in investment banking. There is a great variety of firms to choose from. Banks can be categorized along two main dimensions: the diversity of products they offer and the size and needs of their customers.[5] Some banks offer a broad array of services, while others concentrate their services in a few areas. Some banks serve large, sophisticated corporations that have broad needs and often engage in financial transactions, while other banks concentrate on small companies that have narrower needs and are focused on raising expansion capital through the stock market. Think of firms as falling into a matrix like this one:

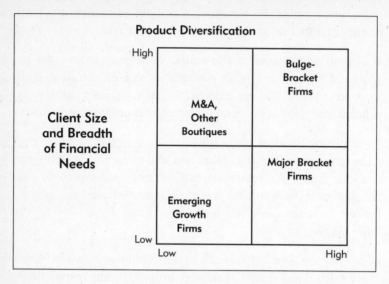

Bulge-bracket firms are large, international, New York–based firms. Examples are Goldman Sachs, Morgan Stanley, J.P. Morgan, Merrill Lynch, and Credit Suisse First Boston. These banks are strong in a broad portfolio of services, including debt and equity underwriting, M&A advisory services, merchant banking, sales and trading, and more. Their clients are sophisticated Fortune 500 companies that regularly tap the capital markets. The name "bulge bracket" comes from the bulge of major investment banks listed at the top of a *tombstone* newspaper advertisement announcing a new securities issue.

Major bracket firms are large, international, and mostly New York–based but are less diversified in their product strengths. While bulge-bracket firms have consistently high market share in all product categories, major bracket firms have much higher market share in some product categories than in others.[6] Examples include Smith Barney, Bankers Trust, DLJ, and Bear Stearns.

Boutiques are those firms that limit their offerings to a particular product, usually a high-margin service whose success is highly dependent on the banker's knowledge and expertise. Accordingly, boutiques often spring up around "star" bankers who leave larger firms. Examples include Wasserstein Perella (an M&A boutique) or D. E. Shaw (a quantitative trading firm). M&A, for example, is a service that requires strategic thinking and is tied to the personal knowledge and connections of the banker. Boutiques typically serve large and medium-size firms seeking product expertise.

Emerging growth banks serve companies in fast-growth sectors such as technology and health care. Although clients can range from small start-ups to well-established industry leaders, the average client is smaller than a bulge-bracket client. Clients are focused on raising money in the stock market or high-yield bond markets rather than tapping the investment-grade bond markets or engaging in more complex transactions associated with mature companies. Accordingly, emerging growth banks engage in basic product offerings and are a good place to learn the fundamentals of investment banking. Examples include Robertson Stephens, Hambrecht & Quist, Alex. Brown, D. H. Blair, and Volpe Welty.

See the company profiles at the back of this book for information on work that each firm performs. Be aware that the quality and quantity of deals you work on will depend on the firm's strength in that area.

~   BASIC INDUSTRY LINGO   ~

Beauty Contest: The series of presentations investment banks make to clients to make themselves more appealing than competitors and therefore win an assignment

Bond: Evidence of a promise to pay back money owed. The issuer of a bond promises to pay the bondholder a specific amount of interest for a specified length of time.

Boutique: A small investment bank that specializes in a product area or a type of client

Broker: An agent who executes orders to buy or sell securities on behalf of clients. *Stockbroker* is used specifically to describe brokers serving individuals rather than institutions.

Bulge-Bracket Firm: The largest, multinational, full-service investment banks, including Goldman Sachs, Morgan Stanley, Merrill Lynch, and J.P. Morgan

Capital Markets: The markets that deal in securities with a maturity of over one year, for example, long-term debt or equity securities

Corporate Finance: The group within an investment bank that provides advice to corporations on a range of financial matters, including raising capital

Debt: An obligation to pay back money owed

Derivative: New, hybrid securities created from underlying, more primitive securities. Options, swaps, and futures are examples of derivatives.

Desk: An area of specialization on the trading floor

Divestiture: The act of selling a subsidiary or a division of a company

The Dow: The Dow Jones Industrial Average. The most frequently quoted indicator of the stock market's performance; it is a number calculated using the stock prices of thirty major industrial companies.

Due Diligence: Investment bankers' evaluation of the financial and other conditions of a company before they help the company issue securities to the public

Emerging Markets: Developing regions such as Latin America and most parts of Asia

Equity: An ownership interest; used interchangeably with "stock"

Fixed-income Security: A debt security such as a bond or a note; these securities pay the holder a fixed amount of interest at regular periods

Futures: Contracts specifying a future date of delivery of a specified amount of products or securities, with the hope of profiting from market price changes

Glass-Steagall Act: A 1934 law separating investment and commercial banking; prohibits investment banks from taking consumer deposits and commercial banks from underwriting stocks and bonds

Going Public: The process of selling shares of a privately held company to the public for the first time. *See* initial public offering.

High-yield Bonds: Otherwise known as junk bonds; pay high interest to bondholders because the issuer's credit quality is poorer and risk is therefore greater

Initial Public Offering (IPO): Selling shares of a privately held company to the public for the first time. *See* going public.

Issuer: The institution selling (offering, or issuing) securities in order to raise capital

Leveraged Buyout (LBO): Buying a company using borrowed funds (sometimes through debt securities). Often the loan is secured by the assets of the company being acquired.

League Chart: A chart used by an investment bank to win business. The chart usually favorably compares the bank's performance in an area against its competitors.

Mergers and Acquisitions (M&A): The process of helping companies merge with, sell, or acquire companies or other properties

Options: The right to buy (call) or sell (put) a fixed amount of a specific security at a specified price within a specified period of time. Options are purchased and traded like securities.

Pitch Books: Small bound documents investment banks use at meetings to try to win business. The books describe the bank's performance and merits.

Private Placement: A stock or bond issue sold directly by a company to an institutional investor but that is not registered with the SEC, underwritten by an investment bank, or offered to the public

Ratings: The evaluation of the credit risk of a security, usually performed by an established rating agency such as Moody's, Standard & Poor's, or Duff & Phelps

Retail Client: An individual investor as opposed to an *institutional* investor, such as an insurance company. Typically used in the context of buying and selling securities.

The Standard & Poor's 500 (The S&P 500): A widely used indicator of stock market performance, using a weighted base of 500 stocks

Securities and Exchange Commission (SEC): The regulatory agency responsible for administering federal securities laws

Security: Evidence that you own a share of property or are owed money (i.e., a stock or bond certificate). Also refers to other financial instruments, such as hybrid combinations of stocks and bonds.

Stock: Evidence of an ownership interest in a property or company

Stockbroker: A salesperson who helps individual investors buy and sell securities

Swaps: Arrangements through which two organizations lend to each other through different instruments: for example, in different currencies and at different rates

Tombstone: Advertisement, usually in a newspaper, announcing a new security issue. Included are the terms, the amount raised, and the names of the underwriters.

Trader: An individual who buys and sells securities for clients or for his firm

Trading Floor: Area of an investment bank where traders and salespeople are located

Underwriting: Investment banks' purchase of a securities issue for resale to investors

Yield: The annual return on an investment, expressed as a percentage of the original investment

---

Consult the Web site for this book, www.thefasttrack.com, for an updated list of articles and books on the industry.

∾   **LIGHTER READING**   ∾

Bronson, Po. *Bombardiers.* New York: Penguin Books, 1996. A fictional account of trading floor life.

Bruck, Connie. *The Predator's Ball: The Junk-Bond Raiders and the Man Who Staked Them.* New York: Simon & Schuster, 1988.

Burrough, Bryan, and John Helyar. *Barbarians at the Gate: The Fall of RJR Nabisco.* New York: Harper & Row, 1990.

Lewis, Michael. *Liar's Poker.* New York: W.W. Norton & Company, 1989. The classic, entertaining description of the Salomon Brothers trading floor.

Stewart, James. *Den of Thieves.* New York: Simon & Schuster, 1991.

~   RECOMMENDED READING   ~

For more articles on individual investment banks, see company profiles.

Bagli, Charles. "Giant Wall Street Merger: The Shake-Out." *New York Times,* February 6, 1997.

Fisher, Anne B. *Wall Street Women.* Knopf, 1990. A must-read for women considering investment banking careers.

Fromson, Brett. "Farm Boy to Financier: Goldman's Corzine Embodies Wall Street's New Meritocracy." *Washington Post,* November 6, 1994.

Himelstein, Linda. "Silicon Valley's Hot Startup Is . . . a Bank." *Business Week,* April 29, 1996.

Holland, Kelley, Leah Nathans Spiro, and Philip L. Zweig. "Waiting for Glass-Steagall to Shatter." *Business Week,* March 27, 1995.

Schifrin, Matthew. "Merrill-izing the World." *Forbes,* February 10, 1997.

Sesit, Michael R. "Top Dogs: U.S. Financial Firms Seize Dominant Role in the World Markets: Tough Competition at Home Sharpens Their Skills, Willingness to Innovate." *The Wall Street Journal,* January 5, 1996.

Uttal, Bro. "Inside the Deal That Made Bill Gates $350,000,000." *Fortune,* July 21, 1986. A behind-the-scenes look at Microsoft's initial public offering and how investment banks work with their clients.

Willoughby, Jack. "The Changing Face of Retail." *Investment Dealers' Digest,* May 1, 1995. A good article for those interested in private client services, the investment bank departments serving very wealthy ("high net worth") individuals.

~   INDUSTRY SOURCES   ~

If you haven't had formal training in economics, finance, or business, you may want to consult some of the sources listed here.

Encyclopedia of American Industries, ed. Kevin Hillstrom. Volume 2: *Service & Non-Manufacturing Industries.* New York: Gale Research, Inc., 1994, pp. 838–845. A well-written, concise explanation of the securities industry.

Harvard Business School Finance Club. *Career Guide: Finance 1997.* Boston: Harvard Business School Publishing, 1997. A useful index of investment banks, including official information on each bank.

Investment Dealers' Digest and *The Wall Street Journal* offer frequent coverage of investment banks among the popular business press.

Little, Jeffrey B., and Lucien Rhodes. *Understanding Wall Street,* 2nd edition. Blue Ridge Summit, PA: Liberty Hall Press, 1987. Well-written explanations of Wall Street fundamentals, geared for the layperson.

Securities Industry Yearbook, 1996–1997. New York, NY: Securities Industry Association, 1997. A comprehensive list of investment banks, also available on the SIA's web site at www.sia.com.

Welcome to Careers in Investment Banking: www.cob.ohio-state.edu/dept/fin/

jobs/ib2.htm. The most comprehensive Internet site on investment banking, written for job-hunters.

Wurman, Richard Saul, ed., with Alan Siegel and Kenneth M. Morris. *The Wall Street Journal Guide to Understanding Money & Markets.* New York: ACCESSPRESS, 1990. Short explanations of financial instruments, good for people who like pictures and graphs.

FOR THE DIEHARDS

Eccles, Robert G., and Dwight B. Crane. *Doing Deals: Investment Banks at Work.* Boston: Harvard Business School Press, 1988. This academic analysis of current management practices in investment banking is appropriate for MBA students who want a very in-depth understanding of the industry.

Ross, Stephen, Randolph Westerfield, and Jeffrey Jaffe. *Corporate Finance,* 4th ed. Chicago: Irwin, 1996. If you want to give yourself a crash course on finance, this is a good graduate-level textbook to use.

NOTES

[1] *Encyclopedia of American Industries,* vol. 2, p. 838; author's analysis.
[2] Ibid.
[3] Robert G. Eccles and Dwight B. Crane, *Doing Deals: Investment Banks at Work* (Boston: Harvard Business School Press, 1988), p. 128.
[4] Peter Truell, "Morgan Stanley's Wall St. Rarity: A Woman With Power," *New York Times,* July 2, 1996.
[5] Eccles and Crane, *Doing Deals,* p. 92.
[6] Ibid., p. 103.

INSIDER INTERVIEW: SPOTLIGHT ON SALES AND TRADING

Rob Bainbridge*
Former Trader, bulge-bracket investment bank

R ob Bainbridge worked in the rough-and-tumble world of trading at a bulge-bracket firm for two years. Rob traded *convertible debt*—bonds that investors can later convert into stock.

*Name has been changed to protect privacy.

How do undergrads typically get hired into the sales and trading areas of a bank?

Through something called an intern program. It's really the equivalent of the analyst program in investment banking. Most new interns rotate for a year, spending three months on each [product] desk and trying to get a permanent offer on one of those desks, looking for a fit. A small minority, about 10 percent, are hired directly to a desk—like me.

How did you land your job?

I was a summer intern on the convertible bonds desk on the trading floor between my junior and senior years. Then at the end of the summer I was offered a full-time position as a specialist for that desk. I liked this desk a lot, and that's why I came back. It really varies how different people come to be specialists. Some desks are really looking for young people, so they're recruiting heavily.

What do interns do?

You get assigned to a desk after a year, but you start by doing a lot of trivial grunt work. A lot of getting coffee for people, getting lunch, sending faxes, and mostly asking a lot of questions. You try to help out and find little things you can do. The really important thing is to find little ways you can add value and support the people around you, since they're not going to let you trade or have accounts for at least a year or so.

Different desks have different ways of training people. Right now, at my firm, everyone who wants to go into equity trading has to spend time on the New York Stock Exchange floor as a clerk. This teaches you quickness, memory skills, how to keep things organized, how to write tickets fast, talk fast, yell, scream, get yelled at—the whole bit. So you're there for six months, and then when a job opens up upstairs at the trading desk, you come up there and become a junior trader.

How are MBAs regarded on the trading floor?

The big mistake MBAs make is thinking that they're going to skip some levels because of their degree. In fact, they're going to get paid twice as much to do the same thing as an undergraduate. They might call you an associate or something like that, but you're going to do the same thing. I was training MBAs to do little jobs for me.

Where I was, in equities, there was no advantage to having an MBA. In equity trading, no one on the desk had an MBA. In fact, in some sections at my firm they might even be at a disadvantage because people might resent them for having an MBA. And they're going to have to listen to people who are much younger telling them what to do. As an MBA I would really be careful about where I went, the culture there, and choosing a firm where they like to make MBAs traders. If there's no premium placed on the MBA, then it's going to be a lot harder of a place to work in.

How would you describe the trading floor culture?

It's a totally different world. It's not like any other job I've heard of. My view of the world is a little warped from it.

There's a lot of drinking involved. It's not stuffy. People are intense, but a lot of cursing goes on, and there's nothing really politically correct about it. You're going to hear a lot of things that might shock you or make you mad, depending on who you are. The MBAs have a hard time doing the grunt work—they've paid $80,000 for a degree and they're still running around getting lunch and sodas for people. It can be humbling, but you have to keep in mind what your overall goal is. If you're looking to make a lot of money quickly, there aren't a lot of better places to do it. The amount of money that people are making three or four years out of business school is pretty phenomenal.

How does the pressure on the trading floor culture compare to the pressure in investment banking?

It's investment banking times ten. Basically all traders think that investment bankers are sissies—they have *lunch hours*. Who knows what the hell they're doing up there? It takes them sixteen hours to do something it would take me ten hours to do. It's actually funny for me to hear people saying that investment bankers are able to work under pressure because we look at them as not having these traits. It's the degree to which those things are true that differentiates investment banking from trading.

When I talk about pressure, I'm talking about maybe you just made a mistake and you just lost $20,000, and now you still have to figure this thing out or you might lose more, and you've got a trader yelling at you, saying "What the fuck is wrong with you?" So many things are happening and you have to do them all in the next five minutes. Pressure, time, how to prioritize five things at once. Listen, talk, and think all at the same time. People only say things to you once, and you're expected to hear it and pick it up. There's a lot of money at stake and every time you make a mistake you're expected to fess up to it.

Could you explain the titles and hierarchy in trading?

You can call yourself whatever you want to in trading. It's not as formalized as in investment banking, where people have strict titles. Basically you're a peon and then you become a trader, then vice president, director, and managing director.

So once you're a trader, what do you do every day?

On the converts desk I was a junior trader, and that meant that I would watch the senior trader's positions when he wasn't there, I'd know where the market was, what prices he would be willing to buy and sell things at. As a junior trader, you're actually placing trades. Since it's the senior trader's "pad," you want to keep in mind what his outlook is and you know that you're generally going to be a buyer while he's gone, unless things change drastically. But something could change in the time he's gone, and you have to decide whether all these bonds are all of a sudden for sale. You use his ideas as a reference point, but you have to keep track of what has changed. What you're not doing is just speculating. You ask for help from people around you so that it doesn't get too out of control.

Who sits on the desk with you?

Typically five or six senior guys and one or two junior guys. Everyone understands each other's jobs, so you can ask for help. You also deal with the sales force of about eight people. The sales force is selling convertible bonds to institutional clients. Some people on the floor don't have college degrees or Ivy League backgrounds, while others do. And you have to work your way between all those people. Traders tend to hire a lot of athlete types. It's important to be quick and forceful in the way you speak, like in team sports. Traders don't put up with a lot of shit. It's a people management and ego management thing.

What can a junior trader do to improve his chances of succeeding?

In the beginning you're really going to need a mentor. You're going to need to build relationships with the people you want to be around or in the groups that you want to get into. Mentors are going to stand up and say, "I want that person on my team." You want a lot of people to say behind your back "He's a good guy, we want him here." If your mentor is someone who's really powerful, you may only need that one person's voice behind you, but the danger is if he leaves then you're unprotected. The broader base of support you can get, the better. That's why interpersonal skills are so important. You have to kiss a lot of ass to get what you want.

How early do people leave this business?

People leave at all points in the game. Although there are not too many people over forty or fifty around. On the equity floor people tend to be older and tend to stay longer. Bond floors tend to be younger, more technical, math-driven, and demanding. To trade stocks, you don't need to know net present value or anything—you just need to be able to count in eighths and add pretty well. The government bond market isn't that complicated, but some of the other bond products get more elaborate. The equity traders tend to make less than the bond traders, so maybe that's the other reason they stay longer. They don't make the kind of money where they could retire early.

One woman on my desk left a year after I got there. She had been in the business for about twenty years, was in her mid-forties, and wanted to leave just to spend more time with her daughter and help her brother finance his new business. No one's ever heard from her since. She was making seven figures for a few years, so not everyone gets to that level. A lot of people cap out making $500,000 or $350,000. Old-timers are those who have spent about twenty years in the business. If you last that long, you probably have enough money to retire at the end.

INSIDER INTERVIEW

Alan Kamal*
Former Analyst, Morgan Stanley

What's it like inside a prestigious bulge-bracket firm? Alan Kamal tells us. He spent two years at Morgan Stanley.

When you were an undergraduate, did you always know you were going to go into investment banking?

No, I was going to apply to law school. I took the LSAT the summer of my junior year. I subsequently realized that I needed three recommendations, and the applications looked too onerous, so I decided to take a couple of years off and then go back to law school if I wanted to. I was just interviewing wherever. I just wanted a job that paid $30,000 to $35,000 a year. Whatever would keep me alive in New York or Boston.

*Name has been changed to protect privacy.

I actually had no idea what Morgan Stanley did the day I interviewed with them. I had not even heard that they were one of the better investment banks or anything. But as it turned out, they were my first investment banking offer.

What does Morgan Stanley look for in people they interview?

All investment banks look for a fit with their culture. When we interviewed people we'd look for fun people, for people who were different. There was this one guy who was trying to sell condoms in Russia. I mean, that really sets you apart.

You know, you don't want to shoot yourself in the foot by wearing a flamboyant suit or something like that. But being interesting is the key, and being fun. You've got to look the part. They hire a lot of people as analysts who don't dress well, but if you want to make it to the next level or if you want to get respect within the firm you have to dress well. You have to look like you're professional.

It's more important to be funny and quick at interviews and have some sort of a repartee rather than be a serious, intellectual kind of person. If you're intellectual you'll do a lot better in consulting. At Morgan Stanley credit is given to a street-smart person who gets the job done and isn't late to the meeting. It's a lot more important to have the book done at 10:30 for an 11:00 flight than to get bogged down in the details.

How would you describe the culture in M&A?

M&A was a big peer support group. There were twenty of us and we were all generalists, not assigned to any particular industry. We took up one whole floor and you literally knew everyone. And you'd go out together every night. We worked hard, but it was a lot of fun.

Did you eat all your meals on the job?

We had a TV room where we ate. It's where we watched *Seinfeld* and *Melrose* and got hooked on them. From 7:30 to 10:30 P.M. was TV time for the analysts in the TV room. And then on Sundays we'd all watch football. On your way in you'd pick up a bagel with lox and then meet there with your friends. We'd literally be there an hour before you had to start work because it was fun.

I've heard a lot of people say that Goldman has a team culture and that Morgan Stanley is a star system. Do you think that's true?

I don't think that's true, frankly. Our work was completely based around teams. What I've seen in investment banking is that every team is hierarchical. Consulting, for example, is completely different—you work in parallel and do your segment of the work, and someone else does their segment and you pull it all together in the end. You're checking in more with people in investment banking.

I don't think anyone else did my work at Morgan Stanley, if that's what you mean by teamwork. If I was working on a deal and I was finished at midnight—I would not stay to help someone if I knew he was going to stay until 4 A.M. In that aspect, there was no teamwork. And although Morgan Stanley's not a star system, you definitely develop a reputation there, which I don't think happens at Goldman. Just comparing us to the analysts from Goldman, there's definitely a difference in culture. The analysts from Goldman are a lot more low key, and they downplay their experience at Goldman Sachs, and you never hear them say anything bad about Goldman Sachs. So in that respect it may be more of a team culture.

Were you given a lot of responsibility at Morgan Stanley?

There really is an effort at Morgan Stanley to make sure you go to every meeting. It was fourteen months into my job at Morgan Stanley when I made a presentation to the board of a major financial services firm. And literally I was walking from our office down the street to the client's building when [my boss] said "Okay, you're presenting." There was no notice or anything. There was no time to be nervous. I think that's partially a function of being in a branch office.

The other thing is that as an analyst, there are things you could never do in other businesses. Even in consulting. As a banker, you get to fly the Concorde sometimes, and you stay at the Ritz and the Mandarin instead of the Hyatt or the Hilton. You always get the best food. Money was no consideration. When you fly, anything more than three hours was first class.

What was the biggest perk you think you ever received?

Oh, man—we could get tickets to a lot of sports events. The meal allowances were also great, and it helped our social life. Also, the people at Morgan Stanley are still my best friends. There's a group of about ten people that I can keep in touch with and who are my friends for life. And the network of sixty analysts that you worked with, you can always call on them, and they will always help. We still have Morgan Stanley analyst vacations. I don't think analysts at other firms do that as much.

What were your total hours like?

In M&A, the advantage was I didn't have to go into work until 10:00 or 10:30 A.M. Plus they could always reach me, since all analysts wore beepers so I could go in whenever. I'd work about 80 per week, on average 10:00 A.M. to midnight—about 14 hours per day, five days a week, plus some on weekends. During bad weeks it could go as high as 110 hours, and during good weeks, it could go down to 50 or 60 hours. I had to fill out a timesheet, so that kept me honest.

Which group do you think teaches analysts more useful skills, corporate finance or M&A?

As a corporate finance analyst you'll see the big picture, if only in the one industry you cover. So if you're interested in industry, corporate finance is a lot more helpful. In M&A, the valuation you do may not be as useful in Corporate America, unless you work for a strategy department of some corporation and you try to buy companies. Corporate finance definitely gives you the bigger picture and lets you speak intelligently on a lot more topics.

Are you positive overall on your investment banking experience?

Yes. It was just a totally great experience for me. I was exposed to things I would never have been exposed to. The people I meet, the people I can call. The responsibility I got. But the downside is the hours. If you're not interested in finance, you couldn't do it.

At the end, I took two months off and went to work for a consulting firm. But I only lasted for four months in consulting. I didn't like it. I was bored to death.

~ 4 ~

GETTING STARTED

ARE THESE CAREERS RIGHT FOR YOU?

Many of your friends, relatives, and career counselors may be pointing you toward careers in management consulting or investment banking. But before firing out résumés, think about whether these fields are right for you. Not only because you'll end up in a job that's better for you, but because you'll have to know *why* you want a job in order to get it. Successful candidates are those who convincingly explain to recruiters, on paper and in person, why they are right for the job, why they are interested in consulting or banking, and why they want to work for the specific company. This tailored approach requires a lot of work and thought. Ruling out any options at all will make your job hunt easier and more successful.

So, how do you decide whether management consulting or investment banking will deliver what you need from a job?

First, think about your career goals. What do you want to learn from your job, and what might you like to do afterward? Are you hoping to stay with your job for just a few years, or longer? What are your values, skills, and interests?

Second, think about enablers. Enablers are the industry or company characteristics that allow you to accomplish your goals. Does management consulting or investment banking provide the enablers that will allow you to meet your goals? The following chart lists some of the key benefits of working in investment banking, management consulting, and sales/trading as well as the typical career paths that people take when leaving the industry.

What Would I Get Out of Management Consulting, Investment Banking, or Sales and Trading?

FIELD	BENEFITS GAINED	TYPICAL EXIT PATHS
Management Consulting (in general)	Knowledge of different industries; how to analyze complex business problems; some work on overseas projects.	
• Strategy Consulting	High-level perspective; entree into top business school; exposure to strategic analysis, business frameworks; work with senior clients	Business school, jobs in client organizations, entrepreneurial ventures
• Information Tech Consulting	Computer and analytical skills; understanding of how companies operate, information technology; client management skills; promotion without an MBA	Jobs at high-tech firms, in client organizations, other consulting firms
• Operations/ Process Consulting	Understanding of how companies operate; client management and communications skills; entree into good business school	Jobs in client organizations, other consulting firms, business school
Investment Banking	Good understanding of finance, accounting, computer spreadsheet modeling, financial analysis, securities industries and markets; good entree into top business school; some ability to spend third year overseas	Business school, finance jobs in client organizations, other investment banks
Sales and Trading	Good understanding of securities markets; promotion without an MBA; ability to gain responsibility and specialization early; shorter hours and less travel than investment banking	Other investment banks, investment jobs at mutual funds and other institutions

The more focused your job search, the more effective it will be. Try to narrow down the companies you're applying to based on whether they will deliver what you need from a job. A good rule of thumb is to focus your efforts on fifteen firms. Better to be thoroughly prepared on fewer firms than underprepared on many. Be realistic, though, and have a few backups. You can get a sense of how you'll do by showing your résumé to a career counselor and asking how you compare to other students.

WHAT TYPE OF RECRUITING PROCESS WILL YOU BE FACING?

The amount of preparation and planning you will need to do to get a consulting or investment banking job depends on where you fit in to the firms' standard recruiting process. Candidates are grouped and reviewed by school. Investment banks and consulting firms "target" their recruiting at certain schools, where they interview on campus. Since firms have limited resources, the thinking goes, they will spend recruiting money on those schools they know the best. Typically, targeted schools are the top universities and business schools in the United States, Europe, and Japan. However, this varies across firms. Andersen Consulting, for example, hires so many undergraduates each year that it must recruit at a broader group of campuses than most other consulting firms.

If you are not currently a student at colleges where firms are collecting résumés or conducting interviews, you are a "nontargeted" or "unsolicited" candidate. You can find out whether a firm targets your school for recruiting by visiting your campus career counseling center and asking for a list of consulting firms and investment banks that will be recruiting on campus. If you graduated from a nontarget or target school several years ago, you are also considered outside the standard recruiting process. You will be considered against a pool of similar "aftermarket" candidates. If you recently graduated from a target school, you could end up grouped with current seniors from that school. You can try applying slightly off-cycle in order to face less competition.

You can get a job offer if you're from a nontarget school or if you've been out of school for a few years, but you will have to work harder to contact firms since you will not have the advantage of direct contact with recruiters through on-campus visits.

A RESEARCH STRATEGY

Your research should aim to find two types of information: information that helps you get the job and information that allows you to decide if the job is right for you. Research doesn't have to be time-consuming if you work smart.

Both targeted and nontargeted candidates should:

- Read the investment banking or management consulting chapter in this book
- Read the profile at the back of this book on the company they're interviewing with
- Look up the company's World Wide Web site on the Internet. Almost every major investment bank and management consulting firm has a Web site. (See Company Profiles for list of Web addresses.) Most contain up-to-date information on recruiting procedures and recruiting managers. Moreover, many sites enable correspondence with the firm through e-mail. Some firms even accept résumés on their Web sites. That's right, you *don't* have to make a long-distance call to request information.
- Attend the company's on-campus information session, a recruiting presentation usually held in September or October. **The information session is not necessarily closed to those from outside the school.** Some campus information sessions are actually held at local hotels or restaurants, and the school can't prevent nonstudents from attending. Call the firm you're interested in and ask where the closest information session will be held in the fall.

The information session will show you how the firm chooses to differentiate itself from competitors and will give you a sense of the firm's culture. In addition, this is your chance to ask recruiters detailed questions about international or regional opportunities, job responsibilities, opportunities for promotion without an MBA, and other topics of interest. Stick around after the information session is over and talk to a recruiter—you'll probably end up making an impression on a recruiter and bagging extra bits of information that haven't been shared during the official presentation. You shouldn't fill the airwaves with lots of specific questions during the presentation. Doing so generally makes a bad impression on peers and makes a neutral (or bad) impression on recruiters. Asking one or two thoughtful questions is fine, but it's best to save very detailed questions for your private discussion with a recruiter afterward. If you really hit it off with a recruiter, he might remember you and look out for your résumé when you send it in.

Nontargeted candidates will need to work hard to contact recruiters and obtain brochures and information. You should take the task of educating yourself about companies very seriously, since you will need extra enthusiasm, initiative, and persistence to find a job. An overall job-hunting strategy for nontargeted students is outlined in Chapter 5, but nontargeted candidates should perform the following extra research steps:

- Look up extra articles on the company you're interviewing with. (See the company profiles at the end of the book for suggestions.)

- Work hard at making connections and consider doing an informational interview.
- Use the industry and firm-specific resources listed in this chapter to research companies further.
- Broaden your search beyond the biggest and most well-known companies. Many smaller, regional investment banks and consulting firms are not listed in this book and do not recruit on campuses. A great place to find them are the Fisher College web sites listed on page 112. You can find additional company names in the Harvard Business School annual reference books on management consulting and finance companies (Harvard Business School Press). Alternatively, look up investment banks on the Securities Industry Association Web site (www.sia.com) or the *Securities Industry Yearbook* (Securities Industry Association). Look up consulting firms in *The Directory of Management Consultants* (Kennedy Publications), *Dun's Consulting Directory* (Dun & Bradstreet), or *Consultants & Consulting Organizations Directory* (GALE Publishing).

Review the firms profiled at the back of this book and find out if any recruit on your campus. For firms that don't, contact them while they're still fresh at the beginning of the recruiting season (August or September). Large or well-known firms usually have two different recruiting managers: one for undergraduates and another for advanced degree candidates. Call the recruiting manager to find out about the firm's hiring needs and résumé deadline, and ask that a brochure and recruiting dates be mailed to you.

MAKING CONNECTIONS

Connections with industry insiders are an important source of information on both banking and consulting and specific companies. At bigger firms, knowing insiders can help you stand out during the recruiting process or alert you to a job opening during the off-cycle; at smaller firms with less structured recruiting processes, connections are often crucial in landing jobs because someone can vouch for your "fit" with the firm. Communicating with industry insiders is a two-way process: You're learning information from them, but they also are evaluating you. Making connections is therefore one of the most effective ways of finding a job. You're preparing for the recruiting process, but you're also making a step forward into the process as well.

There are creative ways of building contacts with banking and consulting insiders. First, look in a school alumni directory to find alumni who are investment bankers and management consultants. If you want to apply for a job rather than simply ask for information, contact the more senior alumni because they can do more to help you. Use your discretion when contacting senior alumni—send a letter and résumé first rather than cold-calling. If the person is not willing to actually help you get a job, you could ask instead for information on his firm and advice on career issues. You even could request an informational interview (as discussed in the next section), which would help you prepare a great cover letter to send to his firm or another firm. Younger alumni a year or two out of school are great sources of information or job-hunting advice. Ask them to share with you their experiences in getting a job at their firm. They are also great sources of inside information that you might not get through official recruiting channels—details on a firm's culture and hierarchy, how happy junior employees are, level of responsibility and respect given to junior employees, and flexibility of project assignments. Business and economics faculty also make good contacts.

Another good way of making contacts is through fraternities, sororities, professional associations, or on-campus professional clubs. Many schools have management consulting or investment banking clubs that organize events to promote consulting and banking. These clubs often have extensive contact with recruiters, because club members organize industry forums or career fairs. So if it's not too late to join and help organize events, do it. Just talking with other members of the clubs may prove useful, as they may be better informed about investment banking and management consulting than an average student.

Finally, think hard about all the people you've met over the past several years. You probably have more connections than you realize. What about the friend who interned at Deutsche Bank one summer, or your friend's uncle who works at Arthur D. Little? Contacting these people might turn up a few good leads, or at least some good inside information on what it's like to work in the industries.

Once you've got a base of contacts, keep track of them. Use computer software or another system to organize names, titles, and notes on discussions you've had. Make sure to follow up with your contacts every few months to keep them up-to-date on what you're doing. Send a personalized thank-you note for their efforts.

THE INFORMATIONAL INTERVIEW

Alumni and other contacts often are willing to meet with you on an informal basis to talk about their jobs and their industries. These meetings are known as informational interviews, but you don't need to call them that when requesting them. Meetings are short (fifteen to thirty minutes) and involve no commitment on the part of the company. Informational interviews are a great way to differentiate yourself from the pack, research a company in-depth, and perhaps make a good enough impression on people to win a real interview.

Most important, if the interviewer likes you, he may be motivated to champion you as a new hire. If you feel that the person will respond well to this, suggest a casual and friendly setting, such as a coffee break—this will allow both you and the interviewer to relax and establish a rapport.

Treat the informational interview professionally: Research the company prior to the interview, bring a résumé (but don't pull it out unless asked), dress as if you were really interviewing for a job, and follow up with a thank-you note (in general, it's best to send thank-you notes to anyone you meet outside the standard recruiting process, and it's safer *not* to send notes to those you meet during the standard process). Keep detailed computer records of people you met and what you talked about.

Some good questions to ask in an informational interview are:

- What do you do on a typical day?
- What are the best or worst aspects of your job and your industry?
- What are the responsibilities of an associate/analyst at your firm?
- What benefits and skills would I gain from an associate/analyst position?
- What would be my options afterward? What have other people done afterward?
- Are there any particular departments or jobs in the industry that would provide better learning experiences than others?
- With my background, what are my chances of getting a job with your firm or with another firm in the industry?
- Are there specific firms or departments that would be more likely to hire me?
- Would you be willing to give me some honest feedback on my résumé? What do I need to improve?
- How do you see this industry changing over the next few years?
- Is there anyone else within the industry that you would suggest I talk to?

FOR THOSE WHO WANT MORE INFORMATION

INDUSTRY INFORMATION

This book has done the legwork for you in describing the investment banking and management consulting industries. If you want more, turn to the "Recommended Reading" sections of Chapters 2 and 3 for lists of a few select articles that you should spend your time looking for.

You also can look for more recent articles to keep up with industry developments. First, consult www.thefasttrack.com, which will list recent articles and books. Second, consult the tried-and-true *Readers' Guide to Periodical Literature* index, which will enable you to locate interesting articles. Even better, use electronic search mechanisms such as Lexis-Nexis, if they are available at your school library.

In general, far more information is available on investment banking and trading than on management consulting. The reason is that most investment banks are publicly traded companies, so their financial and operating information is made available to the public. Many books have been written on finance and investment banking and are available in your school or public library. There have been many fictional accounts of life in investment banking, especially on the sales and trading floor, because this industry lends itself well to outlandish stories. All these books have been listed at the end of Chapter 3. Consulting firms, on the other hand, are privately held companies that are not obligated to disclose any information to outsiders. Few, if any, books have been written on life in management consulting.

The easiest, cheapest way of obtaining additional information on both consulting or banking is through the Internet. Use search indexes like Yahoo or Excite to find World Wide Web sites on management consulting and investment banking, or start at one of the following sites:

- "The Fast Track" site: www.thefasttrack.com. To keep readers of this book up-to-date, this site will list recent articles and books on consulting and investment banking and on specific firms.
- Investment Banking: www.cob.ohio-state.edu/dept/fin/jobs/ib2.htm.
- Management Consulting Online: www.cob.ohio-state.edu/dept/fin/jobs/mco/mco.html. These two sites, operated by the Fisher College of Business at Ohio State University, are good Web sites on investment banking and management consulting geared toward job-hunters. The sites serve as good reference pages where you can find more detailed information on the industries.

FIRM-SPECIFIC INFORMATION

To research a company, determine whether it is public, private, or a subsidiary. Public companies are those whose shares are publicly traded and therefore are required to make a great deal of information available to the public, including filing company financials with the Securities and Exchange Commission. Private companies are those that are privately held—their shares are not available to the public, and information about the companies is kept very confidential. Subsidiaries of public companies are in between—their financial information is sometimes broken out in their parents' public statements.

Most major investment banks are already publicly traded. If a company is public, you can obtain a copy of its *annual report*, or "*10-K*." In the annual report, you can skip to the "Management Discussion and Analysis" section, which contains the more qualitative information that you'll find interesting. You may also want to look up the company's stock price, size, and profitability.

The easy and free way of obtaining a company's annual report is through the Securities and Exchange Commission in Washington, D.C., where these reports are filed. You can obtain reports for free through the SEC's Web site: www.sec.gov. Once on the Web site, search the SEC's Edgar database by using Custom Filing Retrieval Tools. (The direct address for this page is: www.sec.gov/edaux/formlynx.htm.) Enter the name of the company you're researching and the type of form you're requesting, and submit your search. Again, you will receive the most relevant information by requesting a 10-K form, which is the equivalent of a firm's annual report. Once you've downloaded the 10-K, save it as a file on your hard drive so that you can refer back to it later.

A WORD FOR SOPHOMORES AND JUNIORS

If you're reading this as sophomore or junior, you're in a good position. You still have time to build the skills that investment banks and management consulting firms look for rather than just trying to convey them in a résumé. First and foremost, if your grades have been poor in the past, put more time into your academics in order to show some improvement. If you haven't taken any quantitative classes or your SAT math score is weak, consider taking calculus, statistics, or a quantitative business course in order to demonstrate your mathematical competence. Alternatively, take the GMAT exam (the business school admissions test). This will give recruiters a reference point on your quantitative and other analytical skills and will prevent your rejection based on grades and scores alone.

Second, prepare your résumé now and review it objectively against the list of critical skills that recruiters seek, listed in Chapter 6. Are there any serious gaps in your résumé? Try to shore up weaknesses that you think might disqualify you from an interview in consulting or banking. Now is the time to join a campus group to demonstrate leadership or tutor other students to demonstrate communications skills. If you've started an activity, continue it—recruiters like to see consistency.

If none of your previous summer jobs have been in business, you might want to search for a business internship for the upcoming summer. The more similar the internship is to the job you want in terms of skills required, the more it will help you. A finance job will help you win credibility for an investment banking position, and a business operations job will help you position yourself for a consulting position. Look for jobs in economic or commerce-related government agencies, which also make a good impression on employers yet are not limited to those with "connections." Consider nonpaid or work/study internships in business, even during the school year.

Finally, it's not too early to start learning about management consulting and investment banking and why you want to go into these fields. The more you've thought about these issues, the more impressive and mature your interest will seem to the recruiter—and the better decision you will make for your future. Consider applying for a summer internship in consulting or banking (see Chapters 2 and 3 and page 128).

SOME STRATEGIC ADVICE

As you embark on your job-hunt, keep these points in mind:

- Every firm likes to see itself—its culture and people—in a certain way. Research each firm individually and understand the firm's self-image.
- Positions in regional management consulting offices, particularly on the West Coast, are limited and in high demand. Competition for these spots therefore is extraordinarily high. If you're a candidate on the West Coast or the Midwest, you will increase your chances of getting a job offer if you tell recruiters you're willing to be considered for East Coast offices, where more job openings exist.
- To get a job at an investment bank, you'll need to apply to the headquarters office and express a clear willingness to work there, since this is where most job openings exist. Regional assignments typically are made late in the interview process or after you've started working.
- Don't rule yourself out of certain jobs by being too specific about the type of work you'd like to do. For example, you should not say just yet that you'd prefer to work only for consumer products clients at a consulting firm. Instead, project a can-do attitude and an interest in many areas at each firm—who knows, perhaps the firm isn't hiring in the areas you're interested in, but you could receive a job offer in another very interesting area that you hadn't thought about before. Then, after you receive a job offer, you'll have more leverage and can try to negotiate the types of work you will do.
- Don't look down at smaller, newer firms or regional offices. Smaller and newer often means less structure and more opportunity for the recent graduate—both in getting the job and in promotion once you're there. In addition, smaller offices tend to be more personal and more conducive to getting to know senior managers. Many would argue that a smaller firm may present a better opportunity than a large firm. Finally, smaller companies might be less picky about the brand name of a candidate's school.

- To make connections, use educational programs designed by your school to integrate the real world with the classroom. If your course requires you to do a group project that involves interviewing industry experts or spending a day shadowing a businessperson, choose consulting or banking. Some schools require an unpaid internship as part of your coursework. An internship is a great, nonthreatening way to make contacts and impress a potential employer.
- Minorities traditionally underrepresented in business should consider summer and full-time programs designed to introduce them to consulting and investment banking. These programs are a great way to get your foot in the door. For example, Sponsors for Educational Opportunity (SEO) summer positions are available at most investment banks and are good lead-ins to full-time investment banking jobs. There are also specific recruiting conventions organized for African American and Hispanic students; many investment banks and consulting firms send representatives, and this is a good place to develop contacts.

～ 5 ～

PIERCING THE VEIL:
HOW INVESTMENT BANKS AND CONSULTING FIRMS RECRUIT

Investment banking and management consulting grow more popular each year with job-hunters. In fact, these professions are *the* careers preferred by MBAs, with 50 percent of business school graduates taking jobs as bankers or consultants each year.[1] Many large banks and consultancies receive over 5,000 applications each year for analyst and associate positions.[2] To win a job in the face of this fierce competition, you *must* understand how the investment banks and consulting firms make their hiring decisions. As you read this chapter, step outside your shoes and step into the recruiter's. The more you understand the recruiter's perspective, the more you will be able to position yourself appropriately.

Throughout this chapter, I will be distinguishing between the recruiting process for *targeted* and *nontargeted* candidates. Targeted candidates are students at the top schools where firms recruit on campus, while nontargeted candidates are students at other schools or those who have graduated a few years ago.

WHERE ARE THE JOBS?

Investment banks have large headquarters offices, where most employees and jobs are located. Consulting firms, on the other hand, are more decentralized. Employees are distributed around the country in order to ensure that they are near clients, and many jobs will be available outside headquarters.

Like providers of other business services such as advertising and accounting, banks and consultancies are headquartered in major metropolitan areas. The biggest banks are based in New York City and the biggest consulting firms in New York and Boston. But don't despair if you live elsewhere. A number of investment banks and consulting firms are based in Chicago, San Francisco, Los Angeles, and other major business centers. One area rising in prominence is the San Francisco Bay Area, where the growth of high-tech companies is fueling a demand for local investment bankers. In addition, investment banks and consulting firms hire people from around the country to fill their headquarters offices; if you're willing to relocate, you will improve your chances of finding a job. Finally, remember that jobs are available at a wide range of firms, from large firms that everyone has heard of to smaller boutiques and regional companies. Consult Chapter 4 for information on how to find the smaller firms.

WHO RUNS RECRUITING?

One important difference among companies is whether they make hiring decisions on a *centralized* or *decentralized* basis. Most investment banks use a centralized recruiting process while most management consulting firms use a decentralized process.

Centralized Model: The headquarters office manages recruiting for all offices. The headquarters office reviews all résumés, performs interviews, and makes hiring decisions. For the first-round interview, nontargeted candidates need to find their own way to the headquarters office, whereas students at target schools are interviewed by company representatives on campus. For the final round, all interviewees are flown in to the headquarters office at the firm's expense.

Decentralized Model: Although there are uniform recruiting standards throughout the firm, each branch office is responsible for managing its own recruiting process and interviewing students from local schools. The branch office screens résumés, performs interviews, and makes hiring decisions. Candidates are first screened by their local branch office and then forwarded on to the office that the candidate prefers. Chances of students at nontarget schools of breaking into the recruiting process are greater, since it is easier to schedule an impromptu interview at a local office than it is to try to fit into the schedule at a headquarters office 5,000 miles away.

Division vs. Firm: At large firms with diverse businesses, each separate division runs its own recruiting. This is common at investment banks. Investment banking, sales and trading, and other departments each run their own recruiting process. A divided recruiting process is also found at some large consulting firms with separate information technology and strategy consulting divisions, such as Andersen Consulting. If a firm has a division-by-division recruiting policy, you should research each division's different culture, recruiting procedures, and hiring preferences.

THE STANDARD RECRUITING PROCESS FROM YOUR PERSPECTIVE

Now let's review the standard recruiting process used by large management consulting firms and investment banks. Later in the chapter I explain how this process differs for nontargeted candidates.

You're lucky. The major banks and consulting firms have very similar recruiting procedures, so once you understand one, you understand them all. Candidates have *five main points of contact* with the recruiter that provide opportunities for you and the recruiter to assess each other: the campus interview session, the résumé screening, the first-round interview, the final interview, and the selling process. Your leverage increases—and the recruiter's leverage decreases—the further you progress. Here's the whole process from a successful candidate's point of view:

The Campus Information Session: You're a student at a targeted school, and in the fall you attend all the dog-and-pony shows held on campus. During the information session, sometimes called a "Meet the Company" or a "social event," you listen to the firm explain itself and its recruiting procedures. You attempt to discern the differences among firms. Sometimes it's difficult. They all seem to say, "People are our most important asset." You want to make yourself remembered by recruiters, but you watch some classmates try too hard to ingratiate themselves by asking lots of questions during the session and you decide that's not the right approach. Instead, you mingle after the presentation, spending some quality one-on-one time with a recruiter you picked out.

The Résumé Screening: As a student at a targeted school, you submit your résumé to your campus career center by the deadline they specify, and they send the résumé to the companies on your behalf. If you were a nontargeted candidate, you would have to send your résumé directly to the company. You try to use your résumé to communicate why you are different from all the other applicants and therefore worth talking to. Then you wait to see if you're chosen. The résumé screening is the most competitive step in the recruiting process.

The First-Round Interview: Face-to-face with one or two interviewers, you sweat it out for forty-five minutes during the first interview. Since you're a student at a targeted school, the interview is conducted on campus. Nontargeted candidates are interviewed in the company's main office. Now that you have a foot in the door, your job is a little easier: You throw your energy into "selling" yourself and addressing the firm's concerns. If you make the cut, you will be invited to a second-round or final interview.

The Final Interview: The final hurdle in the obstacle course is a difficult one: a grueling day of interviews at the firm's main office a week or two after the first interview. The firm puts a cheery spin on the day that you're dreading, calling it "Super Saturday." But you're also starting to feel a little like a celebrity: You are flown to the firm's headquarters and put up in a nice hotel. You are interviewed by a variety of people, from peers who are just a year ahead of you to high-level managers. Each interview lasts about one hour and tests you in a different area: one covers quantitative skills, another "fit" with the firm. Ten interviews and a social event later, you are on your way home and waiting for The Call. Most firms make decisions immediately afterward, so jobs are offered in the following few days. Some people will be placed on a "waiting list" and won't hear back until offerees have decided whether to join the firm.

The Selling Process: Exhausted, you're happy that the tables have turned and *you* now have the leverage. You've gotten the job offer, and all of a sudden you're receiving phone calls, lots of them, from the firm. They are trying hard to "sell" themselves to you. You're invited to the office, put up at a swank hotel, taken out to dinner and dancing. One analyst has been assigned to be your contact during the sell process.

There are variations on this story. Many investment banks and consulting firms hold three rounds of interviews: two on campus and a final round in the office. A popular model is to invite successful first-round candidates to a second interview that same day or night. Smaller firms or regional offices may use different, and perhaps less formalized, recruiting procedures. It is wise to confirm your understanding of each company's process.

WHAT'S THE RECRUITER THINKING?

You're not the only one competing. Recruiting is strategic for consulting firms and investment banks—what differentiates them, and what drives their reputation, is the quality of their people. Good junior people are important because they are given responsibilities that, if not performed properly, can embarrass the firm or have a serious negative impact on clients. Firms compete vigorously over the best candidates.

While you are on your summer vacation, perhaps backpacking through Europe or playing tennis, firms are thinking about recruiting. To lead recruiting efforts for the year, most firms pick one or two bankers or consultants in addition to a full-time recruiting administrator. Senior management finalizes the number of new people needed for each office, using past years' employee numbers, projected growth in business, and projected turnover. For example, if an unusually large group of analysts is leaving for business school, or if business is expected to boom, the number of analyst hires will increase.

Candidates are grouped and reviewed by school. In the fall, firms assemble teams to cover each target school, the schools where they will recruit on campus. For example, a team would be picked to perform *all* recruiting functions at Northwestern University for the year. Who are the people with the power to decide your fate? They are:

- Full-time bankers and consultants whom the firm has chosen to perform recruiting in their spare time (Don't be surprised if they seem very busy.)
- Chosen because relative to others at the firm, they have the right personality to display to the outside world, they are good communicators, they make firms seem diverse, and they've demonstrated an interest in recruiting
- One or two levels higher than the position the candidates are being considered for
- Alumni of the school the candidates are from, with the idea that alumni can better evaluate school-specific accomplishments—which classes are particularly difficult, which extracurriculars are time-consuming, and which awards are truly considered honors

Recruiting managers schedule interview dates and work backward from the number of jobs they will offer to calculate the number of first-round interviews they will hold. Typical percentages would be as follows: If the recruiters weed out 75 percent of applicants from first-round interviews and 50 percent of applicants from second-round interviews, they know that 12.5 percent of those who are invited to first-round interviews eventually will receive job offers. So if they want to make offers to five students at Dartmouth, they will need to schedule forty first-round interviews on the Dartmouth campus. Just like schools, firms will make more offers than there are positions available, because a certain percentage of candidates will refuse the offer. The more exclusive the firm, the higher its hit rate and therefore the less cushion it needs to build into its number of job offers.

We've looked at the five main recruiting "points of contact" from your perspective. Now, here's what the recruiter is thinking during the standard recruiting process. Of course, there are differences among terms.

The Campus Information Session: I want to reinforce my firm's brand-name recognition on campus and attract the best applicants possible. I'm going to try to differentiate my firm from competitors. I will develop a presentation that conveys a few key points about the firm, and perhaps try some creative presentation methods (multimedia slide shows, informal cocktail parties, etc.) that will create a buzz about us on campus. After the presentation, I'm going to jot down names of students whom I meet who seem to be strong potential candidates. I'll be comparing the school's level of business sophistication relative to other schools and will take this into consideration when we evaluate students.

The Résumé Screening: After the résumé submission deadline, my team meets to review résumés. As head of the team, I sometimes review the résumés first to come up with preliminary picks. Reviewing résumés is a difficult process: We may need to decide on 50 people or fewer out of 300 résumés submitted. On average, I spend one or two minutes reviewing each résumé—more if the candidate is borderline. I search for immediate disqualifiers that make my job easier (e.g., extremely low GPAs or a poorly written résumé or cover letter). After I've chosen candidates, I might review my choices with the rest of the recruiting team, focusing on borderline candidates. We will make small changes after the initial cut in order to balance the diversity of the chosen group. We know that the résumé screen is an imperfect process, because we must evaluate candidates based on a one-page description of their background. We will select many "mistakes" and miss many stars.

The First-Round Interview: This round represents my opportunity to determine whether the candidate meets basic intellectual and personality criteria—if she doesn't, why bother wasting anyone's time during the next round? If I'm a consultant, this means that the "case" question typically dominates the interview. As for personality, I often know within the first two or three minutes of speaking with a candidate whether or not she has the necessary interpersonal skills. Next round I'll focus in on personality more and try to ferret out more deeply hidden personality traits and values. At the end of the interview, there is little time for the candidate to ask questions because I've spent most of our time evaluating the candidate. (One interview alone will decide whether the candidate proceeds to the second or final round.) At the end of the day, the other interviewers and I rank the candidates we've each seen and pick 20 to 30 percent of them to proceed to the next round.

The Final Interview: Now we've narrowed down the pool to people who probably could all work well at our firm. Only small differences exist among these candidates, and we've got to find them. Our interviewing job is more difficult. Subtle variations we see in personality, attitude, or performance on an analytical question will make the difference between two well-qualified people. As a team, we spend time testing interpersonal skills, interest in the industry, and other "soft" characteristics. But each of us may cover different ground: consulting "case" questions, quantitative skills, "fit" with the firm, communications skills, general analytical skills, interest in the industry, or likelihood of taking the offer. We're on our toes at this point because we know that a high proportion of this round's candidates will receive offers. We have to manage candidates' perceptions of the firm carefully. We'll allot more time at the end of the interview to "sell" the firm and answer the candidate's questions.

Like the candidates, we're exhausted at the end of the day. Typically, we remember best the first and the last candidates we saw. All the interviewers hunker down in a conference room with food to rank candidates and swap impressions. We make the easy yes and no decisions, then we debate—and sometimes argue—over borderline candidates. Natural "champions" evolve during this process, and candidates who are championed the hardest or by the most powerful recruiters win out. If we think that a high percentage of people will accept our job offers based on what they've said in the interview, we may reduce the overall number of offers we give. By the time we're done, 50 percent of the final round candidates receive offers. Candidates who are borderline are put on our wait list. Finally, we assign the dirty work. Interviewers who argued strongly against a candidate often are asked to deliver bad news and feedback to the rejected candidate.

The Selling Process: After I make phone calls to winning candidates to deliver the good news, I'm assigned a candidate to convince to join the firm. The mentor is selected to be a good fit or have something in common with the candidate. I'm supposed to arrange a fun social event to woo the candidate, answer the candidate's questions honestly (although I'll try to put a positive spin on everything), and keep the recruiting coordinator up-to-date on the candidate's plans and decisions. Generally, this "selling" process lasts as long as the candidate is undecided. If some turn us down, we extend offers to wait-listed candidates.

Firms *do* vary from the standard process just outlined, which is why you should check with each firm individually. Moreover, companies are constantly changing their managers of recruiting, so that contact names you find in published sources are frequently out of date. The easiest way to find current information is through the company's Web site. Web site addresses are listed in the company profiles at the end of this book.

NONTARGETED CANDIDATES: HOW THE PROCESS WILL DIFFER

As a nontargeted candidate, you will not necessarily have access to on-campus information sessions and will not be able to submit your résumé to firms through a campus career center. Furthermore, you will have to pay your way to a company's offices for a first-round interview. Therefore, your process of submitting a résumé and arranging a first-round interview will differ from the standard targeted recruiting process.

Arranging interviews strategically is an important activity for a nontargeted candidate, especially if you're looking for a job in another town. To hunt for a job economically, you will need to coordinate one job-hunting trip during which you will go through several interviews. One good idea is to arrange interviews for a school vacation, such as Thanksgiving or Christmas. This is a juggling challenge, since you'll need to catch recruiters when they're not on vacation. As a student, you'll typically have more vacation than a recruiter and can work around their schedules.

You'll need to write to firms far in advance in order to leave sufficient time for them to evaluate your résumé and decide whether to offer you an interview. Tell recruiters about your time and travel constraints—this will motivate them to make a decision about your candidacy instead of letting your résumé sit in a file. If they're interested in you, they will make an exception and arrange to interview you separately from other candidates.

If you have just received word that you are being flown to New York for a second-round interview with one firm, use this trip for other recruiting purposes—immediately call other firms to let them know that you will be in town and available for an interview. At the very least, if you are planning a trip on short notice, try to arrange informational interviews with recruiters.

To submit your résumé, send your materials directly to the recruiting coordinator at the firm. Firms assign one recruiting coordinator to undergraduate recruiting and another to graduate school recruiting. At investment banks and some big consulting firms, separate departments within the company have different recruiting managers. For example, the sales and trading or asset management departments of a bank will have a separate recruiting manager from the investment banking department. If you can't decide which department you want to work in, it is acceptable to send letters to several departments, unless the firm specifies otherwise.

Be aware that recruiting coordinators change annually. In order to reach the person you are trying to contact, you must call the company to verify the contact name for the level you're applying to *and* place the title "Undergraduate Recruiting Coordinator" or "MBA Recruiting Coordinator" after the person's name. This way, if by the time you send your letter the coordinator has left the firm or is no longer responsible for recruiting, your letter will be forwarded to his replacement. DO NOT address your letter to the "Personnel Department" or the "Human Resources Department." If you do, most likely the letter will never reach the recruiting coordinator.

If you have an inside connection at the company, send your résumé to him instead (this advice only applies to nontargeted candidates). Include a cover letter addressed to him, with the same formal content that you would have written to a recruiting manager. Ideally, your contact then will forward the letter to the recruiting manager with a note of recommendation attached. No matter how weak the connection, your chances of getting some attention will improve if someone within the company actually passes the résumé on to the recruiting manager. If your school is not a "brand-name" institution, a connection with the company is especially helpful. One way to find a connection is to search through your school's alumni directory. Usually you'll be able to find one graduate from your school at a large company. This person may not have frequent contact with students from his alma mater and may be happy to champion you as a candidate.

What should you include in your envelope if you are sending an unsolicited application to a company? Call and ask the firm, specifying exactly what level you're applying for.

Otherwise, check the company's Internet site for application requirements. If you can't find this information, send at minimum a cover letter and résumé. If your academic transcript is impressive, submit it as well. Including a letter of recommendation is risky; it only makes sense if the recommender's opinion is directly relevant to the job or if the recommender is a high-level client of the firm's. If in doubt, leave it out. *Do not submit anything else: no photograph, no writing samples, no synopses of your work or thesis, nothing.* Banks and consulting firms are conservative businesses and do not take kindly to creative or cutesy submissions.

Since you are sending your résumé directly to the company, double-check the company's address. If you are submitting a résumé for a very specific deadline, send the package via overnight delivery in order to verify that the package arrives on time.

SALES AND TRADING SPECIFICS

Most sales and trading departments do not recruit on campus and have a much less structured recruiting process than the one just outlined. Sales and trading areas usually recruit autonomously, do not use a consistent recruiting process, and do not have highly structured career paths for undergraduates and MBAs. Large bulge-bracket firms such as Goldman Sachs and Morgan Stanley are the exception in that they have more structured, investment banking–style associate and analyst positions that differentiate between MBAs and undergraduates.

To get a trading floor job, plan to send out many résumés and cover letters. You should take three steps (remember, though, to never call a trading floor before 4:00 P.M. EST or you won't get through):

- Call the company to find out the name of the administrator who is handling recruiting for sales and trading, and send him a résumé and cover letter. Specify what type of position (sales, trading, etc.) you are looking for.
- Call the company to find out the name of salespeople or traders who work in specific areas you're interested in (e.g., equity derivatives) and send them a résumé as well. You may have to contact several departments within a single firm.
- If you can develop contacts through alumni associations, clubs, or professional organizations, use them. Write and call your contacts directly to request an interview.

The interview process varies. At firms that have structured hiring programs, the interview process will more closely resemble the three-round process in investment banking. If the process is unstructured, interviews could take the form of conversations with salespeople and traders while they're actually working. Often, candidates will have to pay their own way to the firm for a first-round interview.

SPECIAL INTERESTS

HUNTING OFF-SEASON

If you are a nontargeted candidate, don't despair if you've missed the standard résumé submission period, which runs from October through March. You might have a better chance of winning a job because you aren't being compared to a herd of other candidates.

Firms are somewhat disorganized in recruiting during this period, so it helps to get a referral to gain an interview. Basically, it is a rare firm that won't hire a qualified candidate just because it's the off-season—especially if they have discovered that they underestimated their personnel needs or if too few candidates have accepted their offers. Firms' policies vary. Some bulge-bracket investment banks are so structured that they absolutely will not interview and hire candidates outside the standard recruiting process. March through June will be the most difficult time for someone entering the job market and looking for a job with the McKinseys and Goldman Sachses of the world, since these large firms are completing their final round interviews or have just hired a new crop of graduates. However, very small firms and those with less organized recruiting processes will just be beginning to make hiring decisions.

If you are graduating in the middle of the year from a targeted school, it is better to try to apply upon graduation than to wait until the standard recruiting process begins. Recruiters are accustomed to seeing students graduate in the middle of the year. Recent graduates of target schools with less than one year of work experience should also apply off cycle. If you wait until the regular fall recruiting season, you'll be grouped together with all the new seniors and will face greater competition.

INTERNATIONAL OPPORTUNITIES

One of the most common questions candidates ask is how they can work in an overseas bank or consulting office. There is a lot of competition in landing an overseas job. Three options exist in getting yourself abroad: travel there as part of an assignment, get transferred overseas, or get an overseas job in the first place.

By far the easiest way of ending up overseas is to travel there as part of an assignment. Although this may mean a very short stay abroad, at least you get a taste of international business environments and cultures. Consulting presents the possibility of being staffed overseas on a project that lasts anywhere from a few months to over a year. Persistent lobbying and relevant languages help U.S.-based consultants win these international assignments. In banking, you may travel to visit an overseas client, but you are not likely to spend a long period there.

A second way to work overseas is to begin working in an office in the United States and then push for a transfer or rotation to an overseas location. This method works well for associates or third-year analysts in investment banking. Analysts good enough to be asked to stay for a third year can suggest a preferred location for that year. Likewise, many associates are "rotated" after two or three years and can specify a preferred location. Lucky bankers might get sent to London, Hong Kong, Frankfurt, or Tokyo for a year, because these cities usually have the largest investment banking offices and can absorb extra people. It is much harder to get sent to Paris or other secondary financial centers because offices there are smaller. The transfer method does not work as well for consultants, because rotations are not common and a transfer is seen as more permanent than in banking. Accommodations are made for urgent personal reasons, but in consulting it's difficult to get transferred as an analyst and only slightly easier as an associate.

The third and most difficult method of working overseas is to win a job there in the first place. If you're a foreign national and you speak a language frequently used in business (i.e., French, German, Japanese) fluently, you have a good shot at getting a job overseas through normal recruiting channels. Your chances are even better if you speak a language and are a citizen of an emerging market where offices are just opening (e.g., China, India, and Latin America). You have two options when it comes to finding a job overseas. You can submit your résumé to a U.S. office with the explicit understanding that you are interested in being considered only for an international position. Your résumé will be evaluated at the local office or sent directly to the international office for consideration. If you have doubts about the efficiency or organization of the local office, send your résumé directly to the international office. If they are interested in you, they will ask the local office to conduct a first-round interview with you.

If you're an American and have no fluency in another language, there is almost no chance of getting an investment banking or management consulting job overseas *through normal recruiting channels.* From the firm's point of view, there are several obstacles to hiring an American directly for an overseas office. First, Americans find it difficult to obtain a working visa; in many countries, the company must prove that the American has some important skill or knowledge that a local worker doesn't have. Second, clients do not react well to paying large sums of money for services rendered by an American who can't speak their language well and isn't familiar with local markets and business customs. This is especially true in consulting—consultants have a hard enough time proving their value and convincing clients to change their business processes. Consultants must be native speakers of the language they are working in.

To get an overseas job in such a case, you'll have to follow an unconventional and riskier path. You will need to bypass traditional recruiting channels in the United States, because these will funnel you back toward the U.S. offices. One option is to study at a respected foreign university, then apply directly to local offices of American investment banks and consulting firms. Another option is to contact a bank or consultancy overseas through any connections you can find and offer to start as a lowly, or even unpaid, intern. Finally, you could take a different job overseas first, establish an employment history and hone your language skills, then try to jump to a banking or consulting job. Whichever way you choose, you probably will have to go overseas first, then look for a job once you're there.

FOREIGN NATIONALS INTERESTED IN WORKING IN THE UNITED STATES

Foreign nationals seeking a job in the United States face the same problems as Americans interested in working abroad. If you don't speak English fluently and don't have any special expertise, it will be very difficult for you to break directly into banking or consulting job in the United States. If you have some specialty that an American firm needs and can't find in the United States, the firm will be more likely to sponsor you for a working visa. The best way to get a job as an inexperienced young graduate, however, is to get a degree from an American university or business school. Then, if you make it through the normal U.S. recruiting process, a firm probably would help you get the right working papers, since it already has time and interest invested in you.

It is easier for foreigners to begin working for an American bank or consulting in the region of their origin and then be transferred later to the United

States. Transfers require a history of outstanding performance, fluent English ability, and persistence.

SUMMER OPPORTUNITIES

For Undergraduates: You don't have to have summer experience in banking or consulting in order to get a permanent offer upon graduation. In fact, it might be better to get some experience in an entirely different industry—it would make you a better banker or consultant. But if you have decided to spend your summer in a bank or a consulting firm, plan on a long job search.

From the firm's point of view, recruiting undergraduates for *summer analyst* positions is a distant second in priority to recruiting seniors for full-time analyst positions. Summer opportunities for undergraduates are limited and often unpaid. Even finding out about such positions in the first place takes perseverance—and perhaps connections. Few major investment banks or consulting firms have structured summer intern programs for undergraduates. If a firm does have an intern program, it is likely to be located in the firm's headquarters office and require a similar interviewing process as the full-time analyst position. Smaller firms and regional offices may represent the best chance for the internship-seeker, since they tend to be less rigid in their hiring plans and may respond better to initiative and persistence. Responsibilities and quality of summer experience vary greatly between firms. Juniors have the best shot at snagging summer internships. Check the company profiles at the back of the book or contact firms directly to ask about the availability of summer internships.

The one exception is sales and trading within investment banks: These areas regularly hire undergraduates as summer interns; many interns are then offered full-time positions upon graduation. Summer programs last from ten to twelve weeks and involve rotations to several product areas.

For Graduate Students: Summer recruiting is seen as a way to test people before extending full-time offers and therefore is taken very seriously. Almost all of the leading consulting firms and investment banks offer *summer associate* programs. Summer associate recruiting takes place on MBA campuses a few months after full-time associate recruiting and includes the same steps. Students at nontargeted schools should apply directly to the firms if interested in summer positions.

Summer experience in the industry is important to MBA and other graduate students. You have a better chance of landing a permanent offer (and having one year of tuition reimbursed) if you have some summer

A Recruiting Timeline:

WHAT TO DO AND WHEN

Whether you're applying for an associate or an analyst position, you will go through the same five main points of contact with the major investment banks or consulting firms—you'll just go through the steps at different dates. Use the following chart to look up the typical dates on which events are held for your peer group. Remember that smaller consulting firms and investment banks have less structured recruiting processes; however, generally they recruit at the same time or a month or two later than larger companies.

Important Recruiting Dates

Check these dates with your school career office and with specific firms you're interested in.

Event	2nd-year MBAs Associates	1st-year MBAs Summer Associates	Undergrad Seniors Analysts	Other Undergrads Summer Analysts
Info Session	Sept.–Oct.	Jan.	Oct.–Nov.	Oct.–Nov.
Resume Screen	Oct.	Jan.–Feb.	Nov.–Jan.	Feb.–Mar.
1st Interview	Nov.–Dec.	Jan.–Feb.	Dec.–Feb.	Mar.–Apr.
2nd Interview	Nov.–Jan.	Feb.–Mar.	Jan.–Mar.	Mar.–May
Selling Process	Dec.–May	Mar.–May	Jan.–May	not applicable

What to do two weeks before . . .

THE ON-CAMPUS INFORMATION SESSION: Find out which firms are visiting campus; come up with list of questions to ask at the information session; call firms that are not recruiting on campus to check on recruiting dates and request brochures. Nonstudents should call firms to check on recruiting dates and request a brochure; they also should find out if an information session will be held near them and whether they can attend. Undergraduates applying for summer internships should talk to career counselors to find out which firms offer summer internship possibilities and will be visiting campus for an information session.

THE RESUME SCREEN: Finish your resume; incorporate feedback from other people; finish a basic cover letter if you're a nontargeted candidate (which means having completed some basic research on each company you write to). Contact any connections in management consulting and investment banking, ask them for advice drawn from their own job-hunting experiences.

THE FIRST-ROUND INTERVIEW: Start polishing your interview skills by practicing with a career counselor or friend; research each firm you're interviewing with so that you know what differentiates the firm from its competitors; make a list of questions you will ask during each interview, tailored to the firm. Decide what selling points about yourself you will use in the interview. Also, buy a good interview suit if you don't have one.

THE FINAL-ROUND INTERVIEW: Complete more in-depth research; develop more detailed questions to ask the company; practice more "case" questions if interviewing with a consulting firm; go over your resume to be able to explain every detail thoroughly; come up with points you will make during the interview to address any concerns interviewers may have.

THE SELLING PROCESS (THE "SELL DAY"): Have an opinion or hypothesis about what the firm would be like to work for; come up with some important questions to ask to determine whether the company is right for you; ask career counselors and friends or connections in the industry for their opinions on the company and which questions they would suggest asking.

experience at a firm. About 80 to 90 percent of summer associates will receive offers for full-time positions when they conclude their job. Summer associates are given responsibilities that resemble those of full-time first-year associates.

But if you're taking the summer associate position to judge whether you'll like the work, remember that you won't get an entirely accurate picture of what it's like to work at the firm. Every effort will be made to give you plum assignments, and everyone will be on their best behavior around you.

NOTES

[1]"The Best Business Schools," *Business Week*, October 24, 1994.
[2]Interviews with recruiters.

THE RECRUITER'S PERSPECTIVE

Andrea Terzi Baum
Vice President, Goldman, Sachs & Co.

Mention Andrea Baum's name to any young investment banker on Wall Street, and chances are you'll get a nod of recognition. As the head of the investment banking analyst program at Goldman Sachs—the most prestigious of all investment banks—Baum receives résumés from almost everyone aspiring to be a banker in a given year. In fact, she receives over 6,000 applications each year for Goldman's Investment Banking analyst positions. Many of these candidates pass through her office for an interview.

Baum has grown up in investment banking: She joined one of Goldman's early analyst classes, earned her MBA from Harvard Business School, then returned to Goldman as an associate. In 1990 she was asked to become the full-time manager of Goldman's Investment Banking Division analyst program. With her extensive experience, Baum offers a valuable insider's perspective on the analyst hiring process.

How did you end up as Goldman's head of analyst recruiting?

When I graduated from Brown, I came to Goldman Sachs directly as an analyst. I worked for two years in the Real Estate Department and a third year in the newly formed Pension Services Group. After Harvard [Business School], I came back as a banker in the Real Estate Department. I worked there for over two years and was then presented with the opportunity to come over to the recruiting side. I realized that even though I loved doing real estate deals, what I really found most rewarding was working with people—recruiting for the real estate group, running the summer analyst program, and being a mentor for new hires. That was years ago.

How do you foresee your business and the types of people you need changing?

Our business is becoming more complex, especially in terms of the computer-based tools that are available to us. We are taking a slightly higher percentage of people who have a business background or who come from the hard sciences. But rather than saying we should change the way we hire, I would say that we are providing our people with more effective training.

Should people who are not math or econ majors bother applying for an analyst job?

Oh, absolutely. If somebody is an English major who hasn't touched a number in four years, that's fine. We'll teach them. If you look at some of the people who have been outstanding analysts, many of them have had a liberal arts background. I wouldn't discourage anybody from applying, as long as they are basically comfortable with numbers.

How would you describe your general recruiting philosophy then?

We look for outstanding people who we think would fit in well at Goldman Sachs. We want to hire people who will be very happy here. We have a strong culture, and it's important that people who join us want to be a part of that culture.

How competitive is it to get a job at Goldman?

We get about 6,000 résumés a year just for the Investment Banking Division analyst positions, and we hire around 80 or 90 analysts each year. This is just in the U.S. We hire about 130 analysts total worldwide.

What, to you, are the most important qualifications for landing a job at Goldman?

We look for people with outstanding academic backgrounds who have participated extensively in extracurricular activities and have been leaders on campus. People who have demonstrated a commitment to doing something productive over their summers, be it work or something else. We also look favorably upon students who have been actively involved in the community. On top of that, we look for people with good interpersonal skills and people who have a desire to be a part of a team. Also, we look for those who have a comfort with numbers. But you don't need to be a mathematician.

How do you assess all of this?

We probe deeply into academics, extracurricular activities, and the rationale students have for pursuing such endeavors. We look for those who can work with others and work effectively on a team and obviously those who have a strong work ethic. And you have to be able to juggle. In banking, you have to be able to manage many different projects, so we look for people who have been successful in managing numerous pursuits at the same time as doing well academically.

People think that Goldman has very high academic standards. Is there a GPA cut-off?

Absolutely not. The lower the GPA, however, the more a candidate has to be able to compensate with the less tangible qualities. But we're forgiving. If a candidate had a difficult freshman year and then showed an improving trend, that's meaningful to us. If it goes in the opposite direction, it's a bit more difficult. If you had a bad semester, or something happened, that's okay. Let us know. We're understanding of personal situations that might cause an aberration.

We *do* look for high performers. We think there is a connection between academic performance and doing well on the job. On the other hand, we have hired students with low GPAs who have turned out to be terrific analysts. We will take chances.

How about the thank-you note and cover letter? Do you actually read them?

A meaningful cover letter can be helpful if somebody does not seem to be well suited for the job or it's not clear why they're interested in the job. If you have a background that wouldn't naturally lend itself to investment banking, then a cover letter can help. In addition, the cover letter would be an appropriate place to address any holes in a résumé.

As for thank-you notes, I think there's more downside than upside. I have received so many thank-you notes with my name spelled wrong, poor grammar, and typos. And that can hurt you. I will say that a thank-you note can be helpful if an issue that came up in an interview didn't get completely resolved, and the candidate wants to provide more information.

When you interview someone, what in particular do you look for?

Interpersonal and communication skills, both of those. You want to see how easy somebody is to talk to, how quickly they think on their feet, how composed they are. We do not conduct pressure interviews, but it is interesting to see how people react to a question they've never heard before.

Can you give me an example of one of the tougher interview questions you ask?

I don't actually have standard questions. I used to when I first started interviewing but not anymore. What I like to do is push people to explore themselves, and understand what makes them tick. When people answer a question, I like to follow up and probe beneath the surface. One of the problems is that after the candidates have been out there interviewing with several companies, they've heard all the standard questions. They come in and you push the button, and off they go. I like to ask questions that might be slightly different from how they've heard them phrased before, so that it makes them think.

There is no problem-solving component in the Goldman Sachs interview?

Right. If you get to the final round of Goldman Sachs interviews, you're going to have approximately ten interviews with different people, some of them two on one. And each interviewer has his personal style of interviewing. My own style is to try to get to know someone. To understand their motivations, what excites them, what they're looking for. And based on my experience over the past several years with people who have done well on the job, I try to determine whether the candidate will be successful here.

In terms of interviewing, as a firm I think we're a little touchy-feely. Our interviews are more like conversations. The interview is a time for us to be judging people but it's also a time for them to be learning about us, to be asking us questions.

Are connections crucial to getting a job?

No, not at all. What they can do is get an interview for somebody who might not otherwise earn one. But once you're in the door you're on your own.

How have students tried to capture your attention in creative ways?

First of all, little gimmicks don't help. They make for an interesting story, but that's about it. This one guy, he sent a fish bowl with a live little shark, and attached to the bowl were balloons, and inside the balloons were fake dollar bills. Attached was a letter that said he was as hungry as a shark and that he would make the firm more money than was in the balloons. And you know what, I didn't interview him. First of all, he wasn't qualified. And second, I thought if I interview this guy because I thought the shark was so intriguing, what else are people going to start sending me?

What I want is a solid résumé and a good cover letter. We look at every résumé we get. And if it's not strong enough, even if you get in the door, you probably won't get the job.

What are some important interview DOs?

Research the company before you interview. You don't have to know everything, but you should know something about the company. Know why you're interested, why you're well suited to the industry and the company. Be prepared with several thoughtful questions. Know your strengths and weaknesses. Carry an extra copy of your résumé. Be polite and courteous to *everybody*. People who yell at my secretary . . . you know, she's going to tell me what you said! Be factual and accurate on your résumé and in your discussions. Unfortunately, people sometimes get caught stretching the truth. Be enthusiastic—let people know if you really want the job.

On the don't side, don't be too persistent with follow up calls. Showing your enthusiasm is great, but you don't want to go overboard. Also, don't try to be the person you think *we* want you to be.

But wouldn't a candidate be motivated to pretend that he's right for Goldman?

Look, we're going to see right through it if you're not acting naturally, and you just won't be happy here if you've pretended to be someone you're not.

If a candidate expresses a preference to work in a particular area within the firm, does this lessen his chances of being hired?

It depends on the firm. As far as I'm concerned, if you're totally focused and know what you want to do, then you ought to tell me. But I encourage people to stay open-minded. A lot of the time, you end up finding out about business areas you never even knew existed. Or you might think you know what you want to do, but in our business it's called something else or is housed in a different area.

What's the most memorable interview you've ever conducted?

I hate to say this, but I can't think of one that is the most memorable. What I truly enjoy is when I feel I have gotten to know someone. When I feel I understand how and why they've accomplished what they have. I like it when people are truly open, and when I have more of a conversation with them.

What I don't like is when I ask a question, they answer, and there's silence. And again. And again. I like it when people engage me in a dialogue.

How many interviews do you think you've done over the past five years?

I've seen well over 1,000 candidates over the past five years.

Are the most remarkable candidates those who have done the most interesting things?

I think it's the people who are the most dynamic. After you've done thirteen interviews on a campus in one day, it's the people who really let their personality shine through and who are enthusiastic who stand out. Those people make the thirty minutes memorable.

THE RECRUITER'S PERSPECTIVE

Kate Byrne
Head of Global Recruiting, Monitor Company

An industry veteran of ten years, Kate Byrne has worked in management consulting longer than some consulting firms have even existed. After graduating *magna cum laude* from Harvard with a degree in economics, Byrne cut her teeth on mergers and acquisitions deals at Lazard Frères in New York and then returned to Harvard Business School. Upon graduation in 1987, she joined Monitor Company as a consultant and rose through the ranks to become a Case Team Leader and a Global Account Manager. In 1996, she stepped into the role of head of Global Recruiting for Monitor, where she is responsible for all hiring at the undergraduate and graduate-school levels. Monitor Company is a leading international management consulting firm with over 600 consultants employed worldwide.

What types of people would find management consulting a good place to work?

People with a real intellectual curiosity about business. And people who want a broad exposure to a variety of companies and business issues. If someone is curious not only about finance, but also marketing, production, cost management, and issues of globalization and global competitiveness, then I think consulting is the right profession to pursue.

Do you see the profession of management consulting changing at all, and do you see any potential impact of these changes on people who are now entering the field?

The range of industries and management issues we see are growing, and technological change is happening in the business environment at a very rapid pace, so that the scope of knowledge and expertise required to support global clients is exploding. This is creating a real burden on firms in the industry, and I think different firms are handling this in different ways. Some are developing the knowledge in-house, and they have "industry practices." Some firms, like Monitor, are developing it in-house but are also developing networks outside of the firm to be able to call on expertise when we need it. So that's one thing that I see changing—the rate at which firms need to assimilate knowledge to serve clients.

A second trend is that industry reports or industry structure analysis are a kind of commodity now. The kinds of analysis or insight that ten or twenty years ago you would have seen in the final report of a consulting project are now in the proposal letter. The more challenging aspect of a consulting engagement now is not the solution to the problem but how you make the solution happen in an organization—how you create change. The skill set required for consultants is quite different. You not only need analytical and business skills, but you need the interpersonal skills required to create change.

What is your general recruiting philosophy and how does it differ from other firms?

At both the graduate and undergraduate levels, we are hiring for the Consultant position. What this means for undergraduates is that we're not looking to hire people for two years and then ask them to go back to graduate school. They stay as long as makes sense for them. A lot of undergraduates *do* go back to business school, but it may be after two, three, or four years. And we're interested in having the people who do leave come back after business school. We look to them to be the future leaders of the firm. The way we implement this philosophy is we have a very customized career path. People don't rise in a lockstep fashion through the firm. Once you're here, it's really up to you to figure out how fast you're going to progress, what kind of skills you're going to develop and when. You're in a constant dialogue with a professional development advisor who helps you plan your career.

Are only a few undergraduates given offers to return to Monitor after business school?

Postbusiness school offers are performance-based, but it's a significant number—greater than 50 percent of departing consultants receive the offer.

How many résumés do you receive each year?

We get about 15,000 résumés in North America and 20,000 résumés in total worldwide for the undergraduate consultant position. At the graduate level, we get about 5,000 résumés in North America and 6,000 total worldwide. At the undergraduate level we hire about 100 consultants each year, and at the graduate level, about 50.

What are some of the most important qualities that you look for in consultants?

We look for analytical skills, communication skills, and the ability to work with clients. Another dimension we look for is the ability to learn. Consulting is a very rapid learning environment, and we assume that people don't have most of the skills they need when they join. We provide training for new consultants, but there's also a lot of on-the-job learning that we expect people to be able to handle. We're also looking for people with a sense of initiative or motivation and values that are consistent with our firm's values.

Could you describe the new case interview you've added to the recruiting process?

A lot of firms will give you verbal case questions. We also give a written case. Candidates have twenty minutes to prepare the case, then they discuss it with the interviewer. We are looking to see how candidates can reason through a business problem.

What aspects of the résumé are most important to you?

First, academic performance. We also look for evidence of a high energy level and intrinsic motivation—to what degree the candidate has been involved in extracurricular activities or jobs outside of school. We look for evidence of leadership and action orientation, the ability to get things done. We look for breadth, the ability to balance multiple commitments. We're also assessing whether the candidate has been challenged in their school and work environment.

Are details like cover letters and thank-you notes important? How thoroughly do you read these?

They are important, and we do read them. They reflect that the person has seriously thought about what they want before applying to Monitor. After reading cover letters, we usually know how much the candidate knows about Monitor and how serious they are about pursuing us.

Have people been extraordinarily creative in the ways they've tried to get a job at Monitor?

The candidates I remember the most are the ones who have challenged our hiring decision. There have been instances where people have challenged a decision, and we have reopened the case, done further evaluation, and reversed the decision. So the openness to learning that we value we also apply to our recruiting practices.

Is there anything you wish candidates would stop doing?

The greatest piece of advice I could give is to be yourself. Tell us who you are and what it is you want to accomplish with your life. If you just play back what you think we want to hear, the probability of the relationship being successful for either side is not high.

Which interviews have been most memorable to you?

There are two kinds of interviews that I remember most vividly. One is people who share a personal story that is very high impact that illustrates some part of their personality, values, or commitment. I've heard some fascinating personal stories.

And the other is people who recover well from some blunder. People who really make a mistake and then are extremely graceful in the way they recover from it. First of all, because the blunder is often so memorable, and second, because they're able to recover from it gracefully. It's an indicator of how they might handle themselves in a difficult client situation.

How important are the questions the candidate is asking you?

They are very important, because they reflect how much the candidate has thought about Monitor and the industry. Questions tell us how curious people are and how far along they are in their decision-making process.

When you evaluate a candidate, how important is the name-brand of their school?

It is important that the person come from a high-quality academic institution. There are some schools that don't have great name recognition, but are still high quality. We don't just recruit at Harvard and Princeton. We also go to Williams and Amherst and other smaller schools. What's important is what we know about the quality of the institutions, and even more important, the quality of the programs within the institutions.

Actually, I'm referring to students who come from good schools that don't have quite the same "brand name."

Those people do get hired. Every year. We are very focused in our recruiting efforts, however. There are a limited number of schools where we do on-campus interviews and presentations. We *do* hire a number of people each year from schools where we don't recruit, and we look at all of the résumés we receive very carefully. But in terms of the numbers, there's a lot of competition for a limited number of slots.

What types of candidates do you wish you saw more of?

What we do wish we saw more of is people who are interested in experimenting—taking risks and breaking new ground. Often we see people who are more oriented toward security and how to hedge their bets, and that's an attitude that isn't as exciting as someone who has a lot of self-confidence and really wants to go out and make things happen.

Does that mean that you will look at people who have been out of school and worked in another field for a number of years?

Yes, we hire people like that every year. People who have gone on fellowships and that sort of thing, or who have worked in another industry for a number of years and are now interested in a career change. And they're brought in as consultants just like everybody else.

How should an undergraduate or MBA student decide which job to choose?

I can't answer that for any individual. What I encourage people to do is to think about what's important to them, and write it down. Be very explicit with yourself. Then look at different firms in terms of how well they represent each of those criteria. For certain people, affinity with the firm's people is going to be the most important thing. For other people, name brand is important. For others, it will be the experience—where will they be challenged and stretched the most. But be honest about what matters most to you.

What should people notice about your office when they come in for an interview?

One thing people will notice in most of our offices is the atmosphere is very informal. For example, our Cambridge office is a converted furniture factory with exposed brick walls. Our offices are very much an expression of the personality of the firm, with modern architecture and an in-office casual dress code five days a week. When you're with clients, you'll be expected to dress in whatever is most appropriate for that client. But our philosophy is to allow people to be themselves and be comfortable while they are at work.

How does a Monitor consultant differ from a consultant at another firm?

There is an openness to learning and a willingness to take risks and innovate common to all Monitor consultants. Because of the growth stage Monitor is in and because of the way we run the firm, we are looking to every person who comes in to help us shape the future of the firm. And that does attract a slightly different type of person than the one attracted to firms who are more set in their ways.

~ 6 ~

WHO THE FIRMS
ARE LOOKING FOR

There aren't any hard-and-fast rules as to whom a bank or a consulting firm will hire. Leaf through the firms' recruiting brochures and you'll see employees from a variety of diverse backgrounds.

There are a few caveats, however. The less "brand-name" your school, the stronger your academic and extracurricular record must be in order to win an investment banking or management consulting interview (except in the areas of sales and trading). In particular, academic performance standards are higher for students from schools that a firm does not actively target in its recruiting process. At the MBA level, name brand is even more important; investment banking divisions and consulting firms typically do not hire associates from business schools outside the top tier. Also, if you have absolutely no quantitative courses on your transcript, expect to be grilled more heavily on your quantitative abilities or business interest during an interview. You should emphasize any business summer experience you've had.

CRITICAL SKILLS

When asked about the candidates they hire, bankers and consultants at any firm will mention a few characteristics again and again. I call these "critical skills" because they are the fundamental qualities you need to demonstrate to get a banking or consulting job. Do you think you have these qualities? What examples would you use to show that you do? Here's what recuiters mean when they say they're looking for . . .

"ANALYTICAL SKILLS"

Intelligent; able to find patterns and causal relationships in what appears to be unrelated data; creates hypotheses to drive research; uses clear and logical thinking; draws on past experience to solve problems; applies a creative approach to come up with solutions.

"BUSINESS SENSE"

Entrepreneurial; stays current on major business developments; intuitively understands basic business dynamics; converses easily about business issues.

"CAPACITY FOR CONTINUOUS DEVELOPMENT" OR "QUICK LEARNER"

Solicits and is open to feedback; humble; wants to improve himself; learns from mistakes.

"COMMUNICATIONS SKILLS"

Listens carefully to understand others; uses tactful phrasing and timing when communicating; has a good sense for what people mean; understands how he is being perceived.

"INTEGRITY"

Does not waver on ethical issues; has basic respect for other individuals; is able to maintain confidentiality; follows through on commitments; has high ethical standards.

The Door Is Open for All Majors

MANAGEMENT CONSULTING

Booz•Allen Hamilton is probably typical of most consulting firms in its mix of employees' undergraduate fields:

Undergraduate Major	% of Employees
Engineering	33
Economics	22
Business	14
Science/Math	13
Humanities	12
Computer Science	5

INVESTMENT BANKING

A leading investment bank reports that it hires undergraduates with diverse majors for its analyst program:

Undergraduate Major	% of Analysts
Economics	40
Business/Finance/Accounting	22
Liberal Arts	20
Other	18

Source: "Global Opportunities," 1994 recruiting brochure, Booz•Allen & Hamilton; interview with recruiter at a leading investment bank.

"INTERPERSONAL SKILLS"

Mature; avoids turning business issues into personal issues; genuinely interested in other people; can get along with people from a range of backgrounds; positive in attitude; keeps cool under pressure; thinks before leaping; open-minded; able to put things in perspective.

"LEADERSHIP SKILLS"

Has influence; can make decisions quickly; provides leadership in situations where there's none; understands individuals' positions on issues and how to influence them; able to take risks; takes action when necessary; sets clear goals; rallies people around a shared objective; believes that every problem is surmountable.

"MOTIVATION AND ENERGY"

Enthusiastic; has a "can-do" attitude; has high performance standards; motivates others; willing to work long hours; organizes work effectively; detail-oriented; willing to do grunt work, or unglamorous work.

"QUANTITATIVE SKILLS"

Can apply quantitative thinking to analysis of issues; understands quantitative relationships in business; comfortable performing simple math mentally; some academic training in math.

"TEAM PLAYER"

Likes to work in teams; sensitive and willing to help others; knows when to be a leader and when to be a follower; puts group's priorities before own; shares credit for joint work.

DON'T worry if it seems at first that you don't meet these criteria. Most successful candidates don't *really* possess all these characteristics—many of these skills and characteristics are learned once you've actually started working. But packaging yourself as someone who has these characteristics or the potential to develop them is the difference between receiving a job offer or not.

SPECIFIC SKILLS: ASSOCIATES

The fundamental difference between associates (hired from graduate school) and analysts (hired from university) is time horizon. Associates are expected to have the same critical skills as analysts yet also have qualities that will allow them to be successful in a long-term career at the firm. They should be able to be future leaders of the firm.

- *Managerial ability:* Associates will need to manage teams of analysts almost immediately. It helps if a candidate is able to show some previous management experience and teamwork or a strong potential to be a good manager.
- *Sales ability:* Good salesmanship is important in both banking and consulting, because in a few years associates are expected to start bringing in business. A corollary to this is that prior industry experience helps in consulting—potential clients are more impressed by someone who actually understands their industry or who has had years of general management experience.
- *Leadership:* The firm has to be able to see you as a future managing director, someone who can inspire and influence at the firm. Evidence of unusually rapid career advancements prior to business school will help your candidacy.
- *Commitment:* Since they will invest money and time into training a new associate, firms prefer associates who say they will stick around for the long run.

SPECIFIC SKILLS: INVESTMENT BANKERS

If you're applying to an investment bank, you should demonstrate:

- A *cultural fit with investment banking:* In addition to the critical skills, banks seek people who will get along with clients and colleagues— people who are extroverted, sociable, well rounded, and *not* eccentric. Bankers perform more work alongside their colleagues than consultants, who can spend days working alone on their own separate piece of work. Banks hire many former athletes because they view team sports as good training for the type of teamwork and leadership that banking entails.
- *Enthusiasm for investment banking and the thrill of the transaction:* Investment bankers like to hear that you *really* want to be an investment banker. The hours are brutal and an interest in the job is what keeps you going.
- *Thick skin:* Certain areas of the bank, particularly the trading floor, are harsh environments where there is little time to think about how to say things. Communication tends to be more blunt and less "touchy-feely" than in consulting.
- *Some understanding of finance:* Investment banking focuses on financial issues in which deep, specialized knowledge is important. On the other hand, banks provide less training than consultancies throughout an employee's career because it is harder to pull bankers away from the office for dedicated training time. Therefore, the more you can demonstrate previous knowledge of business and finance, the better off you'll be.

- *Strong quantitative skills:* Banking work tends to be fairly quantitative, and you'll hear that you're supposed to "be comfortable with numbers" in order to do the work. Your grades in quantitative classes will be scrutinized more carefully.

SPECIFIC SKILLS: CONSULTANTS

If you're applying to a consulting firm, you should demonstrate:

- *Outstanding analytical skills:* Firms are hired by clients for ideas and analysis that the client can't come up with himself. Consulting firms therefore need people who are intellectual powerhouses. Average GPAs are much higher than in investment banking, and the range of GPAs is narrower.
- *Individualism:* Although interpersonal skills are valued, there is more room in consulting for slightly more eclectic intellectuals than in banking.
- *Interpersonal skills:* Consulting has the reputation of being kinder and gentler than banking. Treating colleagues with respect and sensitivity is of utmost importance. In addition, you'll need the poise and confidence to work with older clients from day one. One analyst reported that she was sent to interview a client during her first week on the job, whereupon the client asked her, "How the hell old are you, anyway?"
- *Intellectual curiosity:* Unlike bankers, consultants do not necessarily have a completed transaction to look back on when they're finished working with the client. Often, the client does not implement the consultants' recommendations. Consultants need to be satisfied with the intellectual challenge of their work and be comfortable with the knowledge that their client may not follow their advice.

Finally, consulting firms have fewer on-the-ground employees in foreign countries and remote areas. As a result, consultants need to be willing to travel. Those who can't take flying from Chicago to Federal Way, Washington, once a week for six months will burn out quickly. Also, the ability to speak foreign languages is very valuable, as many firms see their employees as one gigantic pool of human resources from which they can draw to staff any project the world over.

SPECIFIC SKILLS: TRADERS AND SALESPEOPLE

Investment banking and trading are not just physically separate worlds. Fast-paced, market-driven, and execution-oriented, sales and trading work demands qualities that are different from those valued in investment banking.

- *Strong quantitative skills:* Important particularly in more technical product areas, such as bonds or derivatives.
- *Effort:* Brightness is not measured primarily through GPA or prestige of school, as it is in investment banking. Instead, intellect is judged through the types of questions you ask and your quickness in understanding markets and products.
- *Interpersonal skills:* An even more important predictor of success than analytical skills in sales and trading. The trading floor is relationship-driven, and those who are able to build the broadest base of support among senior people are most likely to be given good opportunities. Making friends is important from the very beginning: When a new trainee rotates among several different desks, he is trying to win support and a permanent offer from one desk. Insiders report that extremely smart people with no personalities have failed miserably. Recruiters look for outgoing, enthusiastic, confident people who will assert themselves and influence others. In addition, successful traders are thick-skinned enough to be able to deal with egos and a sink-or-swim mentality.
- *Flexibility and speed:* Traders and salespeople are confronted with more change, at a more rapid pace, than investment bankers. You'll hear re-cruiters say they are looking for "flexible" people who can adjust and react quickly to market changes. In fact, salespeople and traders need to move faster physically than most: They talk, act, move, and even eat more rapidly. Sentences become reduced to bullet-point phrases.
- *Thick skin:* As mentioned before, the trading floor can be a blunt, harsh environment. Salespeople and traders need to be able to deal with enor-mous pressure that arises both from the knowledge that large sums of money could be lost instantaneously if a mistake is made and from the demanding and extreme behavior (i.e., screaming and yelling) of the people around them. As one trader at Merrill Lynch described it, "Take the pressure of investment banking, and multiply it by ten."
- *Risk taking:* Because trading is more market-driven and uncertain than investment banking, people need to be able to take calculated risks and be more aggressive. They must seize an opportunity before anyone else does.

DIFFERENCES AMONG CONSULTANTS

I've described the difference between consultants and bankers, but there are differences even among people who work in different types of consulting.

Strategy Consulting: Sheer brainpower can compensate for lack of experience or knowledge, because strategy consulting depends less on detailed knowledge of each industry and more on transferring the same analytical tools from one industry to another. Grades, GMAT scores, performance during the analytical "case" question, quality of school, academic honors, and other evidence of intellect factor heavily into evaluation of candidates. *Characteristics sought: experience in a complex industry or task, talent for intellectual problem-solving, sound analytical skills and lateral thinking, evidence of business sense, superb business judgment.*

Operations Consulting: An operations group of a consulting firm addresses the operational or process problems of a company. Working on these issues often requires knowledge that is unique to the company's industry. Therefore, a firm will look for industry experience in hiring operations consultants, hiring people who have worked in a line, staff, or senior management role. Finally, since operations gurus often implement changes in process or structure, re-cruiters look for those who have had experience in implementing corporate change and interacting with clients. *Characteristics sought: functional or indus-try content experience, experience implementing change, experience in more than one function or industry, indication of innovation, management experience with bottom-line responsibility.*

Information Technology Consulting: Information technology recruiters look for coursework in computer science. Specific experience managing an infor-mation technology project within Corporate America is valued, as is previous experience in information technology consulting. *Characteristics sought: ability to analyze and explain technology as a business issue; previous experience as a consultant or in sales in a service-oriented business; experience in technology proj-ect management, in implementing information systems in software development; management experience with bottom-line responsibility.*

Industry or Functional Specialization: If a firm focuses on a particular indus-try or function, it will look for people who have had experience in this spe-cialty. A consulting firm that provides advice solely to financial institutions, for example, will favor recruits who have worked in a financial institution before. If a firm's focus is providing advice on litigation (lawsuits), then it will seek consultants experienced in legal issues. *Characteristics sought: specific functional or industry content experience, line management experience with bot-tom-line responsibility, previous experience as a consultant or in sales.*

INSIDER INTERVIEW:
SPOTLIGHT ON DAILY WORK IN INVESTMENT BANKING

Beth Bradley*
Former Analyst, major-bracket investment bank based in New York

B eth worked for three years in corporate finance at a leading investment bank. She was in the Financial Institutions Group (FIG),
where she served the M&A and corporate finance needs of financial
institutions such as commercial banks and insurance companies.

Can you describe a typical project that you worked on?

I worked in the financial institutions group at my firm. My work was intensive
in modeling, and we created very thick presentations with lots of graphs and
pictures. Banks are very sophisticated clients. A lot of them have their own
M&A and underwriting departments. If you come in with a book that's not
very good, they see right through it. Plus, all of them have at least three or
four investment banks serving them. There's no loyalty among bank clients. A
lot of times we'd meet other investment banks in the lobby who'd have a
meeting with the client right after us.

My work was very numbers oriented. A typical project would be an M&A
transaction. Huge computer models—pages and pages of models. The industry is very heavily regulated, so that not only do you have to do financial
analysis, but you have to pay attention to all the financial regulations. For
example, are your equity ratios going to be sufficient after the acquisition to
meet required tests? On a typical M&A project I'd go on a due diligence trip
to the client, work on models, and develop relationships with a vice president
or assistant to the CFO or the CFO himself. He would feed me all the information I needed to build the model. Including assumptions and key criteria they
wanted to use to analyze the effect of the transaction. I would keep on punch-
ing numbers into a spreadsheet, probably for eighteen hours a day. I'd go to
meetings. But I'd seldom present my models. I sometimes spoke when the
model was very complicated and no one else could understand and explain it.

Did you find all this work interesting?

Models I found interesting, and it was excellent training, for everything—
learning how to use a computer, understanding accounting and financial anal-

*Name has been changed to protect privacy.

ysis. It's very rigorous. Your clients are so smart and sophisticated that if there's a mistake in your model, they'll catch it. There's a high quality bar.

What did you come away with?

I think analysts at any investment bank develop an ability to work hard and spend time efficiently. But more precisely, I came away with excellent knowledge of spreadsheets, running macros, and other computer skills. I developed a good knowledge of accounting and financial analysis, reading financial statements and making up your mind fairly quickly as to what you think is happening at a company, and what its strengths and weaknesses are. And you develop thick skin. At first you're nervous and you don't say anything and then you get more comfortable with senior management of companies. You gain self-confidence.

Were you encouraged to take on responsibility or speak up in meetings?

Not really, no. They're fairly formal in that respect. I would present my models when no one else could. But they weren't expecting me to lead the presentation or make a big contribution to the meetings. If only for the reason that if you stayed up until 4 A.M. finishing the presentation, you're completely brain-dead during the meeting. The only thing you want to do is sit and relax and hope for the best—that there's no mistake and if there is that no one will catch it.

What were your hours like?

I worked 90 to 100 hours per week in the FIG group, for one entire year. Then, when I became a corporate finance generalist I worked 60 hours per week.

Does anything surprise you about investment banking?

I was shocked by the way people present their jobs to the outside world versus what's going on. You're basically a slave, and on top of that you're sent out to recruit new people. And you're supposed to give speeches about how good it is. Finally, you convince yourself that this job *is* the best. The pressure is high to not say anything to the outside world and preserve the glamour and the myths about investment banking. But if you keep your ears open you can find smaller firms where you can make just as much money and lead a better life.

How do you look after yourself in investment banking?

You have to build allies within your group and with the operating people rather than the administrative people. The administrative people can't do anything to protect you.

What's your opinion of the long-term attractiveness of your specific firm and investment banking in general?

I would go back to investment banking, but not to a big firm like where I worked. There's a lot less politics at a smaller firm. You're more visible and your contribution is more visible. Also, I find the sales and trading culture much more pleasant. They're more matter-of-fact, there's no schmoozing, there's no attitude with the Hermes ties and Porsches and all that. They're regular guys, they make a ton of money, but you'd never know it because they rarely bring it up. And if you do something wrong, they tell you right away, and if you do something good, they tell you also. At my firm, it's very much a corporate finance culture—that was the prestigious thing. They schmooze all the time because that's their job. But it's difficult to get real feedback, to know where you stand, how you're doing compared to the other people. The trading culture is more abrupt. I don't especially enjoy the crude language, don't get me wrong. But I'd rather be in a rough but straightforward environment than in a highly political one.

~ 7 ~

RÉSUMÉ AND COVER LETTER:
THE PACKAGING

Generally there are two schools of thought when it comes to job-hunting. One theory holds that you should be the person each firm wants to see, collect as many offers as you can, and then choose the company that truly suits you—with the job market as tight as it is, you shouldn't be picky until you've gotten at least one job offer. Another theory holds that you should be yourself from the beginning and see which job offers you wind up with—if you've "acted" unlike yourself to approach a firm, you'll be unhappy once you get there.

Choosing an approach is really a personal decision. This chapter is going to assume that if you've bought this book, you want advice on how you can present your background in a manner that demonstrates that you have critical skills, regardless of whether *you* think you have these skills or not. However, this does not mean that you can lie about what you've done. Carefully watch the line between highlighting truths and fabricating untruths.

SELLING YOURSELF

Getting an interview with a consulting firm or an investment bank takes more than a brilliant academic record or blue-chip work experience. One of the most common errors candidates make is assuming that good credentials guarantee an interview or poor credentials rule one out.

As any businessperson will tell you, products often sell because of their packaging. The cold, hard fact is that in the recruiting process, you are the product and banks and consulting firms are doing the shopping. Before they begin interviewing, firms are quickly perusing the shelves to decide which products to examine more closely. Your "packaging" is more than just your résumé: It includes your cover letter and anything else you send to the recruiter when requesting an interview.

Separate your personal feelings and insecurities from the recruiting process. The strongest candidates are those who have perspective and who can see their strengths and weaknesses objectively. Stand back and look at yourself dispassionately as a product. What are your probable strengths in the eyes of the recruiter? What are your weaknesses that you will want to compensate for or downplay? Craft an attractive, dynamic package that highlights positives and compensates for negatives. Your job is to sell the product; how good the product is, is irrelevant to you. The following questions will help you plan your packaging strategy.

~

Why Should the Recruiter Buy **You**?

In assessing yourself as a candidate, answer the following questions:

- What concerns will the recruiter have about me?
- What elements of my background will I highlight to address these concerns?
- What are my biggest assets for a job in banking or consulting?
- What experiences or accomplishments can I use to highlight these assets?

HOW DOES THE RECRUITER EVALUATE YOUR RÉSUMÉ?

To make a decision, recruiters quickly review candidates on critical skills and place them in "yes," "no," or "maybe" piles. *In the face of hundreds of résumés, any small error gives a recruiter the excuse to eliminate the candidate.* Reviewers spend an average of two minutes reviewing each résumé. Basically they are making the easiest decisions first, then going back to review more difficult borderline cases in the "maybe" pile.

Borderline decisions are agonizing for recruiters, who see something appealing in all of the "maybe" candidates. Because recruiters can pull a limited number of candidates up to the "yes" pile, they begin to compare "maybes" closely. This is when small details make a big difference in the process. For recruiters in a hurry—as they all are—the easiest method is to compare quantifiables, such as GPAs or grades in quantitative classes. Recruiters also look at these factors:

- Would candidate add to the diversity of candidate pool?
- Candidate wrote a great cover letter; knows a lot about our firm and is interested in us.
- Has the candidate had relevant summer experiences or hobbies?

The Easy NO

You're a recruiter, and you're sitting down to a pile of 500 résumés that you have to whittle down to 50. Thankfully, some people have made your job easier. They are the "Easy NOs," whose errors rule them out. Here's how they get themselves axed quickly:

- **Forget that banking and consulting are traditional industries.** Firms look for signs that a candidate doesn't understand the traditional business environment. Easy NOs love to use faux-marble, textured, graphics-adorned, colored, or other "different" paper. They also prefer using off-the-wall fonts and a "high-design" look with lots of lines and boxes.
- **Forget to check for typos.** Easy NOs are way too busy with more important things than to double-check their résumé and cover letter, thus letting an astonishing number of typos and grammatical errors remain in place. They address letters to the wrong company or spell the recruiter's name the way *they* think it should be spelled. They love to use inconsistent formatting throughout their résumé, thinking, Who cares? Why not throw in five fonts for fun?
- **Don't understand the company or the job offered.** The "Objective" at the top of the Easy NO's résumé states that he is looking for an engineering job even though he is applying to a consulting firm. (This happens!). Easy NOs write to Merrill Lynch saying that they're looking to work for a small firm, or apply for an analyst job saying that they're looking for a five-year position.
- **Deliberately ignore instructions.** The recruiter specifically asked for an academic transcript to be submitted, but the Easy NO thinks she will be able to get away with not sending one. The recruiter doesn't bother asking twice.
- **Don't explain things clearly.** The Easy NO believes that everyone understands semiconductors the way he does and proceeds to write an unintelligible description of what he did in that industry last summer.
- **Have diarrhea of the pen.** The Easy NO believes that his twenty-one years of life warrant a three-page résumé. Simple activities are explained endlessly. Résumés should be just one page.
- **Exercise questionable judgment.** Easy NOs submit glossy pictures of themselves along with their résumés. They inflate their GPAs on their résumés or state salary requirements in their cover letters.

After deciding on the "maybes," recruiters might conclude by reviewing their "yes" piles once again to make sure their selections are consistent in quality and that the group as a whole possesses a balance of characteristics they seek. Up to the very last moment, recruiters might switch someone in the "yes" pile to the "no" pile or vice versa.

Selecting candidates involves negotiation. Each recruiter will have her favorites and will make a case for those favorites. If you've made a friend at the company sometime before this meeting, it will come in handy. This "sponsorship" phenomenon is also seen in the evaluation of interviews, as I discuss later.

GENERAL STRATEGIES FOR YOUR PACKAGING

Before plunging into the specifics of how to craft either the cover letter or the résumé, let's cover some rules that apply to both. Some of the details mentioned here may seem picky to you, but you'd be amazed at how picky recruiters are. Don't give them the excuse to reject (known in industry jargon as "ding") you just because you don't feel like playing the recruiting game.

DEMONSTRATE CRITICAL SKILLS

In the one or two minutes they spend looking you over, how do recruiters evaluate you? They are looking for evidence that you have skills critical to the job, and they generally have three places to look: a cover letter, résumé, and academic transcript. By comparing these three documents, recruiters put together a quick mental image of you that drives the decision for awarding or denying an interview. Make sure that you have in some way addressed the critical skills listed on the next page somewhere in your package. Critical skills were defined in Chapter 6; here are some tips on how to display them.

The cover letter, résumé, and transcript supplement each other. If the candidate's GPA is mediocre but the rest of her résumé looks great, a recruiter might consult the transcript to see if she has had an upward trend in grades. If the candidate's résumé looks perfect but there is some doubt about her interest in the job, the recruiter might look at her cover letter to see how much thought she's put into it. In other words, play these various documents against each other. If you are worried about something on your résumé, compensate for it in your cover letter.

PRESENTATION

Err on the side of conservatism at all times during your job-hunt so that you don't accidentally rule yourself out of a job opportunity. Investment banks in particular are more conservative in style than advertising, public relations, or other business fields. When you put together your recruiting package, think *The Wall Street Journal*: no colors, no photographs, no fancy fonts, no screaming headlines. Just subdued elegance in black and white.

Résumés and letters on anything besides bond paper in white or cream are

How and Where to Display Critical Skills

"Team player"
Signs you have it: Work in teams, either in academics, extracurriculars, or on the job; participates in team sports; hobbies are people-oriented. *Where you can display it:* resume

"Communications skills"
Signs you have it: Uses tactful phrasing and articulates complex thoughts in cover letter; organizes information well and writes concisely in resume; participates in activities that involve written or verbal communications, such as teaching or journalism; fluent in a foreign language; good verbal SAT or GMAT score. *Where you can display it:* cover letter, resume

"Interpersonal skills"
Signs you have it: Participates in activities that involve interaction with others; demonstrates an ability to get along with people from a range of backgrounds (such as volunteer work or international experiences); positive tone in cover letter; uses tactful phrasing in cover letter. *Where you can display it:* cover letter, resume

"Leadership skills"
Signs you have it: Elected leadership positions; entrepreneurial or extracurricular initiative; has taken risks; successful self-direction in ambiguous situations; has persuaded others to take action. *Where you can display it:* resume

"Analytical skills"
Signs you have it: high grade point average (GPA); rising trend in grades; has performed well in analytical jobs and classwork; has had analytical work experience; uses logical thinking in presenting credentials and writing cover letter; has had business or financial work experience; good SAT or GMAT scores. *Where you can display it:* academic transcript, cover letter, resume

"Quantitative skills"
Signs you have it: Strong grades in quantitative subjects such as math, business, or economics; work experience involving quantitative analysis; good math SAT or GMAT score. *Where you can display it:* academic transcript, resume

"Business sense"
Signs you have it: demonstrated a long-term interest in business, both through classes and through extracurricular activities; knowledgeable about industry and firm in cover letter; enthusiastic about job in cover letter; work experience has provided exposure to major business or financial concepts. *Where you can display it:* cover letter, resume

"The capacity for continuous development"
Signs you have it: Upward trend in grades; challenging classes; built new knowledge on existing knowledge, such as in a study of a foreign language; *Where you can display it:* academic transcript, cover letter, resume

"Motivation and energy"
Signs you have it: Enthusiasm and a bias for action in cover letter; heavy academic load; has juggled many activities; participation in extracurriculars; worked your way through college. *Where you can display it:* academic transcript, cover letter, resume

"Integrity"
Signs you have it: Details on resume seem consistent; hasn't exaggerated accomplishments; hasn't said anything unprofessional or rude in cover letter. *Where you can display it:* academic transcript, cover letter, resume

unacceptable at investment banks or consulting firms. If in doubt, go with white. Nothing should be visible on the paper except for the words printed on it: no speckles, no cute pictures, no heathered or even linen texture. If you're going to use recycled paper, use the kind that is not obviously recycled (i.e., no bits of paper discernible). Monogrammed or otherwise personalized letterhead will scream "pretentious." Go ahead, splurge. Invest in some quality paper. At drugstores, stationery stores, and office superstores, you will find good brands such as Crane's Kid Finish 100% Cotton Fiber Paper or Whisper's Recycled 25% Cotton Fiber Paper. Always use matching paper for résumé, cover letter, and envelopes.

Keep things easy on the eye. Your minimum point size should be 10-point, your maximum 14-point. Don't lose the reader with too many details in sentences that are too long. Try to not pack every corner of the résumé with facts; leave enough "white space" to keep your résumé clean and easy to read.

BREVITY

This rule is simple. Cover letter one page, résumé one page. Under no circumstances should either be any longer. Long résumés are for people who have been in business for ten years or more. Remember that the longer it is, the more likely the recruiter will skim it. Being verbose says to the reader that you're too wrapped up in yourself or in the recruiting process to see things from an outsider's perspective. If you're having trouble editing it down, as you're writing, ask yourself: Does this fact really add something? Is it covered elsewhere?

CONSISTENCY

Check for contradictions, even in small details, that may raise questions about your integrity or your accuracy. Do you say that you worked at a job "in August" on the cover letter and "in July" on the résumé? Do you mention different work objectives in the two documents? Most important, make sure the GPA you list on your résumé is fully accurate. Don't round to the nearest tenth.

ACCURACY

This point can't be stressed enough. Companies have been known to reject on the basis of a typo, spelling error, punctuation problem, or grammatical error. It is especially irritating to the recruiter when her name or her firm's name is spelled wrong. Even inconsistencies in verb tense, capitalization, abbreviation, or other little details bother some people.

Everyone is capable of making a mistake, even those who pride themselves on precision. Double-check and triple-check your materials. Each time, read for a different type of mistake: punctuation, spelling, grammar, typo, wrong company name, address, missing words, and more. That no one can catch all errors in one review is an essential lesson learned as an analyst in investment banking. You're at an advantage if you learn it now.

SAFETY

Play it safe. Unlike in some other fields, where people are advised to use creative tactics to stand out from the pack, in investment banking and management consulting it's best not to try anything too different. Including an extra document such as a recommendation or a writing sample, for example, might give the recruiter a reason to nail you. It's best to let your accomplishments (and how you describe them) speak for themselves.

Also, omit any activities from your letter or résumé that could be viewed as controversial or deal with very personal beliefs. Just to be safe, leave out activities such as leading campus protests or being an activist for abortion rights. These may suggest to the recruiter a cultural mismatch with the investment banking or consulting cultures. Leave out anything that you wouldn't be able to explain positively and thoroughly in an interview. If you worked as an assistant to your professor five years ago and wouldn't recall the details of your findings in an interview, leave the specifics of the job off your résumé (although a better approach would be to remember what you did).

USE SPACE ECONOMICALLY

Assume that the recruiter probably will read your cover letter and your résumé, and don't repeat facts in both. Besides, you're going to want to squeeze too many critical skills into your package to afford saying the same thing twice. Only repeat those two or three things that are critical for the recruiter to remember.

A corollary of this is to stay away from unimportant facts and obvious statements. Don't say that, as a mechanic, you "performed basic mechanics activities such as . . . ," talk about your achievements as a mechanic that were beyond the ordinary and that the recruiter may not be able to figure out herself.

HELP THE READER

A plea to candidates: Help the recruiter understand what you're trying to say. If you attended university overseas, explain the U.S. equivalent of your diploma. If you worked in a particularly obscure scientific field, explain it in layman's terms. Try your explanation out on a friend who knows nothing about the field to see if it works. Recruiters have two or three minutes to look over your résumé and cover letter, and chances are they're not going to reread them. They will move on if they don't understand something.

GET SOME FEEDBACK

As a final important step, get a friend or advisor to take a look at your résumé. Career counselors at your university or alma mater are particularly experienced in reviewing résumés. Ask them to be very honest with you and to approach the résumé as if they were deciding whether to hire you for the specific job you're applying to (i.e., specify whether the résumé is being written for investment banking or management consulting).

What Position to Apply for If You're Neither an Undergraduate Nor an MBA Student

When writing a cover letter to a consulting firm or investment bank, you typically have to specify the position you're applying for. If you're an undergraduate, apply for an "analyst" position. If you're an MBA or law student at a top school, apply for an "associate" position. (Sales and trading areas are a completely different story—titles and positions differ greatly among firms and you need to check on them.)

But what if you're neither? You probably should write a letter to the manager of recruiting for the level you feel you're closest to and make a statement to the effect that you're "interested in a challenging job opportunity at their firm." This won't rule you out of a position and will let the recruiter decide which peer group you may fit in. The danger of specifying that you're applying for an MBA-level position when you don't have an MBA is that you risk being rejected outright. Here are specific guidelines for different types of candidates:

- Undergraduate student: Apply for analyst position. (Verify title with firm.)
- MBA student at top school: Apply for associate position. (Verify title with firm.)
- MBA student at other school: Apply for associate position; firm may decide you should be hired as an analyst.
- Master's degree in another subject besides business: Call or send letter to analyst recruiter; firm may decide you should be hired as an analyst or in an intermediate position.
- Ph.D. in any subject: Apply for an associate position if your degree is related to economics or business; apply for an analyst position if your degree is in something else.
- Graduated from college five years or less ago but do not have a graduate degree: Apply for an analyst position.
- Graduated from college more than five years ago or have significant industry experience: Contact firm for more information, but probably apply for an associate or manager position.

WRITING A WINNING COVER LETTER

Which candidates need to write a cover letter? Most banks and consulting firms recruiting on campus require only a résumé and a transcript of your grades. If you're a targeted student, check with career counselors to find out whether a cover letter is required. If a cover letter isn't required, don't send one in. One typo or well-intentioned mistake in your letter could rule you out. Why take the risk? However, if you're applying outside of an on-campus recruiting process, you *must* send a cover letter to the company along with a résumé.

This section goes over cover letter tips specific to the investment banking and management consulting industries. For more basic information, consult a reference book such as William S. Frank's *200 Letters for Job Hunters* (Ten Speed Press). Also highly recommended is Strunk and White's *Elements of Style* (Macmillan), a classic book that is quick reading and contains invaluable writing advice.

COVER BASIC ISSUES

A lot of candidates forget to answer basic questions that recruiters will be thinking about when reading a cover letter.

1. *Why are you writing to the company?*
   sample answers: to request a brochure or further information; to request an informational interview; to request an interview for a summer or permanent position.

2. *What position are you applying for and when can you start working?*
   sample answers: analyst (pre-MBA) position; associate (post-MBA) position; would like to apply for job in a West Coast office; can start at the end of the summer.

3. *Why do you want to work in the industry?*
   sample answers: to gain exposure to broad business issues; to gain specific industry or functional experience; to build a career in finance.

4. *Why do want to work at the firm you're writing to?*
   sample answers: reputation for having stellar people; strong in areas in which you're interested; offers a great deal of responsibility; some element of the firm's culture is a good match for you.

5. *What are three good reasons why the firm should hire you?*
   sample answers: you have special foreign-language skills or international experience; you are exceptionally enthusiastic about the industry; your summer work experience has prepared you well for the job; one of your accomplishments demonstrates one of the characteristics they're looking for.

6. *What is the next step that will follow the letter?*
   sample answers: you'd appreciate a response from the firm; you will call the firm to follow up; you will be in town and will call the firm then.

GET TO THE POINT QUICKLY

Here's a simple rule to remember: Tell recruiters why you're writing to them in the *first half* of the letter.

Also, the shorter the letter, the better. If you don't believe this, try reading your friends' cover letters. Four or five fat paragraphs will turn you off immediately. Recruiters are in the same position—they have little time, a short attention span, and don't want to read about something that's listed on your résumé anyway. Try to keep your letter to 200 words or less, unless you have a particularly complex story to tell.

PERSONALIZE IT

Companies love to be loved. If recruiters sense your cover letter is a form letter, they will think you're not as interested in the job as another candidate who *has* personalized the letter. When done appropriately, tailoring your letter to the firm can make you stand out. How do you get around this problem without taking up all your time? The best place to personalize the letter is in the sentence where you describe why you'd like to work at the firm. Write a good "base" sentence and change that sentence slightly for each letter. Of course, this involves knowing a few facts about each firm. Here are some examples.

> *Base sentence*
> I am pursuing an analyst position in investment banking. I am particularly interested in . . .
> *Tailored*
> . . . Booz•Allen & Company's small size and collegial atmosphere.
> . . . Merrill Lynch's global reach and expertise in many product areas.

> *Base sentence*
> I am particularly excited about working for [Company XYZ] after attending your information session on campus. I was impressed by [Company XYZ's traits].
> *Tailored*
> I am particularly excited about working for Monitor Company after attending your information session on campus. I was impressed by Monitor's innovative approach to managing people.

Keep in mind that you also can tailor your letter to specific criteria that you think the firm is looking for: entrepreneurial attitude, individualism, and so on. Firms have varying cultural preferences, and after you read a few brochures these will begin to stand out.

DON'T MAKE LAUNDRY LISTS

A very common mistake people make is to get so carried away with the cover letter that they begin to list all their characteristics, which coincidentally happen to match all those the firm has said they are seeking. After reading this list, readers are left with no impression at all—in fact, they can't even remember anything about you. It's better to pick one or two traits and really emphasize them than say you have it all.

TONE

Check for things that come across the wrong way. Showing the letter to your friends or to a career counselor is a good way to do this. Here are some tips:

- Exhibit confidence, not obvious exaggeration: Confidence is saying "I contributed to the SEC's pursuit of insider traders"; exaggeration is saying "I caught an insider trader."
- Avoid the dramatic: "Few candidates share my desire for this job," or "Rescued the company from probable disaster."
- Don't suggest that you're desperate, because firms like people with an aura of success: "Please give me the chance to interview with you," or "I have been pursuing an investment banking job for months."
- Don't try to make expert statements, because they're only going to come across as both obvious and pretentious: "The realities of global consulting demand that your consultants be comfortable in an international setting."
- Don't kiss up too obviously: "I want to work for the company that was able to recognize your intellect" or "My ultimate accomplishment would be to work for McKinsey & Co."

On pages 162 and 163 are examples of our cover letter principles at work. "John Tucker" believes that the recruiter's key concerns about him will be that:

- He doesn't attend a brand-name school where the firm recruits, so his analytical skills and raw intelligence will be in question.
- He is a psychology major and may not have good business sense or an understanding of business fundamentals.

John comes across differently depending on how he writes his letter.

In the "After" version, John subtly addresses the recruiter's potential concerns about his analytical skills and business experience. He replaces his endless list of qualifications with two specific selling points: evidence of his analytical and quantitative skills, and previous consulting experience. He also compensates for the fact that he's not attending a "brand-name" school by adding an element of prestige to his résumé—he mentions an award he has won and the fact that he has been selected for a postgraduation position at the Bright Consulting Group.

"Before" Cover Letter

John Tucker
302 Rose Street
Kingstown, MA 01267

Tracy Ellis
Ace Consulting
50 W. 50th St.
NY, NY 10004

Most prefer "Ms."

Not necessary

Dear Miss Ellis,

Members of your firm suggested that I send my resume to you.

I am currently in my senior year at King College, and I will earn my B.A. degree in Psychology in June of next year. I became interested in management consulting after taking Organizational Behavior, a class which deals with subjects such as managing diversity, creating initiatives, and business culture. I then took Social Implications of Technology, a course which deals with the economic, social, and political consequences of technology, including risk assessment and decision analysis. For this class, I wrote a paper on President Clinton's national technology policy, specifically on the pros and cons of Laura Tyson's view that the government should subsidize high-tech industries.

I have completed and enjoyed several team projects, and feel that I work well in such environments. My courses and research experiences have provided me with strong analytical skills and much practice in problem-solving. In addition, I believe I have the written and verbal communications skills necessary to perform the job well. Although my GPA is not high, my grades have increased significantly this year. I am enthusiastic about consulting and would like to apply my skills to the field.

I have read Ace's brochure and am excited about opportunities at your firm. I must admit I am shocked, but Ace's approach to consulting seems very innovative. The enclosed resume provides details of my education and experience. I would appreciate the opportunity for an interview at your convenience. I can be reached at 222-222-2222. Thank you for your consideration.

Sincerely,

John Tucker

Number is already on résumé

Doesn't suggest next steps

Doesn't get to point quickly

Doesn't explain why he's interested in consulting

Don't need to explain this course; recruiter can figure it out

It's not clear why this is relevant to the job

Endless list of traits is forgettable

Seems like a form letter; no particular interest in Ace; waits until end of letter to say why he's writing

"Shocked" is overly dramatic

"After" Cover Letter

John Tucker
302 Rose Street
Kingstown, MA 01267

Tracy Ellis
Ace Consulting Inc.
50 W. 50th St.
NY, NY 10004 ——— **Preferred title**

Dear Ms. Ellis,

I will graduate in June 1999 with a B.A. in Political Psychology from Kings College. I am interested in applying for a position as an Analyst at Ace Consulting, Inc.

States purpose of letter at beginning

My interest in management consulting has grown out of the courses in business and organizational behavior that I have taken over the past few years. I would like to gain exposure to critical strategic decisions made by companies in a broad range of industries. I am particularly interested in a position at Ace Consulting because of its fast growth and recognized strength in strategy consulting.

More concise; explains why interested in consulting and why Ace

I can contribute to this position previous consulting experience and strong analytical skills. I have worked successfully with a team of classmates to produce a national award-winning psychology study. I have used statistical and other quantitative analysis extensively in both my coursework and my work at the Bright Consulting Group, where I assessed the profitability of expansion plans for a client in the communications industry. I am one of two interns that Bright has invited to rejoin the firm upon graduation. My grades have increased significantly and steadily since freshman year.

Picks a few succinct selling points

Emphasizes quantitative skills; points out increase in grades; hints at caliber of analytical work by mentioning award

I would enjoy speaking with you further about the possibility of an Analyst position at Ace. I have enclosed a resume and will call you next week to follow up on this letter. Thank you for your consideration.

Sincerely,

John Tucker

Suggests next steps

How to Put Your Cover Letter to Work

The cover letter presents an opportunity to (1) answer any concerns a recruiter might have and (2) leave key points in the recruiter's mind to remember you by.

Don't fool yourself. While he's reading your cover letter, the recruiter is subconsciously checking for the absence or presence of critical skills. Reread the critical skills list in Chapter 6 and put yourself in the recruiter's shoes. Which of these skills is noticeably missing from your resume? Is there any chance of displaying these skills in your cover letter? Are there two key points that you want the recruiter to remember about you? The key here is subtlety and appropriateness; a common mistake is to come right out and say that you're intelligent or tactful, thus defeating the purpose.

The following concerns are well-suited to being addressed in the cover letter:

Potential concern: You're a top candidate; how badly do you want to work at *our* firm?

Imply answer in cover letter: You've talked to many people to learn about the firm; you've done research on the firm and are able to explain persuasively why you want to work there; you've put a lot of thought into the cover letter.

Potential concern: You're an art history major with little business experience. How interested are you in business?

Imply answer in cover letter: You explain your interest in the industry persuasively and it seems well thought out and genuine; you give several reasons why you want to work in the industry; you *briefly* highlight relevant aspects of one job you've held that might otherwise not seem related to banking or consulting.

Potential concern: Your résumé suggests strong quantitative skills but not communications or interpersonal skills. How well can you communicate and work with others?

Imply answer in cover letter: You articulate complex thoughts clearly and use clear and logical progression in the letter; you *briefly* mention teaching or other experiences that depend heavily on good communications and people skills.

Potential concern: Your math SAT score is low and you are an English major. How strong are your quantitative skills?

Imply answer in cover letter: You highlight a summer job or class you've had that has involved quantitative analysis (without making it too obvious that this is an area of weakness).

WRITING A WINNING RÉSUMÉ

The résumé is the most important job-hunting document you will write. It is the document most frequently used to compare you against other candidates.

Plan enough time to edit it three or four times before sending it out. Put it aside for a time; you'll invariably recognize potential edits a few days later that you couldn't see before.

This section goes over résumé tips specific to the investment banking and management consulting industries. For more basic information, consult your career counseling center. Unfortunately, the résumés displayed in most reference books are inappropriate for management consulting or investment banking. If you must use such a guide, choose the most conservative sample résumé.

FORMAT

Your résumé should be single-spaced and in a standard business format. Your name, address, and phone number should always be at the top. Arrange your experiences in some logical order, preferably reverse chronological order (most recent to least recent). If you are currently a student, place your education section first; if you have been out of school and working for a while, place your employment experience first.

BE DIRECT

Highlight the *results* or *achievements* of your action. Unlike the cover letter, the résumé shouldn't imply what you want to say; it should be as direct as possible since you need to pack a lot of punch into limited space.

Avoid jargon or technical language if it obscures your point.

Unclear: "Analyzed critical issues as an input for the company's executive visioning session and validated product ideas in alignment with the newly formed corporate vision."

Direct: "Selected issues for executive strategy meeting after in-depth analysis. Used new corporate strategy to validate product ideas."

COVER THE BASICS

Include the following information in your résumé:

- Education
- Experience (could be titled *Employment, Work Experience,* or *Business Experience*)
- Activities (could be titled *Leadership, Volunteer Experience,* or *Extracurricular Activities*)
- Skills (could be titled *Language Skills, Skills and Activities,* or *Additional Information*)

Combine or separate these categories in a manner that best displays your credentials. Don't list an objective at the top of your résumé. This is not standard practice in the consulting or banking industries. Poorly worded or mistaken objectives will cost you the chance to interview, as in the case of the person who wrote to a consulting firm asking for an engineering position. It's not worth the risk.

What to Do If Your Grades Suck

Undergraduate grades are carefully scrutinized, and it will be tough to get a job in consulting or investment banking with a GPA lower than 3.0. However, you don't need a 4.0. The academic performance "bar" depends on the firm. In general, strategy consulting firms tend to be pickiest about your grades. Sales and trading departments care less about grades.

So what can you do to put your grades in a more positive light? Never misstate your grades. But as long as you still list your overall GPA, you can list additional "cuts" at your GPA in order to point out a trend that the recruiter might miss:

- Let's say that you have a rising trend in grades but had a bad sophomore year; you received a 3.3, 2.8, 3.5, and 3.7 in your four years. List your total GPA (3.32), but next to it, highlight your average for your last two years by stating, "GPA during junior and senior years: 3.6."
- Good performance in business, economics, or other quantitative classes will earn you a lot of points among businesspeople, who tend to value the "hard" subjects. If you are an English major but did well in your two Economics classes, calculate your GPA in these classes and list it. You could state, "GPA in Economics classes: 3.7."
- If your major was in a quantitative or business subject and you did well, list your "GPA in Major."

Experience

This section trips people up most often. Candidates become anxious, so they lose perspective and overexplain. Their "experience" section becomes long, disorganized, and unclear.

This section should include summer internships and jobs you have held. Include paid jobs you have held during the school year. Nonpaid extracurricular activities should be included in "Extracurricular Activities," unless they are business-related and relevant to the job to which you're applying (e.g., business manager of the campus newspaper). Unfortunately, recruiters consider certain jobs "menial"; do not list them on your résumé unless you were a manager or accomplished something very impressive. These jobs include janitorial work or work at McDonald's, Taco Bell, and other fast-food restaurants.

Each sentence in your "Experience" section should have a purpose: If you can't explain why the sentence in some way enhances your image, don't include it. Highlight what you accomplished or were responsible for. If you were recognized by your boss in any way or were asked to return the next summer with increased responsibilities, mention it. Recruiters love evidence of success and accomplishment.

One of the hardest things to do is to omit experiences altogether. But if you have plenty of meaty jobs to include and you're stretching the margins to squeeze in "secretarial position" at the bottom of the résumé, forget it. Just leave it out.

Recruiters will be thinking: What in your professional background has prepared you for the job? Have you been recognized for performing well at other jobs? Do you exhibit the business sense, motivation, and analytical skills that the firm is looking for? How well are you able to explain what you've done? How well are you able to organize information?

Activities

This section should include nonpaid activities performed outside of the classroom or outside of work. Unlike the "Experience" section, this section can be arranged in order of significance to you rather than in reverse chronological order. Choose carefully which activities to highlight and what image of yourself you want to create. Do you want to create an image of a well-rounded team player? Then list your soccer experience first. Do you want to seem as if you are intensely interested in business? If so, place your management of the school T-shirt business at the top. Avoid listing only solitary activities, such as running or photography—they will make it seem that you don't like interacting in groups.

One good strategy is to look at the image you've created in your "Experience" section and make sure that image is balanced in your "Activities" section. If you seem highly intellectual in your "Experience" section, make sure you seem personable and outgoing in your "Activities" section. Another good strategy is to think about the people you've met already from the firm you're applying to and project an image that is similar to them. If you've met a lot of jocks at the company, make sure to list some sports in your "Activities" or "Personal" section.

Recruiters will be thinking: How high is your energy level? Have you become involved in interests in the environment outside your work or classroom? Have you shown leadership by being elected by others? Are you a well-rounded person? Is there evidence that you have strong interpersonal and communications skills? Have you worked or played in teams? How consistent have you been over the years in your interests and activities? What activities are important enough to you that you've highlighted them? What are your values?

Skills

In this section, list any relevant skills, training, or knowledge you possess, including foreign languages. If you are computer literate, explain exactly which programming languages or software packages you are familiar with (e.g., C+ +, Microsoft Word, Excel, Lotus, etc.). Don't overstate language ability, as you may be tested on your ability during an interview. One way to get around this is to list languages without specifying level: "Languages: French, Spanish."

Recruiters will quickly skim the "Skills" section for something unusual or interesting and will be asking themselves these questions: Do you have any special skills or speak any foreign languages that match with our business interests? Do these skills provide insight into your choices and values?

But don't be overly concerned if you don't have a laundry list of skills; this section is one of the least important on the résumé. You'll be learning on the job anyway.

Personal

This section is optional, although it's frequently used. This is the place to convey a bit of your personality and show that you are a well-rounded individual who doesn't hide in a cave all day. Mention details that don't fit in elsewhere. If you have lived or traveled overseas, financed your own college education, done four years of volunteer work, or won a chess championship and couldn't fit it into other sections, put it here. Especially good are personal details that convey the qualities the firm is seeking but that you couldn't communicate elsewhere—such as integrity, responsibility, or teamwork. Be wary, though, of listing endless hobbies and being vague. How many times do you think recruiters see "skier and jogger" or "traveled extensively through Europe"? It's better to mention fewer things and be more specific.

Do not include any information that would notify the recruiter of your marital status, children, sexual orientation, national origin, health problems, disabilities, or other personal details.

Honors

Create a separate "Honors" section only if you have won several, and place this section near the "Education" paragraph. Otherwise, wrap your honors into the "Personal" or "Education" section.

References

If you are currently working at a job and are seeking to leave the company, put "References available upon request" at the bottom of your résumé. This will address concerns that you have performed poorly and are leaving involuntarily. It is unlikely that anyone will even follow up on your offer (but just in case, have a few colleagues ready). Students do *not* need to offer references.

TAILORING YOUR RÉSUMÉ FOR INVESTMENT
BANKING AND CONSULTING

If you're applying to more than one industry, write several versions of your résumé, one for each industry. If you're applying to both consulting and investment banking, have two different résumés, each edited slightly to give a different impression. Put your finance coursework at the top of your investment banking résumé and your strategic planning coursework on your consulting résumé. Make prominent the activities, courses, and experience that are most relevant to each job. What if your earliest summer job was with the neighborhood bank and is the most relevant to an investment banking position? Instead of using reverse chronological order, use chronological order so that the investment banker's eye hits the neighborhood bank internship first.

When writing a résumé for a *consulting firm,* emphasize these qualities:

- Evidence of scholarship or intellectual curiosity, such as independent research or thesis
- Analytical ability and experience
- Activities that are communications-based, such as teaching or public speaking
- Entrepreneurial or small-business activities that taught you business fundamentals
- Liking for travel (under "Personal" section)
- Jobs that required you to work well with other people
- Foreign languages

When writing a résumé for an *investment banking* or *sales and trading* department, emphasize:

- Business and highly quantitative courses
- Teamwork, especially through team sports
- Natural leadership ability and interpersonal skills, especially through *elected* positions
- Salesmanship, through sales positions
- Previous experience or interest in finance
- Ability to carry heavy workload, such as hours per week worked on extracurricular activities and jobs (if impressive)
- Ability to juggle many tasks at once

To demonstrate how packaging can triumph over content, let's look at John Tucker again. In his "before" résumé, John does not sell himself enough by making his accomplishments stand out. Instead, he buries his achievements in long-winded sentences and lackluster verbs.

In his "after" résumé, John rearranges information to highlight relevant experience and accomplishments. Just as in the cover letter, he is addressing

"Before" Résumé

John Tucker
302 Rose Street
Kingstown, MA 01267
(222) 222-2222

EDUCATION

Kings College, 1995–1999. Bachelor of Arts in Psychology expected in June 1999. Dean's List. GPA: 3.3/4.0. Courses include Organizational Behavior, Social Implications of Technology. ← Not as concise as it could be

WORK EXPERIENCE

CleanGreen Lawn Mowing Service, Washington, D.C.
Lawn attendant, August 1998.
After one week of training, I began mowing lawns throughout the suburban DC areas. I established a system of mass mailing, securing approximately $2,000 in new business. ← Sounds like a narrative; lacks punch

Bright Consulting Group, Washington, D.C.
Summer Intern, June–July 1998.
I analyzed competitive strategies for clients in the communications industry. Gathered data, assessed profitability of strategies. ← More relevant experience is placed second

Securities & Exchange Commission, Washington, D.C.
Research Assistant, June–August 1997.
Researched records to come up with evidence for cases. Assessed effects on stock price of insiders selling their stock. Demonstrated quantitative skills by developing spreadsheets and graphs. ← Awkward; should mention evidence of quantitative skills, not just say he has them

ACTIVITIES

Writing Tutor, 1996–present
Hold walk-in hours two times a week to help other students revise papers.

Treasurer of Student Council, 1998–1999
Passed a $300,000 budget; negotiated with administration; organized new tutoring system for sophomores. ← Activity more relevant to business is placed second

Kings College Crew
Member since freshman year. Competed in varsity eight since 1997; team has 8–3 record. Captain, spring 1998 to present.

ADDITIONAL INFORMATION

Interests include jogging and art history. Won Bradburd National ← Prestigious award is buried here
Psychology Award. Lived overseas for 4 years during high school.

"After" Résumé

John Tucker
302 Rose Street
Kingstown, MA 01267
(222) 222-2222

EDUCATION

B.A. in Psychology, Kings College, June 1999. Dean's List six of eight semesters. GPA: 3.3/4.0. GPA in Major: 3.6/4.0. Courses include Statistics, Finance, and Organizational Behavior. Awarded Bradburd National Psychology Award for outstanding student paper of the year, 1997.

Puts his grades in more positive light; moves up award

WORK EXPERIENCE

Bright Consulting Group, Washington, D.C.
Summer Intern, Summer 1998.
Assessed profitability of expansion strategy for client in the communication industry; results used by client to make market entry decision. Gathered data through interviews, built spreadsheet, created slides for presentation to client.

By not specifying months, he can place this job first

CleanGreen Lawn Mowing Service, Washington, D.C.
Lawn Attendant, Summer 1998.
Managed accounts throughout the suburban D.C. area. Implemented a mass advertisement mailing that won $2,000 in new business.

Highlights results and responsibility

Securities & Exchange Commission, Washington, D.C.
Research Assistant, Summer 1997.
researched transaction records to build evidence for insider trading cases. Assessed effects on stock prices of executives' stock sales. Developed Excel spreadsheets to analyze stock price movements.

Clearer

ACTIVITIES

Treasurer of Student Council, Kings College, 1998–1999
Won a $300,000 budget through negotiations with college administration; organized new tutoring system for sophomores.

New verbs are more dynamic

Kings College Crew, 1995–present
Elected Captain in spring 1998. Competed in varsity eight since 1997; team has 8-3 record. During season, entails commitment of 20 hours per week.

Emphasizes elected position; explains time commitment

Writing Tutor, 1996–present
Hold walk-in hours two times a week to help other students revise papers.

ADDITIONAL INFORMATION

Interests include art history and basketball. Lived in Japan for 4 years during high school.

Adds one team-oriented activity; specifies which country he lived in the recruiter's potential concerns that he does not have strong analytical skills or business experience. He rewords descriptions to make them sound more impressive.

FOLLOWING UP

Students at targeted schools should follow the standard recruiting process—the firm or the school placement center will call to notify you that you have been selected for an interview. It is best to wait for this notification. The recruiting coordinator will be annoyed that you among hundreds of students feel that you can't wait the standard time for a response.

If you are a "nontargeted" candidate and have sent your résumé to the recruiting coordinator, give the firm two weeks to respond before following up.

Whether you're a targeted or nontargeted candidate, if there are special circumstances that you absolutely must discuss with the company before they were planning to get back to you, call the recruiter and explain your situation very politely. For example, you may have received an "exploding offer" from another firm and may need a response more quickly than usual. Or perhaps you need to leave campus unexpectedly during scheduled interviews and will need to make special arrangements if you're chosen for an interview. Recruiters are generally very understanding of these situations.

Those Pesky Rejections: How to Make the Most of Them

So you've been rejected for an interview. It happens to everyone. Instead of seeing the situation as depressing, try to learn something from your rejections. While most rejections are simply due to competitive odds, you can do some follow-up research to determine whether there is a consistent reason for your rejections. Here's what you can do:

- **Reread the letter and résumé you're sending out.** Rather than continuing to send out a letter that's been unsuccessful, why not review it with a career counselor at your alma mater or at the school you're currently attending? Get some feedback as to what might be causing a problem.
- **Get feedback from a recruiter.** Some recruiters are very willing to provide feedback to rejected students. If your résumé has been rejected, ask the recruiter for an honest critique and suggestions for improvement.

~ 8 ~

BEFORE THE INTERVIEW

... Your first [investment banking] interview might begin with the interviewer asking you to open the window. You were on the forty-third floor overlooking Water Street. The window was sealed shut. That was, of course, the point. The interviewer just wanted to see whether your inability to comply with his request led you to yank, pull, and sweat until finally you melted into a puddle of foiled ambition. Or, as one sad applicant was rumored to have done, threw a chair through the window.

—Michael Lewis, *Liar's Poker*

You dropped your résumé off at the campus career center, and you now receive notice that you're being invited to a first-round interview on campus. The first-round interview is the first in a series of hurdles that you'll need to jump in order to get a job at an investment bank or consulting firm. But take heart—your odds of getting a job have greatly improved since the résumé screening stage. Your chance of progressing from the first round to the next round is close to one in five.

This chapter covers how to prepare for the interview and explains the "soft" skills—communications, clothing, and etiquette—you will need to succeed in an interview. Chapters 9 and 10 focus on the content of the interview: what to say, how to answer specific questions, later-round interviews, and the consulting case question.

In this book, I encourage you to act conservatively during the interview process. Does this mean that all banks and consulting firms are humorless and hidebound? No. But you never know who will be offended by what, and it's better not to take a chance. Play it safe first, and take your risks *after* you've gotten the offer.

Some things have changed since the 1980s, when Michael Lewis penned his memorable description of the Lehman Brothers interview. Consulting firms and investment banks now put on a kinder, gentler face toward students during recruiting. The stress interview is all but gone.

Of course, other "sealed windows" will stand between you and the job. Interviewers walk into interviews with a checklist of skills that they are looking for in a candidate, which we explore later in depth. Typically the interview will be organized into sections testing these different skills. The chart on the next page presents the basic structure of the interview. The segments of the interview will be explained in Chapter 9.

During the interview, the interviewer probably will let you do 75 percent or more of the talking. If you're not familiar with how the first-round interview fits into the overall recruiting process, this may be a good point to review Chapter 5.

LOGISTICS

The company will notify you if you are being invited for a first-round interview. On-campus candidates typically receive a notice from their campus career centers, which manage the interviewing logistics on behalf of recruiting firms. Candidates outside the campus recruiting process will receive a phone call.

Generally, you are given several interview times to choose from. Don't take the first time slot mentioned to you! Your interview order can have a major impact on your chances of making it to the next round. Before you decide on a time, ask the recruiter whether there will be many other candidates interviewing at the firm that day or if you will be the only person seen that day. If you're being squeezed into a day of interviewing with other candidates, you will be competing for attention. One pattern holds true for most interviewers: They remember early candidates and later candidates best. Avoid choosing a slot in the middle of the day, especially since you might be close to an interviewer's lunch hour. Also, try not to get the very first interview of the day, since the interviewer will be the most critical at that point.

One more important scheduling point: If you are applying through an on-campus recruiting process, submit your résumé to a firm or two that you consider less desirable than your top choice. If you are lucky enough to get interviews with several firms, you will then have a few "practice" interviews before your meeting with your top-choice firm. A practice run-through is valuable because interview responses will definitely be rusty the first time they come out of your mouth.

If you are traveling to the company's office, make sure to ask the recruiter for very specific directions, including parking, traffic, and travel time informa-

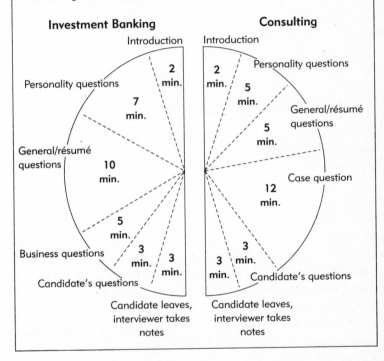

The First-Round Interview

Place: The office (for students at nontargeted schools) or on campus (for students at targeted schools)

Length: From 30 to 45 minutes

People: Conducted by one or two interviewers, usually associates or managers

Purpose: An assessment to weed out easiest "no's" and narrow down the pool for further interviewing. Investment banks will assess personality, energy, and interest in finance; most consulting firms will assess analytical skills through the case question.

tion. Plan on arriving at the office at least fifteen minutes ahead of schedule. Being late for an interview is likely to get you rejected, unless a major disaster prevented you from being on time.

ACTING YOUR WAY THROUGH

Succeeding in an interview requires a good acting performance. Recruiters like people who are similar to themselves: They look for a "pattern" of backgrounds that have been successful in the past at their company. And unfortunately, often they are misled by surface impressions, by the fact that some candidates *look* and *act* like themselves.

Acting is the operative word. To psych yourself up for an interview, picture a stereotype of a consultant or banker. If you have any doubt as to how a banker or consultant speaks or acts, attend a campus information session and watch the presenters carefully—their way of communicating, moving, and dressing. Now, try to adapt some of these characteristics. Avoid saying "like" and other speech patterns that give away how old you are. Carry yourself with maturity, and keep your emotions under control. Imagine that you are in a situation in which you must lead a meeting with senior executives. How would you act out this situation? Walk into your interview with this scenario in mind. You are managing your image to conform to the image the recruiters want. Of course, you still want your natural personality and warmth to shine through.

HEADLINING

Interviewers aren't perfect. They are fallible human beings, and often they make mistakes during the interview process. Put yourself in the recruiter's shoes: You spend eight hours in a row interviewing one student after another, asking the same questions all day. It's hard to even remember candidates' names and faces at the end of the day, not to mention what they said. Frankly, many interviewers find their minds wandering when they are especially tired or bored. Sometimes you literally can see their eyes glazing over. Events that are important to you, the candidate, aren't as important to the interviewer. Candidates magnify every event that happens in an interview, both positive and negative. In reality, the interviewer either didn't notice or didn't care.

Much of the interviewer's assessment, whether he admits it or not, is subjective. Interviewers quickly make up their minds whether they like you as a person and whether you have "presence," and this will make the difference between two candidates who are equally qualified.

The bottom line: You need to make a lasting impression on an interviewer so that all other applicants pale in comparison. To do this, don't approach the interview passively, taking whatever questions are thrown your way; approach it actively with a clear agenda for the interview.

What's your agenda? Come up with *headlines*—a few key points about yourself that will influence the interviewer. Prepare headlines in advance and back each headline up with a well-chosen anecdote that is interesting enough to help the interviewer understand and remember the headline.

Do you want the interviewer to know that you are exceptionally motivated and hardworking? Slip in an anecdote that mentions you worked your way through college. Want him to know that this is absolutely your top-choice firm? Say that you've been talking to friends at the firm for a year about what distinguishes that firm from others. It's up to you to choose which stories to tell about yourself. The key is to slip in points about yourself during *appropriate* moments, not to force them on the interviewer obviously or awkwardly.

The Interview Preparation Worksheet

What is my "story" of why I want to work in this field?

How did I develop an interest in this field?

Why am I interested in this firm?

What headlines about my personality do I want to imply?	How will I communicate these?
•	•
•	•
•	•

What headlines about my analytical skills do I want to imply?	How will I communicate these?
•	•
•	•
•	

What headlines about my business sense and knowledge do I want to imply?	How will I communicate these?
•	•
•	•
•	

What questions about the company will I ask at the end of the interview?

Use the Interview Preparation Worksheet to develop your headlines. Then check your headlines against:

- The skills the firms are looking for—your headlines should suggest that you have these skills;
- The questions firms ask during the interview—so that you have an idea of when you can slip in your headlines;
- The characteristics of the firm you're interviewing with—so that you can tailor your headlines to fit the firm.

You can do this by reviewing the critical skills list in Chapter 6, the interview questions in Chapters 9 and 10, and the company profiles at the end of the book.

The Actor's Wardrobe

Actors must have the right wardrobe and physical image to persuade the audience that they are who they are supposed to be. Job-hunters also must have a credible appearance; they need to look like consultants or investment bankers. The key here is to be attractive and stylish in a very understated, classic way. You want to look conservative, not plain. Pick clothes that won't distract you or your interviewer: If you're constantly tugging at clothes that are uncomfortable, you won't be focused on your performance. Here I outline the safest route in terms of clothing so that you don't accidentally disqualify yourself:

- Play it safe, and stay conservative. Investment banks in particular are bastions of traditional dress.
- Flashy is not good. Avoid easily identifiable brand names and designer clothing or accessories, especially if you're an undergraduate.
- Invest in one high-quality suit. Women may have to spend about $200 to $300 on a suit, and men $300 to $500. Think of it this way: You'll get a lot of use out of this suit, and you'll be able to wear it again once you've gotten a job.
- Your hair, nails, and clothes should look clean and neat. Put a lint remover and a brush or comb in your briefcase, and use them before you walk into the interview or into the company's offices. Always use the restroom before the interview and check to make sure everything is in place. Wear deodorant!
- **Women:** Do not wear pants, just to be safe, even if part of an expensive pants suit. Suits are preferable to dresses, and suit skirts should not be more than one inch above the knee. Suits should be blue, black, or gray. Avoid pastels or other "feminine" colors. Suits should be long-sleeved and fairly conservative. Match your hose to your suit or wear nude-colored hose. Keep an extra pair in your briefcase—your hose will run.

  Match your shoes to your suit or wear black shoes. Shoes should be made of leather or patent leather, in a conservative style. Wear 1- to 2-inch heels if you can walk in them—remember, you may have to walk briskly to a restaurant with your interviewers for lunch. Keep a pair of flats in your briefcase in which you can walk to the interview. Make sure your makeup and jewelry are subdued. Makeup should be used only to make you look healthy and energetic—don't look like you're going out on a date, and don't wear bright lipstick. Dangling earrings and perfume are not considered professional.
- **Men:** Wear dark suits, single-breasted. Polyester and seersucker are unacceptable. Your shirt should be long-sleeved, cotton, and either blue or white. Avoid bow ties, and instead wear a standard tie that doesn't look cheap and isn't too avant-garde. No suspenders, monograms, French-cuff shirts, or anything flashy or used by older men. Facial hair and earrings are frowned upon. Shoes should be in black or brown leather in a conservative style. Wear simple, dark dress socks that reach far enough up your leg that when you sit down, no flesh is showing. Do not wear cologne or after-shave.

THE DRESS REHEARSAL

It's hard for most people to know what tics they have, whether they say "umm" frequently or rock back and forth in their chair when they are nervous. The most important preparation you can do is to go through a dress rehearsal with a friend playing the role of interviewer. Make your real interview *the second time* you explain your thoughts out loud. The smoother you seem, the smarter you'll seem, and the appearance of confidence is critical to landing a job.

Work out your answers to the questions listed in Chapters 9 and 10, then give a friend the list. Tape-record your conversation. Ask your practice interviewer for his impressions of your style: Did you seem genuine? Did you seem nervous? Were you so long-winded that you lost the interviewer's interest? Did you seem energized? On these softer issues, your friend will have some good input. Afterward, listen to the tape and be alert for nervous speech habits or answers that were unclear. Think about how to rephrase an answer so that it fits critical skills listed in Chapter 6.

To practice management consulting "case" questions, try to find a consultant or an experienced businessperson to play the role of interviewer. Use the case questions listed in Chapter 10, and ask your practice interviewer to lead you through the steps in each question as best as possible.

The form on the next page is a good approximation of one that interviewers will use to evaluate you. Try to demonstrate skills in many of these categories during your interview. Ask the friend giving you a practice interview to fill this out, or listen to the tape afterward and evaluate yourself.

THE DAY BEFORE

If you haven't yet, make sure you find out (1) what the company does, (2) how it's different from its competitors, (3) three reasons why you want to work for the company as opposed to its competitors, and (4) five questions to ask the interviewer. If you're really in a rush, the fastest way to answer these questions is to check the company profiles at the back of this book for information on specific firms, and surf the Web and visit the firm's individual site. You can do this preparation easily in an hour or two. Of course, if you're going in for a second- or third-round interview, you should do additional research and preparation.

Make sure to get a lot of sleep the night before the interview and even a few nights before that if possible. Get your preparation and "dress rehearsal" done a day or two early so that you can relax the night before the interview. Do something fun with friends to take your mind off the interview; you'll come across as more rested, positive, and confident the next day.

The Critics Review You

Ever wondered what happens after you walk out of your interview and close the door behind you? Interviewers fill out an evaluation form, which they use to compare candidates at the end of the day.

Interview Evaluation Form

Candidate Name:　　　　　　Date:
School/Employer:　　　　　　Interviewer:
Round:　　　　　　　　　　　Location:

GPA:　　　　SATs:　　　　GMAT:
Location Preferences:

	Outstanding	Good	Average	Poor
COMMUNICATIONS/ INTERPERSONAL	4	3	2	1

Team player, mature, confident, listener, articulate, influential, tactful, tolerant, positive. Reasons:

PROBLEM-SOLVING SKILLS	4	3	2	1

Quantitative, analytical, logical, hypothesis-driven, structured, creative. Reasons:

MANAGEMENT/WORK SKILLS	4	3	2	1

Hardworking, quick learner, organized, good manager, facilitator, juggles multiple tasks. Reasons:

FIT WITH INDUSTRY AND JOB	4	3	2	1

Enthusiastic, experienced, knowledgeable, good business sense, fits with firm, ethical. Reasons:

CLIENT SOLUTIONS	4	3	2	1

Works well with people, practical, results-driven, develops relationships, dedicated to client. Reasons:

	Yes	Maybe Yes	Maybe No	No
OVERALL RATING	4	3	2	1

Did you focus on any particular area?
Key decision criteria/comments/concerns:
Where else does candidate have offers?
Things to test further during next round:

BEFORE YOU WALK IN

If you travel to an office for an interview, you'll probably look a little wind-blown when you arrive. Get there a little early so that you can go to the restroom, comb your hair, and take a deep breath if necessary. Relax, and view this as a fun opportunity to exercise your acting skills and meet some interesting people; remember to visualize yourself as an executive attending an important business meeting. And remember, the world will not end if you don't get the job. If you go in to the interview thinking that this is a life-and-death situation, chances are you will psych yourself out.

DURING THE PERFORMANCE

ATTITUDE

Don't complain or be too negative about anything, even when asked for your "honest" opinion of something. Focus on the positives of all your past experiences—doing so will make you seem like an optimist who makes the best of any situation.

COMMUNICATIONS SKILLS

The unfortunate fact is that interviewers, just like the rest of us, judge messages based not only on content but on delivery. Your interviewer will be deeply influenced by your communications and interpersonal skills, whether he admits it or not. Be aware of the way you communicate and the effect this has on the interviewer. No matter how obnoxious the interviewer is, try to find some redeeming quality about him. Really like the person as if he were a friend. Why is this important? Interviewers like candidates with whom they feel some sort of rapport. Your attitude toward the interviewer will come across on your face and will make or break that rapport.

Nonverbal Communication

- **Eye contact:** Looking at the interviewer strengthens the point you are making. Maintain fairly steady eye contact with the interviewer, especially when you are making a statement where your credibility might be questioned (e.g., ethical dilemma, interest in job). If you are thinking over a question, it's okay to look down or away for a few seconds, because this suggests reflection. When looking at the interviewer, never try to look into both his eyes at the same time; instead, shift your gaze from one eye to the other in order to signal warmth and sincerity.
- **Facial expression:** You want to come across as a happy, well-balanced person, because firms like happy people. Smile occasionally as if you have no worries in the world, and don't let the interviewer read nervousness all over your face. Some interviewers will watch your face for signs of emotions.
- **Gestures:** Subconscious movements, such as waving your arms to make a point, folding a piece of paper, or playing with your hair, are distracting to the interviewer. In addition, they may come off as a sign of nervousness or dishonesty when you're answering difficult questions. Sit up

straight in your chair; slumping conveys a sloppy, laid-back attitude. Lean forward when you want to seem excited or interested.

Verbal Communication

- **Pace:** Many interviewees speed up when they're nervous, and their words become slurred. Pausing for effect will heighten the listener's interest in what you're saying.
- **Space-fillers:** Don't be afraid of silence. Space-fillers like "umm," "uh-huh," "you know," and "like" are both distracting and unprofessional. They also make you seem young.
- **Logic:** At all times, keep in mind the question you're supposed to be answering; if you use a lengthy example, remember to tie the example back to the question. Doing so makes it seem that you had an organized approach to your answer, even if you didn't.
- **Amount:** Cut yourself off when you've made your point. Don't let yourself recite information in five different ways.

Are You a Poor Listener?

The following are bad listening habits that you should be aware of:

- Caring too much about what you're thinking so that you listen only briefly before starting to prepare your own reply while the other person is still talking.
- Losing your concentration and letting your mind wander.
- Letting the physical environment you're in distract you: temperature, noise, clutter, etc.
- Finishing someone else's sentence, because you're impatient.
- Not watching and listening for clues that someone has ended a thought, and interrupting the person.
- Relating everything you see and hear to yourself and letting your own experiences filter what the other person is saying.
- Caring about who the person is instead of what the person is saying: "He looks like someone my age, so he must not know much about consulting."
- Not paying attention to body language, facial expressions, and other non-verbal cues.
- Not answering the question asked.
- Making assumptions about the speaker's goals.

ETIQUETTE

What is considered acceptable in other business fields may not be considered acceptable in investment banking or consulting. The following points will help you brush up your etiquette.

- Don't talk too much about money or perks.
- Crudeness or foul language is not acceptable during the interview, even if you're bonding with the guys. You never know who's going to take offense.
- Just in case, use politically correct terms. Use "women" instead of "girls," and so on.
- Don't sit down until the interviewer asks you to or until he has done so.
- Posing overly tough or critical questions is impolite.
- Be *really* nice to the secretaries or administrators in the office. Besides the fact that this is the right thing to do, it will have an impact on how you're evaluated.
- Don't delve into extremely personal topics or preferences, such as your love life—either yours or the interviewer's.
- Thank the interviewer for his time at the end of the session.

SPIN CONTROL

Too many qualified people rule themselves out because they *think* they lack raw material: They think to themselves, "I haven't had any real leadership experience," or "My business experience isn't as good as John's is." Let's destroy this myth right now—everyone doubts themselves at some point, no matter how great their accomplishments. Those who get jobs are the ones who can put a positive spin on their background. To demonstrate the power of packaging, here is an example of the same accomplishment described in two different ways:

Let's say you were asked the question: *How have you exercised leadership skills during college?*

Just okay: "I was elected as the student representative on a five-person committee that advised the economics department on faculty hiring. We interviewed job applicants on behalf of the economics department and I was there in order to give the department student input."

Better: "I was elected by the economics majors in my class as the only student to represent them on a committee that determined faculty hiring. I spent several hours each week planning questions and issues to discuss with potential faculty members. I interviewed the applicants, summarized my conclusions in short written reports, and communicated these recommendations to the department chair. The majority of our committee's recommendations were adopted by the department."

Notice in the second answer there is an emphasis on using "I," which more powerfully demonstrates what the individual has accomplished. The second answer also is better because instead of just mentioning the position held, it explains the skills demonstrated by holding the position and the results accomplished.

As you develop your answers to each type of interview question, think about ways in which you can put a positive spin on the facts of your life.

THREE METHODS OF COMMUNICATION

You can communicate a point to the interviewer in three ways: directly, by implication, or by demonstration.

- **Directly stated:** "I have strong quantitative skills."
- **Implied:** "For my summer job, I performed a great deal of spreadsheet modeling to quantify the costs of the project we were considering." (The recruiter must make the connection between your previous work and quantitative skills.)
- **Demonstrated:** You answer a quantitative question well during the interview. (This also allows the recruiter to make the connection himself.)

Which of these three methods is the most effective? In this case, the second or third. The listener doubts the validity of the first statement because it seems too carefully planned and therefore not honest. The point is that there is a right time and place to use each method. Some things, such as interest in the job, are better off stated directly. *One of the most common mistakes job-hunters make is using only the first method: They state everything directly.* Personality traits, for example, should be demonstrated, never directly stated. It sounds strange to say "I am a mature, likable person with good judgment." Stating this actually conveys a *lack* of judgment. You should imply qualities—especially interpersonal and communications skills—through your presentation style, or *how* you say things.

The next chapter covers content, or *what* you should say in each segment of the interview.

~ 9 ~

THE INTERVIEW:
ANSWERING THE QUESTIONS

This chapter covers how to answer the questions you will be asked in management consulting and investment banking interviews. The appendix to this chapter presents a comprehensive list of interview questions; Chapter 10 covers consulting "case" questions.

INVESTMENT BANKING VS. MANAGEMENT CONSULTING

The pie chart in Chapter 8 showed that investment banking and management consulting interviews are different. The major difference is that management consulting firms test for strong analytical skills by administering what are called "case" questions. Case questions are scaled-down versions of real business problems that consultants work on, and often they are drawn from the interviewer's projects. The case takes up a good portion of the first-round management consulting interview. *If you're interviewing with consulting firms, it is imperative that you read Chapter 10, which explains how to answer a case question.*

On the other hand, investment banking interviews do not include case questions. Instead, interviewers spend time on résumé and personality questions.

If you're interviewing with both consulting firms and investment banks: Consultants expect you to tell them that consulting is your top choice, and investment bankers expect you to tell them that banking is your top choice. Be prepared with a strong, convincing answer for each. Also, you should review Chapter 6 to understand how to portray yourself differently in consulting and banking interviews.

THE INTRODUCTION

During the first two or three minutes of the interview, interviewers introduce themselves and attempt to "break the ice" by making comments about the weather or other small talk. They also will describe the structure of the interview. It's important to remember that the interviewers are starting with a positive tendency toward you: After all, you have been selected from a large pool of candidates *because they like your résumé*. The introduction is intended to put you at ease, but don't completely let down your guard—many recruiters say that their impressions (positive or negative) are shaped in the first five minutes of the interview. To make a good impression,

- Shake hands firmly with the recruiter (if your palms are sweaty, wipe them off before entering the interview room)
- Relax—the interviewer is looking forward to meeting you after reading your résumé
- Smile, show some warmth, but err on the side of formal rather than informal until you've gotten a sense of the interviewer's style
- If interviewer attempts small talk, make sure to engage in a conversation with him

PERSONALITY QUESTIONS

Put yourself in the interviewers' shoes. They might have to work with you if you are hired, so they want to make sure they like you. This is the major purpose of the personality questions. If interviewers don't like you as a person or you don't really fit in with the culture at the firm, they will find an excuse to reject you no matter how perfect your answers are, no matter if you say what you're supposed to say. *Personality questions and résumé questions form the core of the investment banking interview since investment banks do not use case questions.*

Interviewers also are testing whether they can put you in front of a client without embarrassment. Will you handle sensitive situations with grace and tact? Are you aware of what is appropriate behavior? At every step, interviewers are evaluating whether you'll field a difficult question with poise, because that's what bankers and consultants must do every day with their clients.

You have a big opportunity in this segment of the interview. Personality questions are more open-ended than any other type of question, since they let you choose a response from your life experiences. You can use the discussion to slip in the headlines that you have prepared or address any weaknesses on your résumé. Don't let the conversation ramble; direct it the way you want to.

Critical skills being tested include integrity, interpersonal skills (especially maturity, judgment, and tact), communications skills, and the ability to learn.

Be on the lookout for these common personality questions:

Failure Questions: *What has been your greatest failure? What did you learn from it?* These questions test your maturity, your ability to learn from mistakes, and your ability to handle a seemingly no-win situation. Use this as an opportunity to address weak spots, such as a low GPA—just don't bring up anything that's too negative or personal.

A good answer might be: "My grades dropped during sophomore year, which I consider to be a failure. Afterward, I thought about it and realized that my organization skills weren't where they needed to be in order to handle upper-level courses and that I had overcommitted myself to extracurriculars. [List examples of activities done.] I corrected these problems and my grades increased pretty dramatically the next year. I learned how to budget time better."

Another failure question is: *What would you change about your past?*

Self-Awareness Questions: *What are your strengths and weaknesses?* In answering these questions, honesty is usually left in the dust. But what do recruiters expect for asking such loaded questions? Few recruiters actually think they're going to find out what your real strengths and weaknesses are; they're testing your awareness of how others perceive you and your skill in answering a hard question.

Self-awareness is important because it is crucial to working well with people. If you brag profusely about your strengths or reveal profound weaknesses, you are demonstrating a lack of judgment and a lack of awareness of how you come across to others. So how do you respond? Try to express an old idea in a new way. Rather than say that your weakness is that you are a perfectionist, say "I tend to set expectations for myself and for others that are very high." Don't worry if your answer is somewhat clichéd—interviewers can't fault you for answering a tough question with tact, because they would do the same thing.

No matter what, do *not* imply that you are weak in areas that the firm finds important. Do not say that you are weak in math, analytical or interpersonal skills, work ethic, or confidence. Pick a weakness that has positive implications for the company. Err on the side of creating a driven, workaholic image of yourself rather than a laid-back, lazy image: "My greatest weakness is my tendency to overcommit to projects, which usually leads me to spend less time with my friends than I would like."

In describing your strengths, you have the opportunity to shore up weaknesses by highlighting unexpected qualities. If you have a very technical and dry résumé, you can say: "My greatest strengths are my creativity and ability to get along with people." (Of course, back it up with some persuasive examples.) In any case, you should highlight *a few* strengths that match qualities that the firm is looking for; be selective rather than reeling off a laundry list of qualities that interviewers won't remember.

What concerns you most about working in investment banking/consulting? This is another version of the "weakness" question because you potentially have to reveal something about yourself that doesn't fit the job. Take the response you've prepared as a "weakness" and use it here: "I have a tendency to overwork and leave little time for my friends and family, which I feel bad about. I know that I'll do the same thing in banking because of the long hours." Come up with an answer that interviewers would forgive because they can relate to it: Most investment bankers feel guilty about not spending more time with friends and family.

Other self-awareness questions:

- How would your friends describe you?
- What do you consider to be your three greatest achievements? (Use "I" here, not "we," to highlight what is attributable to you. Use this question to highlight specific strengths that match what the firm is looking for.)

Ethics/Sensitivity Questions: *Describe an ethical dilemma you faced and how you dealt with it.* These questions test both your integrity and your judgment in handling a sensitive situation. A good answer might be: "I knew that a classmate was cheating on every exam in our class. Our university operates on an honor code system, and I felt torn between my loyalty to this classmate and my wish to uphold our system. After all, the other students in the class had studied hard for these exams. I decided to approach this guy and tell him that many people had noticed him cheating and that it would be wise for him to stop before this reached the professor." This is a good answer because the situation is truly a difficult dilemma. Also, you have thought out a pragmatic solution that would work well in a real-life situation.

A bad answer might be: "A friend in my class took the final exam before the rest of the class and then offered me the answers. I thought about it and decided not to accept the help." This is a bad answer because you shouldn't be even hesitating—this is not an ethical dilemma because the right decision is very clear-cut.

Another ethics/sensitivity question is: *A client pulls you aside and tells you that he doesn't like working with women and wants you to replace the women on your team with men. What do you do?*

Fun Questions: *If you were trapped on a desert island for two weeks and could choose any two people in the world to be there with you, who would you choose*

Ten Common Interview Gaffes

Here are ten surefire ways to get yourself rejected:

1. **Not answering the question asked.** This disease is rampant among candidates, who out of nervousness veer off the subject or forget to complete their answer.
2. **Not understanding the job offered.** This is the undergrad-who-wants-to-be-CEO syndrome, where a candidate thinks he's going to be leading meetings instead of crunching numbers. Interpreted at best as ignorance, at worst as pompousness.
3. **Verbosity.** Perhaps out of a fear of silence, this candidate just can't come to a close. One idea leads to another, which leads to another. Agonizing to listen to.
4. **Spewing tons of information without any structure.** A close relative of verbosity. Comes up with a good range of ideas, but disjointedness leaves the interviewer's head spinning.
5. **Not seizing an opportunity to make a point.** Given some great openings to sell himself but he just sits there. If you want to hunt with the big dogs, you've gotta get off the porch. Show some drive and initiative.
6. **Talking about something personal.** Never talk about your family values, love life, deepest feelings, religious beliefs, political leanings, or other sensitive topics.
7. **Crudeness/offensiveness.** Here's a good example of this. When asked, "What was your most memorable experience?", a candidate replied, "Losing my virginity." "Why?" asked the interviewer. "Well, wasn't it for you?" Don't assume the interviewer shares your preferences or sense of humor.
8. **Letting an early mistake ruin the whole interview.** Some candidates act like all is lost when they've made one mistake. But everyone makes at least one mistake during an interview. Forget about it and move on; you'll win even more points.
9. **Thinking professional means cold.** Not smiling or trying to build a rapport with interviewers is a mistake. If they don't like you as a person, they'll reject you no matter what. Try to like interviewers—they'll notice it.
10. **Arrogance.** Acting as if you're going to get an offer (perhaps because someone has led you to believe this) will get you axed.

---

and why? Here the interviewer is trying to get a sense of who you are—your values, priorities, and beliefs. While you don't want to reveal things that are too personal (politics, sex, relationships, etc.), throw the interviewer some nugget about your personality to remember. There are no right or wrong answers here; creative responses are acceptable as long as they don't make you seem too off the wall. Ideally you can give a response that demonstrates creativity, an ability to think on your feet, maturity, and a sense of humor. Displaying a hobby, or interest and knowledge in something besides business, goes over well.

Other fun questions:

- If you had all the money in the world, what would you do besides banking/consulting?
- What do you do for fun?
- What did you do this weekend?

RÉSUMÉ QUESTIONS

Focused on your accomplishments and professional interests, résumé questions form the heart of the investment banking interview and the warm-up of the consulting interview. Interviewers are looking for whether you can communicate a lot of information concisely, why you've made your life choices, what you've accomplished, and whether you've been able to develop insights from each experience. Know your résumé well; be able to explain each choice and provide a few in-depth examples and learnings for each experience listed. Try to draw a clear, logical path of career decisions that are linked together by some type of interest or plan.

In each response, use the time-tested "CAR" approach to make sure you've hit important points:

- Context: *Briefly* set the stage for the example you are going to give. Often people spend too much time on this rather than on what their action was.
- Action: Communicate what you did.
- Results: Explain the results of your action to show interviewers that you made an impact.

Here are examples of résumé questions:

Decision-Making: *Why did you choose to go to [your university]?* This type of question tests your decision-making process and your values. It is important to show some logic in your answer. A rambling answer will be taken as a sign of a rambling mind. On the other hand, if you're asked about a decision that should involve some emotion, don't be overly analytical or you'll seem stiff.

You should be *demonstrating* your strength, *not stating* it: Don't say "I always think very logically and by process of elimination I chose Swarthmore." A better answer would be "I knew I would get a good education at any of the schools I was considering. So I differentiated the schools based on nonacademic factors. My priority was to find a school whose culture and people I really liked. I visited the schools where I had been accepted, and felt that Swarthmore's culture was the best fit for me. People had a great respect for academics but were well rounded." This answer communicates your thought process—and it also tells the interviewer about your priorities, which is the other purpose for decision-making questions.

Other decision-making questions:

- What is an example of a difficult decision you have had to make?
- If you are given an offer, how will you decide whether to accept it or not?

Teamwork: *Give me an example of an experience in which you had to work on a team.* This question is intended to test whether you truly understand the meaning of teamwork and have demonstrated it. Expect this question if you have nothing on your résumé that says "teamwork." A true team player puts the goals of the team above personal goals. In preparing for the interview, think of how to describe your experience in a way that meets this definition. You'll have to imply that you're a team player, not directly state it. These are the only questions where you should use "we" instead of "I."

A mediocre response would be "I was captain of the cross-country team and I worked with my teammates to win the NCAA championships. I very much enjoyed being with my team." A more insightful response would be "I was a member of the cross-country team. Though cross-country is often perceived as a very individual sport, it actually involves a lot of teamwork. Your time and placing is combined with the six other people on your team to result in a team score, so if you drop out or perform poorly the whole team loses. As you're preparing for and running the race, you support other runners because in order to win you all have to win. I really believe our close teamwork allowed us to win the NCAA championships." This answer is better because it shows a good understanding of what teamwork is about. A lot of people confuse teamwork with leadership, reeling off their list of captain, president, and championship credentials without fully explaining how this involves teamwork.

Another teamwork question is: *What was it like to play on the football team (or other sport)?*

Leadership: *Give me an example of a situation in which you demonstrated leadership.* Like the teamwork question, the leadership question rests on whether you really understand what leadership entails. Here's a review: True leadership involves persuading people, not forcing them, to do things. Portray your leadership in terms of *persuasion,* not *dictation.* This is particularly important to consultants and bankers, because they often need to persuade people they don't manage (peers or clients) to help them. Leadership also involves being willing to take responsibility when necessary.

The problem with leadership questions is that often they are traps designed to test your balance between team player and leader. Answering them too confidently can make you sound arrogant and dictatorial. Good examples are relationships in which there is no established hierarchy, and therefore true leadership skills are critical.

"Three classmates and I were working on a group economics project that constituted the major portion of our grade in the class. We were floundering and disorganized, because we hadn't structured our work, divided up tasks, or figured out a timeline. I recognized the cause of our problems and decided to do something about it. I talked to my friends, convinced them that we could do better if we made some process changes, got us more organized, and acted as the "check" to make sure everyone was getting their work done on time. We ended up getting an extremely high grade. I consider this leadership because I stepped up to the plate to lead us in a direction and persuaded my friends to make a decision." This answer is good because it's humble yet shows the candidate is able to lead a group out of danger. As a bonus, the answer also shows that the candidate has good organization skills.

Other leadership questions:

- I see here on your résumé that you "Led basketball team to five wins." What about this experience constitutes leadership?
- What would you do if a client on your consulting project team tells you he doesn't like the goals of the project and refuses to give you information that you need?

Résumé Case: *What would you change about your school?* These questions usually test some experience on your résumé in greater depth. This is to see how fully you've understood and thought about an environment in which you have been immersed, including the structure, key players, and current events of that environment. It is also a test of your ability to think on your feet, perform a quick analysis, structure an answer, and sound confident even if you don't know the answer to a question. (You'll have to do this in front of clients all the time.)

A good answer to the question above is "Though I like [my school] a lot, there is one problem that I've noticed. The academic advisory system is meant to help freshmen and sophomores make major academic decisions, such as choosing a major. But too often this system fails students, and they are left with no one to turn to for advice. I think that this is because those who have been assigned to advise them, junior faculty members, are often too overloaded with other responsibilities to spend quality time providing guidance. A better system might be based on juniors or seniors providing advice. They would understand what new students are going through, having been there themselves, and they could provide advice based on experience." This is a good answer because it is a harmless topic, demonstrates an understanding of key factors in the situation, and offers a practical and defensible solution.

Other résumé case questions:

- I see here on your résumé that you worked as an intern at the SEC. What do you think of the SEC's recent censure of the National Association of Securities Dealers?
- Have you ever had to make a strategic decision?
- Walk me through how you accomplished XYZ on your résumé.

COMMUNICATIONS QUESTIONS

These questions test on the spot your ability to communicate important points concisely or persuade someone. The key here is to remember to structure your answer (you may want to give the interviewer a few key headlines before plunging in), stay as high level with your points as possible, perhaps stopping to give a few well-selected details, stay on track, and summarize quickly at the end of your answer.

- Teach me something. You have five minutes.
- Sell me the lamp on this desk.

BUSINESS QUESTIONS

These questions look for evidence of business knowledge and interest. *Business questions are particularly important in investment banking interviews,* especially for those who are economics or business majors. Investment bankers like people who really want to be investment bankers; remember to show enthusiasm for finance, the securities markets, and the role of an investment banker!

Interest: *Why are you interested in consulting/banking?* This is probably the single most common question asked in the interviews. It is therefore worth investing some time in. You are being tested on your interest in the industry and the company. Take an hour and reflect: How did you initially become interested in the industry? What are the benefits of taking the job, and where might this experience lead you in your wildest dreams? Develop some real excitement that you can project during the interview. Also, how can you portray your past experiences as a long-term chain of events that have led you to your current interest? Once you've developed a storyline, you can use it repeatedly. Nobody will expect you to have a different answer each time the question is asked. This is a topic in which the more directly you answer the question, the better.

A good response for a consulting interview might be "I am an economics major here at Duke, but I have concentrated on theory rather than applied economics. I have increasingly felt over the past year that I would like some 'real-world' business experience—I'd like to learn more about how companies make operations and strategic decisions. I've talked about management consulting with some of my friends who are doing it now, and my sense is that as a consultant I will really learn about how companies operate." *Other reasons for wanting to be a consultant:* exposure to many different industries and issues, learning curve is steep during your entire experience, large degree of client interaction, you like to think about strategic and operational decisions that companies make.

A poor response might be "I heard about it from all my friends, who were applying, so I decided to submit my résumé. Since then I've talked to other friends who are in the industry and I think the work sounds really interesting." Even if it was, don't make your interest sound impulsive or random; make it sound thoughtful and logical.

Reasons for wanting to be an investment banker: You're interested in finance and securities markets, you like the transaction-oriented nature of banking because you like to see concrete results of your work, you will gain strong computer modeling skills, you will be exposed to a variety of companies, you will work with high-level clients.

Other questions that test your industry interest and research:

- What brings you here? Why are you applying to our firm? (Have some reasons that are tailored specifically to the company you're interested in.)
- What other firms are you applying to? (It's a good sign if you're applying to several companies in the industry, since this means you're really interested.)
- What other industries are you considering? (Be careful—don't seem too scattered. You don't need to tell bankers that you're applying to consulting, and vice versa.)
- Follow-up question: Which would you prefer, investment banking or consulting? (If you want a job, tell bankers you'd prefer banking and tell consultants you'd prefer consulting.)
- What do you think a banker/consultant does every day? (See Chapters 2 and 3.)
- Why do you think you would be good at banking/consulting?
- What do you think you would enjoy most about this job?
- I-banking: In which investment banking department do you see yourself? (Tests to see whether you've done some research.)
- What are some differences among consulting/investment banking firms that you have noticed, and which are important to you? How will you make a choice among firms?

Business Knowledge: *How does the government raise or lower interest rates?*
Investment banks rather than management consulting firms often ask business
knowledge questions, particularly because banks are more likely to want some
prior business knowledge than consulting firms. Yet investment banks are not
likely to ask business knowledge questions of anyone except business or economics majors. Business knowledge questions delve into your understanding
of current events or finance or are related to your major. Stay calm and try to
use your personal experiences or what you've read in the media to come up
with an answer. If you haven't heard of or don't understand the subject being
considered, ask first for clarification.

A response to the last question would be "The government affects interest
rates through two main methods: increasing or decreasing the money supply,
which in turn affects interest rates, or directly changing the rate at which the
government lends money to major financial institutions."

Other business knowledge questions:

- What do you think are the major strategic issues in the XYZ industry in
  which you worked last summer?
- What do you think are the major strategic issues banks/consulting firms
  face?
- What do you think of the Morgan Stanley/Dean Witter merger [or other
  situation in the investment banking industry]?

YOUR QUESTIONS

In the last few minutes of the interview, interviewers will ask you if you have
any questions. You are still being evaluated—this is not a time to rest! While
the quality of your questions probably won't make or break the interview, it
does make a difference when interviewers are uncertain about your interest in
or understanding of the job. Poor questions are seen as a sign of little interest
in the job and, even worse, of bluffing: Your until-then enthusiastic performance will seem rehearsed rather than genuine if you end with clichéd or very
basic questions. Resist the temptation to succumb to fatigue during this last
segment of the interview. Nothing is worse than when you ask a question and
then stare at interviewers blankly, repeating "uh-huh" and not truly listening
to the interviewer's response. That's when they know you are killing time and
can't wait to get out of there. Develop questions specifically for each interview.
The best questions are those that are neutral, are tailored to the firm, show
that you have thought about the job, and genuinely interest you.

Good questions for a first-round interview:

- In your opinion, what major changes will occur in the banking/consult-
  ing industry over the next few years?

- How will your firm adjust to these changes? How is your company's approach different from others?
- Could you describe a recent project you've worked on? A typical day on the job?
- It helps me to hear about others' career decisions. What other options were you considering, and why did you choose to join the firm?
- What types of people perform best at the firm? How are analysts evaluated?
- How much client contact would I have? How would this evolve as I progressed?
- Could you describe the project staffing process at your firm?
- I read in your brochure that you assign people to [industry/product/ functional groups]. How is this assignment made? How much interaction is there among groups? (This type of question is tailored to the specific company.)

THE FINAL-ROUND INTERVIEW

After the first-round interview, the firm typically will hold a second-round interview and then a final-round interview. This can all happen in a matter of days. The second-round interview generally is held on campus or in a local hotel the same day or the day after the first-round interview, and the final round is held at the firm's offices a week or two later.

Questions *Not* to Ask

- *Gives away concerns or weaknesses:* "Is it really true that you have to be good at math for this job?"
- *If you're in college, tries to sound expert* (MBAs can get away with more): "Is the industry shifting away from reengineering and toward growth consulting? How will your firm cope?"
- *Tough or negative—interviewer is tired, and you're still trying to get job, not decide on it:* "I've read reports that your firm is very stuffy and conservative. How would you defend yourselves?"
- *Personal or confidential topics:* "Did you get an MBA?" "What is the starting salary for this job?" "How many kids do you have?" "How is the firm handling the current lawsuit?"
- *Presumes that you will get offer or emphasizes perks:* "How much vacation will I get?"
- *Shows your preferences, which don't match job offered:* "Will I be able to transfer to LA in a year?"
- *Too obvious, shows your ignorance:* "Tell me about the firm." "What would be my responsibilities?"

If you have reached a final-round interview, your odds of success have increased to about one in two or one in three. It is worth more investment of time in researching the firm and preparing new questions to ask during the interview. You can start by looking up articles on the firm listed in the company profiles or by visiting the firm's Web site. One person whom you can be sure likes you is your first-round interviewer. When he calls to tell you you're being invited back for a final round, be sure to ask for very specific feedback on your strengths and weaknesses. Ask if he has any advice for the final round, or if there's anyone else at the firm (i.e., peer-level employees) whom you would benefit from speaking with before the final round.

The final round is comprised of a series of four to ten interviews conducted on one day at the firm's office. Each interview lasts from forty-five minutes to one hour. The same critical skills mentioned earlier are being tested, except in more depth. In particular, think of your weaknesses; these are areas where the final-round interviewers are likely to probe.

WHOM SHOULD YOU IMPRESS?

The firm will arrange for you to meet with people from several management levels. Many people assume that they should kiss up to the most senior people they can find, but *those who dominate the decision process are professionals from one level above yours.* If you're an associate candidate, you can expect to be interviewed mostly by managers, with a few associate peers and vice presidents thrown in. If you're an analyst candidate, you'll be interviewed mostly by associates, with a few analyst peers and managers rounding out the mix. This means that although the most senior people have the strongest veto power, they are not necessarily the ones that you need to kiss up to. Many very senior people don't even attend the post interview discussion because they're too busy—they just hand an evaluation form in to the group conducting the discussion. They may not take the time to "champion" your candidacy. Treat all the interviewers you meet with equal respect, but try to establish a strong rapport with one or two interviewers from one level above yours.

Don't let your guard down around alumni, even those whom you knew when they were at school. They may or may not be eager to help you.

VISITING THE OFFICE

The firm generally will pay for your travel expenses to get to the office, but confirm this with them first and save all your receipts. Spend money like it's your own; to do otherwise is extremely unprofessional. It is important to confirm hotel accommodations/reimbursements, the time you're supposed to arrive at the office, directions to the office and the hotel, and parking arrangements/validation.

In packing for your trip, put your suit in a suit bag so that it doesn't get wrinkled during transit. Bring some casual clothes to relax in after your interviews are over and workout clothes if you plan to use the hotel gym.

The firm might plan a social event for all candidates, and though you'll want to have fun and bond with the firm's employees, it's important to remember that you're still being evaluated. This isn't a school social event anymore, this is business. Stories about rowdy candidates make their way back to the head of recruiting. Here are a few simple rules:

- When at a fancy restaurant, don't eat like a slob; you're still being judged.
- Act like yourself.
- Make an attempt to have conversations with others (not just the interviewer, but the other candidates).
- You can drink, but pace yourself and don't get drunk. You're there to get a job.

QUESTIONS TO ASK

There is more opportunity to ask questions now than there was in the first round, because the firm now sees you more as a potential hire and will dedicate time to answering your questions. Also, you can ask a bit more about the job's rewards and compensation. Make your final-round questions more detailed and more tailored to the firm than your first-round questions, and do not use the same questions! Do not ask very basic questions, because the interviewers will wonder why you didn't ask them already during the first round. Continue to be careful not to sound as if you're presuming you'll get the job, and do not give the interviewer a hard time. MBA-level candidates have more latitude to ask challenging questions than undergraduate-level candidates. If you run out of questions to ask, think of asking questions about the interviewers themselves. Most people like to talk about themselves, and this strokes their egos.

AFTER THE PERFORMANCE

The wait begins after you walk out the door. Chances are that if you are going to receive an offer, you'll hear back from the firm within the first few days after the interview. If you haven't heard anything from the firm, wait at least until the date they told you they'd notify you, and then contact them. Be patient! Calling the firm before that date is very annoying to recruiters, unless you have another job offer that you must respond to immediately.

Thank-you letters are unnecessary and are *not* recommended, unless you have something very special to say to an interviewer or you have interviewed outside the standard recruiting process. At best these letters get tossed, and at worst they'll draw attention to something negative—a major typo, for example, or form thank-you letters sent to all the interviewers you've seen at the firm.

Many firms have an official or unofficial wait list. If they tell you that it will take them a few weeks to decide on your case, assume that you're on a wait list. If you are actually told that you're on a wait list, ask how high up you are on the list and whether it's likely that the firm will get to the wait list based on current offer acceptance rates. Also, ask for the name of a person you can contact to get updates on your status. If you need to know their decision sooner because you have an "exploding" offer (one that expires at a certain deadline) at another firm, let the firm know. If you are on a wait list for several weeks or months, it's okay to follow up with the firm every few weeks to show them that you're still interested. In the meantime, assume you're not going to get the offer and pursue other jobs vigorously. If you receive an offer from another firm during your waiting period, call the company and let them know. Sometimes this can hasten a decision on your case.

APPENDIX A: COMPREHENSIVE LISTS OF INTERVIEW QUESTIONS

The General Question Checklist

1. Why are you interested in consulting/banking? (Or: How did you become interested?)
2. Why are you interested in our firm?
3. What three accomplishments are you most proud of?
4. How do your accomplishments show that you have the skills for consulting/banking?
5. Walk me through how you accomplished XYZ. Give me some details.
6. What has been your greatest failure? What did you learn from it?
7. Why did you choose XYZ college?
8. What were your major accomplishments at XYZ job?
9. What is your greatest strength/weakness?
10. What other companies are you interviewing with? Have you received any job offers?
11. Do you have a location preference? Do you have a department preference?
12. What do you do for fun? What did you do this weekend?
13. Describe an ethical dilemma you faced and how you dealt with it.
14. What is an example of a difficult decision you have had to make?
15. How would your friends describe you?
16. What concerns you most about consulting/investment banking?
17. What three issues do you think are important to the consulting/banking industry?

18. What was the last book you read?
19. Do you feel that you'd be more comfortable at a smaller company?
20. In what kind of environment do you work best?

Questions for Post-MBA (Associate) Position

1. Walk me through your résumé.
2. Why did you choose to pursue an MBA? Why XYZ business school?
3. Do you see yourself in consulting/banking over the long-term?
4. Where do you see yourself in five or ten years?
5. Where do you think the consulting/banking industry is headed?
6. How do you think the consulting/banking industry is structured?
7. How would you describe your leadership/management style?
8. I-banking: In which investment banking department do you see yourself?
9. What are some differences between consulting/investment banking firms that you have noticed, and which are important to you? How will you make a choice among firms?

Investment Banking Questions

1. What do you think it takes to be successful in investment banking?
2. What do you think investment bankers do every day?
3. Describe a situation in which you used quantitative skills to solve a problem.
4. Sales/trading: Sell me this XYZ object. Recommend a stock to me.
5. What sources of information do you read on the investment banking industry?
6. How does the government raise interest rates?
7. What do you think of the recent [XYZ situation in the investment banking industry]?
8. What do you think of the way the government treats insider traders?
9. Has the investment banking industry been represented fairly in the press?
10. What do you think of the Morgan Stanley/Dean Witter merger?
11. What are your strengths in business analysis?
12. Can you elaborate further on the accomplishment you mention here on your résumé?

Management Consulting Questions

1. Give me an example of a time you worked in a team. Did you face any obstacles?
2. Give me an example of an obstacle you faced and how you overcame it.
3. What do you think management consultants do every day?
4. Give me an example of a situation in which you analyzed and solved a problem. How did you do it?
5. How would you describe your way of solving problems?

AFTER THE INTERVIEW IS OVER:
WHAT HAPPENS BEHIND CLOSED DOORS

Here is a composite of a discussion in which candidates are evaluated, based on several actual postinterview evaluation sessions.* Consultants have gathered at the end of a day of interviewing undergraduates to decide who will receive job offers at their firm. Out of ten candidates, the group must choose two. There are six people in the room: Patty, the administrative head of recruiting; Troy, the associate who is leading analyst recruiting efforts for the year; Anna, a senior vice president; Teresa, an associate; Steve, an associate; Nigel, an analyst; and William, an analyst.

Each recruiter has ranked their choices from 1 (high) to 10 (low) and has marked these scores on a whiteboard at the front of the room. Total scores have been tallied for each candidate, which has led to an immediate conclusion: There are four clear leading candidates, and the rest will be ruled out. In this excerpt, the group's discussion therefore centers around the top four candidates: Julia, Larry, Bruce, and Vince.

Troy, team leader: Okay, everyone, we have to pick our top two candidates, and we'll also pick two wait-list candidates—the third and fourth best candidates on our list. We'll tell them that they've been placed on a wait list. For people who we give offers to, we'll encourage them to get back to us within two weeks and at least let us know what's going on.

What we should probably do first is look down the rows at the scores that candidates have received and see if there any patterns, like 1s and 2s. We've certainly got a row of 1s here with Julia.

Anna, vice president: She was awesome. And you know what—I think she would take our offer.

Steve, associate: I'm not so sure about that. I think she has an offer at [ABC Consulting Firm] or she'll have one soon and that she's pretty positive on them.

Anna, vice president: I think she'll take our offer. I did a "fit" interview with her, and either she's an excellent liar about what she's really looking for, or else she's going to take our offer. I asked her to explain what she thought were

---

*Names and certain details have been changed to protect privacy.

the differences between us and other companies and she was really able to explain why she thought our approach fit her.

Troy, team leader: Building on that, she asked me the type of questions that indicated that she was very seriously considering us. My gut feeling is that she likes us as a firm, but she's just wondering where people can go after they leave our firm, for example, how many of our analysts get into leading business schools.

Patty, recruiting coordinator: I would have to agree that she likes us a lot. She actually had an offer with another firm that exploded last week, and she put them off and gave up the offer in order to wait and see whether she would get a final round with us.

Anna, vice president: She also declined her offer with [XYZ Consulting Firm].

Troy, team leader: I think we're in violent agreement.

Anna, vice-president: Yes. I think we should make Julia an offer.

Troy, team leader: Okay, let's move on to Larry. Steve, what did you think about him?

Steve, associate: I gave Larry a lot of analysis to work on in my interview, and he was very good with that. But it's going to take him some time to get up to the point where he's fully client-ready. Not that he would explode there, but I think his style is just not one where he seems enthusiastic and ready to work with clients. He seems like he would say "I can do this analysis myself" rather than working with a team well.

Anna, vice president: I have a different perspective on Larry's client-readiness. I think if you gave him something to do with a client team, he would bring it back dead—he would accomplish it. But I'm not sure he would do it in a way that everyone would think is a "win-win" style.

I think his intensity comes from his military background and his familiarity with authority and orders. You really would have to coach him—he can't just go out there and launch a mission at a client site.

Teresa, associate: That's interesting. I had Larry right after you and he made the point that you can't, by virtue of who you are and your rank, expect things of people. He really understood that issue.

William, analyst: I think the thing about his intensity is that it's really improvable through coaching. He's very open, and he listens to feedback.

Steve, associate: What's your thought of how Larry thinks on the fly? Because everything I asked, it was sort of like "Hold on a sec," and he'd scribble something on his little pad. His answers were really good, but he kept using that approach on everything.

Teresa, associate: He did that with me too, and at first I was really concerned. But he did come back with exactly where I was headed, and I wonder if there's a little bit of a language issue, and that he needs to write things down in order to structure his thoughts. English isn't his first language.

Anna, vice president: I think he's a bit afraid of cases. Because when I said I wouldn't be giving him a case, he said "Oh, no cases" and looked rather relieved. I think that writing things down is just his way of handling it.

Troy, team leader: Well, to summarize everyone's comments, he sounds like he has good analytical skills and is potentially coachable on personality issues. Maybe we should put Larry on hold and move on to the next person to evaluate. Let's consider Bruce.

Steve, associate: I have hesitations about Bruce. He did two things that really bugged me. One, he wore those suspenders and that shirt. It would be as if a woman wore a skirt that was too short—you just don't do that, especially on a client site. And second, he walked into his case interview without bringing his notepad. There was no way he could take notes.

Troy, team leader: How did he end up doing?

Steve, associate: He did okay. Bruce is certainly very bright and tries really hard. He has a great presence. He's like the ultimate Xerox salesperson. The bottom line is that he is very intelligent; he did well on my case. We talked about how you would compare the brand equity of Colgate toothbrushes to that of Oral B toothbrushes, and he was able to apply past work experience. But in terms of his judgment, I'm not so sure. If those two incidents hadn't occurred, I would have ranked him much higher.

Nigel, analyst: Why don't we address your two issues, Steve? The suspenders—all right, that could have been a bad judgment call. But as for the notepad, Bruce could have forgotten one, and if you really wanted to, you could have given him a notepad.

William, analyst: I think that the headline for me with Bruce is, he's a little immature. And maybe the suspenders issues falls into that. I'm on your side, Nigel, in terms of the notepad—during my case, he was assertive to ask for paper, and so that's a nonissue as far as I'm concerned. But I felt a little uncomfortable talking to him, and it wasn't the way he dressed or anything, it was who he was. And that concerns me a little. I felt that Larry was more coachable.

Nigel, analyst: I think Bruce is more presentable. Thinking of my last couple of clients, I could see sending him to any part of the client organization, saying "Go talk to these people," "Go talk to those people," and I feel like he'd come back with the necessary information.

Anna, vice president: Did Jacob [another vice president who interviewed Bruce] leave any comments behind for us on Bruce before he left?

Troy, team leader: Jacob's comments on Bruce were, and I'll read them from his notes: "Extremely presentable, could lead the client through different situations." Maybe we should next discuss our third-ranking candidate based on these scores and then try to make some decisions.

Troy, team leader: Let's talk about Vince next.

Teresa, associate: I personally had a tough time deciding between Vince and Larry, making them two and three on my list after Bruce. I thought Vince had a very nice style, good analytical structured thinking. I gave him my Taco Bell case. He did a very good job in answering clearly. The only negative that I saw was that as he was going through the case he made a couple of assumptions, because he's foreign and isn't that familiar with Taco Bell, and he didn't validate these assumptions with me to ask if they were reasonable. But that was really my only negative on him.

Anna, vice president: The only reason why Vince ended up number three on my list was because I saw the Energizer Bunny—Larry—before him. In comparison, although I thought Vince was very solid and had a good fit and very client presentable, he was a little bit nervous. I'm not sure why. Vince was more reserved than Larry.

Troy, team leader: I thought the same thing. Vince got into a little bit of trouble on my case. He was nervous, and I think that's why he didn't structure his answer the way he would have been capable of. But I still think he was presentable and has had experience in which he has had to interact with clients.

Anna, vice president: He's done a lot of analysis, actually, in his prior work experience. And he's taken a lot of initiative.

Steve, associate: The one problem I had is that Vince's thought wasn't as strategic as I would have expected. His thought process and the rigor he put around the strategy aspects of my case were not strong. I thought he was very confident and had a very operational notion of how a business should be run, but I didn't see him thinking, "What would be the implication of this company action, and what would occur?"—strategic thinking didn't seem to come naturally to him. Vince got the answers, but I always had to push him on it. I asked him, "You have an organization that has a lot of brand loyalty from its customer base and you have a major competitor coming into the market. What are some of the issues you would face?" He got flustered and wasn't able to work through this issue. I think that I could put him in front of a client, but I would actually pick Bruce over him, except for those two issues I mentioned about him. I would drop Vince and take Bruce and Larry.

Patty, recruiting coordinator: What do we think the chances are of Bruce and Larry taking an offer from us?

Nigel, analyst: I don't know about Bruce. He seemed more focused on consulting, but I don't know what his other choices are. Larry seems to be talking to other firms, and he's definitely talking to investment banks, but I don't have an indication where he'll go.

William, analyst: Larry told me that he's been interviewing for six weeks, which tells me that either he doesn't like the offers he's been given, or he hasn't been given any good offers. And he repeatedly said he was getting tired of interviewing. So I think he's probably very "susceptible" to taking our offer.

Anna, vice president: I asked Larry what he was looking at, and he said investment banks and other consulting firms. My sense is that he has a bit more of a natural fit with an investment bank, in terms of the hierarchy thing.

Steve, associate: I sat next to Larry at lunch and asked him what he wanted to do with his future. And definitely investment banking was one part of the future and management consulting was another part of that future. He had a wide variety of ideas, including starting his own business. Bruce was more focused on this job and on being a consultant.

Troy, team leader: So, let's try to wrap up. Is there any consensus? We're going to take Julia from the very beginning of our discussion, but which one of these people—Bruce, Larry, and Vince—would you want to fill the other spot? Which one would you rather work with on a team?

Anna, vice president: Well, when it comes down to it, I compare Bruce and Larry and I think that style and forgetfulness are easy to coach. Running over a client is harder to coach. Steve, would you strongly object to us giving Bruce an offer?

Steve, associate: No, I think you guys have done a good job of making the case for Bruce. He's confident and self-assured and focused on consulting.

Troy, team leader: I guess it sounds like unless there's disagreement, we should make offers to Julie and Bruce and put Vince and Larry on the wait list. We'll divide up the calls and make them tonight.

~ 10 ~

THE MANAGEMENT CONSULTING CASE QUESTION

Case questions represent the heart of the management consulting interview. What's their purpose? *They are supposed to test your ability to take a bunch of random data and, in a structured manner, derive a conclusion—in sum, test your analytical skills.* Interviewers will be watching to see whether you think logically, can come up with a structured problem-solving approach, are comfortable with numbers, and can communicate your thoughts clearly. Since management consulting is an intellectually demanding job, your interviewers want to make sure you have the basic skills to succeed. There are three main types of case questions: the standard business case question, the numbers question, and the brain teaser.

Most people dread case questions. But they don't have to be terrible, humiliating experiences. First, although you may think that you need to find that one perfect answer, there are actually several equally good, individualistic ways to analyze and answer each question. Second, interviewers are hoping that you'll do well, so often they give you hints and additional information to help work through the problem.

Last, and most important, attitude is paramount. The secret to doing well on case questions is to approach them with confidence and not overthink them or take them too seriously. The most successful candidates report that they went into the interview thinking that case questions would be a fun brainstorming session, an opportunity to be creative and discuss interesting ideas with smart people. You don't want to constrain your answers by worrying about whether your answer is "right" or not—you may worry yourself into a box. Since the interviewer will welcome almost any creative idea and you may hit upon a good idea by accident, feel free to throw out as many ideas as you can think of. You also will need to state your opinions with conviction so that you persuade the interviewer that you can be placed in front of clients and win their confidence.

Now let's cover each type of case question in depth.

STANDARD CASE QUESTIONS

In the case question, the interviewer presents you with a hypothetical business problem and asks you for your opinion. Case questions mimic actual consulting projects and often are drawn from a case the interviewer has worked on. The case question is the most commonly used type of problem-solving interview question. It is also the longest segment of the interview, usually lasting at least ten to fifteen minutes. You'll want to seem calm, cool, and intelligent even though you're under significant pressure.

Remember, try to see the case question as an opportunity for fun rather than as a test. The back-and-forth of the case resembles more of a discussion than an oral exam.

The case question has fairly standard components:

- *Opening*—The interviewer briefly describes the business problem to you and what question you are to answer. You must demonstrate here that you are a good listener. Do not immediately jump to a response; instead, open with a framework for decision making.
- *Your questions*—You are expected to analyze the problem by asking thoughtful questions in key areas that you think are important. The interviewer may use your questions as an opportunity to drive you toward the solution. Typically he will give you more information, at which point you can either analyze this information and ask for feedback or ask further questions. The interviewer will assess your creativity and your ability to process and analyze new information, pick out critical factors in the case, think on your feet, and interpret graphical or numerical data.
- *In-depth exploration of a branch*—if you've asked a question that is in an area the interviewer wants to explore, the interviewer may answer your question and then ask you a follow-up question that will explore this area more deeply.
- *Analysis and conclusion*—Generally a specific area of the mock client's business is critical to the solution of the problem. The interviewer will either drive you toward this area or let you know when you've reached it by asking you follow-up questions. He may present you with a final question that gets to the heart of the problem, and ask for your analysis. Always state your assumptions clearly if you are presenting an opinion.
- *Communication*—The interviewer may ask you to summarize your conclusion as if you were recommending it to the client in order to test your ability to communicate.

～
Help—I Need a Framework!

Since a structured response will win you big brownie points, it's good to think of two boilerplate structures that you can use to organize your thoughts. Doing so can really help out when you don't know what to say. Consultants call these boilerplates "frameworks." Here are two frameworks to remember—use them to highlight key issues and lay out your path of analysis at the beginning of the case and as a mental checklist to ensure that you haven't forgotten anything important during the rest of your analysis.

Porter's Five Forces: From Michael Porter's classic book *Competitive Strategy.* The five forces are the key structural features of an industry that determine how competitive and how profitable the industry is. Use the framework to answer questions about introducing new products, entering new industries, or addressing declining sales or profitability. The five forces are: **suppliers, buyers, competitors, substitute products,** and **new entrants.** You can think about the bargaining power of buyers and suppliers as well as the threat of competitors, substitutes, and entrants. *Note: Don't actually tell the interviewer "I'm going to use the Porter Five Forces Framework to solve this problem"; make it seem as if you naturally are aware of these factors.*

Profitability Analysis: Profits = Revenues − Costs. This simple framework is useful to keep in mind when answering questions about sudden changes in a company's profitability or operations. Problems can lie on either or both the revenue or cost sides, driving poor results:

- *On the revenue side,* you can think about price and quantity sold. Also think about the 3Cs—Customers (who they are and why they buy the product), Company (what are its competitive advantages), and Competitors (what they are doing). Also think about the 4Ps—Pricing (in comparison to competitors), Promotion (advertising message and positioning), Product (features), and Place (does the product reach the consumer cost-effectively, what distribution alternatives are there).
- *On the cost side,* you can think about the composition of cost, average cost per unit, breakdown between variable and fixed costs, how costs compare to competitors, capacity utilization, and economies of scale.

Five qualities distinguish great case responses from good ones:

- *A structured response.* Why is this important? Because it demonstrates that you think clearly and can make sense of an ambiguous situation, and because it allows you to remain composed.
- *A broad perspective* on the situation analyzed, mentioning all possible avenues of exploration and not focusing immediately on nitpicky questions or narrow paths that you think are right. Consultants call this "big-picture thinking."
- *A concise and linear* manner of thinking and communicating.[1]
- *Business judgment.* Demonstrate that you can identify and prioritize likely high-impact areas of the case to investigate first.

- *Unusual and creative insights* into the case. Show that you were able to come up with ideas proactively, without having the interviewer push you toward them.

We will now go through two practice cases, step by step. As you proceed, cover up the answer immediately following each question (the text not in italics) and come up with an answer of your own before consulting the answer. You might even want to give the second question to a career counselor or a friend in consulting and ask them to play the role of interviewer in a practice case interview. *Note: These responses are designed to show you what an A+ interview would look like, so don't be discouraged if you can't come up with the same answers—they don't need to be as good in order to get a job.*

PRACTICE CASE 1

1. Opening. *A semiconductor manufacturer that has been increasingly profitable over the past three years has experienced a sudden decrease in profitability over the past few quarters. How would you analyze what's happening?*

At this point, the recruiter is looking for big-picture thinking and structure in your response. Don't jump immediately to what you think is the right answer based on some past experience you've had, because chances are it isn't. Do not get stuck on one answer this early in the interview! You'll have a chance to drive to a conclusion later on. Take a few seconds to think about how you will structure your response. Use a framework (see the box on page 208) to break down the problem into parts. This is a profitability problem. Either costs have risen or revenues have decreased, so the revenue-cost framework is a good approach here.

Mention your framework and several possibilities and then ask questions that will help you decide which part of the analysis you want to focus on.

"If profitability is decreasing, there could be problems either with the company's sales or with its costs. On the sales side, I would examine the company's sales to determine whether there has been a downturn and when it occurred. On the cost side, I'd like to see their cost structure and analyze how that's been changing over the past few years. I would find out whether that breakdown has changed and which costs have gone up. Do we have historical data on their sales and their costs?"

2. Exploring one branch deeply. The interviewer responds: *Actually, their costs have been pretty stable lately. But let's say that they have seen a drop in sales. What measures or indicators do you think you should look at to analyze what's happening to the manufacturer's revenues? You've mentioned sales trends, but what else is there?*

You now know that the interviewer is interested in pursuing revenues, not costs. Take this hint—do *not* stubbornly insist on returning to the cost side. You can tell from the phrasing ("what else?") that he is fishing around for specific answers. Open your mind to any possibility you can think of; don't dismiss ideas because you're afraid they're too simple. Many candidates hurt themselves by failing to mention all their ideas.

The interviewer is again testing your ability to prioritize information and bring up the most important things first. For example, if in this example you thought of two sales indicators, total market share and sales of specific product lines, mention the high-level indicator first—total market share. Explain your answer fully. What interviewers don't see, they don't know: They won't understand that you have insight into the case unless you explain your reasoning. Remember, the interviewer is testing your ability to analyze the situation logically.

"Well, I think it's important to look at market share to see whether the revenue downturn is specific to the company or to the industry as a whole. If the company's market share is stable but its revenues have gone down, that means the entire industry's revenues have decreased. If the company's market share has decreased, then they're losing business to competitors, and they would need to address that problem."

3. Processing a new piece of data. *That's a good point. How would you interpret data saying that the company's market share hasn't really changed and that their number of units shipped was staying level in the period of falling revenues?*

Now is the time to get specific! The interviewer is testing your willingness to take a position, to craft a hypothesis based on the new data provided. The interviewer is watching to see if you have a facility with business concepts and quantitative data. Use the data provided to craft a specific hypothesis.

"The data suggests that the entire industry is showing decreasing revenues and the company's problem is not unique. Also, since until shipments are level but revenues are falling, the company's price per unit must be falling. That would suggest to me that the company is lowering its prices. Maybe there is too much supply in the market? Probably all the companies in the market are feeling the effects of an oversupply, since the company's market share isn't changing."

How would you interpret the fact that all the companies in the market are within a 4 percent pricing band? What does that suggest about the type of market this is?

"That would suggest that this semiconductor product is a commodity, because there is extremely little differentiation among products and therefore among pricing. If some companies were able to charge a lot more for the same product, it would mean that their product was somehow better. Customers would be paying a premium for that added value. Industries with more differentiation would show a greater range of prices. The fact that this is a commodity market also would explain why prices are dropping fairly evenly among all companies and therefore revenues and market share is not changing. If this were a noncommodity product, then the impact on prices would vary according to the company's product."

Let's say that in addition to what you've found already, you see data that shows that although a competitor's revenues are falling, they're not falling as sharply as the company's revenues. How would you explain this?

Now the interviewer is throwing in a little twist, a piece of data that contradicts the scenario laid out so far, to see how you will respond to a sudden challenge. He is testing your calm under pressure, your analytical skills, and your ability to see the other side of the issue. You need to be able to derive a conclusion from this data and find your way to an answer. You'll want to analyze the situation deeply, but don't get lost in the details; always keep in the back of your mind the question that was asked.

"I guess I would have to ask, is the competitor's product less sensitive to price fluctuations, and if so, why? If the competitor's prices are not falling as sharply as the company's, the answer might lie in the product. Perhaps the competitor has added value that makes their semiconductors more valuable to the customer—add-ons like great customer service or quality. If the competitor's prices *are* falling as fast as the company's, then you have to think that perhaps their market share is increasing or that their total revenues are supplemented by some other product that is not doing as badly as this semiconductor product is. The competitor is basically more diversified."

4. Coming up with a conclusion or solution, and recommending it to the client. *Okay, say that you are right on your first explanation of the problem: The competitor is both better diversified and his products have more added value. What solutions would you suggest to the company, and how would you implement them? How would you describe these recommendations as if you were speaking to the client?*

In this last step, the interviewer is testing whether you can come up with a realistic solution for the client. This involves good judgment and perspective. He wants to see a range of solutions that are logical conclusions from your previous points. And he wants to see that you are thinking about cost-benefit trade-offs, that you think about the client's profitability before implementing a solution. Finally, the interviewer is assessing your ability to communicate in a clear and concise manner.

"I would say to the client, you are in a commodity industry that is vulnerable to price shifts caused by changes in supply and demand. If you want to hedge yourself against price downturns, you might want to consider diversifying your product line into higher value-added products or offer specialized services along with your existing products. We could examine what the customer values and would be willing to pay for and perform a cost-benefit analysis to choose the types of new goods and services to offer."

"We should find out what the customer truly values and would be willing to pay extra for. This would involve customer interviews or surveys and an examination of what exactly the competitor provides. The customer might value increased timeliness or fewer defects in the product. Perhaps they'd like scheduling flexibility or better payment terms. If it was decided that quality and timeliness were the issues, then you'd want to review your processes to see exactly how you can improve. Timeliness could be improved by increasing inventory. Or quality could be improved through a better testing process. In both cases, we'll want to weigh the cost of making these changes—in time, money, and opportunity costs—against the predicted revenue increase you'd get for them."

PRACTICE CASE 2

Again, cover up the responses (the text not in italics) and try to think through the major issues of this case yourself. When done with one part of this case, move on and uncover the next part.

1. Opening. *Your client manufactures electric switches that are put on machine tools as an emergency, fail-safe mechanism to stop the machine if necessary. Your client has $600 million in revenues and for ten years has remained flat in terms of revenues and profits. You've been hired to generate profitable growth for the company. Where would you start? We have access to some data, so you can ask me questions.*

The main focus here is growth, so you might structure your first response by suggesting several broad growth strategies, each of which can be evaluated.

"There are several ways to grow a business. We could take market share away from a competitor, stimulate primary demand and therefore increase the size of the market as a whole, or use our technology to develop new products and therefore expand into a new market. We could look at each strategy and see how well it fits with the current market conditions and dynamics of this industry."

2. Explore one branch deeply. At this point, the interviewer would ask you which one of your three suggestions you'd like to pursue, and then you could talk about the pros and cons of each suggestion. More likely, the interviewer will suggest a path to follow and ask you to evaluate that option: *This is just a switch manufacturer. They can't do much to affect primary demand. And they're not very technological. So that leaves the third option—let's look at increasing* *market share. How would you go about analyzing that option? Here is some data for you to look at—the current competitors and their respective market shares. Your client is Company B. Also, I will tell you that the switch market has been flat and that there are only three companies in this market, all of whose market shares have been stable. No company has been gaining market share at the expense of others. But first, by the way, what is the total size of the switch market in revenues knowing these numbers?*

Market Share

Company A	60%
Company B	30%
Company C	10%

The interviewer is slipping in a test of your quantitative skills before you get to the question about market share. You know that 30 percent of the market is equal to $600 million, because the interviewer previously mentioned that your client, Company B, generates $600 million in revenues. So you know that 10 percent of the market is equal to $200 million. So 10 times $200 million equals $2 billion, which is the total size of the market.

Great. Now let's get back to our question—how would you increase the company's market share?

Now, in order to figure out how to increase market share, you need to figure out what is compelling to customers to make them switch to your switch from a competitor's. If your product is very different from your competitors' products, you could try to convince customers based on superior product characteristics. If this is a commodity market, price could be a compelling reason for switching, so you could ask the interviewer a question to determine whether it is a commodity market.

"First, I'd want to figure out whether this is a commodity business, because if it is, then price is very important. Commodity means that one product is replaceable with another very easily, so I want to find out if there are any major differences that would keep a potential customer from changing from a competitor's switch to my switch."

On an engineering level, there is no difference between the products. Physically, a customer could very easily take a competitor's switch out and put yours in, or vice versa. But you haven't seen much of that kind of switching. As a matter of fact, your customer base hasn't changed in ten years.

So although there is no physical differentiation between products, there is something that differentiates the switches from each other. You should probe into this.

"I'd want to find out why customers are so loyal to a particular vendor. I'd like to ask our existing customers about what is important to them in a switch manufacturer."

3. Processing a new piece of information. *Customers have been using your switch for years and they love it. It's a very small but important part of a very expensive machine. Because it's an emergency switch, any failure could lead to injuries and lawsuits—a risk nobody wants to take. They've never had a problem with your switch and will change vendors only if there is a quality problem with your switch.*

Here's some key information! You now know what drives the customer's decision and can plan a strategy. Note that this strategy is actually not market-share focused: Rather than trying to gain new customers, you will increase revenues by raising prices for existing customers.

"If the customer is obsessed with quality and doesn't want to switch to a competitor for fear of lowering quality, maybe there is room to raise our prices without scaring them away to a competitor. What do prices currently look like in the market?"

4. Coming up with a conclusion or solution. *Their prices look like this. What recommendation would you make regarding prices?*

Company A	$21
Company B	**$20**
Company C	$18

Obviously, your client's prices are not as high as they could be. For example, Company A is getting away with a $21 price, so maybe you could raise prices as well. So you need to determine how much the price can be raised. Instead of sticking to one number, propose a mechanism to determine a range.

"My basic recommendation to the client would be to raise prices, since we have a captive group of customers and Company A actually is charging more for the same product. A fair amount of research would need to be done to determine the optimum price point, but we could start by defining a range. Company A is charging $21 and still has 60 percent share, so $21 is definitely okay. So we could use this as a benchmark and at least raise prices by 5 percent to $21 and not lose any customers. Determining the high end of the price increase is a little more complicated, and we probably should look at what percent of total machine costs the switch represents in order to figure out how much more the customer could bear."

There may be some other discussion, but that would be icing on the cake. You got the main point of the case!

NUMBER QUESTIONS, OR GUESSTIMATES

The biggest myth about number questions is that they assess your quantitative skills. In fact, they test your number-crunching ability only marginally—basically, your multiplication and addition skills. Most interviewers don't even know the right answer to the number question. They couldn't care less. They are examining instead the logic you use to move from one step to the next, your creativity, and your ability to perform simple multiplication and addition. In fact, the interviewer would rather that you arrive at a wrong number with a good analytical technique than provide the right answer because you just happened to learn it in class last week.

A typical number question asks you to estimate something through a rough ("back-of-the-envelope") calculation. You are supposed to reach your end calculation through a series of narrowing assumptions. The assumptions may or may not be true in real life; that is irrelevant. Interviewers won't give you any real data to help build assumptions, nor do they like it if you ask for data. It *is* important to develop a line of reasoning you will use to proceed through the problem and then explain the logic behind each successive assumption you make. It's fine to take a few seconds at the beginning of the question to think up your approach. As you're progressing through the calculation, you will narrow your numbers further.

A couple of tips for number questions:

1. *You* are determining the numbers. Pick estimates that allow you to easily do math in your head. For example, choose round numbers such as 50 percent instead of 55 percent. Choose combinations that are easy to work with: 30 percent of 120 instead of 33 percent of 120.
2. The multiplication and addition in these questions are very elementary, but if you freeze under pressure, try to do some practice beforehand in doing math in your head. Otherwise, ask the interviewer if it would be okay to take notes during the interview.
3. It helps to know a couple of basic facts that you can work from on any question. You should know the population of the United States (250 million).
4. Start with key drivers of the object you're estimating, then think of substitutes for that object that would lessen your estimate.
5. Don't forget to finish the question. Many candidates do well until the very end, when they forget to convert their answer to the right number of units or otherwise answer the question asked.

Examples of number questions:

- How many gas stations are there in the U.S.?
- How many bagels do Americans eat every day?

- How many children are born each day in the U.S.?
- How much does a fully loaded 747 weigh?

There are many great ways to answer each number question. Here's an example of one question, answered with two different strategies.

How many tombstones were sold in the U.S. last year?

Strategy 1: Break It Down

1. I would first try to figure out how many people in the U.S. die each year. I know that the U.S. population is around 250 million, and I would guess that about 1% die each year. 1% seems reasonable to me given the size of the elderly population. 1% of 250 million makes 2.5 million deaths each year."
2. "Now I have to figure out how many of those people are buried. If we assume that the majority of Americans are still buried, and perhaps only .5 million of that 2.5 million are cremated, that leaves 2 million who are buried."
3. "Then I want to find out how many are buried with gravestones. Out of the 2 million, let's assume that some are buried with grave markers besides gravestones. Let's say that 75% are buried with gravestones. So my guess is that 1.5 million tombstones are sold in the U.S. each year."

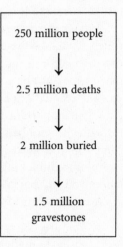

Strategy 2: Build It Up

1. "If I look at the town of [Town], Ohio, I think that there are about two mortuaries serving a population of 25,000 people. Those mortuaries probably do about 3 funerals each per week, and I think that most deaths in [Town] are handled by them. That makes a total of 24 people dying each month and about 300 people dying each year in [Town]."
2. "Let's say that 50 of the deceased are cremated, since burial is still more popular. That leaves 250 people who are buried, of which I think the majority, probably 4 out of 5, are buried with a gravestone of some kind. So that means 200 gravestones are sold each year in [Town]."
3. "If we assume that [Town] is a representative sample of the rest of the country, which I think it is based on its demographics, then we can extrapolate from [Town]'s numbers. Since [Town] has 25,000 compared to a U.S. population of 250,000,000, then [Town]'s 200 gravestones suggest a total of 2 million gravestones sold in the U.S. each year."

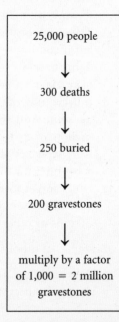

Be prepared for a common follow-up question: If you were asked to walk out of this room and find the real number, how would you do it? The interviewer is testing your resourcefulness and creativity in finding information and solutions. This is an important part of the actual consulting job, as often you are asked to answer "impossible" questions.

BRAINTEASERS

Brainteaser case questions seek very specific and structured answers and are therefore more close-ended than normal case questions. You need to demonstrate the same qualities as you would in a normal case question: logical thinking, clear communication, and creativity. Here is an example of this type of question:

- Why are manhole covers round?

There are at least three commonly accepted answers to this question:

1. Because you can more easily transport a round cover by rolling it around on its edge.
2. No matter how you place it in the hole, it fits without needing to be rotated.
3. Because a round object will not fall into a similarly shaped hole, whereas any other shape would.

∿ APPENDIX: MORE CONSULTING CASE QUESTIONS ∿

---

1. If you had to choose the CEO of a truck manufacturing company, what factors would you consider? Would you choose someone from marketing, finance, or operations? How would your answer change if you were choosing the CEO of an advertising firm?
2. A manufacturer/retailer of baby clothes has seen its retail sales plummet over the past two years. How would you identify the cause of this problem, and what would you recommend that the company do?
3. If you were considering moving an insurance company's location from City A to City B, what factors would you take into account to make the decision? City A is an urban area on the East Coast, while City B is in a rural area also on the East Coast.
4. An American satellite services provider wants to enter developing countries in Asia, specifically by providing telephone service to consumers through satellite links. What does the company need to know before making the decision to enter this market? If it chooses to enter, what might a good strategy be?

5. Interpret these two graphs. What does each tell you? What might you hypothesize about these companies?

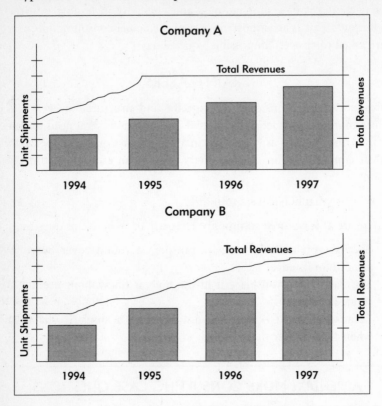

Answer: Company A's revenues have leveled off after 1995 yet unit shipments are increasing every year. This suggests that its price per unit is falling. Company B, on the other hand, shows steadily increasing shipments and revenues and therefore either stable or increasing prices. You can come up with all sorts of hypotheses to explain these graphs; one is that Company A is in a commodity business that is subject to price fluctuations of the market or that a competitor has entered Company A's market and driven prices down, whereas the same thing has not happened to Company B.

 NOTES

[1]"How to Ace the Case Interview," Bain & Company, Inc.

Bob Simonelli*

Former Consultant, Bain & Company, Inc.

B ob joined Bain out of business school. Here he shares a post-MBA perspective on the management consulting industry. After he was interviewed, he left Bain for a start-up company.

Does your family ever express confusion about what you do?

Yes. My dad once said while we were talking about my job, "We'll have to talk more sometime about what you actually do." It's hard to conceptualize that a consultant could just come in to a client company and be useful in such a broad range of areas. I've worked on things like an industry strategy assessment that asks "What is the future of financial services?"—and that's so heady and abstract—way down to strategic things like "We need to eliminate 20 percent of cost out of our factories." And I've worked on all the stuff in between: Evaluate this company as an acquisition, evaluate this market, or reorient our division.

What is your favorite project to date?

Probably working for a beef farmer and marketer.† We were asked to do a domestic strategy case. They were under some profitability pressure because they're exporters and the export prices had dropped terribly because of producers overseas who produce fifty times what they make. These competitors could mass-produce beef and undercut our client's prices. The company was faced with the challenge of selling more here in the domestic market, and they were uncertain what was going to happen. They asked us to do a market assessment. So what we did was pretty classic. We interviewed the whole management team, ten people, and asked what they thought was happening in the market and how the company operated and met the challenges of the market. We formed our hypothesis—Bain operates on an "answer-first" principle— then gathered some initial data and evaluated our hypotheses. We did a huge interview in the market. We gathered information from the distributors and

*Name has been changed to protect privacy.
†Product has been changed to protect privacy.

also from purchasers like restaurants, supermarkets, and caterers. Actually, our answer changed very little.

To give you an example, we had a product strategy, which advised our client to develop more value-added products like precut steaks in addition to its regular supply of beef. In terms of distribution channels, we thought they should exploit the growing catering and retail channels. And in terms of operations, we advised them to build a new value-added factory, which would produce the precut steaks and other value-added products, and basically start up a separate operation.

Did you actually get to travel and visit the farms?

We spent time with the management, who taught us a lot about cattle ranching. We took a fantastic tour of the company's facilities. We were the envy of the office. I've been getting these big steaks sent to me as gifts from the client.

So you had a lot of interaction with clients and vendors.

We did a lot over the phone but we also went to the big markets and did in-person research. The education was important because it's a small company. In a big firm like an auto company you might say it's not as important to get a feel for the culture, but here it was. We were looking at individuals.

Do you feel accepted by client organizations, or is it a battle to win credibility each time?

It's a mix. Clients who have hired consultants before are shaped by their previous experiences. If they've been burned before by consultants, they can have a pretty tough view. If they've had a good experience before, then they tend to be welcoming.

You've worked in investment banking previously. What do you think are the key differences between investment banking and consulting?

First, investment banking is an execution job. You know what your product is, so at the beginning you set up the work plan and it's the same every time. In consulting, it's more project dependent and creative. There's a lot more variety in the projects, so there's no generic execution.

Which do you like better?

You get a rush in investment banking that you won't find in consulting. Consultants talk about the crunch in getting ready for board meetings but it's not the same as doing a divestiture, a takeover, or an IPO [initial public offering].

It's not as immediate in terms of the impact. In investment banking, you see the results right in front of you. The company has $100 million more than when you started working for it. In consulting, even though we say we have great results, you don't see them right away. I like the greater breadth of consulting projects, though. You get more client exposure. In consulting it's not how much can you execute, but can you do the right kind of thinking to structure the project.

What are some of the biggest misperceptions people have about consulting?

I've actually been pretty surprised by how creative the consulting job is. You have to develop your own structures to solve problems. So it's a struggle for some people. And it's very different from having the structure handed to you like in banking. I was thinking the other day that if I couldn't hack it in consulting, I could go back to investment banking, and that wouldn't require the same sort of intellect.

What mistakes do you think candidates make in the recruiting process?

People don't seem to do a lot of research about the firm. At business school, you can always find someone who's been at the firm to talk to. There are lots of candidates who come in and say consulting sounds interesting but don't really know what it is. So I would recommend that people spend more time researching what consultants do.

What's an example of a "case" question you ask candidates during an interview?

We have a good one now that we use, which is "How would you evaluate the market for disposable diapers in the U.S.?" And you take the candidate from key market drivers, to substitutes, and through to a market estimate. We're testing more the ability to do 80–20 analysis, the ability to use common business sense. The candidate might respond, for example, that there are 250 million people in the U.S., that there must be 25 million people under ten years old, and that babies wearing diapers are one to three years old and there must be five million of them. And finally, we test the ability to synthesize findings. We ask, "Let's assume you have thirty seconds to deliver this message to the CEO, what are you going to say?" The point is for people to communicate in clear, sharp points.

Another question I ask is: "You're on a desert island with no one else except for an average-size supermarket. How long can you survive on the food in that supermarket?" I get pretty interesting answers to that one. I'm looking for someone to be able to go from the size of the supermarket, to the square meters of food, to how long it will last them. I'm looking for the ability to structure the problem. Eighty percent of the success of the interview will be around structuring.

What is the most important characteristic you're looking for from a candidate during an interview?

I'm looking for aptitude and cultural fit. On aptitude, I look for the ability to structure problems and good business sense, and on the fit side, I look for people who are entrepreneurial and results-oriented.

How would you distinguish a Bain consultant from a consultant at a competing firm?

They're enjoyable to be around. Though there's stress in their lives, it's work hard, play hard. They're fun, interesting people. All the way from the partners to the first-year people. I have other data points. I think the culture at McKinsey, for example, is a lot more formal than at Bain.

Where do you think this job fits into your overall career path?

In the short term I might still be at Bain, up to manager. But more likely this is a stepping-stone to me doing my own business.

~ 11 ~

CHOOSING THE
RIGHT JOB

I f you're picking from several banking or consulting job offers, congratulations. You've made it through an enormously difficult test, and you should feel proud of your accomplishment. Now you need to be aware of the selling techniques that firms will use to convince you to accept their offer. Many former analysts feel retrospectively that this is the part of the job search where they knew the least and made the greatest mistakes. Don't slack off in your investigation: The irony is that all your efforts spent winning a job could be wasted if you choose one that isn't right for you. Analyst and associate positions involve at least two years of commitment, and this is time that could be spent on something else.

A couple of ground rules: Cautiously evaluate firms' claims. Don't let a firm pressure you; take your time in making a comfortable decision. This is the one and only time in your relationship with a firm that *you* have some leverage; use this to make sure you get the information you need to make your decision. Any firm that discourages you from taking your decision too seriously because you're "just an analyst" is probably not a firm that will take your career seriously.

THE NUTS AND BOLTS OF THE OFFER

Consulting firms and investment banks make job offers over the phone. A senior recruiter will call you to give you basic information about your offer. Information includes:

- base salary

- signing bonus—a once-only bonus that is paid when you join the firm
- indication of yearly bonus—many firms divide the yearly bonus into two components, individual performance and the firm's overall performance

Other details you should listen for include vacation time, health insurance, 401(K) or profit-sharing plans, and relocation expense reimbursement. Listen carefully to details. For example, analysts at a firm that shuts down during the week of Christmas and gives employees two weeks of additional vacation probably end up taking more vacation than those at a firm with three weeks of vacation time. This is because people often feel peer pressure not to take all their allotted vacation time but if the firm shuts down everyone is forced to take time off.

Two particular aspects of the offer are very important:

- First, most consulting firms will allow you to remain a generalist (someone who works on projects in different industries) for several years. However, investment banks will require you to join a group. Banks will either make you an offer in a specific department or make you a general offer with the condition that you will be assigned to a specific department once you've arrived. As discussed in Chapter 3, your investment banking department assignment will make or break your experience.
- Second, if you're an analyst, watch for time limits placed on your tenure at the firm: Some companies state outright that theirs is a two-year analyst program, while others leave it more open-ended. Why is this important? Open-ended offers provide a cushion in case you don't get into business school or can't immediately find an appealing new job in another company.

THE SELLING PROCESS

The minute a firm decides they want you, it's as if they can't live without you. The firm will assign one or two people to act as your "mentor." Soon after you receive a job offer, you will begin getting phone calls from these people day and night. You'll start to use your answering machine to screen out calls. Technically, the mentor is responsible for answering your questions and putting you in contact with other employees if you have questions he can't answer. Realistically, the mentor's role is to "sell" you—to persuade you to join the firm. Your mentor will court you until you've made up your mind. Mentors, like recruiters, are picked for their loyalty to and success at the firm. The mentor cannot help but feel the pressure to sell you on the firm because he will be recognized for a successful job. Therefore, mentors are not natural candidates for providing you with a representative sample of opinions on the firm.

The highlight of the large firm's selling process is the "sell day": The company pays your way to visit the office, stay in a posh hotel, and schmooze with current employees. One unspoken objective is to impress (and entice) you with luxuries you are not accustomed to, to create an image of banking or consulting that is fast paced and glamorous. During the sell day, the firms will trot out extremely senior people to make you feel important. Sometimes, these bigwigs won't remember your name once you've joined the firm. All of the people you talk to will be friendly, positive, and happy with their jobs—people who are unhappy with the company are not included in recruiting. Some firms also may massage your ego, trying to flatter you into taking the job. Be cynical.

Although you should discount at least half of the official information you hear, you *can* pick up valuable information by carefully observing the subtleties of what people are saying and doing. Listen to your gut instinct when evaluating your surroundings. Use the selling process to fill in informational gaps.

THEIR SALES TECHNIQUES

The importance of an *unbiased* career decision can't be stressed enough. Some very intelligent people feel that their rational thinking fell victim to banks' and consulting firms' sales techniques. Whether during sell day or other recruiting functions, be aware of the effect of these techniques on your thought process:[1]

- *"Attending our sell day event doesn't mean you're obligated to join us. We just want a chance to answer your questions."* This is a classic case of escalation of commitment. The objective is to break down one large act of commitment (your taking the job) into several smaller acts of commitment so that you can more easily stomach the large commitment. Once you arrive at sell day, you may find yourself seriously listening to the arguments put forth by the firm's employees. The firm has therefore won a share of your attention by convincing you to take an initial step.

- *"We love our jobs."* Human beings like to see themselves as consistent. There would be a large contradiction between hating a job and doing it anyway, especially when explaining one's actions to others. Therefore, analysts and associates justify their actions by claiming that they love their jobs. They want to love their jobs because they've already chosen them and are doing them. This is especially true of first-year analysts, who still care that their college classmates see them as having chosen the right path.

- *"Carefully consider whether you're cut out for this job, because not every-one can make it here."* This technique plays on your ego, your machismo. It challenges you to try to succeed, an offer that tempts overachievers. Also, describing the analyst program as difficult builds mystique around it and makes outsiders want to belong to a "club" of people who have succeeded in this experience. The analyst program is made out to be a special and separate world from the outside.

- *"We had one analyst out of sixty last year who was so good and worked so hard that he was promoted to the associate position without an MBA."* The firm will create myths around certain people and elevate them as role models. This communicates to you what the firm's values are—hard work, sacrifice—and may tempt you to try to resemble these mythical analysts. And become a legend yourself.

- *"Look at it this way—you're going to be working long hours anywhere you go, but it's better to be working at our bank that at XYZ bank."* Translation: It's better to be low on our totem pole than on someone else's. This argument presents your choice solely as one between investment banks rather than as a choice between investment banking and something completely different. Once this argument has narrowed your perspective to just investment banks, it appeals to exclusivity and encourages you to pick the best of investment banks. This argument is also used by consulting firms. Remember, you don't have to do anything you don't want to. Evaluate any job offer in absolute, not relative, terms.

- *"But you told me that you'd join our firm if you got an offer."* Be careful what you promise during an interview or any other contact with the firm: It will come back to bite you. Firms like it when you make very public, verbal acts of commitment. When they challenge you later by recalling these statements, they rely on the fact that you don't want to see yourself or have others see you as flaky. This ignores the fact, of course, that it is perfectly reasonable to change your mind.

Other, subtle, self-imposed factors also may influence your decision:

- *Sunk costs:* You already have put so much time and effort into interviewing with this firm, do you really want to go through the process all over again with another firm and waste your precious effort?
- *Peer concerns:* Your friends on campus know that you have been interviewing—how will it look to them if you change your mind all of a sudden about what you've been doing and decide that banking and consulting aren't right for you? It's better to change course now than to be miserable later.

What to Watch For

Keep these questions in mind when you're visiting the firm on sell day:

Hierarchy/responsibility ☐

Are junior people (e.g., analysts) speaking at meetings? Do they appear comfortable expressing opinions in front of managers? Do they act servile or obsequious around their managers? Do professionals interact in a friendly, easy manner with secretaries and administrative staff?

Culture ☐

How comfortable do you feel around the firm's people? Can you see yourself socializing with them? Are they obliged to socialize with each other after work? How much do you like the people in the department in which you have an offer?

Firm's integrity (i.e., how much you trust their sales pitches) ☐

How comfortable are you with the firm's selling methods? Do you feel that the firm is exerting too much pressure or using smarmy selling techniques? Do you trust the people you meet on a gut level? Do people's claims of incredibly short hours or great assignments seem surprising or too good to be true? Do their assertions seem completely out of line from what you've seen at other firms? Have employees' statements contradicted each other?

Quality of colleagues ☐

How intelligent, knowledgeable, well-spoken, and charismatic do the firm's people appear compared to people at other firms?

Quality of life/job satisfaction ☐

Are only the happy analysts and associates involved in recruiting? Do those who are not involved appear to be stressed out or dejected when you see them at work? How many analysts choose to return to the firm after business school?

Learning ☐

Are analysts and associates able to explain clearly what they have learned from the past few years? Does what they're saying make sense to you, or do you think they are B-S-ing to cover up their lack of good learning experiences?

Business school acceptance ☐

How many of the analysts you meet have applied to business school? How many have been accepted at a top school? (Assume that over 50 percent of second- and third-year analysts apply to graduate school.)

- *Public failure or success:* You want to show that you've succeeded in an immensely competitive process, and often this means accepting one of the jobs you've won. This pressure is especially high for people who are very self-conscious.[2]

ON SELL DAY

If there are specific people of whom you'd like to ask questions, call your mentor in advance to arrange a meeting during sell day. *If a firm has made you a department-specific job offer, make sure to meet as many of the people in that department as possible.* Some candidates have accepted their offers only to arrive at their assigned department and find that the one person they met was not indicative of the rest of the clan (or, worse yet, has left the department).

If your offer is a general one but you will be assigned to a group later, make sure to investigate thoroughly how assignments are made, which groups tend to be more sought after among analysts, and why. MBAs should actively try to influence their department assignment if they haven't already; a good justification for stating a preference now is that you have gathered information during the recruiting process and have come to a conclusion. Undergraduates, if they have a strong preference, should get as much of a commitment as possible from the firm that they will receive this assignment. This should happen before taking the job; once you have accepted the job, you have no more negotiating leverage.

One word of caution: Behave professionally at all times during selling events, even around junior businesspeople who will be your peers. Firms often take successful candidates out for a night on the town, and this often involves drinking. You need to stay in the good graces of your possible future employer. Getting plastered in front of the firm's representatives will be remembered for a long time.

See the appendix to this chapter for a comprehensive list of questions to ask during sell day.

WHAT'S NEGOTIABLE?

Can you negotiate the offer you get? It depends.

Undergraduates and others applying for entry-level analyst positions have almost no room for negotiation, with the following exceptions:

- Unstructured recruiting programs, or job offers from smaller firms or regional offices, may have more room for negotiation.
- If you are absolutely opposed to the department assignment you have

received, it may be possible to change it. This has happened in a few cases. If you receive an offer in a specific department, ask to talk to as many people in that department as possible. If you have serious concerns about the group assignment, ask how flexible the assignment is and express an alternative preference as a condition of taking the job. If your offer is a general one, ask how department assignments are decided and express a preference up front, before you accept the job. If possible, try to get an indication or commitment as to whether you'll get your preferred assignment.

- Firms are not flexible when it comes to salary and title. They may be more flexible regarding less important components of the offer, such as relocation expenses and starting date. It is reasonable for you to request reimbursement of relocation expenses, particularly if you are planning a long-distance move. It may be possible to delay your start date if you have very important reasons for doing so. Some firms even will allow you to defer your start date for a year in order to make use of a prestigious scholarship such as the Rhodes or Marshall.

MBAs from second-tier business schools, advanced degree candidates in other fields, and those who have been working for several years often find themselves in a predicament. If you're in this group, presumably you set expectations up-front with the firm as to whether you'd consider working as an associate or an analyst. If the firm has interviewed you as one or the other throughout the entire recruiting process, it will be hard to change their image of you now that you've gotten your offer. There is almost no way to raise yourself up from an analyst to an associate offer, except perhaps if you have a competing offer at another, higher-ranking firm. However, it may be possible to bring you on at a slightly higher salary since you have more experience or education. Also, since you are interviewing outside the normal group of targeted candidates, it's possible to negotiate other aspects of your offer, such as signing bonus, start date, and department assignment.

Sometimes a firm will give this in-between group a special formal title: senior analyst, for example, or junior associate. In this case, it is practically impossible to get your offer raised up to the full associate level, and frankly you should be thankful that you don't have to settle for the analyst title.

MBA students have the most leverage in negotiation, because the firm sees you more as a long-term investment and because the experience and skills of MBA candidates vary more widely than those of undergraduates. While you cannot increase the offered base salary or bonus, you can negotiate one of the biggest perks of all: reimbursement of part or all of your business school tuition by returning to a firm where you've worked as a permanent or summer employee. In addition, MBAs frequently have been able to alter start dates simply in order to travel, relax, or do some other work for a year. By talking to members of the firm, they have been able to evaluate and influence their placement in particular departments.

CULTURE AND PEOPLE

You will hear this many times, but it bears repeating: Among similar job offers, you should choose the firm whose culture and people you like best. Why? Because success very much depends on how well you mesh with the company culture.

At school, your individual performance can be quantified fairly objectively through tests and projects that you prepare alone. At work, this changes. Especially at a junior level, you work as part of a team and have few assignments that you alone are responsible for (aside from photocopying and proofreading). In addition, the work your team has accomplished is difficult to grade because there are a few immediate quantitative measures of a client's satisfaction. (They will pay you the same fee, no matter how much they liked your work.) There are no exams, no papers, and no class rankings. As you can imagine, performance measurement tends to be much more subjective at work than at school. In addition, you'll be judged by one or two managers at work versus four or five professors at school, so your evaluation becomes less balanced. Most important, you no longer can control your performance based solely on your individual effort; in order to get your job done well, you will rely on other people's help.

Because the work performance review is so subjective, and because you need cooperation from others, it is critical to build strong work relationships with your colleagues, managers, and mentors. It is especially possible to do so if you have an underlying friendship. Those who are able to joke around, go out for beers, try a great restaurant, or play golf with their colleagues—in other words, relate to them on a personal level—are at a great advantage. Unfair as it seems, friendships carry over into the work environment and will affect colleagues' perceptions of you and your work. People who like you will champion your cause, look after you, and cooperate with you.

In conclusion, this means that you should look for people with whom you can bond and build strong relationships. Seek firms whose culture and people you're comfortable with, whose style you would want to emulate. Seek an environment in which you won't feel that you're hiding your true self every minute of the day. If your gut is telling you that the culture doesn't fit you right now, the culture probably won't ever fit you. Don't make the mistake of thinking you can succeed at a firm based on your performance and regardless of the other people there: Remember, now performance is a subjective thing.

How to Really Evaluate the Money

The money *sounds* great: $40,000 for your first year as an analyst, or $80,000 as an associate. But what does that really amount to? Don't just look at salary; consider these factors too:

- **Location:** Associates and analysts in New York report that the cost of living is so high that it is significantly harder to save money. Your dollar will go farther in other cities.
- **Per diem:** All your client-related travel costs (including dry-cleaning, hotel, meals, and transportation) are reimbursed. The more you travel, the more you get. For consultants, who can be on the road for an entire year, this can add up. There are stories of consulting analysts not even renting an apartment because they are always staying in hotels, and just leaving their stuff with Mom and Dad.
- **Frequent traveler points:** Don't underestimate the value of these bonuses. A two-year consulting analyst can come away with hotel and airline points worth several thousand dollars, which is no small percentage of their total compensation. Investment bankers will not travel nearly as much.
- **Business school reimbursement:** Don't overestimate this perk. Most analysts end up wanting to make a career change after business school, so they turn down the reimbursement offer. Anyway, if you work at another firm during your business school summer, usually they will offer you some form of reimbursement if you join them after graduation.
- **Long-term salary increases:** If you're an associate or otherwise interested in staying put for a while, compare the salary cap reached over the long term in management consulting versus investment banking: It is dramatically lower.

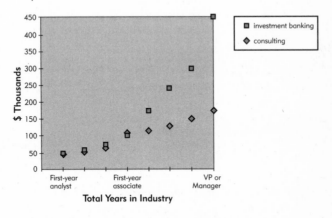

Note that as a third-year analyst, salaries are higher in investment banking.

CLOSURE

After you've accepted a firm's offer, do one more thing to bring an end to the recruiting process: Call each firm from which you've received an offer. At least give them the courtesy of turning down their offer directly, rather than leaving a message on voice-mail. Firms will appreciate it, especially after putting a lot of time, thought, and money into recruiting you. Believe it or not, some recruiters become attached to candidates they'd really like to see join the firm.

Besides courtesy, these calls make business sense. You don't want to burn any bridges, since you might end up knocking on these people's doors again—perhaps after business school or if your initial job choice is disappointing. You might even want to send a personalized thank-you note to recruiters with whom you had significant contact.

Now you can go out and do some real relaxing. Enjoy! You've reached the fruition of a lot of hard work.

 APPENDIX: QUESTIONS FOR UNDERGRADUATES TO ASK DURING SELL DAY

General Questions

- What do you like most and least about your job?
- How many analysts will be in my analyst "class"?
- How will my performance be evaluated?
- How will my work and responsibilities change over my two years as an analyst?
- How many analysts were accepted last year at Harvard, Stanford, and other leading business schools?
- What support does the firm provide to analysts applying to business school?
- Do you have a business school reimbursement policy? How many people receive this option?
- Typically what percentage of analysts each year are asked to stay for a third year?

Questions Specific to Investment Banking

- How do you determine which department I'm assigned to?
- How would you describe the differences between M&A, corporate finance, and other departments?
- Can I meet more people in the department that I have been assigned to?

Questions Specific to Management Consulting

- Please describe your staffing process. How will I interact with staffing coordinators?

- How many projects can I expect to work on during my two years as an analyst? What is the longest project you've heard of an analyst working on?

Questions Specific to Sales and Trading

- How quickly would I be assigned to a specific product desk permanently?
- What types of training would I receive during my first few months at the firm?

∼   **NOTES**   ∼

---

[1] These ideas are based on theoretical frameworks taught in Professor Joel Podolny's Organizational Behavior class at the Stanford Graduate School of Business.

[2] Robert B. Cialdini, *Influence: Science and Practice* (New York: HarperCollins), 70.

INSIDER INTERVIEW

Rajesh Gupta*
Former Analyst, strategy consulting firm

R ajesh graduated from an Ivy League school, worked for a year at a small company, then joined a strategy consulting firm for two years. Just after he was interviewed, Rajesh left consulting to pursue his entrepreneurial interests at a well-known start-up company.

How does working at a small firm affect your experience?

First, there's a greater range of things that a new analyst can do at our company. It's a very young place, so we don't have as many senior people. There's more upside for new people than there would be at some other places in terms of responsibility. Second, because I've been able to work with some pretty senior-level people, I've gotten thrown in early into thinking strategically about business. And that's great.

On the downside, you don't have the guidance of more experienced people because we're all young. Also, we may not have the range of clients that a larger firm might have.

*Name has been changed to protect privacy.

How has your role evolved since you started?

On my first case, I was assigned a very discrete piece of analysis, and I was managed by somebody else who had designed the overall piece. They checked my work. My first few cases were like that. After I had been at the firm for four to six months, I started to do some of my own work-planning and helped to design analysis. And now that I've been here for about a year and a half, I'm overseeing the work of first-year analysts, and I have more freedom.

What have you learned in consulting?

A friend of mine showed me this cartoon. It's entitled, "How a consultant asks a woman to marry him." The first picture is this guy showing a bar chart to his potential bride that's titled "How my love for you has grown over time." The next one is a 2 by 2 matrix called "My love for you versus other women." And then the last one says "How I feel about spending time with you versus other activities," and it shows golf, sailing, and all these things. This is his presentation to try to win her over! While that's a little extreme, the point is that consulting really hammers into you a structure for how to think about business or anything else in life. Regardless of whether people are planning to go into business or public policy or whatever, it's extremely valuable to have the ability to think logically.

Another thing you get from consulting is concrete, general business skills. You can come off of two years at our firm and have a conversation with someone from marketing, operations, or accounting and have a pretty good talk with them and understand what it is that they do.

Finally, you get thrown into situations that are the equivalent of someone inviting you to come play baseball, where you're playing on their field in front of their fans, and you've seen it played but you've never really played it yourself. And you're playing for a million dollars, and they've been playing for twenty years and are pretty good. And after you've done that a couple of times, you get the self-confidence of knowing that given three or four days, you can come off sounding pretty knowledgeable. That ability is an ingredient you'll find in CEOs and senators, I believe. It's taking limited information and sounding credible and developing intelligent views.

When the senior guys at consulting firms come in toward the end of a project, they'll take what several other people have done, and package and market it extremely well to the client. There are two types of senior guys at our firm. There's one type who's just a brilliant business analyst in general and then there's another who isn't. But one thing they have in common is they can both tell a very good story.

What has surprised you about consulting?

I didn't understand the whole lifestyle issue. At first, when I heard that consultants travel four days a week, I thought it sounded pretty cool. Now I've been traveling two days a week and I think four days would be really difficult. So as for lifestyle, it's hard to have a good sense for it until you're actually doing it. Some of the undergrads I've interviewed say things like: "The lifestyle doesn't seem so bad in consulting—it's about seventy-five or eighty hours a week." They have no idea what they're talking about. That's a lot of hours, and you definitely feel it.

Second, I have found that there are some businesses I really enjoy working in and others I don't. Consulting firms work with a lot of industrial companies in businesses like chemicals, steel manufacturing, or plastics. These companies hire consultants because they make big capital spending decisions and don't have the allure to draw in talented young people for their own full-time staffs. If you're a bright young person, the prospect of working with those firms isn't particularly exciting. It can be really frustrating. If you end up working with some steel company for over a year, it's almost like you're working *for* them. You're really immersed in their culture. Out of college nobody would say "Hey, I'll go work for some steel company," but somehow you end up doing that anyway through consulting. So in general, you're not able to control the nature of the consulting assignment you're going to get. If I were analyzing which consulting firm to join, I would want to know what the expertise of the firm is, and I'd also like to know how much control I'm going to have over my assignments.

A friend of mine got stuck in the salt industry, and during this first conversation with his clients they tried to convince him that salt is not really a commodity product. You're working with these forty-five-year-old managers who have been in the salt business for twenty-five years and you have to figure out how you are going to get motivated to learn about the business.

How would you describe your colleagues? What traits do they share?

Well, consultants in general, I would say that they're not quite as aggressive or social in general as investment bankers. They're more reserved and academic. I've met people who did well in investment banking who I don't think would do well in consulting.

I've noticed that in consulting people talk a lot about how smart someone is. Intellectual horsepower is important. In high school, people talked a lot about how good-looking someone is. And in college it was how cool you are—instruments, sports, that kind of thing. In consulting, people really admire others' intelligence. They are smart and passionate and interested in things.

So you've bonded with your colleagues?

Yes, but I've found that there are only about four or five people I would want to hang out with after work. One thing that does happen in a small office is that people rely on others in the office for their own social life, even to the point of dating people in the office. It's almost like an extension of college. One other thing is that people really care where you went to school. There is some elitism.

What advice would you give to someone deciding which consulting firm to work for?

You want to think about the brand name on your résumé—ten years from now, what are people going to think? The major reason for going into consulting is to leverage it into another career.

   If you go to a more established company, there's more stability. You'll be more actively managed and there will be more senior people on your team. The downside is that although they treat people well, they have more room to muscle people around and they're just not as responsive to individual needs. At smaller, less well-known firms, there's more of an opportunity to rise up, but you'll be less actively managed. Also if you do well there, there's more upside financially as well.

How do consultants at your firm feel about their experiences?

One negative thing is the lack of diversity within our firm. Especially racial diversity. There's a limited number of black and Hispanic consultants. We have a council trying to work on that. But the problem is, in the pool we interview from, there are very few black or Hispanic candidates we can interview.

How do you think women find working at your firm and in consulting?

The experience will depend on the client you're working with. For example, if you're working with a big industrial client in the Midwest and you're young and you're a woman, there's going to be an additional hurdle you have to get over in winning over the client. But I think women speak very highly of our firm and our culture. It's a very sensitive and politically correct place, and about as different as you can imagine from an investment bank.

   But one story might illustrate the problems women face in consulting. There's a woman at our firm who went to business school after being an analyst, and a partner came to visit her and took her to dinner and asked what they could do to recruit her back to the firm, and she said that her decision was primarily going to based on lifestyle issues, because she wanted to raise a family. She didn't want to trade off not having a family. And he said, "What trade-off? I see my kids twice a week, every week!" And he was bragging about that.

Where does this job fit in with your overall career path and where would you like to be in a couple of years?

I want to work in the technology industries, but I want an MBA, too. I've heard it's hard to get into business school with just two years of consulting. So I'll do two years here and then a stint at a medium-size company, or I'll do four years here and then move on to business school.

INSIDER INTERVIEW

Gillian Chen*

Former Analyst, bulge-bracket investment bank

G illian worked in New York at a bulge-bracket investment bank for three years. Afterward she attended a top business school, worked in management consulting between two years at business school, and currently works for a small company.

You've said you considered going into consulting. Why did you choose investment banking instead?

I wanted breadth, and I felt like I would get exposed to different industries and companies in investment banking, whereas in consulting I would get stuck on one project for two years. The last straw was comparing the type of grunt work I'd be doing in each industry. Some consultant told me a story about standing outside McDonald's for two weeks counting parking spaces and keeping track of what people ordered. And I decided, you know what, I'd rather write a [computer] model. Which, in retrospect, I don't know if I still believe. It was just that, at the time, consulting sounded tedious.

Why did you choose to join your particular firm?

I had offers from several brand-name firms and Kidder Peabody. I ruled out Kidder Peabody immediately. Since my job was going to be a big résumé

*Name has been changed to protect privacy.

builder and launch my career, I thought it was real important that the firm I chose was going to hold its value as a *name* over time. So it came down to two firms—Company X and Company Y, the one I joined. My decision was based partly on the culture of the firms and partly on the positions they offered me.

What did you perceive to be the cultural differences between Company X and Company Y?

I felt that Company X was really "fratty," like a fraternity. When I visited the firm, I noticed a lot of guys that I felt were aggressive—they talked about having beer in the office on Fridays and that sort of thing, like in a locker room. I wasn't impressed with the women there either. The women were scarce, and they acted more like men—they were forced to act that way. I remember thinking that they weren't women there like me. And people had told me that there was a "star system" at Company X as opposed to a team culture. Company Y I thought of as being good guys, nice relationship bankers. It didn't seem to me to be like *Liar's Poker* at Company Y. Of course, I interviewed with people from Company Y that I loved, and then I got in there and I had never seen the people I was actually going to work with.

How did your role as an analyst change over time?

As a first-year analyst, I crunched numbers, managed and analyzed large amounts of information, analyzed comparable deals, prepared a lot of exhibits. As time went on, I did less assisting in developing presentations and client relationships and more of taking these roles on fully. When I was a first-year analyst, for example, a vice president would ask me to develop four exhibits for a presentation on Tuesday. Sometimes I was invited to the presentation, sometimes I wasn't. By the time I was a second-year, there were times when they would say, we want you to make a presentation next Tuesday, let's talk about what the content should be. And I would get to make decisions about the content.

What do you want to tell people about the culture in investment banking?

I think your perception of the culture depends on what type of person you are. But to summarize *my* opinions, I think that banking is by necessity team-oriented because no one person can get all the work done. I think that investment banking is a little locker room-ish; there are a lot of guys high-fiving and people standing around playing in football pools and fantasy baseball leagues. There's definitely a lot of male bonding that goes on, which alienates a lot of women. It's male-dominated, and many women bankers feel the need to emulate the men that work there. Also, I think that people have real strong work ethics. There's not a whole lot of understanding about what's going on in your personal life. It's looked down on to bring your personal life to work. I think there's some spirit of helping people to develop professionally, but I don't think it's as evident as in other business settings.

What other skills or assets helped you to be successful in investment banking?

You need to be pretty confident in your abilities, because people don't fork out a lot of praise. You need to be relatively tough. People will eat you alive if they think you're weak or can't take what they're dishing out. They'll talk about you and joke about you and be less likely to want to work with you if you're not tough. I remember reviews where they'd read me comments like she's "tough" and has got "killer instincts." It wasn't what I wanted to be known for, but they thought this was positive feedback. Being very detail-oriented is also important. People will never forgive you for putting the wrong company name on a book, or making a mistake on a number. Forever you'll be known as the person who is careless. People form impressions very early, and for two years you'll have to live with those impressions.

What's the biggest perk you receive in investment banking?

You get a big stamp of approval on your résumé. Everyone assumes you're a hard worker, you're smart, and no one ever questions your analytical skills. It gets you over a lot of hurdles in getting into business schools and getting jobs later in life. And contacts, too, great contacts.

So the biggest perks aren't the money and other material goods?

The money at first was really impressive to me, but then I saw how fast it went. It's fleeting. I definitely liked taking chauffered cars home and using car phones and going to the Plaza for lunch. But it wears a little thin when you realize that a two-hour lunch at the Plaza means you're going to be at work for two extra hours that night.

Did it ever seem weird to you that at twenty-two, you were making $50,000 a year and staying at Ritz Carltons across the country?

It always felt to me like our company was buying my time. They were buying those years from me. What they were doing was paying me to live there and give up my personal life. So, the Ritz Carlton and all the rest of the compensation didn't strike me as odd because I felt early on that I deserved those things. They bought my life.

Exactly how many of your hours did they buy each week?

I think I worked on average from 7 A.M. until 10 P.M. Just enough time to get eight hours of sleep, but not enough time to do anything social. To give you a point of reference, our company pays for a chauffered ride home if you work past 8 P.M. I only took the subway home twice in my entire first year. I'd also work one day on the weekends.

Could you summarize the positive and negative impacts on you of working in banking?

On the positive side, you carry around a stamp of approval for the rest of your life, and it gets you into business school. I learned that I was tougher than I thought I was. I gained a lot of confidence dealing with senior people. I developed strong quantitative and project management skills.

On the negative side, I think my attention span was permanently shortened. It was so fast-paced that you didn't have the time to do planning and analysis, and I adjusted to that. I think I have less patience for long-term analysis.

What were your managers like—did they help you develop professionally?

There's an emphasis on short-term, monetary results in investment banking. The questions that are asked are "What have you done for me, what money have you made for the company, what transactions have you closed?" There are people who are horrible managers who can make managing director because they're profit centers unto themselves. They have no social skills, never contributed to anyone's development, and it doesn't matter because they're getting deals done.

Where has the analyst job led you?

Well, as I said, it helped me get into business school. In terms of getting a job, I think that the banking experience would have helped me a lot more had I wanted to stay in finance. After business school, I had a lot of opportunities in principal investments, business development, and other finance-oriented jobs. But my experience didn't help me get a job in marketing beyond just a general stamp of approval.

That's interesting. Would you therefore recommend to undergraduates to take a job in a field that they might be interested in pursuing long term?

That's always my advice to people. If you know what you want to do, get in there and get some experience and credibility. There were so many people coming out of business school with me who *only* had consulting or banking in their backgrounds, and no recruiters wanted to talk to them about doing marketing or operations or line jobs. They wanted to talk to them about strategic planning or finance. The good news is that once I was able to work my way into a marketing position, the fact that I had done consulting and investment banking gave people the impression that I was a high-quality employee, that I was responsible and reliable. It's given me a cachet for life.

How to Use the Company Profiles

The companies profiled here have fact-checked their profiles, but the viewpoints and insider interviews were independently gathered and developed by the author. I've randomly selected "insiders" to provide their personal opinion of each company. *I have included these interviews to provide you with an honest point of view that you don't typically get in the recruiting process, but they should not be taken as absolute truth.* Interviews are by nature very subjective, and other insiders might disagree vehemently with the opinions expressed in them.

How can you use the profiles to help you? Be diligent in getting your résumé to the right person. Recruiting for the prestigious positions you are applying for is generally run as a separate process from recruiting for other departments within an investment bank or consulting firm. The company profiles list the name and title of the person you'll need to send your résumé to, as of 1997. However, *recruiters and international offices change frequently,* sometimes every few months. It is absolutely imperative to call the company or visit its Web site to verify names and locations before sending out your package.

When calling investment banks and large consulting firms, even if you give the receptionist the title of the person you are looking for, your call might be forwarded to the Human Resources Department. Do not send your résumé there, since they typically do not run the recruiting process for the prestigious analyst and associate positions.

Other information about the company profiles:

- "Recruiting" indicates whether the company's recruiting process is centralized (all résumés screened at headquarters) or decentralized (each office screens résumés and runs its own recruiting process). Investment banks tend to have centralized recruiting processes, so you should send your résumé to the recruiting contact at the headquarters office.
- For consulting firms, the recruiter at the headquarters office is listed, but often you can apply to other offices directly. In this case, call the headquarters office to get a phone number and name for the regional office, or visit the company's Internet site.
- "Summer Jobs" indicates whether the firm has summer positions for either undergraduates or graduate school students.
- "Undergrad Title" and "Grad Title" indicate which titles the firm is using for the "analyst" and "associate" positions. Check this before writing your cover letter so that you can properly refer to the position you are applying for.
- Use the profile for three things: good reasons for why you want to work for the company, good questions to ask at the end of the interview, and an understanding of the firm's culture so that you can present yourself in a way that's compatible.

Room no. 519

$12,950
12,950 (taxes)
1036 Title
43
14029

18GCMS648SA1478O8
4

$2001
GPA
$2001

07 grad. prog.
06 MEGA   *Drums*
03 Com. Secy'   *Teams*
02 Cult.
00 Placement
99 MEA
98 LDS
97 Secy'

* Organization to
* Person to Person
* Environment (team building)
  - tone
  - Everyone is imp
  - Influsing my vision
* Assess

* Counseling
* Innate

PROFILES OF
THE LEADING
CONSULTING
FIRMS

Andersen Consulting

NAME: **Andersen Consulting**

ADDRESS: **1345 Avenue of the Americas, 8th Floor, New York, NY 10105, (212) 708-4400**

WEB SITE: **www.ac.com**

◆

RECRUITING: **For Strategy, apply to New York office. For Technology or Process/ Change management, apply to office of interest. Apply to one office** *only.*

SUMMER JOBS: **Undergraduate and Graduate levels**

GRAD RECRUITING CONTACT (STRATEGY): **Sara Karlen Lacombe, National Director of Campus Recruiting**

GRAD RECRUITING CONTACT (TECHNOLOGY, PROCESS/CHANGE MANAGEMENT): **Apply to office of interest. See Internet site for address.**

GRAD TITLE: **Consultant (Strategy, Technology, Process/Change Management)**

UNDERGRAD RECRUITING CONTACT (STRATEGY): **Sara Karlen Lacombe, National Director of Campus Recruiting**

UNDERGRAD RECRUITING CONTACT (TECHNOLOGY, PROCESS/CHANGE MANAGEMENT): **Apply to office of interest. See Internet site for address.**

UNDERGRAD TITLE: **Business Analyst (Strategy); Analyst (Technology, Process/ Change Management)**

◆

RELATED READING: "Consulting Giant's Hot Offer: Jobs, Jobs, Jobs," *Wall Street Journal,* March 6, 1996. Richard Melcher, "Who Says You Can't Find Good Help?" *Business Week,* January 8, 1996. "Inside Andersen's Army of Advice," *Fortune,* October 4, 1993.

OTHER OFFICES: (Domestic) Atlanta, Boston, Chicago, Cincinnati, Cleveland, Dallas, Denver, Detroit, Hartford, Houston, Kansas City, Los Angeles, Minneapolis, Nashville, New York, Palo Alto, Philadelphia, Phoenix, Portland, Raleigh, San Francisco, Seattle, St. Louis, Washington, D.C.; (International) Auckland, Bangkok, Beijing, Brussels, Buenos Aires, Caracas, Frankfurt, The Hague, Hong Kong, Jakarta, Johannesburg, Kuala Lumpur, London, Madrid, Manila, Melbourne, Milan, Paris, São Paulo, Seoul, Shanghai, Singapore, Sophia Antipolis, Stockholm, Sydney, Taipei, Tokyo, Toronto, Zurich

PART I: ANALYSIS

If you're going to remember one thing about Andersen Consulting, remember that it is the largest consulting firm in the world. Netting over $5 billion each year in revenues, Andersen is bigger than many of the clients it serves. Andersen's size has several major implications for you as job-hunter and junior employee. Andersen offers a highly diversified group of services to clients and, luckily, a large number of jobs to graduating students. "Being [the] one stop for a multitude of major corporations," the *Wall Street Journal* argues, "has enabled Andersen to be among the most aggressive and successful recruiters on college campuses." Andersen is hiring over 5,000 college students each year.* Given these numbers, it is worth your while to apply to Andersen.

Size has other ramifications. Andersen trains hundreds of fresh-faced students en masse at its corporate campus in Illinois—then "deploys armies of consultants"† to projects around the world. If you're looking for an intimate work environment, you may want to look elsewhere. Engagement teams can range in size from three people to 200. But Andersen offers employees an instantly recognizable brand name and excellent resources. For example, consultants use a proprietary network, the Knowledge Xchange™, to quickly call up research gathered by colleagues around the world. This type of technology can greatly improve an analyst's work (not to mention work hours). According to figures the firm has provided, Andersen spends $250 million annually, or 7 percent of its fee base, on training employees. Finally, there are hints that Andersen's capital also provides a bigger buffer against hard times; the firm never has had a major downsizing.

For a firm that built its reputation on technology consulting, Andersen has diversified widely to provide "one-stop shopping" to clients. First, the firm expanded successfully into reengineering and other operations consulting areas. Now, seeing a future full of promise for strategy consulting, Andersen is building up its Strategic Services practice.

Andersen's business is organized into four practices in order to provide clients with an integrated approach: Strategic Services, Process, Technology, and Change Management.

Strategic Services has little contact with the other practices and there is little movement between Strategic Services and other groups. Strategic Services is seen as more competitive to break into. Strategy professionals account for approximately 5 percent of Andersen's total workforce but apparently generate 20 percent of total revenues. Competitors remain skeptical about Andersen's credibility as strategy consultant given its technology roots—they claim that Andersen uses strategic consulting as simply a front to sell more technology work.‡ But the firm points to a personnel growth rate of 33 percent in Strategic Services as evidence of its growing success with clients and suggests that if the Strategic Services practice stood alone, it would be second in size to McKinsey in the strategy consulting market. Andersen is paying more and conferring fancier titles to strategy consultants than to consultants in other practices in order to attract top-notch brains away from the elite strategy firms.

Each of the four practices performs its own recruiting, so it is important to call

*"Consulting Giant's Hot Offer: Jobs, Jobs, Jobs," *Wall Street Journal*, March 3, 1996.
†"How 10 Leading Consulting Firms Stack Up," *Business Week*, July 25, 1994.
‡Interviews with consultants at strategy firms.

the recruiting contact listed and ask for the right contact person for the practice in which you're interested. Andersen also has six industry coverage groups that crisscross its functional practices: products (industrial and consumer), health care, utilities, government, communications, and financial services.

Junior Andersen professionals work on one client project at a time. Most consultants on the systems side of Andersen are assigned to one specific industry group, where they are encouraged to develop industry expertise. Systems consultants tend to be on client site five days per week. A typical systems project team is much bigger, with even the smallest systems teams reaching ten to twenty people.

Consultants typically are hired from business schools or with significant previous business experience. Some systems consultants have been promoted from within without an MBA. Strategy consultants are promoted to manager on average after three years, to associate partner after another three years, and to full partner after another three or four years.

Analysts (Technology, Process, and Change Management practices) or *business analysts* (Strategic Services practice) are recruited from undergraduate institutions. Since technology consulting remains a large proportion of Andersen's business, most undergraduates are hired into the Process and Technology practices rather than into the Strategic or Change Management practices. A relatively high number of Andersen analysts have degrees in engineering, computer science, or other "hard" subjects.* Liberal arts majors, though, should still feel very welcome applying to Andersen. Analysts in the Technology, Process, and Change Management practices may have the opportunity to build a long-term career with the firm without an MBA, while business analysts are expected to remain with the firm for two years, then return to business school.

Numbers: ANDERSEN CONSULTING

Founded: 1989 (Separated from Arthur Andersen)   **Ownership Structure:** Partnership

Sample Clients: Astra/Merck, Dow Chemical, London Stock Exchange, Hong Kong Telecom, Deutsche Bahn AG, Allstate Insurance, BP Exploration, Sony Corp., Harley-Davidson

	1996	1995	1994	1993	1992
Net Revenues ($M)	5,300	4,224	3,452	2,876	2,772
No. of Employees	44,000	38,000	32,711	29,296	26,730

Roles: Analyst/Business Analyst   Consultant   Manager   Assoc. Partner   Partner
⟶

Sources: *Wall Street Journal, Business Week,* Andersen Consulting

---

*"Consulting Giant's Hot Offer: Jobs, Jobs, Jobs," *Wall Street Journal,* March 3, 1996.

PART II: INSIDER INTERVIEW

This former analyst worked on technology issues, as opposed to Strategic Services, at Andersen.

How would you describe the people and the culture at Andersen?

I had a good experience with the people I met. You're dealing with motivated, intelligent people who are team players. You got done what you had to and it wasn't for your own personal gain. It was a work-hard, play-hard mentality, and it's definitely a conservative atmosphere.

How would you summarize the positives and negatives of working at Andersen?

The negatives were that when I went into the home office, I wouldn't know what floor to go to or who to talk to. I once spent an hour figuring out where to sit down and where to put my coat. It's just such a vast enterprise that you have a hard time really relating to the overall company. Every time I went to a division meeting, I would know about 40 people, and the other 2,000 I didn't know at all. What really mattered was who you were working with. If you had a good manager, you were happy. The positives were you got put in positions where you had a lot of responsibility. They had twenty-four- or twenty-five-year-olds working on multimillion-dollar projects. Also, it was really a team atmosphere, which I liked. Andersen was a great experience.

PROFILE

Arthur D. Little, Inc.

NAME: **Arthur D. Little, Inc.**
HEADQUARTERS: **25 Acorn Park, Cambridge, MA 02140, (617) 498-5000**
WEB SITE: **www.arthurdlittle.com**

◆

RECRUITING: **Centralized through Cambridge**
SUMMER JOBS: **Graduate level only**
GRAD RECRUITING CONTACT (HEADQUARTERS): **Tracy Keogh**
GRAD TITLE: **Consultant**
UNDERGRAD RECRUITING CONTACT (HEADQUARTERS): **Tracy Keogh**
UNDERGRAD TITLE: **Business Analyst**

◆

RELATED READING: "The 10 Best Outfits for You to Join—and Then Quit," *Money Magazine,* May 1996. Joann Lublin, "Midsize Consulting Firms Lose Out to Both Big Guys and Boutiques," *The Wall Street Journal,* March 6, 1996.

OTHER OFFICES: (Domestic) Arlington, Chicago, Houston, Los Angeles, New York, Philadelphia, San Francisco, Santa Barbara, Washington DC; (International) Berlin, Bogota, Brussels, Bombay, Buenos Aires, Cambridge, Caracas, Gothenburg, Hong Kong, London, Madrid, Mexico City, Milan, Monterrey, Moscow, Munich, Paris, Prague, Riyadh, Rotterdam, São Paulo, Singapore, Seoul, Stockholm, Sydney, Tokyo, Toronto, Vienna, Wiesbaden, Zurich

PART I: ANALYSIS

Founded in 1886, Arthur D. Little is the oldest management consulting firm in the world. The company's roots in science are long and proud too: A.D. Little pioneered contract research and eschews the lastest consulting fads and management theories for good old-fashioned common sense, scientifically proven ideas, and knowledge based on experience.

A.D. Little's culture is conservative, its image traditional. Common sense, hard work, and practicality are valued, and "prima donnas" don't last long. Clients are heavily integrated into the consulting process. One difference from other consulting firms is critical: The company has a strong emphasis on knowledge and training and consultants with years of industry expertise or specialized academic training since they can speak credibly to clients about specific fields. Many consultants at A.D. Little hold advanced degrees in engineering, medical, and scientific fields, and environmental management, among other areas. The company has product and technology development laboratories in Cambridge, Massachusetts, and Cambridge, UK.

A.D. Little is the only management consulting firm to own and operate an accredited school of management, developed originally to train government workers from Africa. At A.D. Little's program, one can earn a one-year master's degree in management. This school also conducts A.D. Little's intensive, career-staged training of employees.

A.D. Little finds that its business is increasingly international, with 60 percent of revenue generated overseas.* This is more of a generalist consulting firm than most, offering services in three very different areas: Management consulting; technology and product development; and environmental, health, and safety consulting.

The Technology and Product Development division often performs research under contract. This area encompasses sophisticated research facilities and laboratories in the United States and abroad. Technology and Product Development helps clients assess technology-related opportunities and make technology investment decisions. The Environmental, Health, and Safety division helps companies comply with their responsibilities by combining management and scientific expertise; it provides services such as environmental, health, and safety auditing and safety and risk management.

However, the firm has a management consulting emphasis, with 75 percent

*Presentation at Stanford Business School, October 14, 1996.

of revenue generated through management consulting fees. Within management consulting, A.D. Little employs a matrix structure of crisscrossing functional and industry "practice areas." There are eight core functional areas: strategy, organizational management, customer management, technology and innovation management, manufacturing management, supply chain management, information management, and corporate finance. New employees are hired into an industry practice area but build up their knowledge of functional practice areas. The areas in which the company excels are those in which they can leverage their technology expertise: in particular, the automotive, chemicals, telecommunications, and health care industries.

A.D. Little has been experiencing a compound annual growth rate in income of about 14 percent since 1991, and expects to mushroom in 1996 and 1997 and expand its staff by 35 percent.

A.D. Little consultants work on more than one "case" at once. A typical A.D. Little case team consists of three to ten people, at a variety of levels. The "consultant" position is the equivalent of the "associate" MBA-level position at other firms. A.D. Little hires a broader mix of people than other consulting firms: Ph.D.'s, lawyers, and others are hired in addition to the more traditional MBA recruits. Although progression of five levels in five years is not unheard of, a more typical path from consultant to director takes eight years. *Analysts* are recruited from undergraduate institutions. They are expected to remain with the firm for two or three years.

Firmwide employee turnover is reported to be about 12 percent.* Long-term consultants are rewarded with ownership of A. D. Little stock; the company is 100 percent owned by employees. Most consultants are located close to headquarters, with about 65 percent of the North American staff living in the Boston area.

Numbers: ARTHUR D. LITTLE, INC.

Founded: 1886   **Ownership Structure:** Partnership

Sample Clients: Thomas Cook Group, British Gas, Scott Aviation, Northern Telecom

	1996	1995	1994
Net Revenues ($Millions)	574	514	428
No. of Consultants	1,272	1,095	975

Roles: Analyst   Consultant   Manager   Sr. Manager   Assoc. Director   Director
→

Sources: A.D. Little Press Release, March 5, 1996; A.D. Little "Pathway to Performance"; A.D. Little "Finding the Right Path"; A.D. Little, *Consultants News*

---

*Presentation at Stanford Business School, October 14, 1996.

PART II: INSIDER INTERVIEW

How would you describe the company's culture?

I would describe the company as a group of distinctive individual personalities rather than a school of identical fish. It's relatively light on the political bullshit. I always felt that there were open lines of communication.

What did you like best about your experience at the firm?

I liked the fact that I had the opportunity to join an industry practice and focus. In my case, for someone who is not particularly drawn to consulting per se, it was nice to be able to specialize in an industry of preference. Generally speaking, A.D. Little allowed people to "carve their own paths" of interest. Also, I found A.D. Little a friendly environment to work in; there were nice people and very happy clients.

What would you like to have changed about your experience at the firm?

I would have preferred cases with a bit more focus on implementation. Also, training was weak, although this is improving substantially.

What do you think A.D. Little looks for in its new hires?

They look for creativity, strong individual personalities who enjoy working in team settings, and strong technical acumen or interest in technology—since they focus so much on technology-intensive industry clients. They like people with intensity and ambition but who are not sharks.

What advice would you give someone seeking a job at A.D. Little?

They are not the slickest or smoothest consulting firm in terms of their recruiting efforts, particularly toward MBAs and undergraduates, so you have to be patient and pursue them aggressively. Have your own opinion; they don't need a bunch of cookie-cutter clones or slavish classical strategists.

PROFILE

A.T. Kearney, Inc.

NAME: **A.T. Kearney, Inc.**
HEADQUARTERS: **222 West Adams Street, Chicago, IL 60606, (312) 648-0111**
WEB SITE: **www.atkearney.com**

◆

RECRUITING: **Centralized through Chicago; state in cover letter your office of interest**
SUMMER JOBS: **Graduate level only**
GRAD/UNDERGRAD RECRUITING CONTACT: **Christi Brewton, Recruiting Coordinator**
GRAD TITLE: **Associate**
UNDERGRAD TITLE: **Business Analyst**

◆

RELATED READING: Ronald Yates, "Kearney Finds Life with EDS Fulfilling," *Chicago Tribune*, September 30, 1996. Joann Lublin, "GM's EDS Has Been Courting Kearney, A Bigger Management-Consulting Rival," *The Wall Street Journal*, February 17, 1996. Tim Dickson, "A Blend of Aggression and Tradition," *The Financial Times*, June 12, 1995. Joann Lublin, "EDS Unit's Bid For Kearney May Create a Culture Clash," *The Wall Street Journal*, May 5, 1995. John Byrne, "Lock the Doors, It's EDS," *Business Week*, September 19, 1994.

OTHER OFFICES: (Domestic) Alexandria, Atlanta, Boston, Cambridge, Chicago, Cleveland, Corapolis, Costa Mesa, Dallas, Denver, Detroit, Englewood, Houston, Los Angeles, Miami, Minneapolis, New York, Ottawa, Philadelphia, Phoenix, Plano, Redwood City, Rosslyn, San Diego, San Francisco, Santa Clara, Southfield, St. Louis, Stamford, Washington DC; (International) Amsterdam, Barcelona, Beijing, Berlin, Brussels, Buenos Aires, Caracas, Copenhagen, Dusseldorf, Helsinki, Hong Kong, Kuala Lumpur, Lisbon, London, Madrid, Melbourne, Mexico City, Milan, Moscow, Munich, Oslo, Ottawa, Paris, Prague, São Paulo, Seoul, Singapore, Stockholm, Stuttgart, Sydney, Tokyo, Toronto, Warsaw, Wellington, Zug

PART I: ANALYSIS

Looking for a firm where assertive new hires can move up the ladder quickly? A.T. Kearney might be the consulting firm for you. There have been major changes at this Chicago-based management consulting firm over the past few years, driven primarily by its 1995 merger into Electronic Data Systems. Even before the EDS acquisition, Kearney had been growing at double digits for several years. The new opportunities created by the merger, coupled with Kearney's intense organic growth, have created an environment that is extremely dynamic. Much of the future of the "new" Kearney is yet to be defined. This growth constitutes an opportunity to have an immense impact on the company's direction and internal processes.

A.T. Kearney is a firm that represents not only change but also old-line tradition. The firm is actually a very early spin-off from McKinsey & Co., the strategy consulting firm. A.T. Kearney, Inc., was born when McKinsey partners Andrew Thomas Kearney and Marvin Bower agreed to go their separate ways, with Bower continuing to operate McKinsey's office out of New York and Kearney opening a separate company in Chicago. The firm began operating in Europe in 1964 and in Asia in 1972. Although it remained a sleeping giant for many years, A.T. Kearney has experienced explosive growth from the 1980s to the present. Between 1983 and 1988 alone, the firm tripled in size.

While McKinsey is known for strategy consulting, Kearney is a firm known for its strength in operational consulting. The firm's 1996 revenues were comprised of

40 percent operations and organizational design, 35 percent strategy, 15 percent information technology strategy, and 10 percent marketing and sales.* Providing tangible results to clients is of great importance to Kearney and has served the company well at a time when clients are requiring consultants to implement change rather than simply make recommendations. Combined with EDS's strength in information technology consulting, Kearney now stands as one of the few firms that can credibly offer a fully integrated consulting offering.

Although now a subsidiary of EDS, much of Kearney remains intact. The firm's headquarters remain in Chicago, and former Kearney chairman Fred Steingraber remains as CEO. Most important, the Kearney name stays on the door, which helps it leverage its brand-name recognition.

Kearney consultants have traditionally been known as independent, self-reliant, and pragmatic. Consultants take a hands-on approach to solving clients' problems. Has the integration of two cultures—individualistic consulting firm and large technology company—been successful? So far, no major fireworks have erupted, and few employees have lost their jobs. The passage of time also will help, especially since EDS is predisposed to hiring consultants aggressively and populating itself with new blood. Before the merger, EDS had built a 1,300-person firm from scratch in two years.

The company's strategies for the future will continue to evolve. Kearney is targeting the automotive, financial institutions, and communications and electronics industries as its highest priorities for growth. According to an internal Kearney newsletter, it hopes to derive 50 to 60 percent of its business from clients in these industries by the year 2000. In particular, the firm will focus on technology convergence and the way it impacts several sectors.

Kearney consultants are assigned to Industry or Regional account teams, such as Consumer Products or the Midwest. Besides working on project teams, consultants also have the opportunity to help the firm develop its methodologies and research—its "intellectual capital." Consultants are rotated into these types of internal projects.

Business analysts typically are hired from undergraduate institutions. They are expected to remain at the firm for two years before returning to school for a graduate degree. The firm makes offers to outstanding analysts to return after business school. *Associates* join A.T. Kearney with an MBA or other relevant postgraduate degree and between two and four years of work experience. Associates typically are promoted to *manager* after two to four years, then to *principal* after another three years. New associates and business analysts participate in a training program when they arrive at the firm. Mentors are assigned to guide new employees and help them through the performance review process.

Consultants News, September 1996.

Numbers: A.T. KEARNEY, INC.

Founded: 1926   **Ownership Structure:** 100% owned by EDS

Sample Clients: Federal Express, Sony, Bank of America, Sears, Spring, General Motors, Chemical Bank, Chase Manhattan, Rolls-Royce, Westpac, BP Oil

	1996	1995	1994	1993
Net Revenues ($Millions)	870	650	346	278
No. of Consultants	2,300	2,095	1,007	925

Roles: Business Analyst   Associate   Manager   Principal   Officer

Sources: A.T. Kearney, A.T. Kearney brochure "Facts about A.T. Kearney," interviews with former employees, *Consultants News*

PART II: INSIDER INTERVIEW

How would you describe the company's culture?

A.T. Kearney's culture is down-to-earth and results-oriented. The firm has a strong implementation focus, which manifests itself in the large amount of time that consultants at all levels spend working on client sites. There is a real roll-up-your-sleeves type of commitment to clients.

What did you like best about your experience at the firm?

People, responsibility, and exposure, in that order. A.T. Kearney attracts some of the brightest and most dynamic, and at the same time most down-to-earth, people I have met. The responsibility is extraordinary. As an analyst, you work face-to-face with the client right from day one and will be asked to lead client teams and present to management after a very short time. The wide scope of A.T. Kearney's engagements also allows for a breadth of experiences, be they different industries, function, or geography.

What did you like least about your experience at the firm?

Traveling is what lures many people into consulting, but after a while it really loses its luster. Because A.T. Kearney consultants are usually on-site, they travel *a lot.*

What types of candidates do you think the firm prefers?

A.T. Kearney tries to target candidates with exceptional academic and professional records. At the analyst level, there is no preference as far as area of study is concerned. It's your academic performance that counts. As with all consulting firms, interpersonal skills are equally, if not more, important, especially because consultants work directly with clients on a daily basis.

PROFILE

Bain & Company, Inc.

NAME: **Bain & Company, Inc.**
HEADQUARTERS: **Two Copley Place, Boston, MA 02116, (617) 572-2000**
WEB SITE: **www.bain.com**

◆

RECRUITING: **Apply to Boston or to local office; mention geographical preference**
SUMMER JOBS: **Graduate and Undergraduate levels**
GRAD RECRUITING CONTACT (HEADQUARTERS): **Cris Pontes-Alzes, Recruiting Manager**
GRAD TITLE: **Consultant**
UNDERGRAD RECRUITING CONTACT (HEADQUARTERS): **Jennifer Fulton, Undergraduate Recruiting Manager**
UNDERGRAD TITLE: **Associate Consultant**

◆

RELATED READING: "Wouldn't It Be Better to Work for the Good Guys?" *Fortune,* October 14, 1996. "The Ways Chief Executive Officers Lead," *Harvard Business Review,* May 1, 1996. "Bain & Company: International Expansion," *Harvard Business Review,* November 28, 1994. Glenn Rifkin, "Don't Ever Judge This Consultant by Her Cover," *The New York Times,* May 1, 1994. "Orit Gadiesh: Pride at Bain & Co.," *Harvard Business School case,* January 14, 1994. Paul Hemp, "Did Greed Destroy Bain & Co.?" *The Boston Globe,* February 26, 1991. Keith Hammonds, "Can Bain Consultants Get Bain & Co. Out of this Jam?" *Business Week,* February 11, 1991.

OTHER OFFICES: (Domestic) Atlanta, Chicago, Dallas, Los Angeles, San Francisco; (International) Beijing, Brussels, Geneva, Hong Kong, London, Madrid, Milan, Mexico City, Moscow, Munich, Paris, Rome, Seoul, Singapore, Stockholm, Sydney, Tokyo, Toronto

PART I: ANALYSIS

Bain & Company is a well-known name in the consulting industry and one of a prestigious group of Boston-based strategy firms. Founded in 1973 by former BCG consultant William Bain, the company was once nicknamed "the KGB of consulting" for its secretive practices: In Bain's early days, partners did not carry business cards and clients were referred to by code names. The firm's services were pricey, partly because of the exclusivity of its services: Bain set a policy of working for only one company at a time in any industry in order to prevent conflicts of interest. One of the first consultancies to emphasize the *implementation* of strategic advice, Bain consultants preferred to work on increasing a company's market value rather than simply handing clients a list of recommendations. To win business, Bill Bain liked to show prospective customers the increase in stock prices of companies that Bain had advised.

The company hit a rough spot in the 1980s, when it found itself overstaffed and facing soft business conditions. Restricted by its one-client-per-industry policy, Bain also was hurt by having to turn down business. In the meantime, competition was increasing from firms that had adopted Bain's implementation focus. Moreover, the firm's founders had created an employee stock ownership plan, borrowed against it to take out cash for themselves, and saddled the firm with debt. In 1990 Bain laid off about 15 percent of its employees, including recent college graduates. In response to increasing demands of junior officers for a share in management and profits, Bain shifted ownership of the company from its eight original owners to the company's then seventy officers, making them partners.

Since then the company has recovered and thrived. Job-seekers, take notice: Bain jobs may be some of the most secure in the industry, since the firm seems determined at all costs not to repeat its 1990 layoffs. Since many clients did not see it as an issue, the firm has somewhat relaxed its policy of serving only one client per industry. Bain has remained focused, resisting the temptation to diversify—although it does a mix of strategy and operations work, the majority of its revenues are derived from corporate strategy. Bain still emphasizes increasing the shareholder value of clients, proudly charting the stellar stock performance of its clients relative to the S&P 500. If you interview at Bain, you'd better say that you're focused on results—Bain doesn't write reports. The firm also has a principal investors advisory practice that helps clients assess the strategic value of properties being purchased, perform due diligence, and develop profit improvement plans.

According to insiders, Bain's culture is down-to-earth and spirited. Outgoing young Bainies, as they are known, reportedly are fun to work with. Senior managers are known to socialize with younger colleagues after work. "I would enjoy having a drink with just about anybody in the company," one Bain consultant commented during an interview. Offices are largely self-governed and develop their own unique atmosphere. There is acceptance of individualism at Bain, starting at the top: Orit Gadiesh, chairman of the board at Bain, is widely known within the firm for both a colorful style *and* for being a respected leader and strategist.

After leaving Bain, many consultants start their own companies. One insider estimates that 50 percent of consultants who leave are departing for entrepreneurial ventures or venture capital, whereas at other firms the same number might be leaving for Fortune 500 companies.

Bain is organized in a matrix structure of overlapping functional and industry groups:

- "Practice," or functional, areas: including competitive strategy, organizational effectiveness and change strategies, customer loyalty, logistics, information technology, mergers and acquisitions
- "Industry" areas: including industrial products, consumer goods, financial services, manufacturing, health care, and technology

However, industry affiliation plays a more dominant role in a consultant's career. Consultants are hired as generalists and over time will develop expertise in an industry area. For the most part, Bain consultants serve one client at a time. Teams spend some time on-site each week with clients.

Note that Bain has the reverse of titles used at other firms. *Consultants* are recruited from leading business schools, law schools, and other graduate programs. *Associate consultants* (known as ACs) are recruited from leading undergraduate institutions and are expected to remain with the firm for two years before returning to business school. Bain seems to hire undergraduates from a wider range of schools than other strategy consulting firms.

Bain has the distinction of pioneering the hiring of undergraduates, as it realized early on that it could recruit extremely bright young people to perform high-impact work. Associate consultants are provided with a two-week worldwide off-site training program sometime during their first few months. Many associate consultants are asked to stay for a third year. One insider estimates that in his class, 90 percent of the associate consultants stayed for a third year. Some associate consultants are promoted without an MBA, but most prefer to go back for an MBA. Bain often sponsors its associate consultants for an MBA.

Numbers: BAIN & COMPANY, INC.

Founded: 1973   **Ownership Structure:** Partnership

Sample Clients: DEC, American Trans Air, Continental Airlines, Dell, Eagle Snacks

	1996	1995	1994
Net Revenues ($M)	450	375	300
No. of Consultants	1,350	1,200	1,030

Roles: Associate Consultant   Consultant   Manager   Vice President   Director   →

Sources: *Consultants News*, Bain brochure "People Distinguish the Way We Work," *Business Week, Aviation Week, Fortune, Supermarket News*

PART II: INSIDER INTERVIEW

How would you describe the company's culture?

The company is very entrepreneurial. Corporate careers are considered to not be very exciting, and many Bainies aspire to run their businesses. The client is king—at all levels of the firm employees are expected to show total dedication to clients.

How would you describe the typical Bainie?

Young—although there are some older partners, oftentimes Bain feels like a school. Smart—the selection process is very tough and Bain is very strict on analytical abilities. Energetic—there are some workaholics around. Fun—Bainies love to party, and it is somewhat promoted by the firm's culture. It is okay to drink at a corporate event and have a good time.

What did you like best about your experience at the firm?

The exposure to the very top-level issues at great client companies and making lifelong friends among my Bain colleagues.

What would you like to have changed about your experience at the firm?

I would like to have had more control over my personal life. Sometimes it was hard to predict whether I would have a weekend off.

What do you think Bain looks for in its new hires?

People who are smart, analytical, comfortable with numbers, and can think logically. They should also be presentable to a client, mature, and show good team skills.

PROFILE

Booz•Allen & Hamilton, Inc.

NAME: **Booz•Allen & Hamilton, Inc.**
HEADQUARTERS: **101 Park Avenue, New York, NY 10178, (212) 697-1900**
WEB SITE: **www.bah.com**

◆

RECRUITING: **Apply to New York or local office if firm doesn't recruit on your campus**
SUMMER JOBS: **Graduate level only**
GRAD RECRUITING CONTACT (HEADQUARTERS): **MBA Recruiting Department; call for updated contact name**
GRAD TITLE: **Associate**
UNDERGRAD RECRUITING CONTACT (HEADQUARTERS): **Undergraduate Recruiting Department; call for updated contact name**
UNDERGRAD TITLE: **Consultant**

◆

RELATED READING: "Booz•Allen & Hamilton: Vision 2000," Harvard Business School case, March 25, 1996. "Mapping Corporate Brainpower," *Fortune*, October 30, 1995. "Merger Mania in Medialand," *Forbes*, October 23, 1995. John Byrne, "The Craze for Consultants," *Business Week*, July 25, 1994. Peter Coy, "Oh, What a Lovely War Game," *Business Week*, February 1, 1993.

OTHER OFFICES: (Domestic) Chicago, Cleveland, Dallas, Houston, Los Angeles, San Francisco, Washington DC; (International) Amsterdam, Abu Dhabi, Bangkok, Bogota, Buenos Aires, Caracas, Dubai, Dusseldorf, Frankfurt, Hong Kong, Jakarta, Kuala Lumpur, Lima, Melbourne, Mexico City, Milan, Mumbai, Munich, Paris, Santiago, São Paulo, Seoul, Shanghai, Singapore, Sydney, Tokyo, Vienna, Warsaw

PART I: ANALYSIS

Booz•Allen is a generalist management consulting firm that offers clients a "triple crown" of services: advice on strategy, operations, and technology. If you work at Booz•Allen, be prepared to provide clients with *integrated* solutions.

Booz•Allen is a good place for those who want a well-recognized name on their résumé. It is one of the oldest firms in the management consulting industry, founded in 1914 by Edwin Booz soon after he graduated from Northwestern University. Booz's vision for his start-up company was to perform statistical analysis and market research for corporations such as Goodyear Tire & Rubber and the Canadian Pacific Railroad. He also applied his skills to the country's benefit—in 1917 he was drafted into the army and helped reorganize the various bureaus of the War Department. On the eve of World War II, Booz provided consulting advice to the navy, beginning a long-term relationship with the government that continues to this day. In 1959 *Time* magazine dubbed Booz•Allen & Hamilton "the world's largest, most prestigious management consulting firm."

For many years, Booz•Allen was known as the sleeping giant of the industry. But its efforts to reinvigorate itself are evident: The firm has implemented a "vision 2000" strategy to lead it into the next century and has revamped its corporate image and recruiting brochures. Although it serves large Fortune 500 companies, Booz•Allen has a sizable government clientele, which distinguishes it from other strategy consulting firms. Booz•Allen is also unusual in that its people are specialists in industry or functional areas. Even undergraduates are hired into specific industry groups on the premise that clients will prefer consultants who have deep knowledge. Booz•Allen is a dominant player in consulting to the media industry, with a greater than 50 percent market share.

Booz•Allen is a traditional, mature, and efficiently run company. This is a company where structures are in place to make sure things don't fall through the cracks—and where you will find some "gray-hairs" whose backgrounds are in Corporate America rather than business school.

The firm is organized into two sectors: the Worldwide Technology Business (WTB) and the Worldwide Commercial Business (WCB). The Commercial Business provides business expertise primarily to major international corporations, while the Technology Business provides technology expertise primarily to the government. Insiders say that the Commercial Business is regarded as the more prestigious of the two divisions and that it hires from a very different background—mostly top colleges and MBA programs.

Commercial Business consists of six *practice groups:*

- Four industry strategy groups: Communications, Media, and Technology (CMT); Energy, Chemicals, and Pharmaceuticals (ECG); Financial Services (FSG); and Marketing and Engineering (MEG).
- Two functional strategy groups: Information Technology Group (ITG), which provides expertise in information technology across all industry groups and hires people with some technology experience or background; and Operations Management Group (OMG), which assists clients in developing competitive operations capabilities.

Client engagements are cross-functionally staffed so that you will at least get to work with consultants from other functional groups. For example, as a consultant in the Financial Services group, you would serve clients in the financial services industry; you wouldn't work with consultants in the Energy and Chemicals group, but you might work with consultants from the Operations Management or Information Technology groups to deliver an integrated product to the client. By all accounts, this system works smoothly, with consultants from different groups working together well.

One of the first things a new recruit does at Booz•Allen is attend "New Hire Orientation," a weeklong off-site program that provides an introduction to the firm's methodologies and ways of doing business.

All consultants are staffed on one engagement at a time and typically work on two or three engagements per year. According to insiders, initiative is rewarded at Booz•Allen: Those who ask for opportunities get them. The amount of travel depends on the engagement. Consultants are not required to spend a certain number of days each week at the client's offices.

Associates are hired from business and other graduate schools. There is apparently an informal "lead consultant" title between the graduate and undergraduate levels; if you are an advanced degree candidate in a field other than business, you should ask if you can apply for the lead consultant level rather than the straight undergraduate level.

Consultants are recruited from undergraduate institutions and are expected to stay at the firm for at least two to three years. There are not as many undergraduates at Booz•Allen as at other comparably sized firms, since apparently the Booz• Allen undergraduate recruiting structure is not as developed. But when it does recruit undergraduates, Booz•Allen hires highly intellectual and bright students with strong grades from top schools. Booz•Allen asks for SAT scores and a transcript from all undergraduate applicants. There is some indication that the firm may promote more undergraduates without an MBA than most consulting firms. Consultants do not join a general research pool but instead are assigned immediately to engagement teams.

Undergraduates should find out whether Booz•Allen is recruiting on their campus; if not, they should apply directly to the headquarters office. Undergraduates should include a cover letter, résumé, transcript, and standardized test scores in their packages, and should feel free to express preferences for specific offices.

Numbers: BOOZ·ALLEN & HAMILTON, INC.

Founded: 1914   **Ownership Structure:** Partnership

Sample Clients: Allied Signal, General Dynamics, Caterpillar, American Express, AT&T, Corning, Blue Cross/Blue Shield, Procter & Gamble, Viacom

	1996	1995	1994
Net Revenues ($Millions)	720	785	475
No. of Consultants	5,685	5,200	2,200

Roles: Consultant   Associate   Sr. Associate   Principal   Vice President
→

Sources: Booz·Allen materials, *Business Week*, Booz·Allen Web Site, *Consultants News*, Booz·Allen & Hamilton

---

PART II: INSIDER INTERVIEW

How would you describe the company's culture?

This is a stuffy company at the senior levels, but at the junior levels it is a pretty fun place to work. The company tries to be "PC" toward women.

What did you like best about your experience at the firm?

The people—there are great junior people to work with. Practices differ a lot. The Marketing group tended to be younger and more "hip" in every way. Operations and Information Technology were not as young. There was a bit of self-selection going on—it seemed as if all the new recruits wanted to go into Marketing. It was always perceived as the "coolest" thing to do.

What did you like least about your experience at the firm?

Sometimes as a junior person at Booz, I felt as if the firm really didn't listen to me. It was hard to get things done at the firm for consultants—the firm clearly cared more about associates (post-MBAs).

What types of candidates does the firm prefer?

The firm generally prides itself on hiring really smart people. Nailing the case questions in the interview is critical!

What advice would you give someone seeking a job at the company?

Practice case questions. Also, you have to play the recruiting game. You need to know which offices have stronger groups (and thus would tend to hire). For example, don't go into San Francisco wanting to work for the media group—there isn't one. Recruit smartly—it's a pretty random process when Booz gets so many good résumés. Talk to people and make sure the consultants (not just the recruiting coordinator in New York) know you and think you'd be fun to work with.

PROFILE

The Boston Consulting Group, Inc.

NAME: **The Boston Consulting Group, Inc.**
HEADQUARTERS: **Exchange Place, 53 State Street, Boston, MA 02109, (617) 973-1200**
WEB SITE: **www.bcg.com**

◆

RECRUITING: **Decentralized, office by office**
SUMMER JOBS: **Graduate level only**
GRAD RECRUITING CONTACT (HEADQUARTERS): **Call local office for name of Graduate Recruiting Coordinator**
GRAD TITLE: **Consultant**
UNDERGRAD RECRUITING CONTACT (HEADQUARTERS): **Call local office for name of Undergraduate Recruiting Coordinator**
UNDERGRAD TITLE: **Associate**

◆

RELATED READING: John Byrne, "The Craze for Consultants," *Business Week,* July 25, 1994.

OTHER OFFICES: (Domestic) Atlanta, Chicago, Dallas, Los Angeles, New York, San Francisco, Washington, D.C.; (International) Amsterdam, Auckland, Bangkok, Brussels, Budapest, Buenos Aires, Dusseldorf, Frankfurt, Hamburg, Helsinki, Hong Kong, Jakarta, Kuala Lumpur, Lisbon, London, Madrid, Melbourne, Milan, Monterrey, Moscow, Mumbai, Munich, Oslo, Paris, Seoul, Shanghai, Singapore, Stockholm, Sydney, Tokyo, Toronto, Warsaw, Zurich

PART I: ANALYSIS

Founded in 1963, The Boston Consulting Group (BCG) is a patriarch in the relatively young consulting industry. It is also McKinsey's most-often mentioned competitor. BCG is accustomed to giving McKinsey a run for its money in the prestigious "strategy" stratosphere of the consulting industry: In the early 1970s, BCG practically invented modern strategy consulting when it pioneered the development of consulting "products"—specific tools with hip names such as the "experience curve" and the "portfolio matrix"—and marketed them to corporate CEOs. This raised the stakes for all other consulting firms that had until then sold themselves simply on the basis of their intelligence. To this day, BCG consultants will tell you that a major difference from competitors is their creativity in solving problems. The firm is a leading recruiter of the brightest undergraduates and MBA students.

When presenting itself to clients, BCG stresses its creativity, its strength in competitive strategy, and its integration of the client into the consulting process. Most of BCG's clients are Fortune 500 companies or international corporations of comparable size, and BCG develops deep relationships with the CEOs of these companies. According to the firm, over 90 percent of its top fifty clients in 1993 retained the firm again for services in 1994. Though BCG is known primarily as a strategy advisor, it has diversified into process, or operations, consulting to the point that about 40 percent of its revenues come from operations consulting. The firm has helped companies make the organizational and operational changes needed to implement new strategies. For example, BCG was behind many cost-reduction efforts at leading companies in the 1990s. One of the company's major operations methodologies was "time-based competition," emphasizing a company's ability to produce and deliver products quickly as a major competitive advantage.

Like other strategy firms, BCG is secretive and low profile. A BCG consultant's style is polished and buttoned-down enough to fit in at the corner office. However, BCG is also known for having room not only for the "mainstream" person but also for the more quirky intellectual with a unique background. Each BCG office is self-governed, has developed a different culture, and staffs its consultants primarily on cases in the local region.

BCG consultants are generalists for their first few years at the firm, working for clients in many different industries. They usually work on two engagements at a time, particularly during their first few years at the firm. Because they are split between two engagements, BCG consultants cannot spend four days at one client's offices, and therefore they travel less than consultants at competing firms. New consultants attend one-week, off-site international workshops to introduce them to the firm. Consultants also benefit from ongoing workshops on oral presentation, writing skills, and specific analytical tools. In addition, more senior consultants participate in annual off-site training sessions.

Notice that BCG has the reverse of titles used at most consulting firms. The average new *consultant* at BCG has a master's degree in business or law and two to four years of work experience. After six to eight years at the firm, consultants are likely to have reached the *partner* level. Those who leave have moved on to jobs in large client corporations or in start-up companies.

Associates are recruited from undergraduate institutions and typically leave for business school after two or three years. Insiders report that you don't need to be a "star" in order to be asked to stay a third year. But even stars need to go back and get an MBA; very few associates are promoted without it.

Befitting its intellectual image, BCG is known for giving very case-intensive interviews. Instead of using the first-round interview to test your "fit" with the firm, BCG focuses on your analytical skills by taking up most of the interview with a case. Later rounds will then cover personality and résumé questions.

~

Numbers: THE BOSTON CONSULTING GROUP, INC.

Founded: 1963   **Ownership Structure:** Partnership

Sample Clients: Aetna, GTE, NYNEX

	1996	1995	1994	1993
Net Revenues ($Millions)	600	550	430	340
No. of Consultants	1,550	1,320	1,125	925

Roles: Associate   Consultant   Case Leader   Manager   Officer →

Sources: BCG, BCG Web site, BCG recruiting materials, *Business Week*

PART II: INSIDER INTERVIEW

How would you describe the company's culture?

BCG is a place where what matters are the people and what you can do. Compared to most places, BCG is apolitical, and face time has no value.

How would you describe the typical BCG consultant?

Fairly intellectual, down-to-earth, friendly, and eclectic.

What did you like best about your experience at the firm?

By far, the people I worked with made working at BCG worthwhile. BCG consultants often form real and long-term friendships with other people within the firm. For anyone considering consulting, BCG is a great place to work.

What do you think BCG looks for in its new hires?

BCG looks for demonstrated leadership, intellectual strength, and then that "something different."

PROFILE

CSC Index

NAME: CSC Index

HEADQUARTERS: Five Cambridge Center, Cambridge, MA 02142-1493, (617) 520-1500

WEB SITE: www.csc.com/index

◆

RECRUITING: **Centralized; apply to Cambridge**
SUMMER JOBS: **Graduate level only**
GRAD RECRUITING CONTACT (HEADQUARTERS): **Pauline Johnson, Director of Campus Recruiting**
GRAD TITLE: **Associate**
UNDERGRAD RECRUITING CONTACT: **Pauline Johnson, Director of Campus Recruiting**
UNDERGRAD TITLE: **Research Associate**

◆

RELATED READING: Joseph White, "Next Big Thing," *Wall Street Journal,* November 26, 1996. Alex Markels, "Champy, Management-Book Author, Quits CSC Index to Join Perot Systems," *The Wall Street Journal,* August 20, 1996. Joann Lublin, "Midsize Firms Lose Out to Both Big Guys and Boutiques," *The Wall Street Journal,* March 6, 1996. Willy Stern, "Did Dirty Tricks Create a Best-Seller?" *Business Week,* August 7, 1995.

OTHER OFFICES: (Domestic) Atlanta, Chicago, Dallas, New York, San Francisco; (International) Brussels, London, Munich, Paris

PART I: ANALYSIS

CSC Index is the management consulting arm of Computer Sciences Corporation, a large multinational firm that provides information technology-related services.

Until recently CSC Index was the home of James Champy, the coauthor of *Reengineering the Corporation* and the man who started the corporate reengineering craze of the early 1990s. Champy and coauthor Michael Hammer coined the term "reengineering" to describe their suggested radical redesign of companies' processes, organization, and culture. Reengineering advocated the elimination of corporate hierarchies and the use of vertically integrated product teams made up of marketing, manufacturing, and other functional areas. CSC Index rode reengineering's wave of popularity, enjoying a pace of growth twice the industry's average. According to company information, the firm nearly doubled its staff in the year following publication of *Reengineering the Corporation,* and produced revenues of $115 million in 1993.

Facing competitors who had successfully mimicked reengineering and a decline in client interest in reengineering, Index's growth slowed in 1994 and 1995. Then its reputation was affected in 1995 when *Business Week* published an article alleging that the firm had attempted to manipulate sales of its new book, *The Discipline of Market Leaders,* to make it appear on the *New York Times* bestseller list. Reacting to slumping revenues, the firm stopped recruiting second-year MBA candidates, decreased its number of vice presidents, and closed its office in Japan.

Today the firm's revenues stand at about $200 million. James Champy has left Index and the firm is moving beyond reengineering. In the consulting industry overall, engineering is "out" and a new management fad has replaced it: a corporate emphasis on growth. Index is responding by working with CEOs to define and implement growth strategies. The firm is focusing on service offerings such as strategic cost reduction, supply chain solutions, I/T strategy and outsourcing, and business process outsourcing. The company is also building up its consultant ranks again and has resumed recruiting second-year MBA students.

Culturally, the firm is a nonhierarchical, let-your-hair-down sort of place. It values confidence without arrogance and seems to turn out down-to-earth, likable consultants who aren't afraid to use unconventional approaches in their problem-solving. Because of the firm's flexibility, there is great opportunity for up-and-coming young consultants.

CSC Index integrates four consulting functions: Business strategy, Operations, Information Technology, and Change Management.

Sixty percent of the firm's business involves serving clients in the energy, financial services, health care, and information technology industries. As a consultant at Index, therefore, there is a high probability that you would work on a project in one of these industries.

Average project teams consist of three to six consultants, including one or two associates and one principal. Index consultants usually spend Mondays through Thursdays at the client site. The firm's partner-to-consultant ratio is approximately one to five.

Associates typically are hired from graduate schools or with significant previous business experience. New associates become generalists but later on develop industry specializations. *Research Associates* are recruited from undergraduate institutions and are expected to remain with the firm for two or three years.

Numbers: CSC INDEX

Founded: 1969   **Ownership Structure:** 100% subsidiary of publicly traded Computer Sciences Corp.

Sample Clients: Agway, Amoco, Hallmark, PepsiCo

	1996	1995	1994	1993
Net Revenues ($M)	200	175	140	115
No. of Employees	350	400	400	300

Roles: Analyst   Associate   Senior Associate   Managing Associate   Principal   Partner

Sources: CSC Web site, interviews with insiders, CSC Index, *Business Week*

PART II: INSIDER INTERVIEW

How would you describe the company's culture?

CSC Index prides itself on being a little offbeat, a little more fun and more creative in its problem-solving approach with the client. I feel that CSC Index consultants are very upfront, genuine, and are well received by our clients because we are perceived as trustworthy. Consultants I have worked with give their client an honest look in the mirror, which some other firms may not—because they are afraid to lose business. I think this makes us click well with clients who really do want to make things improve, as opposed to the type of client who just wants a consultant to stamp approval on their preconceived notions.

How would you describe the typical CSC consultant?

Many of us have unique career paths to CSC Index. I think for this reason there is no typical consultant. Some attributes are in common, however. Dedicated to teamwork and team process, highly creative, good synthesizing of ideas. People I have worked with are very intelligent but not snobbish. The breadth of backgrounds, styles, and opinions is what keeps us from being one-minded. I think this is good for our clients.

What did you like best about your experience at the firm?

Variety and being actively coached by fellow consultants. I worked in many industries in a variety of capacities, ranging from on-site work at a factory to analytical work regarding market entry.

What would you like to have changed about your experience at the firm?

I don't think I would have changed anything, which sounds canned, but I learned a lot from mistakes I made and everyone I worked with. If I had navigated around those experiences I would have learned a lot less.

What do you think CSC looks for in its new hires?

The person should have an acute business sense, an ability to work well with other consultants, and come across credibly to clients of many levels of seniority, really from the shop floor to the president's office. This means the person should not be arrogant. I also think we look for people with personality. One thing I like that a colleague said is that "Index is for people who hate the typical management consultant who takes a lot of client time and money, then dumps a bound report on the client's desk. Index is for people who hate that type of insincerity and ineffectiveness."

PROFILE

Deloitte & Touche Consulting Group

NAME: **Deloitte & Touche Consulting Group**
HEADQUARTERS: **10 Westport Road, PO Box 820, Wilton, CT 06897, (203) 761-3000**
WEB SITE: **www.dttus.com**

◆

RECRUITING: **Graduate: Centralized through Headquarters; Undergrad:
Decentralized through local office**
GRAD RECRUITING CONTACT: **Jack Beighley**
GRAD TITLE: **Senior Consultant**
UNDERGRAD RECRUITING CONTACT: **Jack Beighley**
UNDERGRAD TITLE: **Business Analyst / Systems Analyst**

◆

RELATED READING: Lee Berton, "Deloitte to Separate Consulting Practice From Its Auditing and Tax Operations," *The Wall Street Journal,* February 2, 1995.

OTHER OFFICES: (Domestic) Atlanta, Austin, Boston, Chicago, Cincinnati, Cleveland, Dallas, Detroit, Houston, Kansas City, Los Angeles, Minneapolis, New York City, Parisppany, Philadelphia, Pittsburgh, San Francisco, Seattle, Stamford, Washington D.C.; (International) Toronto, Montreal, London, Brussels, Paris, Singapore, Hong Kong, Sydney, Aukland, Johannesburg

PART I: ANALYSIS

The Deloitte & Touche name may sound very familiar to you. Perhaps it's because Deloitte & Touche Consulting is a division of one of the "Big Eight" accounting firms, Deloitte Touche Tohmatsu International—an impressively large organization with over 60,000 people and $6 billion in annual revenues worldwide.

Although they traditionally have been computer jocks, advising companies on computer systems and software that support and enable organizations, the Big Eight have now moved up into managers' offices to provide advice on operational issues and on implementing changes.

Deloitte & Touche Consulting Group exemplifies this trend. Aggressive and fast-growing, the company has been hiring newly minted MBAs and attempting to expand into strategy consulting from its core operations business. The company impresses clients with its ability to implement operational changes and, especially in the era of technology, redesign a company's business processes and systems to make new strategies work. In 1995 the firm reorganized, making Deloitte & Touche Consulting Group a subsidiary of its tax and accounting sister companies. This reorganization makes the consulting arm more independent and better able to deliver its consulting services worldwide. Insiders say that the partners in the Consulting Group share profits almost entirely with each other, not with the tax and audit partners. In the future, Deloitte & Touche must continue to work at the task of building a name for itself as a strategy consultant.

Are you put off by the "every man for himself" tendencies needed to survive at other consulting firms? Deloitte & Touche is a good place for those who want a kinder, gentler consulting firm with procedures in place to make sure people don't fall through the cracks. The company states boldly in its recruiting materials, "We have none of the politics, back-stabbing, and cut-throat competition that make life miserable at other firms."

Deloitte & Touche has won several awards for being one of the most enlightened employers in the United States. You'll find an uncommon commitment to people at the firm. Consultants are assigned both a *development counselor,* a senior member of the firm, and a *mentor,* a more junior colleague, to provide them with advice. The firm takes great pains to allow employees to live balanced lives through an initiative called the "Work/Life Balance." Consultants work fifty to sixty hours per week on average. Weekend work is minimal. Since Deloitte & Touche has a strong emphasis on implementing changes and redesigning companies' processes, much of their work is done on-site: Consultants typically spend four or five days per week at the client's locations. Women interested in balancing families with careers may find Deloitte & Touche a particularly friendly environment. Twenty-five percent of the firm's partners are women, an extremely high number compared to other consulting firms.

Deloitte & Touche Consulting Group provides clients with services in these areas: Business Process Reengineering, Strategy, Value Chain and Logistics, Client/Server Solutions, World-Class Financial Management, Change Management, Enterprise Resource Planning, and Reorganization Planning.

Most new consultants join Deloitte & Touche as generalists and work on projects in any of the service areas just listed. The company also provides corporate strategy consulting through Braxton Associates, its strategy practice "brand name." Deloitte & Touche consultants and Braxton consultants are sometimes staffed on projects together.

The firm makes the decisions on your initial assignments as a new employee; after you prove yourself, you have more input into your staffing. Typical engagement teams have ten to fifteen consultants, larger than teams at pure strategy firms.

After a few weeks or months on the job, new employees are trained at the Deloitte & Touche Consulting Group Development Center at the Scottsdale (AZ) Conference Resort. During their career, employees attend seminars regularly to

---

Numbers: DELOITTE & TOUCHE CONSULTING GROUP

Founded: 1985   **Ownership Structure:** 100% Subsidiary of Deloitte & Touche, USA

Sample Clients: General Motors, Monsanto, Rockwell International, Merrill Lynch, Bayer, Sears, CNA, Prudential, AT&T, PacBell, State of Kentucky

	1996	1995	1994	1993	1992
Net Revenues ($Millions)	1,550	1,160	1,056	887	754
No. of Consultants	8,857	7,483	7,305	6,474	5,755

Roles: Analyst   Consultant   Sr. Consultant   Manager   Sr. Manager   Partner

Sources: Deloitte & Touche disk materials, *Consultants News,* Deloitte & Touche Web site, interviews

update their skills and knowledge. This training is aligned with a consultant's level in the firm so that instruction is matched to current job requirements.

Deloitte & Touche Consulting Group is much less snobby about the schools it will hire from than the strategy consulting boutiques—so if you're an outstanding student at a school that has less of a brand name, you will still have a chance of being hired. Most new *senior consultants* join Deloitte & Touche with an MBA and between two and four years of work experience. Deloitte & Touche is more likely than a strategy firm to hire candidates with years of experience in an industry but no MBA. *Business analysts* (general consulting) and *systems analysts* (information technology) join Deloitte & Touche with undergraduate degrees in a variety of majors.

PART II: INSIDER INTERVIEW

How would you describe Deloitte & Touche Consulting Group's culture?

Deloitte & Touche's culture is actually pretty laid-back. Of course, there will be the occasional seventy-hour week, but everybody at the firm knows and acknowledges the fact that a seventy-hour week *sucks* and is something to be avoided. In fact, if people are consistently working that hard, they are generally viewed as inferior or inefficient. The best thing about the culture is that most everybody there is really just plain old fun to be around. That stems from the fact that we place a premium on making sure the clients genuinely like us, not just that they pay us. It's considered a failure to walk away from a project with an important person at the client not totally happy with the team that did the work.

Do you think young hotshot MBAs or older veterans of Corporate America dominate the firm's culture?

Young hotshot MBAs are not hired by D&T. Young, down-to-earth, energetic MBAs are, and they are truly beginning to shape how D&T operates. However, there are the stodgy types still around. They are the ones who have been slow to realize that you don't necessarily have to suffer to make partner. They think something like "Well, if I had to put in ungodly hours to make it where I am, then so should you." Most people can't wait for those types to die or retire. Unfortunately, those types still control the firm.

What do you think Deloitte & Touche excels at?

D&T is an operations consulting firm to its core. Few firms have the ability to implement process improvement like D&T can. And I'm not just talking about manufacturing lines. I'm talking about things like call centers, accounting functions, sales forces, and product development processes. D&T has mastered the ability to understand the day-to-day operations of a client, identify its inefficiencies, and come up with truly effective solutions. This type of expertise goes a long way.

What did you like best about your experience at the firm?

The people, the people, the people. They really try hard to hire people who fit the nonarrogant, down-to-earth, likable culture that has grown up.

What did you like least about your experience at the firm?

The types of clients the firm has. In my experience, D&T suffered from not being considered among firms like McKinsey and BCG. We didn't often work for CEOs. We weren't hired by the COOs or the CFOs or the president of a subsidiary. Also, operations work was sometimes not as interesting or glamorous as strategy work.

What advice would you give someone seeking a job at the company?

Don't refer to D&T as a Big Eight firm. We really have become separate from the accounting side and are trying to compete more with the "pure" consulting firms. Also, be friendly and open. Don't be arrogant. Show an interest in operations and in implementation.

PROFILE
Gemini Consulting

NAME: **Gemini Consulting**
HEADQUARTERS: **25 Airport Road, Morristown, NJ 07962, (201) 285-9000**
WEB SITE: **www.gemcon.com**

◆

RECRUITING: **Hybrid: Apply to office nearest you; Summer Undergrads apply to Cambridge**
SUMMER JOBS: **Graduate and Undergraduate levels**
GRAD RECRUITING CONTACT: **Karleen Mussman, Campus Recruiting Coordinator, 5 Westbook Corporate Center, Suite 600, Westchester, IL 60154, (708) 531-8826**
GRAD TITLE: **Senior Consultant**
UNDERGRAD RECRUITING CONTACT: **Linda Toyias, Recruiting Coordinator, Suite 600, 124 Mount Auburn Street, Cambridge, MA 02138, (617) 491-5200**
UNDERGRAD TITLE: **Consultant**

◆

RELATED READING: Joseph White, "Re-Engineering Gurus Take Steps to Remodel Their Stalling Vehicles," *The Wall Street Journal*, November 26, 1996. Joann Lublin, "Midsize Firms Lose Out to

Both Big Guys and Boutiques," *The Wall Street Journal,* July 11, 1995. Gilbert Fuchsberg, "Business Bulletin: Management Consulting," *The Wall Street Journal,* May 19, 1994.

OTHER OFFICES: (Domestic) Cambridge (MA), Morristown (NJ); (International) Barcelona, Brussels, Frankfurt, Johannesburg, Lisbon, London, Madrid, Milan, Munich, Oslo, Paris, São Paulo, Stockholm, Tokyo, Utrecht, Zurich

PART I: ANALYSIS

Gemini Consulting is an international consulting firm that was formed in 1990 out of the union of the MAC Group, a strategy consulting firm, and United Research, an operations consulting firm. The intent of the merger—still the key driving principle behind the firm today—was to respond to clients' demands that consultants not only provide strategic advice but implement it. By merging, Gemini became one of the few consulting firms to offer a full complement of expertise in strategy, operations, and information technology. Gemini consultants spend four days per week at their clients' offices to put their advice into practice.

Gemini is constantly transforming itself to fit changing times. For a while, it was in the headlines because it was the fastest-growing company around, expanding 88 percent from 1991 through 1993. The company's hiring exploded as well. But faced with a downturn in the market for reengineering (or "business transformation," as it is known within the company) and a slump in domestic revenues of 23 percent in 1995, Gemini found itself overstaffed. The company shrank its North American consultant workforce by over 15 percent.

Redefining itself as ever, Gemini has moved toward increased emphasis on smaller projects that allow it to "earn the right" to work on larger engagements. (Previously, Gemini focused on large transformation or reengineering assignments.) It is also focusing its efforts on a selected number of service offerings and attempting to be the leading provider in those offerings. And the company maintains its ability to offer clients a triad of strategy, operations, and information technology advice.

Gemini is a unit of the French holding firm Cap Gemini Sogeti. The company's consulting business is extremely strong in Europe and South Africa. U.S.-based consultants who have requested European assignments have frequently gotten them. The firm has less of a presence in Asia and Latin America, however.

There is no heavy wood paneling, no conservative furniture at Gemini offices. This mirrors the firm's culture: Gemini does not have the hierarchy, structure, or sacred cows of its older consulting peers. Senior managers roll up their sleeves and work to support junior colleagues. The company is fairly decentralized, with each office having a unique culture. Overall, Gemini is a good place for people who can thrive and guide themselves in a fairly unstructured environment. Since the company is relatively young and fast-changing, significant opportunity and responsibility exist for the new recruit.

Some cultural differences lingered between employees of the two original entities from which Gemini was formed. MAC Group employees were traditionally young turk MBAs, strong in serving the financial services and telecommunications industries. United Research employees were veterans of American industry, with strengths in the oil, gas, and chemicals industries. These differences are fading with time as natural turnover brings in new people, but insiders say that of the two cultures and business practices, United Research's has prevailed.

The firm is generous to employees in terms of training and just plain winding down. Many consultants have been sent to Key West, Bermuda, and other sites for fun and education in the sun. All new consultants attend the two-week Gemini Skills Workshop, a training session that alternates between London, England, and Morristown, New Jersey—during which consultants are introduced to the firm's consulting methodologies and to each other. Gemini offers paid sabbaticals and voluntary reduced work schedules to longtime consultants.

Home base for a Gemini consultant is, first and foremost, his office. Offices serve as a base for the training, evaluation, and promotion of consultants. Consultants are hired into either the Strategy or Operations divisions. The company also has industry practices such as Oil & Gas and "C4" (communications, electronics, and high technology). However, most analysts and associates are generalists who rotate from one industry practice to another. Consultants are staffed by level through a central staffing team, but connections with senior managers help influence assignments.

At Gemini, the graduate school title is *senior consultant* and the undergraduate title is *consultant*. Recruiting is handled by each office individually and linked to local campuses. Senior consultants are hired primarily from business school. Gemini hires a fair number of people with significant business experience who do not come from the traditional MBA track; these nontraditional candidates are hired sometimes as senior consultants or at higher levels and are staffed primarily on operations or process projects. Senior consultants act as generalists and are promoted to *managing consultant* after two years and then *principal* after two to three years. Gemini maintains an up-or-out policy.

Consultants are recruited from undergraduate institutions and are expected to remain with the firm for two years before returning to business school; on rare occasions they will be asked to stay for a third year. They remain generalists during their tenure with the firm, unless they happen to hit it off with senior members of an industry practice and get staffed consistently on projects in a certain industry. Undergraduates hired by the Cambridge office are assigned during their first six months at the firm to "The Shop," a Cambridge-based research group that provides market and industry information to consultants in the field. After gaining experience, they are assigned to projects and begin work on client sites. Undergraduates are given significant responsibility in comparison to other firms—such as leading project workstreams, managing other undergraduates, or presenting to senior clients. In general, everyone at Gemini—including junior consultants—

enjoys a much higher level of interaction with clients than is typical at other firms, since so much time is spent working at clients' offices.

Successful candidates in the Gemini recruiting process must first meet the firm's analytical standards by performing well on the case question. Candidates must also be likable, demonstrating strong interpersonal skills and the ability to win over a wide variety of people, since Gemini consultants spend much time with clients.

Numbers: GEMINI CONSULTING

Founded: 1974   **Ownership Structure:** 100% subsidiary of Cap Gemini Sogeti

Sample Clients: DuPont, Union Carbide, British Telecom, Rolls-Royce, Coca Cola, Inland Steel

	1996	1995	1994
Net Revenues ($M)	600	548	551
No. of Employees	1,550	1,400	1,700

Roles: Consultant Sr. Consultant Mng. Consultant Principal Vice Pres. Sr. Vice Pres.

Sources: Gemini Consultants Web site; *Consulting News;* "Craze for Consultants," *Business Week; Management Today*

PART II: INSIDER INTERVIEW

How would you describe the company's culture?

Gemini prides itself on being very "people oriented." Also, the organization is not very hierarchical. It is not uncommon for most undergraduate consultants to be leading client teams, giving presentations to executives, and, in general, taking on the role of a post-MBA or more senior employee.

What did you like least about your experience at the firm?

The irrational attachment to being on the client site even when this was in many instances the least productive way to get work done. Five days a week on-site did not make sense; nor did the notion that clients could not be convinced that consultants worked when they were not on-site.

What did you like best about your experience at the firm?

The opportunity to work overseas and to take on responsibility beyond that of the traditional analyst. For the potential employee, Gemini offers more responsibility than at many competing firms.

PROFILE

McKinsey & Company, Inc.

NAME: **McKinsey & Company, Inc.**
HEADQUARTERS: **55 East 52ⁿᵈ Street, 17ᵗʰ floor, New York, NY 10022, (212) 446-7000**
WEB SITE: **www.mckinsey.com**

◆

RECRUITING: **Apply on campus or to office nearest you; if no office near you, apply to headquarters**
SUMMER JOBS: **Graduate level only**
GRAD RECRUITING CONTACT: **Julie Healy**
GRAD TITLE: **Associate**
UNDERGRAD RECRUITING CONTACT: **Patricia Evans**
UNDERGRAD TITLE: **Business Analyst**

◆

RELATED READING: John Byrne, "Sexual Harassment at McKinsey?" *Business Week*, December 9, 1996. "Everything in the Garden's Lovely," *The Economist*, July 27, 1996. John Byrne, "The Craze for Consultants," *Business Week*, July 25, 1994. John Huey, "How McKinsey Does It," *Fortune*, November 1, 1993. "The McKinsey Mystique," *Business Week*, September 20, 1993.

OTHER OFFICES: (Domestic) Atlanta, Boston, Chicago, Dallas, Houston, Los Angeles, Minneapolis, New Jersey, Orange County, Pittsburgh, San Francisco, San Jose, Stamford, Washington D.C. (International) Amsterdam, Bangkok, Barcelona, Beijing, Berlin, Bogota, Bombay, Brussels, Buenos Aires, Budapest, Caracas, Cologne, Copenhagen, Dublin, Dusseldorf, Frankfurt, Geneva, Gothenburg, Hamburg, Helsinki, Hong Kong, Istanbul, Jakarta, Johannesburg, Kuala Lumpur, Lisbon, London, Madrid, Melbourne, Mexico City, Milan, Monterrey, Montreal, Moscow, Mumbai, Munich, New Delhi, Osaka, Oslo, Paris, Perth, Prague, Rome, São Paulo, Seoul, Shanghai, Singapore, Stockholm, Stuttgart, St. Petersburg, Sydney, Taipei, Tokyo, Toronto, Vienna, Warsaw, Zurich

PART I: ANALYSIS

McKinsey & Company is the management consulting industry's standard-bearer. Neither the oldest nor the largest consultancy, McKinsey is instead known for being the most successful, elite, and high priced. This secretive firm provides advice to CEOs of Fortune 500 companies, leaders of governments, and even the Vatican. It generates the largest amount of revenues per consultant of any firm.

McKinsey & Co. was founded in 1926 in Chicago by James O. McKinsey, an accountant who wanted to apply himself to the new "science" of business management. When McKinsey left to run Marshall Field in 1935, he was succeeded by Marvin Bower, who managed the spin-off of competitor A.T. Kearney, Inc., and led McKinsey for several decades.

The firm has deep, long-standing relationships with senior management of companies around the world. Clients are typically large, Global Fortune 500 companies. McKinsey is also known for providing free advice to educational and other nonprofit organizations, such as the American Red Cross, Habitat for Humanity, and the Nature Conservancy. Although the elite business of advising corporate CEOs on strategy is what the firm is best known for, McKinsey is now a generalist consulting practice, offering advice on strategy, operations, and information technology. The firm's engagement mix is approximately 29 percent organization, 22 percent strategy, 20 percent marketing and sales, 18 percent operations, and 5 percent finance.* McKinsey has had particularly strong experience working with financial institutions, consumer products, health care, and electronics industries. (See interview with Kenichi Ohmae, pages 15–21.)

Like Goldman Sachs in the investment banking industry, McKinsey is a private partnership run by an elite group of directors. Only one in five consultants who join McKinsey will ever make it to partner, and only one in ten will make it to director. The company believes in an up-or-out policy, but those who can't make it are taken care of: They have access to a vast and impressive McKinsey alumni network which seems to run most of Corporate America.

On the one hand, McKinsey is decentralized: No office is considered headquarters, and all offices are considered equal and self-governed. Culture is reportedly fairly different among offices. On the other hand, McKinsey prides itself on being "One Firm" and has built revered internal institutions—such as a series of governing committees—that are typical of a highly structured company. Although it has a reputation for being buttoned-down and conservative, McKinsey is also one of the few leading consulting firms to publicly welcome gay and lesbian applicants; over the past few years it has hosted recruiting dinners for gay and lesbian students at Harvard Business School, Wharton, and Stanford Business School.

Like other consulting firms, McKinsey has grown significantly overseas, with over 60 percent of revenues generated outside the United States. The company is truly global in other ways: Managing director Rajat Gupta, the firm's leader, was born in India, educated in the United States, and has lived in both the United States and Europe.

McKinsey is a secretive firm, its culture shielded. The McKinsey style is traditional and understated. Some have described McKinsey as a "hard" culture in which quantitative skills are valued. Certainly the firm's people are highly intellectual. McKinsey's halls are filled with Rhodes scholars and other brainy types, and it recruits not just MBAs but those holding Ph.D.'s and other advanced degrees. McKinsey invests substantially in management research, running its own mini-business press and publishing the highly respected *McKinsey Quarterly*, a management journal. Like most other consulting firms, McKinsey is mostly governed by men: Only a small minority of partners and directors are women.

McKinsey traditionally has shied away from making senior consultants specialize in certain industry groups; instead, the firm has preferred to state that its

*Presentation at the Stanford Graduate School of Business, 1996.

consultants are trained in problem-solving. However, the firm offers employees both specialist and generalist career paths, and its efforts to hire experienced professionals are increasing. Consultants typically spend four days per week at their clients' offices.

Recruiting is handled by each office individually. People around the world are pounding on the firm's doors to get in. McKinsey receives job applications from over 50,000 people per year, of which very few are hired. *Associates* are hired from business schools, law schools, other graduate schools, or with significant previous experience. Non-MBA associate hires are provided with a four-week "mini-MBA" program. Associates are generalists and are promoted to engagement manager after a few years. *Business analysts* are recruited from undergraduate institutions and are expected to remain with the firm for two or three years. Some offices hire non-MBAs as business analysts.

Intelligence and high grades are very important to the firm. Preparing for an interview? Note that one manager at the firm has stated that McKinsey seeks people who are "insecure and thus driven by their insecurity."*

Numbers: McKINSEY & COMPANY, INC.

Founded: 1926   **Ownership Structure:** Partnership

Sample Clients: AT&T, Swiss Reinsurance, IBM, the Vatican, Royal Dutch/Shell, Nestlé, Daimler-Benz, Volkswagen

	1996	1995	1994	1993	1992
Net Revenues ($M)	2,100	1,800	1,500	1,300	1,200
No. of Consultants	3,944	3,553	3,116	2,977	2,772

Roles: Business Analyst   Associate   Principal (partner)   Director (senior partner) ➞

Sources: McKinsey & Co. Web site; "The Firm Walks Tall," *Eurobusiness;* "A Career with McKinsey & Co.," McKinsey Recruiting Brochure; "Craze for Consultants," *Business Week; Consultants News,* McKinsey & Co.

PART II: INSIDER INTERVIEW

How would you describe the company's culture?

McKinsey is definitely a meritocracy. The culture is very collegial; there is a big emphasis on helping others, both in terms of your own team members or other teams that are doing work in your area. It is a culture that values highly self-motivated individuals.

*Ron Daniel quoted in "How McKinsey Does It," *Fortune,* November 1, 1993, p. 72.

What did you like best about your experience at the firm?

It would have to be the people. I worked with some amazing people who were both really smart and a lot of fun. I also found that senior people were willing to take the time out to coach and counsel me.

What would you like to have changed about your experience at the firm?

I personally wish that I had explored a wider variety of industries. When I chose studies, I chose based on the people, not the industry. As a result, I had great teams but did most of my work in an industry I am not particularly interested in as a career.

What do you think McKinsey looks for in its new hires?

I think that leadership experience is very important. They want to see that you can do more than just get good grades. I also think that they value, in the case interviews, a structured, logical thought process.

Anything else you'd like to add?

I would give careful consideration to your office selection because I think different offices can offer different experiences in terms of their overall size, peer group size, industries served, and lifestyle.

PROFILE
Mercer Management Consulting, Inc.

NAME: **Mercer Management Consulting, Inc.**
HEADQUARTERS: **1166 Avenue of the Americas, New York, NY 10036,**
  (212) 345-8000
WEB SITE: **www.mercermc.com**

◆

RECRUITING: **Centralized: Apply to Washington, DC, office, 2300 N Street, NW,**
  Washington, DC 20037, (202) 778-7400
SUMMER JOBS: **Graduate and Undergraduate levels**
GRAD RECRUITING CONTACT: **Cathy Baker, Director of North American Recruiting**
GRAD TITLE: **Associate**
UNDERGRAD RECRUITING CONTACT: **Cathy Baker, Director of North American**
  Recruiting
UNDERGRAD TITLE: **Research Analyst**

◆

RELATED READING: David Gaylin, "South African Business Gets Back on Track," *The Wall Street Journal,* December 2, 1996. Ron Frank and John Porter, "Leadership for Growth," *Strategy & Leader-*

ship, September/October 1996. Duncan McDougall, "Know Thy Customer," *The Wall Street Journal*, August 7, 1995. Joao Baptista and Dwight Gertz, *Grow to Be Great: Breaking the Downsizing Cycle*, The Free Press, 1995. John Byrne, "The Craze for Consultants," *Business Week*, July 25, 1994.

OTHER OFFICES: (Domestic) Boston, Chicago, New York, San Francisco, Washington, DC; (International) Hong Kong, London, Madrid, Montreal, Munich, Paris, Toronto, Zurich

PART I: ANALYSIS

Part of the worldwide consulting conglomerate Marsh & McLennan, Mercer Management Consulting is a general consulting firm serving large international corporations. Mercer Management Consulting was formed out of the merger of Strategic Planning Associates and Temple, Barker & Sloane, which were both acquired by Marsh & McLennan Companies. The firm adopted its present name in 1992.

If you work at Mercer, be prepared to help companies focus on strategies for growth. Mercer was touting growth strategies as early as 1993, when much of the rest of the consulting industry was still pushing reengineering; in 1996 corporate growth became the major focus of the industry. Mercer has a service-industry orientation rather than a manufacturing one; this means that as a consultant at Mercer, you would be more likely to serve clients in such industries as financial services and telecommunications. Recently, however, the firm has been expanding its client base in such industrial sectors as oil and chemicals, automotive, and consumer-product manufacturing.

An example of Mercer's consulting methodologies is Customer Franchise Management, which assesses a company's customers and performs economic analysis to evaluate which customers are most profitable. This methodology, which involves switching from evaluating costs on a product line basis to a customer basis, can be used to reallocate resources toward serving the most profitable customers.

Mercer provides a range of consulting services to its clients: strategy consulting, process and reengineering consulting, and change management.

The firm seems to offer a strong possibility for foreign travel and work. A priority for the firm is growth in Europe and Asia, and many U.S. analysts have been sent to Asia for long-term projects.

Insiders say that Mercer's culture is nonhierarchical, collegial, and focused on developing people. *Associates* typically are hired from graduate schools. New associates join the Central Resource Group, a generalist group, and are assigned to cases in many different industries. *Research analysts* are recruited from undergraduate institutions and are expected to remain with the firm for two or three years.

Consultants are assigned mentors to help oversee their career development. The firm does not require consultants to spend a specified number of days on-site with the client each week.

Mercer apparently has a remarkably open interview process, in which interviewers are willing to debrief candidates on their performance at the end of the interview. Candidates can expect two interviews in the first round: one case interview and one noncase interview.

Numbers: MERCER MANAGEMENT CONSULTING, INC.

Founded: 1970   **Ownership Structure:** 100% subsidiary of March & McLennan Cos.

Sample Clients: British Rail, Chemical Bank, Sara Lee, US West

	1996	1995	1994
Net Revenues ($M)	1,159	1,004	889
No. of Employees	9,241	8,872	8,251

Roles: Research Analyst Consultant Assoc. Sr. Assoc. Principal Vice Pres. Director

Sources: Mercer Management Consulting career brochure, Mercer Management Consulting Web site, interviews with former employees, *Consultants News*, Mercer Management Consulting, *Business Week*.

PART II: INSIDER INTERVIEW

How would you describe the company's culture?

While we must have worked at least as hard as other consulting firms (since there are only so many hours per day one can possibly work), Mercer higher-ups really seemed interested in the morale level and in developing junior staff. There were detailed reviews at the end of each case, career reviews every six months, and "upward" reviews. I'm sure many consulting firms have these processes in place, but I really had the feeling that everyone in the firm took these seriously and managers both tried hard to provide constructive feedback.

Even the upward reviews seemed to be given credence among the partners, as managers who repeatedly "burned out" case teams were openly expected by the partners to improve their management style. In addition, partners made an effort to respect scheduled vacation or other plans whenever possible.

Particularly, my office was quite a fun, collegial place when I joined because it was small and had a charismatic office head. We all learned from each other among the junior staff, because there was no middle management to speak of to provide day-to-day training and mentorship. As a result, we were a very tight group.

Mercer is fairly nonhierarchical. Case team discussions were generally treated as a "competition of ideas," and junior people were expected to speak up, even to contradict more senior members of the firm, even when it impeded the efficient progress of meetings.

What did you like best about your experience at the firm?

The touchy-feely culture. I really feel that Mercer was a great place for me to learn how to work in a professional environment. I was helped and developed by a series of associates, senior associates, managers, and partners during my four years. I received frequent informal feedback and became friends with most of the people for whom I worked. I always felt relaxed, secure, and willing to say or do whatever I felt was appropriate to get the job done.

What did you like least about your experience at the firm?

Over and over at Mercer, I experienced or witnessed case teams pulling all-nighters because the partner who sold the case had overpromised deliverables either at the outset of the project or during a subsequent redefinition of scope. It also happened when no one overpromised, but because events or resources were not scheduled properly to assure timely completion of the project. There seemed to be the sense that since consultants are used to working overtime and being available at all hours, it is not too important to try to manage projects so that their time is used efficiently.

What types of candidates do you think the firm prefers?

Smart people who are not abrasive in any way and do not have ego problems. One key factor, besides intelligence, strong educational background, and articulateness, is the ability to get along easily with colleagues and (most important) the client.

What advice would you give someone seeking a job at the company?

Practice case interviews, be self-deprecating (although don't go too far given that you need to impress them), and emphasize past experiences that demonstrate your ability to be a strong team player.

PROFILE

Monitor Company

NAME: **Monitor Company**
HEADQUARTERS: **25 First Street, Cambridge, MA 02141, (617) 252-2000**
WEB SITE: **www.monitor.com**

◆

RECRUITING: **Apply to Cambridge or nearest office**
SUMMER JOBS: **Graduate and Undergraduate levels**

GRAD RECRUITING CONTACT (HEADQUARTERS): **Colette Pervais, Global Recruiting Administrator**
GRAD TITLE: **Consultant**
UNDERGRAD RECRUITING CONTACT (HEADQUARTERS): **Colette Pervais, Global Recruiting Administrator**
UNDERGRAD TITLE: **Consultant**

◆

RELATED READING: "Targeting Support to Needs of Firms," *Boston Globe,* January 28, 1997. "Prophet of Profit," *Far Eastern Economic Review,* November 21, 1996. "The Craze for Consultants," *Business Week,* July 25, 1994.

OTHER OFFICES: (Domestic) New York, Santa Monica (CA); (International) Amsterdam, Frankfurt, Hong Kong, Johannesburg, London, Madrid, Milan, Paris, Seoul, Tokyo, Toronto

PART I: ANALYSIS

Monitor Company is a young consulting firm, founded in 1983. Nevertheless, it has quietly established itself in the most elite "strategy" echelon of the management consulting industry. The firm's success can be attributed partly to its blue blood: Monitor was cofounded by Michael Porter, the Harvard Business School professor who authored the consultant's bible *Competitive Strategy.* Porter still sits on the firm's board of directors and does much of his consulting through Monitor. Monitor also has found success by sticking closely to its roots; unlike other Cambridge-based strategy firms that diversified into reengineering and information technology, Monitor is still a strategy purebred. Monitor consultants are a highly intellectual bunch who employ cutting-edge business thinking to solve clients' problems. The firm has close ties to leading business professors, such as Harvard's Chris Argyris, and is populated with graduates of prestigious schools such as Harvard and Williams.

But don't mistake Monitor for a stuffy, hidebound firm. Its innovative and flexible management policies set it apart from competitors and make it a good place for those who might chafe under the restraints of a more traditional firm. Read its recruiting brochure and you'll quickly notice Monitor's unconventional approach: "We think it arbitrary, silly, and wasteful to lump people into rigid, inflexible boxes on rigid, inflexible timetables of promotion defined by rigid, inflexible expectations about acceptable performance or rates of development." Strong words for a consulting firm. Even its offices are different—headquarters in Cambridge are housed in a renovated warehouse with open-face brick walls.

No distinctions in title exist at Monitor; undergraduate and MBA hires alike are known as "consultants." For junior employees, this means that there is the opportunity to be a "star" and to take on significant responsibilities at an early stage. The possible downside is that less confident, less aggressive people will not progress as quickly in this flexible environment.

There is no strict career path for each entering "class" of new employees.

People move up at their own pace, and compensation among each class varies more than at other firms—for example, bonuses range from 0 to 50 percent of base compensation for new MBA hires. There is no "up-or-out" policy either. Undergraduates hoping to build a long-term career without an MBA, take notice: Monitor is probably the only leading consulting firm that truly puts no cap on how long you can stay. Monitor is famous for the flexibility it affords employees; some have taken sabbaticals or worked part-time in order to pursue other interests.

Although much has been made of Monitor's consulting relationship with AT&T, the firm's client base actually is highly diversified. The breakdown of the firm's revenues in 1996 was as follows: telecommunications, 24 percent; consumer products, 18 percent; media and entertainment, 8 percent; raw materials processing, 7 percent; and financial services, 7 percent. As a Monitor consultant, you *do* have a high chance of working on a telecommunications-related project. The firm is not organized along industry or functional lines; instead, all consultants are generalists and rely on a "network" of outside experts for specialized knowledge. The firm has three small subsidiaries: Decision Architects, a software arm; Strategic Market Research, a market research arm; and Monitor University, which conducts training seminars for both Monitor consultants and outside corporate executives. Finally, the Monitor Institute is an internal group that provides consulting work for nonprofit organizations; occasionally consultants are staffed in this group for short periods.

Monitor offers a full complement of corporate strategy services to its clients:

- *Corporate strategy:* Addressing both overall corporate strategy and business unit level strategy, assessing customer groups and their needs, reshaping corporate portfolios (for example, new market entry, acquisitions, or divestiture strategy)
- *Aligning process and organization with strategy:* Designing logistics, distribution, organizational structures, and processes in order to implement new strategies.
- *Human elements of strategy:* Addressing the behavioral elements of changing strategies.
- *Software:* Developing technical tools to solve strategic problems.

Monitor consultants are known for working hard: They reportedly work to sixty hours per week on average and eighty hours per week during crunch times. But consultants travel less than at other firms: Undergraduates should expect to travel several days per month during their first year and two to three days per week in subsequent years.

Monitor's hiring practices really distinguish the firm from competitors. Monitor is the only consulting firm to hire both undergraduates and advanced degree students as *consultants,* albeit at different salary levels and with different performance expectations. The firm recruits candidates from diverse academic backgrounds. Monitor uses highly unusual exercises to test candidates' interpersonal skills. Recent interviews have consisted of a thirty-minute first round of personality and résumé questions and an hour-long second round with a data-heavy case question. The final round has been known to consist of a variety of questions, including a critique of a video of a consultant interacting with a client and an exercise in team problem-solving. Candidates likely to succeed in the Monitor interviewing process are not only intelligent but take risks, voice opinions, and seek a different approach to solving problems. (See interview with Kate Byrne, pages 135–140.)

A consultant's development is overseen by an assigned Professional Development Advisor, who helps set performance targets and development goals.

~

Numbers: MONITOR COMPANY

Founded: 1983   **Ownership Structure:** Privately held

Sample Clients: AT&T, BASF, Coca Cola, Government of Canada, Navistar, Nissan, Pacific Telesis

	1996	1995	1994	1993
Net Revenues ($Millions)	181	147	115	90
No. of Consultants	700	610	450	340

Roles: Consultant   [no titles in between]   Director

————————————————————————————————→

Sources: Monitor Company, *Consultants News, Business Week*

PART II: INSIDER INTERVIEW

What have you learned as a consultant at Monitor?

I've learned a lot about working with people and especially with clients. Sometimes there were meetings I would run with the client's plant general managers, and you know there's no way in any other job where as a twenty-two-year-old you would be running a meeting like that. I've also had to learn about many different industries really quickly.

How would you describe Monitor's culture?

It's laid-back in the sense that people really have fun with each other and try to get to know each other. There are definitely different "groups" within the office, but it's not incredibly cliquey. Some people do things together outside of work and others don't. Either is completely okay.

The people who have done really well are praised because they're bright and they work really hard, and they don't complain at all. You have to have your own opinion and stand up for yourself. To do well you have to be aggressive— aggressive and hardworking.

What do you like least about your experience at Monitor?

The downside has to do more with the industry in general: I do not like the hours. I do not like the travel. Sometimes I think that people are too cocky for their worth. You meet some people who think they have the right answer at age twenty-four, and that bothers me.

What do you like best about your experience at Monitor?

There's a great network to help you if you're having problems. For example, I could talk through issues with the person in charge of allocations [assignments] and to my Professional Development Advisor.

And you felt like they were listening?

Definitely. One day a director came to my office and asked "How are you doing?" and I felt comfortable saying "I don't like this and this and this," and he actually changed things.

Other Worthy Mentions

The Advisory Board Company

NAME: **The Advisory Board Company**
ADDRESS: **600 New Hampshire Avenue, NW, Washington, DC 20037, (202) 672-5600**
WEB SITE: **www.advisory.com**

◆

RECRUITING: **Centralized through Headquarters**
SUMMER JOBS: **Graduate and Undergraduate levels**
GRAD RECRUITING CONTACT: **Career Management Staff**
GRAD TITLE: **Senior Consultant**
UNDERGRAD RECRUITING CONTACT: **Rachel Rodin, Undergraduate Recruiting**
UNDERGRAD TITLE: **Consultant**

◆

OTHER OFFICES: (Domestic) None; (International) London

Cornerstone Research

NAME: **Cornerstone Research**
ADDRESS: **124 Mount Auburn Street, 4th Floor South, Cambridge, MA 02138, (617) 491-4411**
WEB SITE: **www.cornerstone.com**

◆

RECRUITING: Local by office
SUMMER JOBS: Graduate and Undergraduate levels
GRAD & UNDERGRAD RECRUITING CONTACT: Professional consultant in charge changes yearly. Call office of your choice and ask for name of Professional Recruiting Coordinator.
GRAD TITLE: Associate
UNDERGRAD TITLE: Analyst

◆

OTHER OFFICES: New York, Menlo Park (CA)

Dean & Co.

NAME: Dean & Co.
ADDRESS: Fairfax Square, Tysons Corner, 8065 Leesburg Pike, Suite 500, Vienna, VA 22182, (703) 506-3900
WEB SITE: www.deanco.com

◆

RECRUITING: Centralized through Headquarters
SUMMER JOBS: Graduate level only
GRAD RECRUITING CONTACT: Director of Recruiting
GRAD TITLE: Associate
UNDERGRAD RECRUITING CONTACT: Director of Recruiting
UNDERGRAD TITLE: Analyst

◆

OTHER OFFICES: none

First Manhattan Consulting Group

NAME: First Manhattan Consulting Group
ADDRESS: 90 Park Avenue, 19th Floor, New York, NY 10016, (212) 557-0500
WEB SITE: www.fmcg.com

◆

RECRUITING: Centralized through Headquarters
SUMMER JOBS: Undergraduate level only
GRAD & UNDERGRAD RECRUITING CONTACT: Linda Chang, Recruiter
GRAD TITLE: No formal MBA position; senior staff are Consultants
UNDERGRAD TITLE: Analyst

◆

OTHER OFFICES: none

KPMG Peat Marwick

NAME: **KPMG Peat Marwick**
ADDRESS: **345 Park Avenue, New York, NY 10154, (212) 758-9700**
WEB SITE: **www.kpmg.com**

◆

RECRUITING: **Centralized through Headquarters**
SUMMER JOBS: **Undergraduate level only**
GRAD & UNDERGRAD RECRUITING CONTACT: **Elizabeth Motzenbecker, Recruiting Manager—Financial Services; Robert Johnston, Recruiting Manager—Health Care & Life Sciences; Paula Gatti, Recruiting Manager—Manufacturing, Retailing & Distribution; Paula Gatti, Recruiting Manager—Public Services; Paula Gatti, Recruiting Manager—Information, Communications & Entertainment**
GRAD TITLE: **Consultant**
UNDERGRAD TITLE: **Analyst**

◆

OTHER OFFICES: More than 1,000 offices worldwide. Please see Web site for listings.

Marakon Associates

NAME: **Marakon Associates**
ADDRESS: **300 Atlantic Street, Stamford, CT 06901, (203) 978-6600**
WEB SITE: **www.marakon.com**

◆

RECRUITING: **Centralized through Headquarters**
SUMMER JOBS: **Graduate level only**
GRAD RECRUITING CONTACT: **Denise Le Van, MBA Recruiting Coordinator**
GRAD TITLE: **Associate**
UNDERGRAD RECRUITING CONTACT: **Eileen Farren, BA Recruiting Coordinator**
UNDERGRAD TITLE: **Analyst**

◆

OTHER OFFICES: (Domestic) Chicago, New York; (International) London

Mitchell Madison Group

NAME: **Mitchell Madison Group**
ADDRESS: **520 Madison Avenue, New York, NY 10022, (212) 372-9000**
WEB SITE: **www.mmgnet.com**

◆

RECRUITING: **Centralized through Headquarters**
SUMMER JOBS: **Graduate and Undergraduate levels**
GRAD RECRUITING CONTACT: **Carol Labi, Recruiting Manager**
GRAD TITLE: **Associate**
UNDERGRAD RECRUITING CONTACT: **Tricia Iglesias, Undergraduate Recruiting Coordinator**
UNDERGRAD TITLE: **Business Analyst**

◆

OFFICES: (Domestic) Boston, San Francisco; (International) Frankfurt, Paris, London, Melbourne, Munich, Sydney

Price Waterhouse, L.L.C.

NAME: **Price Waterhouse, L.L.C.**
ADDRESS: **Management Consulting, 1177 Avenue of the Americas, New York, NY 10036, (212) 596-7000**
WEB SITE: **www.pw.com**

◆

RECRUITING: **Centralized through Headquarters**
SUMMER JOBS: **Graduate and Undergraduate levels**
GRAD RECRUITING CONTACT: **Jean-Marie Callanan, Change Integration Recruiter**
GRAD TITLE: **Consultant**
UNDERGRAD RECRUITING CONTACT: **Dana Hagendorf, Undergraduate Recruiting Manager**
UNDERGRAD TITLE: **Consultant**

◆

OTHER OFFICES: Chicago, Minneapolis

Strategic Decisions Group

NAME: **Strategic Decisions Group**
ADDRESS: **2440 Sand Hill Road, Menlo Park, CA 94025, (415) 854-9000**
WEB SITE: **none**

◆

RECRUITING: **Local by Office for Grad, Centralized through Headquarters for Undergrad**
SUMMER JOBS: **Graduate level only**
GRAD RECRUITING CONTACT: **Sandra Dallas, Recruiting Coordinator**
GRAD TITLE: **Associate**
UNDERGRAD RECRUITING CONTACT: **Sandra Dallas, Recruiting Coordinator**
UNDERGRAD TITLE: **Business Analyst**

◆

OTHER OFFICES: (Domestic) Boston, New York; (International) Caracas, London

PROFILES OF
THE LEADING
INVESTMENT
BANKS

Bear, Stearns & Co., Inc.

NAME: **Bear, Stearns & Co., Inc.**
HEADQUARTERS: **245 Park Avenue, New York, NY 10167, (212) 272-2000**
WEB SITE: **www.bearstearns.com**

◆

RECRUITING: **Centralized: Apply to Headquarters**
SUMMER JOBS: **Graduate level only**
GRAD RECRUITING CONTACT (HEADQUARTERS): **Jennifer Rolnick, Recruiting Coordinator**
GRAD TITLE: **Associate**
UNDERGRAD RECRUITING CONTACT (HEADQUARTERS): **Jennifer Rolnick, Recruiting Coordinator**
UNDERGRAD TITLE: **Analyst**

◆

RELATED READING: Debra Sparks, "The Cowboy's New Clothes," *Financial World,* November 18, 1996. Alan Greenberg (chairman of Bear Stearns), *Memos from the Chairman* (New York: Workman Publishing, 1996). Leah Nathans Spiro, "Can Bear Stearns Trade Up?" *Business Week,* November 27, 1995. James E. Cayne (CEO of Bear Stearns), "Investment Banking's Ingredients for Success," *Investment Dealers' Digest,* May 22, 1995.

OTHER OFFICES: (Domestic) Atlanta, Boston, Chicago, Dallas, Los Angeles, San Francisco; (International) Beijing, Buenos Aires, Geneva, Hong Kong, London, Lugano, Manila, Paris, São Paulo, Shanghai, Singapore, Tokyo

PART I: ANALYSIS

Historically, "the Bear" has earned its keep through trading and through the relatively unglamorous business of securities "clearing"—the processing of trades for other broker dealers and professional investors. Bear Stearns's mighty clearing operations account for a large percentage of the daily volume of the New York Stock Exchange.

Recently, however, Bear Stearns has made headlines for its gains in investment banking areas traditionally dominated by bulge-bracket firms, and analysts are waiting to see whether these gains will be long-lived. Bear Stearns's investment banking division made tremendous strides in 1996, particularly in mergers and acquisitions where it leaped to an impressive fourth in 1996 rankings. Its high-yield business is also reportedly very strong. Investment banking now accounts for 20 percent of Bear Stearns's total revenues.* One of Bear Stearns's particular strengths is in serving the investment banking needs of the gaming and entertainment industries.

Insiders say that the Bear Stearns culture still reflects its roots as a trading house. The individual is king at Bear Stearns. The firm has been called "scrappy"

*Leah Nathans Spiro, "Can Bear Stearns Trade Up?" *Business Week,* November 27, 1995.

and "entrepreneurial," and is known to place more value on individual accomplishments and ideas than on title or precedent. Steep differences in pay exist between performers and nonperformers. Less elitist than other Wall Street houses, Bear Stearns has embraced as its CEO a former scrap-iron salesman and professional bridge player who never received a college degree.* But unlike other trading houses, Bear Stearns is a conservative firm that has avoided risky ventures and has avoided layoffs for seventy-two years. Strong performers have been rewarded with stock options, and the company is 37 percent employee-owned. Prima donnas won't do well here; Bear Stearns people are forthright and plain-speaking and don't use a lot of euphemisms or put on airs.

Bear Stearns's policies and people are highly individualistic. Chairman Alan Greenberg, who in his spare time is an amateur magician and yo-yo enthusiast, sends memos to Bear Stearns employees using a fictitious "dean of business philosophers" named "Haimchinkel Malintz Anaynikal" to make his points. Bear Stearns requires senior executives to contribute 4 percent of earnings to charity, auditing tax returns to ensure compliance.† It encourages employees to blow the whistle on dishonest colleagues or managers.

What does the future hold for Bear Stearns? The company has one of the highest returns on equity in the securities industry but a relatively small capital base and limited international revenues. Moreover, to succeed in investment banking, the firm will move toward a more team-oriented culture and a longer-term approach to building client relationships. If the firm can't sustain its investment banking gains, current speculation holds that the firm eventually may be bought by a European commercial bank seeking to break into the U.S. investment banking market.

Bear Stearns offers a full range of investment banking services. Divisions that offer jobs to undergraduates and MBAs include: Investment Banking (includes Equity and Debt Underwriting, M&A, Public Finance, High Yield), Institutional Equities (includes Sales and Trading), and Fixed Income (includes Sales and Trading).

Bear Stearns's investment banking division typically recruits *associates* from business schools and other graduate schools. Over the past few years, Bear Stearns's investment banking *analyst* program has been a work-in-progress that has increasingly resembled the programs of the bulge-bracket firms. Analysts are recruited from undergraduate institutions.

PART II: INSIDER INTERVIEW

How would you describe the company's culture?

The culture is synonymous with the virtues of Alan Greenberg, the Chairman of the Board, who preaches the importance of increasing the bottom line through

*1996 Bear Stearns Annual Report.
†Debra Sparks, "The Cowboy's New Clothes," *Financial World,* November 18, 1996.

Numbers: BEAR, STEARNS & CO., INC.

Founded: 1923   **Ownership Structure:** Publicly Traded (BSC-NYSE)

Total Consolidated Capital (1994, $M): 5,810

Sample Clients: Planet Hollywood, Donna Karan International, Lucent Technologies, Guangshen Railway Company Limited, Cablevision Systems Corporation, Mohegan Tribal Gaming Authority, Unisys

	1996	1995	1994	1993	1992
Net Revenues ($M)	2,982	2,075	2,416	2,143	1,844
No. of Employees	7,749	7,481	7,321	6,306	5,873

Note: Revenues include interest income and dividends, net of interest expense.

Roles: Analyst   Associate   VP   Assoc. Dir.   MD   MD/Principal   Sr. MD
➤

Sources: Bear Stearns 1996 Annual Report, *Institutional Investor*, April 1995

---

common sense and consistent customer service. You feel it from day one—on your first day you are given a bag of paper clips and rubber bands with a memo from the chairman advising you to use these resources sparingly, because they are the last ones the company will provide for you. The image of high-flying investment bankers does not exist at Bear Stearns. The chairman sits on the equity trading floor amid traders, not in some inaccessible office.

What did you like best about your experience?

Bear Stearns is less hierarchical than the larger bulge-bracket firms, and I feel I had a much broader exposure not only to various industry and product groups but also to higher-level responsibilities. . . . Bonuses were generous compared to other banks—although well deserved as I felt Bear Stearns analysts worked more hours and in an environment with more "rough edges" than the average Wall Street analyst.

What did you like least about your experience?

My biggest complaint has to do with the industry—the romance of having a job with long hours ended almost immediately and the lifestyle began to wear me down physically and emotionally. Contact with the outside world was minimal, so I felt like I began to suffer from tunnel vision and lost perspective. As far as Bear Stearns in particular, analysts receive little administrative support—for example, no secretaries.

What types of candidates does the firm prefer?

It sounds clichéd, but Bear Stearns looks for self-starters with a proven capacity for a tremendous amount of work. All analyst programs are rigorous but compared to peers at other investment banks, I felt Bear Stearns was toward the high end of the scale in terms of hours spent in the office. In addition, because of the smaller size of the analyst pool compared to the bulge-bracket firms, quantitative skills and previous relevant experiences are in particular very highly valued.

What advice would you give someone seeking a job at the company?

Apply skin thickener! While I had a very positive experience there, Bear Stearns is not for everybody. If you are comfortable in a sink-or-swim environment, however, Bear Stearns can be a great place to start your career.

Is the Bear Stearns recruiting process unusual in any way?

Bear Stearns's investment banking analyst recruiting efforts were only recently organized with a full-time recruiting coordinator and as such still lacks many of the bells and whistles you see at other firms. But, as I said before, Bear Stearns is not a bells-and-whistles firm.

Anything else you'd like to say?

When comparing analyst programs, don't be naive and think that all banks offer equal opportunities. That could not be farther from the truth. It's hard to turn down the prestigious firms, but make sure you are comfortable with the people you have met and the structure of the program. Get to know as many people as possible before you take the job. Don't underestimate the importance of feeling comfortable with your colleagues! Since you spend every waking hour over the next two years in your cubicle, the quality of your relationships with superiors and peers will truly make or break your experience.

PROFILE
Credit Suisse First Boston, Inc.

NAME: **Credit Suisse First Boston, Inc.**
HEADQUARTERS: **11 Madison Avenue, New York, NY 10010, (212) 325-2000**
WEB SITE: **www.csfb.com**

◆

RECRUITING: **Centralized: Apply to New York**
SUMMER JOBS: **Graduate level only**
GRAD RECRUITING CONTACT (HEADQUARTERS): **Christine Snyder, Manager MBA Recruiting**
GRAD TITLE: **Associate**

UNDERGRAD RECRUITING CONTACT (HEADQUARTERS): **Margaret Thomas, Undergraduate Recruiting Manager**
UNDERGRAD TITLE: **Analyst**

◆

RELATED READING: Philip Maher and Ron Cooper, "The New Bulge Bracket," *Investment Dealers' Digest*, November 25, 1996. Anita Raghavan, "Wheat Brings Tensions, Profit to First Boston," *The Wall Street Journal*, April 26, 1996. Leah Nathans Spiro, "Did Someone Say Abandon Bank?" *Business Week*, April 8, 1996. Nicholas Bray and Glenn Whitney, "Trimmer CS First Boston Gets Tougher," *The Wall Street Journal*, June 20, 1995.

OTHER OFFICES: (Domestic) Atlanta, Boston, Chicago, Houston, Los Angeles, Philadelphia, San Francisco; (International) Amsterdam, Auckland, Beijing, Budapest, Frankfurt, Geneva, Hong Kong, London, Madrid, Melbourne, Mexico City, Milan, Moscow, Osaka, Paris, Prague, São Paulo, Seoul, Singapore, Sydney, Tokyo, Toronto, Vienna, Warsaw, Wellington

PART I: ANALYSIS

Credit Suisse First Boston is a large, multinational investment bank offering a broad array of corporations and governments. Credit Suisse First Boston's name is very well recognized, and having it on your résumé will open doors later.

Credit Suisse First Boston has a long and colorful history. First Boston was created in the 1930s out of a merger between the investment banking subsidiaries of the First National Bank of Boston and the Chase National Bank. Known for creating deep relationships with blue-chip clients, the company's fortunes surged with the mergers and acquisitions market in the 1980s. In the late 1980s the firm was saddled with the collapse of the junk bond market and failed bridge loans. To gain stability and capital, the firm merged with its European affiliate, Credit Suisse First Boston, in the 1980s to form a new company named CS First Boston. In 1990 Credit Suisse's parent company CS Holding increased its stake in CS First Boston to a majority one, becoming the first foreign firm to take majority position in a major U.S. investment bank. CS Holding invested $300 million in capital to save the firm. In 1994, a year of disappointing results for CS First Boston, CS Holding invested an additional $400 million. Disagreement over bonuses—too high by CS Holding's standards, too low by CS First Boston employees' standards—led to defections of more than fifty CS First Boston traders, salespeople, and bankers in 1996. But 1995 and 1996 profits improved with President Allen Wheat's strategy to cut costs and move the firm toward higher-margin businesses and proprietary trading. In 1997, CS First Boston was shifted completely under the umbrella of Credit Suisse. The firm was renamed Credit Suisse First Boston and is a wholly owned business unit of the Credit Suisse Group.

Credit Suisse First Boston is relationship focused and better known for its capabilities in investment banking than in sales and trading. Within sales and trading, it is known for being stronger in fixed income than in equity.

Culturally, the firm is traditional in the style of the major New York investment houses. This bank values highly its relationships with corporate clients, and its relationship focus is evident in its culture. Offices are elegant and people are polished and buttoned down.

Credit Suisse First Boston offers opportunities for recent graduates in several areas:

- *Corporate and Investment Banking:* Raising capital, advising on mergers and acquisitions
- *Equity:* Sales, trading, and research of equity securities (stocks) and convertible securities
- *Fixed Income:* Includes the sales, trading, and research of debt securities, foreign exchange, and emerging market securities
- *Credit Suisse Financial Products:* Raise money for clients by structuring, selling, and trading derivative products

Not all of these divisions hire undergraduates. As at other investment banks, each area performs its own recruiting and has a slightly different recruiting, training, and job assignment process. Applicants should call the firm to obtain the specific recruiting contact for each of the areas.

Associate and *summer associate* opportunities exist for MBA and other graduate students in investment banking, sales and trading, and other areas. Investment banking *associates* are recruited primarily from business and law schools or have relevant prior experience.

Investment banking *analysts* are recruited from undergraduate institutions and are expected to remain at the firm for two years before returning to business school. Outstanding analysts are invited to stay at the firm for a third year. Investment banking associates are given job offers in a specific industry or product group, while analysts are given general offers.

Numbers: CREDIT SUISSE FIRST BOSTON, INC.

Founded: 1932   **Ownership Structure:** Subsidiary of Credit Suisse Group

Total Consolidated Capital (1996, $M): 8,500 E

Sample Clients: IBM/Lotus, Cox Communications, Seagram/MCA, DuPont, Walt Disney, MetLife, Raytheon, California Energy, Time Warner

	1996*	1995	1994
Net Revenues ($M)	5,307E	2,221	2,119
No. of Employees	10,000E	5,033	6,555

Roles:	Analyst	Associate	Vice President	Director	Managing Director

→

Sources: CSFB 1995 Annual Report, CSFB recruiting brochure
*1996 numbers reflect reorganization of Credit Suisse Group

PART II: INSIDER INTERVIEW

How would you describe the company's culture?

CSFB in general has a cooperative, team-oriented culture.

What did you like best about your experience at the firm?

I was given a tremendous amount of responsibility very quickly. The people I worked with were very nice, interesting people. CSFB is a well-respected name, and a new graduate can get good experience there.

What would you like to have changed about your experience at the firm?

The way the firm is run tends to create little fiefdoms that do not cooperate with each other. Also, the flip side of getting a lot of responsibility is that there weren't a lot of senior, experienced people that I could learn from.

Anything else you'd like to add?

CSFB has a good program for technical people who are interested in sales and trading or investment banking. It's a technical analyst career path. Graduates with degrees in areas like engineering, computer science, or math are put in the information technology department for a year or two and are then given the opportunity to move into the business areas. I know of several computer programmers who became traders in the equity department.

PROFILE

Goldman, Sachs & Co.

NAME: **Goldman, Sachs & Co.**
HEADQUARTERS: **85 Broad Street, New York, NY 10004, (212) 902-1000**
WORLD WIDE WEB: **www.gs.com**

◆

RECRUITING: **Centralized: Apply to New York office**
SUMMER JOBS: **Graduate level only**
GRAD RECRUITING CONTACT (HEADQUARTERS): **Alissa Burstein, Associate**
GRAD TITLE: **Associate (All Divisions)**
UNDERGRAD RECRUITING CONTACT (HEADQUARTERS): **Andrea Baum, Vice President; Alissa Burstein, Associate**
UNDERGRAD TITLE: **Financial Analyst (Investment Banking); Analyst (Equities, Fixed Income, Asset Management, Research)**

◆

RELATED READING: Anita Raghavan, "Goldman Sachs Abandons Public Sale Amid Younger Partners' Opposition," *Wall Street Journal*, January 22, 1996. Joseph McCarthy, "The Natural: Interview with Goldman Sachs Senior Partner Jon Corzine," *Chief Executive*, October 1995. Phillip Zweig, "Where Does Goldman Sachs Go From Here?" *Business Week*, March 20, 1995. Brett Fromson, "Farm Boy to Financier," *The Washington Post*, November 6, 1994. Michael Carroll et al. "Inside Goldman's College of Cardinals," *Institutional Investor*, October 1994. Larry Light, "The Street's Big Holdout May Have to Go Public," *Business Week*, November 25, 1991.

OTHER OFFICES: (Domestic) Boston, Chicago, Dallas, Houston, Los Angeles, Memphis, Miami, Philadelphia, San Francisco, Washington D.C.; (International) Beijing, Frankfurt, Grand Cayman, Hong Kong, London, Madrid, Mexico City, Milan, Montreal, Osaka, Paris, São Paulo, Seoul, Shanghai, Singapore, Sydney, Taipei, Tokyo, Toronto, Vancouver, Zurich

PART I: ANALYSIS

The preeminent investment bank of the 1990s is blessed with a name that sounds like money. Goldman Sachs, a full-line investment bank headquartered in New York, is widely regarded as the most prestigious firm on Wall Street. One of a handful of true bulge-bracket firms, Goldman operates in and dominates a variety of product areas. The firm has its pick of clients, advising kingdoms and Fortune 500 companies and sometimes turning away business. Money is what Goldman is known for producing; its pretax *profit* reached an eye-popping $2.7 billion in 1993. To put that in perspective, Goldman made more profit than the gross domestic profit of Nicaragua and many other countries.

Goldman was founded as a commercial paper firm just after the Civil War by German Jewish immigrant Marcus Goldman. The Depression was hard on Goldman Sachs, but the firm was managed ably by Sidney Weinberg, who started as a janitor and worked his way up to the chairman's seat. Guided by Weinberg and later leaders including Weinberg's son John, John Whitehead, and current Treasury Secretary Robert Rubin, the firm built a reputation around integrity and putting clients' interests first—the fourteenth and first tenets, respectively, of the Business Principles that the firm lives by. Goldman refused to work on the acquisition side of hostile takeovers during the 1980s.

Goldman is the last private partnership on Wall Street, and this makes the firm what it is. Why? The Goldman partnership is the most exclusive club on the Street—the prize that everyone within the firm, down to the most junior banker, dreams of. It represents guaranteed riches: Even new partners make a few million dollars a year, and senior partners make much more. But more important, the mystique surrounding the partnership is central to Goldman's culture. Every other year in the fall, speculation mounts as employees attempt to guess who will make partner. Employees huddle around The List when it is distributed, and new partners are inducted at a special meeting during which the secrets of Goldman's finances are finally revealed to them.* It has been argued that the partnership

*Patrick McGeehan, "Wall Street Lifts Hiring to a Record," *Wall Street Journal*, December 12, 1996.

is what keeps Goldman's people extraordinarily motivated—and thrifty, since expenses ultimately come out of partners' pockets.

A visitor to Goldman might expect glitziness or other visual evidence of greatness. Instead, Goldman's halls are filled with understated furniture and conservative antiques. Goldman's investment bankers are on the whole highly polished, articulate, conservative team players—never flashy.

Goldman is not without faults. Profit in 1994 fell to $508 million due to trading losses and disappointing results from new overseas offices. Chairman Jon Corzine, who took the helm in late 1994, admits that the firm strayed too far into proprietary trading. Under his leadership, the firm recalibrated its balance between banking and trading and recovered well. Observers are constantly speculating that Goldman will have to go public in order to raise capital it needs to compete in an increasingly competitive and global banking arena. Goldman has avoided most of the large-scale scandals that have engulfed other firms but has been sued on gender discrimination charges.

Goldman serves mostly very large multinational companies and governments. The firm is organized around several divisions: Investment Banking, Equities, Fixed Income, J. Aron Currency and Commodities, Asset Management, and Operations, Technology, and Finance.

The Investment Banking Division includes services in mergers and acquisitions, corporate finance through debt and equity underwriting, real estate, and principal investments. The division encompasses specialized industry groups including those serving the financial services, energy, power, telecommunications, media, health care, high technology, transportation, and retail sectors.

In investment banking, the vast majority of *associates* are hired from business schools. Goldman is one of the very few investment banks to recruit on campus at leading law schools. *Analysts* are recruited from undergraduate institutions and certain master's degree programs, and are expected to remain with the firm for two years, after which some are asked to remain with the firm for a third year. Other analysts leave for business school or other job opportunities. (See interview with Andrea Terzi Baum, pages 130–135.) Goldman investment banking analysts find a great deal of success in business school admissions.

Goldman is known among investment banks for placing a higher emphasis on undergraduate grades, and analyst candidates are asked to provide a college transcript. Goldman makes efforts to recruit qualified minority candidates, visiting campuses such as Howard University and Spellman College. One distinguishing feature of Goldman's hiring process is that investment banking associates and analysts are made job offers in specific groups, as opposed to receiving group assignments after they've joined the firm. In the fall of 1996, Goldman led a wave of firms in increasing the investment banking pay offered to MBAs—reported to include a salary of $75,000, a year-end bonus of $25,000, and a signing bonus of $20,000.

Numbers: GOLDMAN, SACHS & CO.

Founded: 1869   **Ownership Structure:** Limited Liability Partnership

Total Consolidated Capital (1996, $M): 17,685

Sample Clients: Ford Motor, Estee Lauder, AT&T, Kingdom of Sweden, The Upjohn Co., World Bank

	1996	1995	1994	1993	1992
Net Revenues ($M)	6,129	4,483	3,537	5,764	3,937
No. of Employees	8,976	8,159	8,998	8,103	7,202

Roles:	Analyst	Associate	Vice President	Managing Director

Sources: Goldman Sachs Web site, Goldman Sachs 1995 Annual Report, Goldman Sachs, Moody's "US Securities Firms," January 1996

PART II: INSIDER INTERVIEW

How would you describe the company's culture?

The clichés about Goldman are true: It's teamwork-oriented, client-driven, and a real meritocracy. However, within the firm, each department has its own identity and subculture, which is a unique derivation of the firm's overall culture.

What did you like best about your experience at the firm?

Senior people at the firm were earnestly concerned with the analyst experience. People made efforts to ensure that I worked with a variety of people, had a life outside of work, and learned all facets of the business. After my two-year program, senior people, including partners, took the time to help me with recommendations for business school, look for third-year positions within the firm, and assist me with a job search outside of Goldman. Today many of these same people are helping me in my summer job search now that I am at business school.

What would you like to have changed about your experience at the firm?

I had a very good experience from my first day to my last. That being said, I can't think of much that I would change. However, if you pushed me, I would have liked the opportunity to have had greater exposure to products outside of my department.

What do you think Goldman looks for in its new hires?

It seemed that they looked for an ability to handle many tasks at the same time, interpersonal skills, unique experiences, and quantitative aptitude. They look for team players and hard workers.

What advice would you give someone seeking a job at the company?

The cards are stacked against an applicant based on sheer numbers; however, an applicant can gain an advantage by having a deep understanding of the business and Goldman in particular. Goldman is a very proud company. Convince an interviewer that you know and like the culture and are committed to working in that type of environment. At the end of the day, Goldman knows the type of candidate it is looking for and is very effective at finding those individuals from the thousands of résumés it receives every year.

PROFILE
Hambrecht & Quist Group

NAME: **Hambrecht & Quist Group**
HEADQUARTERS: **One Bush Street, San Francisco, CA 94104, (415) 576-3300**
WORLD WIDE WEB: **www.hamquist.com**

◆

RECRUITING: **Centralized through Headquarters**
SUMMER JOBS: **No formal program**
GRAD RECRUITING CONTACT (HEADQUARTERS): **Sharon Henning, VP Professional Recruiting**
GRAD TITLE: **Investment Banking Associate**
UNDERGRAD RECRUITING CONTACT (HEADQUARTERS): **Sharon Henning, VP Professional Recruiting**
UNDERGRAD TITLE: **Investment Banking Analyst**

◆

RELATED READING: Linda Himelstein, "Silicon Valley Seeds Itself," *Business Week,* March 11, 1996. Peter Sinton, "S.F. Investment Bank Goes After Europe," *San Francisco Chronicle,* January 16, 1996. Peter Truell, "Guppies Who Swim with the Wall Street Sharks," *The New York Times,* October 9, 1995. David Kalish, "Investment Banking the Hands-On Way," *San Francisco Examiner,* October 2, 1995. Hal Lux, "Hambrecht & Quist Adds Notch In Belt With Netscape IPO," *IDD Magazine,* August 21, 1995.

OTHER OFFICES: (Domestic) Boston, New York, San Diego; (International) Bangkok, Hong Kong, London, Manila, Paris, Singapore, Taipei, Tokyo

PART I: ANALYSIS

Hambrecht & Quist (H&Q) is based on the West Coast and generates about $350 million in annual revenues. Although it is considerably smaller than the bulge-bracket investment banks, H&Q has made waves because of the business it is in. H&Q serves "high-growth" companies—those in rapidly evolving industries such as technology and health care. The equity market boom of the mid-1990s, and in particular the increase in high-technology companies' initial public offerings (IPOs), thrust H&Q and other growth-focused investment banks into the public spotlight. H&Q has consistently taken first or second place as underwriter of new technology stock offerings, outranking Goldman and others in the process. The firm has grown rapidly since 1992, more than tripling in revenues. In August 1996 H&Q managed one of its most important deals ever—taking itself public to raise capital for ongoing expansion and to create a more liquid market for its shares.

Founded in 1968, H&Q differs somewhat from other West Coast–based banks in that its roots lie in venture capital. Cofounders William Hambrecht and George Quist developed relationships with early-stage companies and provided them with both private and public capital. H&Q initially funded companies as a venture capital investor, then grew along with its clients in order to serve their increasingly broad financial needs. To this day, the company is highly relationship-oriented and counts as a competitive advantage its ability to identify promising companies early on. If you're looking for a place where you can work closely with entrepreneurs and small companies, this is it.

Heard of Netscape? H&Q comanaged its hot IPO. H&Q has advised companies that are leaders in their field as well as smaller companies at the forefront of emerging technologies. Genentech, Biogen, Adobe, and Apple are examples of other clients that H&Q has worked with. H&Q's branded consumer goods practice is small, but it has done deals for young, glamorous companies such as Boston Beer (Sam Adams), Robert Mondavi, Cannondale, and The North Face.

As for its culture, H&Q might be called the Nice Guy company. H&Q is known as "the kindler, gentler investment bank" and, according to insiders, lives up to that moniker. If you want to make it at H&Q, you'd better be a true team player with a calm, polished exterior. The firm likes to reward employees with stock options: Some employees receive 20 percent of professional bonuses in stock, with a three-year vesting period. Insider ownership of the company is 70 percent, an extremely high figure. (By comparison, similar figures for DLJ and Lehman are 6 percent and 17 percent, respectively.)

H&Q specializes in four growth sectors: technology, health care, business information and outsourcing services, and branded consumer products. The firm likes to call its focus "granular," meaning that instead of serving high tech or health care in a broadly defined manner, the firm establishes expertise in very sharply defined subsectors within those industries. For instance, within the software industry, H&Q has assigned bankers to focus on Internet software, consumer software, and design and automation software. Functionally, the firm traditionally has been strong in the high-margin businesses of underwriting, IPOs, and venture capital.

Hambrecht & Quist LLC is structured around three principal divisions: Investment Banking (including private placements, IPOs, debt and equity offerings, M&A, financial advisory work), Syndicate, Sales and Trading, and Research (divided into Technology, Health Care, Information Services, and Branded Consumer).

Investment banking services are provided out of the San Francisco, New York, Boston, London, and Asia/Pacific offices. The vast majority of investment banking *associates* are hired from business schools, but some are hired off-cycle through other channels. All associates are hired as generalists. Investment banking *analysts* are recruited from undergraduate institutions and are expected to remain with the firm for two years. Opportunities to remain with the firm for a third year sometimes are available for outstanding analysts.

H&Q's formal training program consists of three weeks for associates and four weeks for analysts. Since the firm staffs leanly and may not have the time and cushion needed to train people, it is important to emphasize a real interest in finance, prior experience, or familiarity with financial concepts when applying. Evidence of being a team player is also a plus.

Numbers: HAMBRECHT & QUIST GROUP

Founded: 1968   **Ownership Structure:** Publicly Traded (HMQ-NYSE)

Total Consolidated Capital (1996,$M): 226.7

Sample Clients: Netscape, Intuit, Adobe, US Robotics, ImmuLogic, Cannondale

	1996	1995	1994	1993	1992	1991
Net Revenues ($M)	390	220	119	110	125	82
No. of Employees	725	498	426	350	327	291

Roles: Analyst   Associate   Vice President   Principal   Managing Director

Sources: H&Q 1996 Prospectus, *Investment Dealers' Digest*

PART II: INSIDER INTERVIEW

How would you describe the company's culture?

H&Q has a very open, friendly atmosphere. A flat hierarchical structure allows analysts to interface with principals and managing directors on a daily basis. Even Dan Case, the CEO, is accessible.

H&Q bankers realize that analysts are human beings, not machines—they don't ask for information they don't really need, there's hardly any "busy work," and the senior bankers actually feel a little bad about asking you to pull an all-nighter or to spend an entire weekend getting a project out the door. That doesn't mean that there is any less work, but morale is better because analysts feel like the senior bankers care about them.

Above all else, H&Q is a meritocracy. The sooner you can show that you can handle a lot of responsibility, the sooner the senior bankers will readily hand off important projects or clients to you.

What did you like best about your experience at the firm?

The best parts of working for H&Q include the huge amount of responsibility an analyst can get if the senior bankers think he or she can handle it. We get to work with some exciting, cutting-edge companies and have the opportunity to constantly update our industry knowledge—you never stop learning. Analysts get lots of contact with the most senior executives of H&Q's clients.

What did you like least about your experience at the firm?

H&Q doesn't have the same rigorous training programs as larger banks. You need to be proactive to learn different models and techniques, and you need to be comfortable asking for help, otherwise your work will be of lower quality and may take longer than necessary.

What types of candidates do you think the firm prefers?

It didn't seem like you needed an economics, finance, or technical background to work for H&Q. Some of the best analysts were English and Political Science majors who exhibited a fascination with the technology or health care industries. The bottom line is that H&Q hired analysts that the bankers liked to hang out with in their spare time.

What advice would you give someone seeking a job at the company?

The associate or VP in charge of recruiting is incredibly busy with the normal deal load as well as with recruiting. Don't get discouraged if your messages aren't returned immediately—keep plugging away. It is essential that a job-seeker make it as easy as possible for the recruiter to set up a meeting. A good idea is to offer to be available for a telephone interview at the recruiter's convenience—that's the toughest thing to turn down, and you'll avoid getting strung along if you don't fit the recruiter's profile.

Do you think the company's recruiting process is unusual in any way?

Recruiting at H&Q is ridiculously selective. I believe that H&Q typically looks at around 2,000 résumés for ten analyst positions. H&Q conducts on-campus recruiting at seven or eight campuses and a large majority of hires come from this pool, although anyone with a very strong résumé will get serious consideration.

PROFILE

J.P. Morgan & Co., Inc.

NAME: **J.P. Morgan & Co., Inc.**
HEADQUARTERS: **60 Wall Street, New York, NY 10260, (212) 483-2323**
WEB SITE: **www.jpmorgan.com**

◆

RECRUITING: **Centralized through New York**
SUMMER JOBS: **Undergraduate and Graduate levels**
GRAD RECRUITING CONTACT (HEADQUARTERS): **Gregory Pepe (Investment Banking)**
GRAD TITLE: **Associate**
UNDERGRAD RECRUITING CONTACT (HEADQUARTERS): **Anne Grant (Investment Banking)**
UNDERGRAD TITLE: **Analyst (Investment Banking, Research)**

RELATED READING: Philip Maher and Ron Cooper, "The New Bulge Bracket," *Investment Dealers' Digest,* November 25, 1996. Stephen Frank, "J.P. Morgan's Make-Over Has Left Investors Puzzled," *The Wall Street Journal,* June 4, 1996. "Recasting the House of Morgan," *The Financial Times,* January 26, 1996. Robert Teitelman, "Morgan Enters the Warner Era," *Institutional Investor,* January 24, 1996. Michael Sesit, "U.S. Financial Firms Seize Dominant Role in the World Markets," *The Wall Street Journal,* January 5, 1996. Ron Chernow, *The House of Morgan* (New York: Atlantic Monthly Press, 1990).

OTHER OFFICES: (Domestic) Boston, Chicago, Houston, Los Angeles, Newark (DE), Palm Beach, San Francisco, Washington DC, Wilmington; (International) Amsterdam, Bangkok, Beijing, Bombay, Brussels, Buenos Aires, Caracas, Cayman Islands, Frankfurt, Geneva, Hong Kong, Jakarta, Johannesburg, London, Madrid, Manila, Melbourne, Mexico City, Milan, Nassau, Osaka, Paris, Prague, Rome, Rio de Janeiro, Santiago, São Paulo, Seoul, Shanghai, Singapore, Sydney, Taipei, Tokyo, Toronto, Warsaw, Zurich

PART I: ANALYSIS

Founded over 150 years ago, J.P. Morgan has a pedigree that is quite distinguished. J.P. Morgan was instrumental in the financing of such pillars of American industry as U.S. Steel, General Electric, and AT&T; it also served as financial representative for the French and British governments during the two world wars. When the Glass-Steagall Act was enacted after the Great Depression to separate commercial and investment banking, J.P. Morgan was forced to curtail its activities to commercial banking. The House of Morgan split, with a few partners forming a separate investment bank, Morgan Stanley—one of J.P. Morgan's major rivals today. Now, with privileges granted to J.P. Morgan to conduct investment banking activities (and Glass-Steagall gradually dying anyway), the firm not only is back in investment banking, but is recognized as being among the bulge-bracket firms in the industry.

What are J.P. Morgan's strengths? The firm's reputation is top shelf. It is willing to commit capital to support its deals, and it has a lot of capital to commit. Its treatment of employees is the best in the industry. Finally, its corporate culture, though becoming diluted, is still unique.

This is a firm that is as international as it claims. J.P. Morgan has its roots in the London merchant banking firm of George Peabody and Junius Morgan. In 1861 J. Pierpont Morgan, for whom the firm is named, established a New York sales and distribution office for his father's firm. J.P. Morgan was the first U.S. American investment bank to open an office in Paris, over 125 years ago. Unlike in the United States, J.P. Morgan was never forced to halt its investment banking services abroad and thus has been building its investment banking reputation and experience outside the country. J.P. Morgan's name is better recognized outside the United States than most other American investment banks.

J.P. Morgan's roots as a commercial bank have a significant influence on the company. First, the firm is well capitalized and has one of the highest credit ratings of any Wall Street bank. This gives it a strong foundation as it enters a period of intense consolidation and competition in which larger investment banks with access to capital will survive. Already, after only a few years of being allowed to participate in securities markets, the company has made enormous strides in debt and equity underwriting and mergers and acquisitions and is challenging the traditional investment banking powerhouses.

Morgan, as it is called in the industry, is a kind, gentle, and classy firm, where big egos and boisterous behavior are not received well. The firm has a powerful Human Resources department, which results in an environment where the "little people" are protected from abuse and receive a great deal of career guidance and mentoring. Morgan's mothering is famous: Employees in the New York office receive a free lunch every day. As in commercial banking, J.P. Morgan likes to grow its people from within and doesn't require them to have MBAs to progress up the career ladder. Investment banking *analysts* are hired for three years, longer than at most banks, and are more likely to be promoted without an MBA than at other firms. Because it views analysts from a longer-term perspective than other banks, Morgan invests more in their training: It usually rotates investment banking analysts through two assignments so that they may learn several aspects of the business.

Morgan offers job opportunities for recent graduates in several areas, including:

- *Investment Banking:* Advisory and financing services for corporations and governments

- *Equity Research:* Industry-based research, investment recommendations
- *Municipal Finance:* Advice and financing for public sector clients
- *Markets:* Sales and trading of equity and debt securities
- *Investment Management:* Manages investment funds for institutional investors

However, applicants can apply only to one area, so it's worthwhile to do some research before you send out your cover letter and résumé. According to the firm, recruiting coordinators change very frequently, so candidates should check Morgan's Web site for new contact names. When ready to apply, those who attend schools where J.P. Morgan is not recruiting on-campus should send their résumé and cover letter directly to the recruiter for one of the career areas listed above.

Investment banking *associates* are most typically hired from business schools or with significant relevant experience. *Summer associate* positions are available to MBA students. Investment banking *analysts* are recruited from undergraduate institutions. J.P. Morgan is unusual in that it offers investment banking *summer internships* to college juniors in the United States. Submit an application for summer internships between January and March of your junior year in college.

Numbers: J.P. MORGAN & CO., INC.

Founded: 1861 (in the U.S.) **Ownership Structure:** Publicly Traded (NYSE-JPM)

Total Consolidated Capital (1996, $): 15,144 billion

Sample Clients: Ford Motor Company, Westinghouse, Hoescht, General Motors, General Electric

	1996	1995	1994	1993	1992
Net Revenues ($M)*	5,153	3,901	3,536	4,499	2,950
No. of Employees	15,728	15,613	17,055	15,193	14,368

*Net of interest expense

Roles: Analyst/Trainee Associate Vice President Managing Director
————————————————————————▶

Sources: J.P. Morgan 1995 Annual Report, J.P. Morgan Web site, JP Morgan

---

PART II: INSIDER INTERVIEW

How would you describe the firm's culture?

Many aspects of the J.P. Morgan mentality are holdovers from the commercial banking days. In the old days, bankers were more like Renaissance people: well educated, cosmopolitan, and with an "ideal pedigree." When I was at J.P. Morgan a year ago, most of the people were "home grown." People were promoted from within the institution. An MBA was not considered essential.

What types of candidates do you think the firm prefers?

In my experience, J.P. Morgan looks to hire well-rounded people. I was a humanities major. I suppose the firm felt that whatever I didn't know about finance or economics I had the capacity to learn through their training program. You can teach people to be bankers, but you can't teach people to be people.

J.P. Morgan was the only investment bank that was offering a career track position for undergraduate hires—not a typical two-year churn-and-burn program. Senior people were very serious about developing junior people: You were encouraged to attend client meetings; you were asked your opinion.

What did you like best about your experience at the firm?

Opportunity was abundant. Many of the senior bankers were holdovers from the commercial banking days and therefore were still new to investment banking and the latest financial products. As a junior person, if you knew what you were doing, you were given the appropriate level of responsibility.

The bank was serious about its pristine reputation. J.P. Morgan refused to be in deals for the casino and gaming sector. Lewd behavior inside and outside the bank was unacceptable. It was not okay to take a client to a local strip club, for example. I was proud to tell people that I worked for J.P. Morgan.

What did you like least about your experience at the firm?

Politics played too great a role in assignments and promotion. Often people were promoted who weren't the best performers but were the most well connected internally. Furthermore, the bank clung to several old and senior bankers from the commercial banking days who burned resources with nothing to show for the effort. The internal bureaucracy was bulky, slow, and unwieldy, and information was always disseminated slowly.

What changes at J.P. Morgan should candidates be aware of?

The bank is becoming more like a typical investment bank. They no longer hire undergraduates for a career track position but for a three-year analyst program. I believe that the bank is placing a greater emphasis on MBAs and will continue to increase the number of MBA hires over time.

PROFILE

Lehman Brothers Inc.

NAME: **Lehman Brothers Inc.**
HEADQUARTERS: **3 World Financial Center, New York, NY 10285, (212) 526-7000**
WEB SITE: **www.lehman.com**

◆

RECRUITING: **Centralized through New York**
SUMMER JOBS: **Graduate level only**
GRAD RECRUITING CONTACT (HEADQUARTERS): **Dorine McManus (Investment Banking)**
GRAD TITLE: **Associate (Investment Banking)**
UNDERGRAD RECRUITING CONTACT (HEADQUARTERS): **Jennifer Edwards (Investment Banking)**
UNDERGRAD TITLE: **Analyst (Investment Banking)**

◆

RELATED READING: Michael Siconolfi, "Lehman Sought Merger Partners," *Wall Street Journal.* "Can Lehman Survive?" *Fortune,* December 11, 1995. Ken Auletta, *Greed and Glory on Wall Street: The Fall of the House of Lehman* (New York: Random House, 1986).

OTHER OFFICES: (Domestic) Atlanta, Boston, Chicago, Dallas, Houston, Jersey City, Los Angeles, Miami, Newport Beach, Orlando, Philadelphia, San Francisco, Seattle, Washington, D.C.; (International) Bahrain, Beijing, Buenos Aires, Dubai, Frankfurt, Geneva, Hong Kong, London, Madrid, Mexico City, Milan, New Dehli, Osaka, Paris, Santiago, São Paulo, San Juan (PR), Seoul, Singapore, Taipei, Tel Aviv, Tokyo, Toronto, Zurich

PART I: ANALYSIS

Lehman has one of the longest, most distinguished histories on Wall Street. The firm was founded as a cotton brokerage in 1850 by three German brothers in Montgomery, Alabama. By the turn of the century, the firm had diversified into securities underwriting. The firm was managed by a series of family members until the 1950s. In 1973 former Commerce Secretary Peter Petersen was hired to manage Lehman, and the firm prospered. At this point, Lehman was known as "the bank of banks," perhaps the strongest on Wall Street in client advisory relationships and corporate finance. In 1977 Lehman merged with Kuhn Loeb, another historic investment bank. Legendary trader Lew Glucksman assumed the helm in 1983, and under his stewardship the firm was sold to American Express in 1984.

American Express's strategy was to combine Lehman's strength in investment banking and institutional sales with the retail sales strength of Shearson Loeb Rhodes, which it had acquired earlier. Shearson Lehman, the new entity, had an enormous network for selling stocks and was building a strong franchise in stock underwriting. But Shearson Lehman produced uneven results—and Amex decided to exit the securities business by first selling Shearson, then Lehman. Lehman became an independent company again. But it lost the retail sales network it had gained through Shearson. This, combined with a poor compensation plan that drove away many of the firm's top equity analysts, caused Lehman's stock underwriting business to plummet.

Now Lehman is back to being strong mainly in bonds but is building on this strength to improve its equity underwriting business. To remain competitive, the firm has downsized and reorganized at all levels, from support staff to senior management. Results for 1996 showed great improvement, with return on equity rising to 20.6 percent in the fourth quarter compared with 9.3 percent the year before.

So what does all this turmoil mean for you, the junior employee? It is reportedly very important to get into a strong group at Lehman, because the weaker groups may see less deal-flow and bankers may spend more time writing pitch books than doing deals. If you're an undergraduate, the firm's overall performance probably has little impact on you since you will be at the firm for a short stint anyway. If you're an MBA student, the long-term choice of Lehman involves some uncertainty about the firm's future but also greater opportunity: You will be able to have a big impact in a firm that welcomes new ideas to solve its problems. Moreover, Lehman's name on your résumé will be better recognized than many of the small boutiques or newer specialist investment banks.

The firm has four primary lines of business: Investment Banking (including Public Finance), Fixed Income (including sales and trading), Equities (including sales and trading), and Private Client Services.

Within each business, bankers are further organized into industry, product, and geographic groups. According to a former analyst, the firm is very strong in serving the telecommunications/media, natural resources, health care, and high-technology industries.

Recruiting is structured somewhat differently. Candidates apply to the following recruiting groups:

- Investment Banking (distinguishes between "Investment Banking Associates/Analysts" and "Public Finance Associates/Analysts")
- Sales, Trading, and Research (hires for Fixed Income and Equities)
- Private Client Services (title is "High Net Worth Sales Associate")

Investment banking *associates* typically are hired from leading business schools. A major strength of Lehman's program is that associates join a generalist program and rotate through several groups, then receive specific assignments after assessing different groups. An associate is asked to name three top choices, and the assignment decision is then made based on the firm's needs and the associate's preferences. Regional or international hires must perform a rotation in the New York office for four months to two years before settling into a regional office.

Investment banking *analysts* are hired from undergraduate institutions and master's programs in any subject other than business. Last year over eighty analysts worldwide were hired. This number remains fairly consistent over time. Analysts join the firm as generalists, then help choose their group assignment after the training program. Analysts are expected to remain with the firm for two years, then return to business school or be promoted. However, Lehman invites more analysts to remain for a third year than most investment banks. About one third of second year analysts are given an opportunity to stay for a third year; the program is very flexible, with many third-year analysts offered stints in regional offices or exotic international locales. Compensation for a third-year analyst is reportedly close to an associate's pay. In addition, Lehman is the only major investment bank to offer a tuition reimbursement program to analysts returning from business school.

Numbers: LEHMAN BROTHERS INC.

Founded: 1850   **Ownership Structure:** Publicly Traded (NYSE-LEH)

Total Consolidated Capital (1996, $M): 19,796

Sample Clients: Digital Equipment Corporation, Bellcore, World Bank, Eastman Kodak, USX Corporation, Deutsche Postbank, Republic of France

	1996	1995	1994	1993	1992
Net Revenues ($M)	3,444	2,942	2,738	3,555	2,853
No. of Employees	7,700	7,771	8,512	N/A	N/A

Roles: Analyst   Associate   Vice President   Senior Vice President   Managing Director

Sources: Lehman Brothers 1996 Annual Report, *Wall Street Journal*, Lehman Brothers, interviews with analysts

---

PART II: INSIDER INTERVIEW

What did you like best about your experience at Lehman?

People were fairly atypical. I've met a lot of bankers from Goldman and Morgan and they strike me as polished, wealthy, socially exposed, well-rounded people who are able to express themselves. Lehman people are a bunch of people who are international, people who sometimes could not speak English well, who are good with numbers. But people were characters. They weren't your typical WASP bankers. They were a very diverse group. They were pretty cool people. And fun.

You can definitely socialize with the higher-ups. They're very approachable. A lot of people participated in jogging events, ski events, and stuff like that. There was a lot of hierarchy in front of the clients, but when you were in the office you could joke around with the associates and VPs. We'd have food fights all the time. It was very casual.

What do you think a student needs to know about Lehman?

People are willing to help you and aren't cutthroat. But you do need to start day one building relationships and building trust with their groups, because those are the people who are going to help you. Also, you're going to have three years at most at the firm. Only one or two people each year get promoted to associate without an MBA. In my class, I believe that about 28 percent got an offer to stay for a third year.

What did you like least about your experience at the firm?

I wouldn't say that Lehman's the type of company that takes care of you in the sense that it wants you to grow. I think they see you as replaceable and exchangeable. You get what you come for, I guess—a little bit of money, and a good name on your résumé.

What types of people did you see being hired at Lehman?

They like athletics, high grades, and high scores just like anyone else. Also, they really want fresh meat for their analyst program. If you've been out more than two years, especially if you haven't been working in a relevant field, it's questionable whether you'll be hired. If you've gotten an MBA from anywhere other than a top school, you should work at a smaller firm, because I don't think Lehman's going to give you much credit for it.

PROFILE
Merrill Lynch & Co., Inc.

NAME: **Merrill Lynch & Co., Inc.**
HEADQUARTERS: **World Financial Center, 250 Vesey Street, New York, NY 10281,**
   (212) 449-1000
WEB SITE: **www.ml.com (career information under "Merrill Lynch Online")**

◆

RECRUITING: **Centralized through New York**
SUMMER JOBS: **Graduate level only**
GRAD RECRUITING CONTACT (HEADQUARTERS): **Joy Andal (Investment Banking).**
   Please call firm to verify contact name.
GRAD TITLE: **Associate (Investment Banking)**
UNDERGRAD RECRUITING CONTACT (HEADQUARTERS): **Joy Andal (Investment**
   Banking). Please call firm to verify contact name.
UNDERGRAD TITLE: **Analyst (Investment Banking)**

◆

RELATED READING: Matthew Schifrin, "Merrill-izing the World," *Forbes,* February 10, 1997. "At Merrill, A Gatekeeper Determines Client Contact," *Investment Dealers' Digest,* April 1, 1996. Shawn Tully, "Merrill Lynch Bulls Ahead," *Fortune,* February 19, 1996. "Magnificent Merrill," *The Economist,* April 15, 1995.

OTHER PRINCIPAL OFFICES: (Domestic) Chicago, Houston, Los Angeles, San Francisco; (International) Hong Kong, London, Mexico City, São Paulo, Singapore, Tokyo. These are the primary offices from which Merrill Lynch conducts its investment banking activities. The company has hundreds of additional locations and retail branches. Please see Web site for more information.

PART I: ANALYSIS

Merrill Lynch enjoys the unique position of being all things to all people. The firm is the world's largest underwriter of stocks and bonds, a sophisticated bulge-bracket investment bank based in New York. But of all the major Wall Street firms, this is the one that your aunt in Idaho is most likely to have heard of, because Merrill also has retail power—a network of over 13,000 brokers across the country. These brokers generate commissions from selling mutual funds, stocks, and bonds to individuals like you and me. Merrill holds over $730 billion in assets in customer accounts. Its relatively stable retail business creates a nice cushion during downturns in investment banking.

Merrill Lynch was formed in 1914 by partners Charles Merrill and Edmund Lynch. After the 1929 stock market crash, the firm focused on underwriting instead of brokerage services. But after World War II, Merrill expanded its retail business organically, training brokers in the art of customer relations. Donald Regan (who later left to become President Reagan's treasury secretary) led the firm in the 1970s and helped it acquire the prestigious firm of White Weld and expand into real estate, insurance, and other financial services. In the 1980s Merrill Lynch built up its investment banking business.

In the late 1990s the firm has ensconced itself in the bulge bracket with Morgan Stanley and Goldman Sachs. But unlike Goldman and Morgan Stanley, its culture has a strong brokerage orientation. Merrill is a bit more street-smart and down-to-earth than its neighbors. This starts at the top, where you'll find senior managers who didn't attend elite schools or come from blue-blood lineages: President David Komansky grew up in a tenement and never received a college degree. CEO Dan Tully grew up in Queens and spent his youth studying on the subway because his family's apartment was too small.* He rose at Merrill through brokerage operations.

Merrill Lynch is a leader in stock and bond underwriting, partly because its enormous sales force gives corporations confidence that it will be able to place shares with the best buyers at the best prices. But Merrill does not dominate the mergers and acquisitions business because it doesn't have the history of close relationships with senior corporate executives that Goldman Sachs and Morgan Stanley have.

The firm also has a global presence, with more than 11 percent of its employees located outside the United States. With its industry-leading $27 billion in capital at the end of 1996, Merrill stands to win even if the investment banking industry becomes consolidated as is predicted.

*Shawn Tully, "Merrill Lynch Bulls Ahead," *Fortune*, February 19, 1996.

Merrill Lynch's Corporate and Institutional Client Group serves corporations, governments, and institutional investors worldwide and offers the most employment opportunities to recent graduates. The group is organized into the following areas:

- Investment Banking: Includes corporate finance (debt and equity underwriting), mergers and acquisitions, real estate, private equity, and high yield finance
- Institutional Client: Securities sales force serving more than 6,000 institutional investors worldwide
- Institutional Investment Management Services: Asset management and mutual funds
- Global Client Products, including:
  Debt Markets: Trades debt (bond) related products and derivatives, structures and originates public finance, money markets, project finance
  Equity Markets: Trades equity- (stock-) related products and derivatives, convertibles
  Capital Markets: Acts as liaison between sales/trading and investment banking

The firm also offers employment opportunities in its Private Client Group (serving wealthy individuals).

Within investment banking, people are further divided into industry groups such as Utilities and Financial Institutions and transaction groups such as Corporate Finance or Real Estate. New hires joining Investment Banking are hired directly into a specialty group. Most new hires joining sales or trading within Equity or Debt Markets will rotate through various sales and trading groups for a few months before receiving a final placement on a desk.

Numbers: MERRILL LYNCH & CO., INC.

Founded: 1914   **Ownership Structure:** Publicly Traded (NYSE-MER)

Total Consolidated Capital (1996, $M): 27,008

Sample Clients: Daimler-Benz, Blockbuster Entertainment, Macy's, Fannie Mae, Toyota, Japan Rail, Hyundai, Government of China, KLM Royal Dutch Airlines

	1996	1995	1994	1993	1992
Net Revenues ($M)	12,961	10,265	9,625	10,558	8,577
No. of Employees	49,800	46,000	43,800	41,900	40,100

Roles: Analyst Associate Vice President Executive Vice President Managing Director

Sources: Merrill Lynch brochure "Graduate Opportunities at Merrill Lynch," Merrill Lynch Web site, Bloomberg, 1996 Annual Report

Investment banking *associates* typically are hired from business schools or with significant previous experience. New associates are put through an extensive five-week training program that resembles a mini-MBA. Unlike at Goldman Sachs and other less sales-and-trading–oriented firms, all associates at Merrill must take the Series 7 exam, which qualifies them to sell securities in the United States. *Summer associate* positions at the firm's New York headquarters are available to MBA students and last ten to twelve weeks. Investment banking *analysts* are recruited from undergraduate institutions and are expected to remain with the firm for two years.

PART II: INSIDER INTERVIEW

What did you like best about your experience at the firm?

There were two things that really enhanced my experience at Merrill Lynch. Analysts are generally given a great deal of responsibility, and the people that I worked with were great to work with. Senior bankers were always very accessible.

What did you like least about your experience at the firm?

What I liked least about my experience is common industrywide. The worst projects were the internal "studies" and "puff" material (also known as league tables) showing why Merrill Lynch should be involved in a transaction.

What types of candidates do you think the firm prefers?

Merrill Lynch prefers candidates that have some familiarity with accounting and math, or some quantitative subject, and show a willingness to work hard and are easy to get along with—this is required because the hours are so long.

What advice would you give someone seeking a job at the company?

The only advice I would give would be to be very familiar with your résumé and be prepared to answer any questions concerning "holes" (or inconsistencies) in your résumé. It is important that you have a clear, thoughtful reason why you want to go into investment banking. It's best to talk to people in the industry to get a good idea of what analysts do.

PROFILE

Montgomery Securities

NAME: **Montgomery Securities**
HEADQUARTERS: **600 Montgomery Street, San Francisco, CA 94111, (415) 627-2000**
WEB SITE: **www.montgomery.com**

◆

RECRUITING: **Centralized: Apply to San Francisco**
SUMMER JOBS: **Graduate and Undergraduate levels**
GRAD RECRUITING CONTACT: **Maggie Woodward, VP**
GRAD TITLE: **Associate**
UNDERGRAD RECRUITING CONTACT: **Maggie Woodward, VP**
UNDERGRAD TITLE: **Investment Banking Analyst**

◆

RELATED READING: Anne Evers, "Growth on the Horizon: Montgomery Securities," *Buyside Magazine,* March 1997. Scott McMurray, "What Makes Montgomery Run?" *Institutional Investor,* February 1997. Linda Himelstein, "Silicon Valley Seeds Itself," *Business Week,* March 11, 1996. Nanette Byrnes, "Too Much, Too Soon?" *Business Week,* October 23, 1995.

OTHER OFFICES: (Domestic) Boston, New York

PART I: ANALYSIS

On the very last page of Montgomery Securities's 1994 brochure lies a glimpse into the spirit of the firm: a picture of the Supermarine Spitfire, a World War II prop plane that was "legendary in its ability to outmaneuver, outrun, and outfight larger warplanes." Prone to symbolism, Montgomery's brochures emphasize the power of the individual to effect change and surpass boundaries.

What is all this positive energy directed at? Montgomery Securities is one of four investment banks dominating the West Coast, along with Robertson Stephens, Hambrecht & Quist, and Alex. Brown. But if CEO Thomas Weisel has his way, Montgomery will become as large and as powerful as the New York bulge-bracket firms. Already, the firm is attracting attention from job-hunters around the country.

Upstart Montgomery is named for the other Street, Montgomery Street in downtown San Francisco. Weisel cofounded its predecessor, Robertson, Colman, Siebel, & Weisel, in 1969. In 1971 Weisel and partner Sanford Robertson split, dividing Robertson Stephens and Montgomery Securities into two separate companies. Since then Montgomery has been known for a trading orientation and Robertson for an investment banking orientation. Montgomery has grown from just $104 million in revenues in 1990 to over $700 million in 1996. Its goal is to hit $1 billion by the year 2000.* Its unique offering: investment banking services for select industries, and sales and trading execution capabilities that are on par with the bulge-bracket firms. Montgomery is the nation's largest industrial equities brokerage outside of New York City.

Montgomery's culture mirrors the personality of Weisel, an athlete and art collector who isn't afraid to speak his mind. Montgomery encourages individuality, competitiveness, self-expression, and the emergence of "stars." Those who lack confidence or can't be aggressive may want to look elsewhere. And about sports:

*Nanette Byrnes, "Too Much, Too Soon?" *Business Week,* October 23, 1995.

The firm is filled with former athletes, so many that industry insiders joke that you have to be an athlete to get a job here. After-work events are often sports-centered. The firm even has an in-house gym. In its recruiting brochure, Montgomery states that it "believes there are similarities between success in athletics and success in business. Many of the qualities for success in athletics—long-term commitment to a goal, discipline, preparation, performance under difficult circumstances, and teamwork—are part of any successful business strategy." Take this to heart when preparing your résumé.

Montgomery's investment banking is very focused. It serves five high-growth sectors: technology, health care, financial services, consumer goods, and media and communications. Want to work for a West Coast investment bank but in something other than high tech? Montgomery is known for its strength and experience in serving consumer goods companies, specialty retailers, hotels, and restaurant companies.

Montgomery performs three main functions: It develops moneymaking ideas for institutional investors and high-net-worth individuals, meets the investment banking needs of growth companies, and creates strong asset management vehicles. Montgomery has recently expanded its high-yield debt business in response to client demand. Montgomery is known as a trading house, but contrary to popular belief, the firm does not actually engage in proprietary trading (trading on its own behalf).

Will Montgomery be able to achieve its aggressive growth targets while serving a very focused group of clients? The firm thinks so, pointing out that the "in the 1990s, more than 3,200 companies have gone public, doubling the universe of growth companies."*

The company's principal divisions are: Investment Banking (private placements, equity underwriting, M&A, high-yield debt underwriting); Research; Sales, Trading, and Convertible Securities; Private Client Department; Prime Brokerage Services; Montgomery Asset Management; and Clearing Services.

Investment banking *associates* typically are hired from business schools or with significant previous banking experience. New associates become generalists but after six months are assigned to one of the five sectors. *Investment banking analysts* are recruited from undergraduate institutions and are expected to remain with the firm for two or three years. They begin as generalists but soon specialize in one of the five sectors. Undergraduates are also hired for limited "clerk" positions in sales and trading.

Those likely to be successful in the recruiting process are confident, competitive, well-rounded overachievers with winning personalities. A background in sports is a big plus. Street-smart, entrepreneurial skills are also valued. While Montgomery recruits a variety of majors, it is looking for those with some familiarity with financial concepts.

*Montgomery Securities, *1996 Corporate Review*.

Numbers: MONTGOMERY SECURITIES

Founded: 1971   **Ownership Structure:** Limited Partnership

Total Consolidated Capital (1996, $M): 160

Sample Clients: StrataCom, Mirage Resorts, Doubletree, HFS, Wells Fargo, Orchard
Supply Hardware, Staples, Lone Star Steakhouse & Saloon

	1996	1995	1994	1993	1992
Net Revenues ($M)	705	467	306	304	208
No. of Employees	1419	982	800	691	528

Roles: Analyst   Associate   Vice President   Principal   Managing Director
———————————————————————————————▶

Sources: Montgomery brochure "The Other Street," Montgomery Web site, Montgomery Securities

---

PART II: INSIDER INTERVIEW

What adjectives would you use to describe Montgomery's culture?

Aggressive, competitive, political, and entrepreneurial.

What should someone applying to Montgomery know about the firm?

Montgomery prides itself on having an athletic culture. Thom Weisel, the founder and CEO, is an avid cyclist and skater and wants that athleticism to flow throughout the firm.

What did you like best about your experience at the firm?

I had the ability to act like a vice president, even though I was an associate. There are no hangups at Montgomery about someone being too young or inexperienced to be in front of clients. Everyone is so stretched that it happens naturally. Montgomery's senior management is intelligent, aggressive, and very strategic. I think they are making a legitimate run at the bulge bracket.

What would you like to have changed about your experience?

Being based on the West Coast, the travel schedule to visit clients across the country is ugly.

What do you think Montgomery looks for in its hires?

Montgomery looks for successful New York bankers who want more of a life, who are more well rounded and family-oriented.

Is there any advice you would give someone applying to the firm?

Show enthusiasm for Montgomery!

PROFILE

Morgan Stanley

NAME: **Morgan Stanley (a division of Morgan Stanley, Dean Witter, Discover & Co.)**
HEADQUARTERS: **1585 Broadway, New York, NY 10036, (212) 761-4000**
WEB SITE: **www.ms.com**

◆

RECRUITING: **Centralized through New York**
SUMMER JOBS: **Graduate level only**
GRAD RECRUITING CONTACT (HEADQUARTERS): **Patricia Palumbo (Investment Banking)**
GRAD TITLE: **Research Analyst (Equity Research); Associate (all other divisions)**
UNDERGRAD RECRUITING CONTACT (HEADQUARTERS): **Patricia Palumbo (Investment Banking)**
UNDERGRAD TITLE: **Financial Analyst (Investment Banking)**

◆

RELATED READING: "Brains and Brawn: Morgan Stanley Group and Dean Witter plan an $8.8 Billion Merger," *The Wall Street Journal,* February 5, 1997. Leah Nathans Spiro, "Why Morgan Stanley Bought a Case of the Blahs," *Business Week,* July 8, 1996. Peter Truell, "Morgan Stanley's Wall St. Rarity: A Woman with Power," *The New York Times,* July 2, 1996. Anita Raghavan, "Morgan to Pay $745 Million for Fund Firm," *The Wall Street Journal,* June 24, 1996. Leah Nathans Spiro, "Global Gamble," *Business Week,* February 12, 1996.

OTHER INVESTMENT BANKING OFFICES: (Domestic) Chicago, Los Angeles, Menlo Park, Philadelphia, San Francisco; (International) Beijing, Bombay, Frankfurt, Hong Kong, Johannesburg, London, Luxembourg, Madrid, Melbourne, Milan, Montreal, Moscow, Paris, Seoul, Shanghai, Singapore, Taipei, Tokyo, Zurich. The company has hundreds of additional locations and retail branches.

PART I: ANALYSIS

Do you want to work on the biggest investment banking transactions of the year, the kind that make the front page of *The Wall Street Journal?* Morgan Stanley may be the place for you. This large, international firm is one of three in the bulge bracket and is known for its preeminence in investment banking. Morgan Stanley is a leader in several important corporate finance and advisory markets, especially mergers and acquisitions. Its investment bankers advise governments and blue-chip global corporations that frequently tap the financial markets. And Morgan Stanley has a powerful retail distribution network too: In early 1997 the bank announced its merger with Dean Witter, Discover.

Morgan Stanley was formed in 1935 by Howard Stanley and Henry S. Morgan, son of J.P. Morgan, who left J.P. Morgan & Co. after the Glass-Steagall Act forced a separation between commercial and investment banking. J.P. Morgan became solely a commercial bank in the United States, while Morgan Stanley became a separate company focused on investment banking. Over the years Morgan Stanley developed a reputation as a "white-shoe," WASP-y bank that refused to participate in stock syndications unless it was named lead manager. The firm finally moved into the rough-and-tumble world of trading in the 1970s and went public in 1986. Although it lost some of its underwriting lead in the 1980s, Morgan Stanley is now back at the top of the league tables along with Goldman Sachs and Merrill Lynch. Seeking to expand its asset-management business, Morgan Stanley acquired Miller Andersen & Sherrerd and mutual fund manager Van Kampen American Capital in 1996.

Since its founding, Morgan Stanley has changed in significant ways. The company is aggressively expanding into new markets, particularly overseas. A significant portion of the firm's revenues are generated outside the United States, and approximately one-third of employees are located in Europe and Asia. Morgan Stanley is considered the premier investment bank serving emerging markets such as Mexico and China. Asia, in particular, is a top Morgan Stanley priority for business development.

While Goldman Sachs is known on Wall Street as a team system, Morgan Stanley has been called a "star system," in which assertiveness and individualism are rewarded and people develop reputations quickly within the firm. As Morgan Stanley states in its 1996 recruiting brochure, "Strong personalities thrive." Bankers there work hard for their money, and analysts wear beepers in order to be reachable when they're out of the office. Morgan Stanley's new headquarters in New York seems to embody its bold image: a glass-and-steel box wrapped in bands of moving, real-time neon stock quotes. And the building is located in Times Square, not on Wall Street. Individualism doesn't mean there isn't camaraderie; Morgan Stanley's New York M&A group is famous for the "bonding" that occurs among bankers.

Morgan Stanley offers job opportunities for recent graduates in many of its divisions:

- *Equity Research:* Industry-based research, investment recommendations
- *Equity Sales and Trading:* Sales and trading of equity securities
- *Fixed Income/Foreign Exchange:* Sales, trading, and research of debt securities and currency
- *Investment Banking:* Includes corporate finance, M&A, equity, real estate, and debt capital markets group that links corporate finance to trading floor
- *Private Client Services:* Investment advice and other personal financial services for wealthy individuals
- *Strategic Planning Group:* An internal management consulting unit that designs strategies for the firm

Investment banking *associates* typically are hired from business schools or with significant previous business experience. Most associates are hired initially into the New York, London, Hong Kong, or Tokyo offices, but there is some movement later to other offices worldwide. Investment banking associates are hired into a generalist group nicknamed "The Pool," where they spend one year before being placed as a product, regional, or industry specialist in Corporate Finance, MARD (mergers and acquisitions), Equity Capital Markets, Debt Capital Markets, or Real Estate. Associates are generally promoted to vice president after their fourth year. *Summer associates* serve as generalists during their ten- to twelve-week tenure at the firm. Summer associate positions are also available to MBA students in Equity Research, Equity Sales and Trading, Fixed Income, Foreign Exchange, Information Technology, and Private Client Services.

Investment banking *analysts* are recruited from undergraduate institutions and are expected to remain with the firm for two years. Investment banking analysts receive general offers but must choose a group before they begin work; they stay in this group for two years. Outstanding analysts are asked to stay for a third year, but almost none are promoted to the associate position without an MBA. Because of Morgan Stanley's brand name, investment banking analysts are accepted at the best business schools in the country. Equity Research, Public Finance, and other divisions at Morgan Stanley also recruit undergraduates.

Numbers: MORGAN STANLEY

Founded: 1935   **Ownership Structure:** Publicly Traded (NYSE-MS)

Total Consolidated Capital (1996, $M): 18,917

Sample Clients: NYNEX, Deutsche Telekom, Lucent Technologies, People's Republic of China, Time Warner, American Home Products

	1996	1995	1994	1993	1992
Net Revenues ($M)*	5,776	3,623	3,501	3,019	2,159
No. of Employees	11,613	9,238	9,685	8,273	7,421

*Net of interest expense

Roles: Financial Analyst   Associate   Vice President   Principal   Managing Director

Sources: Morgan Stanley "Career Opportunities," Morgan Stanley 1994 Annual Report, Morgan Stanley 1995 and 1996 Annual Reports

---

PART II: INSIDER INTERVIEW

How would you describe the company's culture?

It's a typical investment bank—rough, tough, and a lot of egos flying around. There's no room for "misfits." You lead a very fast life, especially in New York

City with the clubs, drinking, and eating expensive food. It's an all-around extreme environment.

What did you like best about your experience at the firm?

The skills that I developed. Also, the companies that I worked with. The clients are generally a lot more respectful than clients in consulting. Banking clients really view you as an expert—providing financial advice on things they know little about. Overall, Morgan Stanley is a good bank with a strong reputation. If you want to work for a bank, it's up there with Goldman and will get you far in the world.

What did you like least about your experience at the firm?

My investment banking group was filled with stressed-out people—there was a lot of yelling going on for things that were beyond an analyst's control.

What types of candidates did you see hired at Morgan Stanley?

Finance, accounting types who are assertive and willing to play the game and try to fit in. They like people who buy into the "glamour" of the job.

What advice would you give someone seeking a job at the firm?

Talk to as many honest people who have worked in the industry as you can. Try to get all sides of the story. I know people who really liked the hours, the lifestyle, and the work. Make sure that you can physically, emotionally handle the job—and get ready for a roller-coaster ride.

PROFILE

Robertson Stephens & Company

NAME: **Robertson Stephens & Company**
HEADQUARTERS: **555 California Street, Suite 2600, San Francisco, CA 94104, (415) 781-9700**
WEB SITE: **www.rsco.com**

◆

RECRUITING: **Centralized: Apply to San Francisco**
SUMMER JOBS: **Graduate and Undergraduate levels**
GRAD RECRUITING CONTACT (HEADQUARTERS): **Maggie Alexandre, Vice President of Human Resources**
GRAD TITLE: **Senior Associate (Corporate Finance, Sales & Trading); Junior Analyst (Research)**

UNDERGRAD RECRUITING CONTACT (HEADQUARTERS): **Maggie Alexandre, Vice President of Human Resources**
UNDERGRAD TITLE: **Analyst (Corporate Finance, Sales & Trading); Associate (Research)**

◆

RELATED READING: Peter Sinton, "B of A Buys Robertson, Sells Unit to Travelers," *San Francisco Chronicle*, June 10, 1997. Daniel Levine, "Investment Banks Ride Sizzling IPO Market to New Heights," *Banking & Finance Quarterly*, August 30, 1996. Linda Himelstein, "Silicon Valley Seeds Itself," *Business Week*, March 11, 1996.

OTHER OFFICES: (Domestic) Palo Alto, New York, Boston; (International) Tokyo, London, Singapore [1997]

PART I: ANALYSIS

Robertson Stephens & Co. is one of a new breed of successful specialist investment banks. It was originally founded in 1969 as Robertson, Colman, Siebel, & Weisel. In 1978 partners Sanford Robertson and Thomas Weisel split, dividing Robertson Stephens and Montgomery Securities into two separate companies. In 1997, Robertson was purchased by Bank of America—giving Robertson a greater capital base and access to new customers and products. Insiders say that B of A plans to invest $200 million in Robertson over the next three years.

Sometimes called the "four horsemen" of the West Coast, Robertson, Montgomery, Alex. Brown, and Hambrecht & Quist are grouped together because they specialize in serving corporations in high-growth industries and often find themselves competing with each other for business. Robertson, for example, is involved only in the technology, health care, consumer products, and real estate sectors. The number of high-technology initial public offerings (IPOs) has skyrocketed in recent years as small start-ups hit the big time, driving up the fortunes of Robertson and the other investment bankers serving them. Robertson is extremely strong in corporate finance and has a growing franchise in mergers and acquisitions.

Culturally, Robertson is described as being most similar to Hambrecht & Quist. Both firms are fairly small and entrepreneurial and foster camaraderie among employees. You will find much less formality at Robertson than at the bulge-bracket New York investment banks. Offices are modern and functional, with no mahogany paneling or brass letters on the wall. (Instead, the headquarters office in San Francisco has a sweeping view of the San Francisco Bay Bridge.) Robertson's lack of formality may be a positive or negative, depending on your need for structure and ceremony in the workplace.

Robertson's business is organized into several functional areas, with job opportunities available for recent graduates in most areas: Investment Banking (which includes M&A and corporate finance), Equity Research, Sales and Trading, Venture Capital, and Asset Management.

Robertson has a particularly strong research department. Research is central to Robertson, which as a smaller bank must provide value and information to clients that the big Wall Street banks cannot.

Are you hoping to be in the middle of the action in high-tech investment banking? Robertson would be a good place for you: The firm is a leader in the high-technology IPO market and takes advantage of its proximity to Silicon Valley to call on clients frequently. Senior mergers and acquisitions bankers at Robertson, for example, must keep up-to-date with recent developments in technology, develop a network of contacts in the Valley, and develop a point of view about technology-related industries in order to identify acquisition opportunities and new technologies for their clients.

Corporate financiers at Robertson find themselves needing a generalist portfolio of skills, since they frequently call on entrepreneurs who are less financially sophisticated and need guidance on a broad array of financial issues. This differs from the needs of the client base of a Goldman Sachs or Morgan Stanley—bankers at these bulge-bracket firms typically serve global corporations with large finance staffs who need specialized advice on complex financial products. Robertson is therefore a good fit for those who would prefer to serve the fundamental financial needs of young entrepreneurial companies rather than serve the companies that are the pillars of American industry.

Senior associates typically are hired from business schools or with significant previous investment banking experience. Some senior associates are hired into specific departments, while others are hired as generalists. *Analysts* are recruited from undergraduate institutions and are expected to remain with the firm for two years. About 30 to 40 percent of analysts are asked to stay at the firm for a third year; they are paid extremely well (insiders say over $100,000 in annual salary) and are given significant responsibility.

According to insiders, Robertson's recruiting process is still less structured than that of other firms but is being systematized quickly. This may present an opportunity for young job-hunters with unique backgrounds hoping to break into investment banking.

At the senior associate level, the firm is reputed to prefer candidates with a demonstrated previous interest or experience in investment banking. There is no training program for new senior associates. Robertson tends to be staffed leaner and therefore has fewer resources available to watch over junior bankers; insiders say that the firm seeks people who can hit the ground running and work independently. Summer opportunities exist for both undergraduate and graduate students.

PART II: INSIDER INTERVIEW

How would you describe the culture of the firm? Does it feel like a small firm?

I would say people travel so much that it feels small because if you look around the offices, two-thirds of the senior people are out at any given time, and a ton of the analysts are out on any given day. I would say that the culture is pretty serious and professional but it's also a "star system" in the sense that we have some really

---

~

Numbers: ROBERTSON STEPHENS & COMPANY

Founded: 1978   **Ownership Structure:** Limited Liability Corporation

Total Consolidated Capital (1996, $M): N/A

Sample Clients: Chiron, Excite, E-Trade, The Men's Wearhouse, Whole Foods Market, Pixar, Ascend Communications, US Office Products, Homedco, Nellcor

	1996	1995	1994
Net Revenues ($M)	350E	258	135
No. of Employees	765	524	396

Roles: Analyst Associate Senior Associate Vice President Principal Managing Director

——————————————————————————————————▶

Sources: *Banking & Finance Quarterly*, interviews with Robertson employees, Robertson Stephens & Company

---

young principals. There's definite potential for people, once they've been through the business school process, to just rocket up. On the other hand, having a star system implies that there are individual, entrepreneurial business units within the company, and that's not quite the case. We try to be very team oriented.

Analysts get really close, you know, just like any analyst program. Tomorrow we don't have to work because it's Good Friday, so all the first-years are all fired up to go out tonight. It's pretty close—like being in a frat, you know, where you develop this bond.

Is there anything about Robertson that you wish were different?

Work fewer hours. There's no doubt about it: It's a lifestyle trade-off. People are scheduled flat-out and it's tough to get anyone to support you in a pinch. I wish we had our act together more with regards to recruiting. And give necessary attention to non–revenue-producing activity. Things do change, though. A few years ago, I would have said we needed more infrastructure and support. But we've pretty much addressed that now.

What do you think the firm looks for in the candidates they interview?

Some people walk into the investment banking interviews thinking "I am so quantitative, I am such a stud. They've gotta hire me." People don't really understand what we're looking for. We're really looking for people who are smart and willing to work hard.

There's a lot of contact with clients; sometimes you're the sole representative of the firm at a meeting. So we want people with composure and personality, who can carry themselves well and have good judgment. People don't understand this.

Sometimes they'll play intense because they think that's what we want, and that can often backfire.

For senior associates, I think we look for people who can run a transaction. We've been so busy that if we hire somebody at that level, we want to make sure we get instant leverage out of him. I'd say it's the unusual exception that we hire a senior associate into Robertson without prior investment banking background.

PROFILE
Salomon Brothers, Inc.

NAME: **Salomon Brothers, Inc.**
HEADQUARTERS: **Seven World Trade Center, New York, NY 10048, (212) 783-7000**
WEB SITE: **www.salomon.com**

◆

RECRUITING: **Centralized through New York**
SUMMER JOBS: **Graduate level only**
GRAD RECRUITING CONTACT (HEADQUARTERS): **Lisa Burke, Recruiting Administrator (Investment Banking)**
GRAD TITLE: **Associate (Investment Banking); Trader (Sales & Trading); Research Associate (Market Analysis); Analyst (Company Research)**
UNDERGRAD RECRUITING CONTACT (HEADQUARTERS): **Patricia Harley, Recruiting Manager (Investment Banking)**
UNDERGRAD TITLE: **Financial Analyst (Investment Banking, Sales & Trading); Research Assistant (Market Analysis); Junior Analyst (Company Research)**

◆

RELATED READING: Greg Burns, "Salomon Steps into the Daylight," *Business Week,* May 5, 1997. Jill Dutt, "The Wipeout That Wasn't," *The Washington Post,* October 6, 1996. 1996 Salomon Inc. Annual Report. Leah Nathans Spiro, "Turmoil at Salomon," *Business Week,* May 1, 1995. Elizabeth Lesly, "Salomon's Creative Write-Off Course," *Business Week,* February 20, 1995. Michael Lewis, *Liar's Poker* (New York: W.W. Norton & Co., 1989).

OTHER OFFICES: (Domestic) Atlanta, Boston, Chicago, Dallas, Los Angeles, San Francisco; (International) Bangkok, Beijing, Bombay, Frankfurt, Hong Kong, London, Madrid, Melbourne, Milan, Osaka, Paris, São Paulo, Seoul, Singapore, Sydney, Taipei, Tokyo, Toronto, Zurich

PART I: ANALYSIS

The subject of Michael Lewis's famous *Liar's Poker,* Salomon Brothers, is a major investment bank founded in 1910 and headquartered in New York City. Salomon's sales and trading capabilities have always been its hallmark: Its corporate finance department was not started until 1969, and until the 1980s, "Solly" was a niche player in bond trading. The firm's roots are still evident, its culture still known on

Wall Street as more trading-oriented than that of other banks. However, insiders (especially those in investment banking) say that *Liar's Poker* overstated the firm in terms of how cutthroat and tough it is.

In the 1980s Salomon broadened its investment banking capabilities in a bid to enter the industry's top tier. A rash of problems, however, tarnished Salomon's rising star. In August 1991 Salomon was gripped by a government bond scandal. The firm admitted to submitting false bids in U.S. Treasury auctions; CEO John Gutfreund and other senior managers were forced to resign. Bookkeeping errors and poor risk management contributed to a 1994 loss of $399 million. Finally, the firm suffered defections of top managers in 1994 and 1995.

But the worst seems to be behind Salomon. The firm managed to produce earnings of over $400 million in 1995 and over $600 million in 1996, a very strong comeback. As always, its sales and trading franchise dominates the industry. Salomon's leaders claim they have no interest in participating in the mergers sweeping the investment banking industry; they'd prefer to go it alone.

Salomon offers a range of investment banking services, including advisory, capital raising, research, and trading services. In addition, Salomon trades on its own behalf. Divisions that offer job opportunities for undergraduates and MBAs include:

- Investment Banking (U.S. Corporate Finance, Capital Markets, Financial Institutions, and International Investment Banking)
- Sales and Trading
- Research

Each of these divisions has a different recruiting process, so be sure to confirm the appropriate contact name and information before applying.

Numbers: SALOMON BROTHERS, INC.

Founded: 1910   **Ownership Structure:** Publicly Traded (NYSE:SB)

Total Consolidated Capital (1995, $M): 18,992

Sample Clients: PacTek, DirecTV, Kimberly Clark, Northrop Grumman, Orange County, CBS, VLSI, Qantas Airways, General Motors, State of Israel, BellSouth

	1996	1995	1994	1993	1992
Net Revenues ($M)*	4,367	3,199	1,321	4,169	3,860
No. of Employees	7,146	7,007	7,562	6,880	6,844

*Net of interest expense

Roles   Financial Analyst   Associate   Vice President   Managing Director

$\longrightarrow$

Sources: Salomon 1994–1996 Annual Reports Interviews

Salomon's investment banking group typically recruits *associates* from business schools. Associates help determine their own department assignments and are promoted to vice president after three or four years. Investment banking *financial analysts* are recruited from colleges and universities, are assigned by the firm to a department, and are expected to remain with the firm for two or three years. According to a former Salomon Brothers analyst, approximately 5 percent of financial analysts are promoted to the associate level. Salomon offers positions in sales and trading and several other areas to undergraduates.

PART II: INSIDER INTERVIEW

How would you describe the company's culture?

Salomon has an aggressive culture where you can get buried if you are not confident. I feel that the firm is not relationship-driven but, rather, driven entirely by muscle.

What did you like best about your experience at the firm?

It built wonderful discipline and taught me a lot about what I wanted to prioritize in my life. I would recommend an analyst experience to anyone looking to build a background in business fundamentals. The best thing about Salomon was the great quantitative skills that it built. Furthermore, my work had to be incredibly precise. I developed skills that I will use forever.

What did you like least about your experience at the firm?

I think the aspect of Salomon that I hated the most was what it did to me as a person. Perhaps it is the same in any analyst program, but I felt that I lost balance in my life. I also felt that my managers didn't take the time or have the interest to become quality mentors.

What types of candidates do you think the firm prefers?

In my experience, Salomon prefers street-smart people who are aggressive and a little rough around the edges. You will not find many traditional "bankers" at Salomon.

What was your perception of the company's recruiting process?

From what I saw, the recruiting process started with a committee of mostly analysts who reviewed the résumés from their individual schools. After this, they set up individual interviews and called back about 15 percent of the candidates.

PROFILE
Smith Barney Inc.

NAME: **Smith Barney Inc.**
HEADQUARTERS: **388 Greenwich Street, New York, NY 10013, (212) 816-6000**
WEB SITE: **www.smithbarney.com**

◆

RECRUITING: **Centralized: Apply to headquarters**
SUMMER JOBS: **Graduate and Undergraduate levels**
GRAD RECRUITING CONTACT: **John Rae, Senior Vice President (Investment Banking)**
GRAD TITLE: **Associate**
UNDERGRAD RECRUITING CONTACT: **Wendy Chapman, First Vice President (Investment Banking)**
UNDERGRAD TITLE: **Financial Analyst**

◆

RELATED READING: Kirsten Downey Grimsley, "26 Women Sue Smith Barney, Allege Bias," *The Washington Post,* November 6, 1996. Leah Nathans Spiro, "Can Jamie Dimon Turn Smith Barney into a Wall Street Dynamo?" *Business Week,* October 21, 1996. Anita Raghavan, "Weill's Smith Barney Snaps at Merrill's Heels," *The Wall Street Journal,* September 19, 1996. Geoffrey Smith, "It's Nice to Have This Stuff in Your Blood," *Business Week,* August 12, 1996. Michael Siconofli and Anita Raghavan, "Small Change: Smith Barney Fails to Crack Big Leagues of Investment Banking," *The Wall Street Journal,* March 23, 1995. Robert Lenzer, "Sandy Weill," *The New York Times—Late Edition,* November 7, 1993.

OTHER INVESTMENT BANKING OFFICES: (Domestic) Chicago, Los Angeles, San Francisco; (International) Beijing, Hong Kong, Israel, London, Mexico City, Seoul, Tokyo, Toronto

PART I: ANALYSIS

Change is a constant in the investment banking industry, and Smith Barney has had its share of it. The New York–based firm is a subsidiary of The Travelers Group and is heavily influenced by Travelers CEO Sandy Weill. By all accounts, Weill is the driving force behind Smith Barney's bid to become an investment banking powerhouse.

Smith Barney offers a full line of investment banking services and falls into the "major bracket" category of the industry. The firm has ridden a roller coaster of change over the past few years. It began in 1993 when the firm bought the retail brokerage arm of Shearson Lehman Brothers, acquiring a sales network of over 8,000 brokers that grew in size to rival Merrill Lynch's (Merrill Lynch has the largest retail brokerage network of any investment bank.) Also in 1993, Weill hired former Morgan Stanley president Bob Greenhill as Smith Barney's CEO in order to build up the firm's investment banking operations. Given a blank check to attract talent, Greenhill brought over twenty other Morgan Stanley investment bankers using fat guaranteed paychecks as bait. Greenhill himself was pricey, receiving a three-year pay package of $86 million. Differences in pay quickly created tension, with the old Smith Barney bankers resenting the new Morgan Stanley bankers for consuming much of the firm's bonus pool due to fixed pay contracts. In the meantime, results were slow in coming from the expensive acquisition of Morgan Stanley talent. Greenhill resigned in January 1996 and was replaced by Jamie Dimon, a Harvard MBA who was homegrown at Smith Barney as Weill's protégé.

In 1995 and 1996 Smith Barney reaped some rewards from its strategy. The firm vastly improved its equity underwriting standings. It leaped to second place in the initial public offerings rankings and to fourth place in U.S. common-stock offerings. In particular, Smith Barney's investment banking group serving the health care industry is now known for being the best on the Street. The firm still has challenges in front of it, including expanding its M&A and international presence. Smith Barney made an attempt to buy the failed Barings PLC, and industry observers believe it will try again to buy expertise overseas.

Smith Barney's culture is entrepreneurial and young. The firm is flatter, more flexible, and less bureaucratic than its more established Wall Street peers. Smith Barney recently made headlines because it is facing charges of sexual harassment in a class-action suit brought by twenty-six former employees.

The firm recruits undergraduates and graduate students for the following areas:

- Investment Banking Division
- Public Finance: Raises capital for municipalities, public projects, infrastructure
- Capital Markets Division: Includes institutional sales and trading
- Research Division
- Investment Management Division: Creates mutual funds, other investment vehicles

For those interested in investment banking, the Investment Banking Division is split into industry groups such as Energy and Health Care, product groups such as High Yield and Private Finance, and advisory groups such as Mergers & Acquisitions.

Investment Banking and Public Finance *associates* are recruited primarily from MBA programs. Smith Barney cares less about the name brand of the schools it hires from than other firms; a much wider variety of schools is represented within its halls. Public Finance associates spend one or two years as generalists after which they specialize in an industry group, while Investment Banking associates are immediately assigned to specialty groups when they are hired. Capital Markets associates complete a training program and a rotation program before being assigned to a desk.

Analysts are recruited from undergraduate institutions and are expected to remain with the firm for two years before returning to business school. Many analysts are asked to stay for a third year, and a few are then promoted to the associate position. Public Finance analysts are generalists, working on a variety of projects, while Investment Banking analysts specialize in one group. Capital Markets analysts complete a training program before being assigned to a desk.

Five-week training programs are provided to analysts and associates, starting in mid-summer for analysts. Summer hires typically work in the New York City office, and many are offered the opportunity to return to the firm upon graduation. Of all the investment banks, Smith Barney has a recruiting brochure that is probably the most honest. It is highly recommended for its description of the highs and lows of working in investment banking.

Numbers: SMITH BARNEY INC.

Founded: 1873   **Ownership Structure:** 100% subsidiary of Travelers Group, Inc.

Total Consolidated Capital (1996, $M): 2,500

Sample Clients: Kohlberg Kravis Roberts, Enron Corporation, Healthsouth

	1996	1995	1994	1993	1992
Net Revenues ($M)*	6,295	5,434	4,764	3,094	1,677
No. of Employees	28,000	28,000	27,500	N/A	N/A

*Net of interest expense

Roles: Financial Analyst   Associate   Vice President   Director   Managing Director
→

Sources: Travelers Annual Report, Smith Barney, Smith Barney recruiting brochure

---

PART II: INSIDER INTERVIEW

How would you describe the company's culture?

It's a solid firm that is young and fresh—a rising star that is taking business from the more established firms.

How were associates and analysts assigned to specialty groups once they joined?

Basically, there were no real generalists at Smith Barney. After you got an offer from the firm and accepted, you had to interview with a specific group and list your top three preferences. The groups ranked who they wanted and came up with a match.

Did most analysts return to business school after two or three years?

Yes, most left after two or three years, but my impression is that it is less stringent than at Goldman or Salomon. If you did a decent job, it was easy to get a third year. But it was much more difficult to get an associate position—they had to really like you.

What did you like best about your experience at the firm?

I worked on some interesting transactions with people who I really enjoyed working with and respected.

What did you like least about your experience at the firm?

The associates and senior managers on a power trip. And losing high-profile deals to other banks often.

What do you think Smith Barney looks for in its new hires?

Strong quantitative skills, strong communication skills, and essentially all the skills favored at other firms.

What advice would you give someone seeking a job at Smith Barney?

Just as at any investment bank, try to get assigned to one of the groups that dominate their respective industries, such as health care at Smith Barney. These groups are well worth working for. If you end up in a struggling group, it can be a frustrating two years.

Other Worthy Mentions

Alex. Brown & Sons Inc.

NAME: **Alex. Brown & Sons Inc.**
HEADQUARTERS: **1 South Street, Baltimore, MD 21202, (410) 727-1700**
WEB SITE: **www.alexbrown.com**

◆

RECRUITING: **Centralized through Headquarters**
SUMMER JOBS: **Graduate and Undergraduate levels**
GRAD RECRUITING CONTACT: **Christina Peters, VP of Investment Banking**
GRAD TITLE: **Associate**
UNDERGRAD RECRUITING CONTACT: **Christina Peters, VP of Investment Banking**
UNDERGRAD TITLE: **FinancialAnalyst**

◆

OTHER OFFICES: (Domestic) Annapolis, Atlanta, Baltimore, Boston, Chicago, Dallas, Fishkill, Greenwich, Jacksonville, Los Angeles, New York, Philadelphia, Richmond, San Francisco, Washington, West Palm Beach, Wilmington, Winston Salem; (International) Geneva, London, Tokyo

Cowen & Co.

NAME: **Cowen & Co.**
HEADQUARTERS: **Financial Square, New York, NY 10005, (212) 495-6000**
WEB SITE: **www.cowen.com**

◆

RECRUITING: **Regional by East/West Coasts**
SUMMER JOBS: **Graduate level only**
RECRUITING CONTACT (EAST COAST): **Laura Hevesi—New York Office**
RECRUITING CONTACT (WEST COAST): **Wendy Ruggiero—San Francisco Office, Four Embarcadero Center, Suite 1200, San Francisco, CA 94111**
GRAD TITLE: **Associate**
UNDERGRAD TITLE: **Analyst**

◆

OTHER OFFICES: (Domestic) Albany, Atlanta, Boston, Chicago, Cleveland, Dayton, Houston, Phoenix, San Francisco; (International) Geneva, London, Paris, Tokyo, Toronto

Donaldson, Lufkin & Jenrette, Inc.

NAME: **Donaldson, Lufkin & Jenrette, Inc.**
HEADQUARTERS: **277 Park Avenue, New York, NY 10172, (212) 892-3000**
WEB SITE: **www.dlj.com**

◆

RECRUITING: **Centralized through Headquarters**
SUMMER JOBS: **Graduate and Undergraduate levels**
GRAD RECRUITING CONTACT: **Elizabeth K. Derby, Director of Recruiting (Investment Banking)**
GRAD TITLE: **Investment Banking Associate**
UNDERGRAD RECRUITING CONTACT: **Deborah A. McCarroll, Manager of Recruiting**
UNDERGRAD TITLE: **Investment Banking Analyst**

◆

OTHER OFFICES: (Domestic) Annapolis, Boston, Chicago, Dallas, Houston, Los Angeles, New York, San Francisco; (International) Bangalore, Buenos Aires, Hong Kong, Johannesburg, London, Mexico City, São Paulo

Lazard Freres & Co., L.L.C.

NAME: **Lazard Freres & Co., L.L.C.**
HEADQUARTERS: **30 Rockefeller Plaza, New York, NY 10020, (212) 632-6000**
WEB SITE: **none**

◆

RECRUITING: Centralized through Headquarters
SUMMER JOBS: Graduate level only
GRAD RECRUITING CONTACT: Suzanne Zywicki, VP (Investment Banking)
GRAD TITLE: Associate
UNDERGRAD RECRUITING CONTACT: Suzanne Zywicki, VP (Investment Banking)
UNDERGRAD TITLE: Financial Analyst

◆

OTHER OFFICES: (Domestic) Chicago, Los Angeles, San Francisco, Washington D.C.; (International) Beijing, Bombay, Frankfurt, Ho Chi Minh City, Hong Kong, London, Milan, Moscow, Paris, Singapore, Tokyo, Warsaw

Paine Webber, Inc.

NAME: Paine Webber, Inc.
HEADQUARTERS: 1285 Avenue of the Americas, 13th Floor, New York, NY 10019, (212) 713-2000
WEB SITE: www.painewebber.com

◆

RECRUITING: Centralized through Headquarters
SUMMER JOBS: Graduate level only
GRAD RECRUITING CONTACT: Kelly Decker, Assistant Vice-President
GRAD TITLE: Associate
UNDERGRAD RECRUITING CONTACT: Kelly Decker, Assistant Vice-President
UNDERGRAD TITLE: Financial Analyst

◆

OTHER OFFICES: (Domestic) Chicago, Houston, San Francisco; (International) Hong Kong, London, Taiwan

Piper Jaffray Cos., Inc.

NAME: Piper Jaffray Cos., Inc.
HEADQUARTERS: 222 South 9th Street, Minneapolis, MN 55402, (612) 342-6000
WEB SITE: www.piperjaffray.com

◆

RECRUITING: Centralized through Headquarters
SUMMER JOBS: Graduate and Undergraduate levels
GRAD RECRUITING CONTACT: Mary Nease, MBA Corporate Employment Rep.
GRAD TITLE: Associate (Investment Banking)
UNDERGRAD RECRUITING CONTACT: Jennifer Piehl, Undergraduate Corporate Employment Rep.
UNDERGRAD TITLE: Corporate Finance Analyst (Investment Banking)

◆

OTHER OFFICES: Chicago, Minneapolis

Union Bank of Switzerland

NAME: **Union Bank of Switzerland**
HEADQUARTERS: **229 Park Avenue, New York, NY 10171, (212) 821-3000**
WEB SITE: **www.ubs.com**

◆

RECRUITING: **Local by office**
SUMMER JOBS: **Graduate and Undergraduate levels**
GRAD RECRUITING CONTACT: **Erica Blechschmidt, Recruiting Coordinator**
GRAD TITLE: **Associate**
UNDERGRAD RECRUITING CONTACT: **Erica Blechschmidt, Recruiting Coordinator**
UNDERGRAD TITLE: **Analyst**

◆

OTHER OFFICES: (Domestic) Houston, Montreal, San Francisco; (International) Abu Dhabi, Bahrain, Bangkok, Beijing, Beirut, Bogota, Budapest, Buenos Aires, Caracas, Dubai, Frankfurt, Hong Kong, Jersey, Johannesburg, Kuala Lumpur, Labuan, Lisbon, London, Luxembourg, Madrid, Mexico City, Milan, Monte Carlo, Moscow, Mumbai, Osaka, Paris, Prague, Rio de Janeiro, Santiago de Chile, São Paulo, Seoul, Shanghai, Singapore, Sydney, Taipei, Tehran, Tokyo, United Arab Emirates, Warsaw, Zurich

Wasserstein Perella & Co., Inc.

NAME: **Wasserstein Perella & Co., Inc.**
HEADQUARTERS: **31 West 52nd Street, New York, NY 10019, (212) 969-2700**
WEB SITE: **none**

◆

RECRUITING: **Localized by Office or through Headquarters**
SUMMER JOBS: **Graduate and Undergraduate levels**
GRAD RECRUITING CONTACT: **Fran Lyman, Recruiting Manager**
GRAD TITLE: **Financial Associate**
UNDERGRAD RECRUITING CONTACT: **Fran Lyman, Recruiting Manager**
UNDERGRAD TITLE: **Financial Analyst**

◆

OTHER OFFICES: (Domestic) Chicago, Dallas, Los Angeles, San Francisco; (International) Frankfurt, London, Paris, Tokyo

INDEX

To the Reader

Feedback on *The Fast Track* is welcome. Please send your comments to Mariam Naficy, c/o Broadway Books, 1540 Broadway, New York, NY 10036, or send an e-mail to the author through *The Fast Track* Web site: www.thefasttrack.com.